cognitive–behavioral

group

therapy

FOR SPECIFIC PROBLEMS AND POPULATIONS

cognitive–behavioral

group

therapy

FOR SPECIFIC PROBLEMS AND POPULATIONS

Edited by John R. White and Arthur S. Freeman

American Psychological Association
Washington, DC

Published by
American Psychological Association
750 First Street, NE
Washington, DC 20002

Copies may be ordered from
APA Order Department
P.O. Box 92984
Washington, DC 20090-2984

In the U.K., Europe, Africa, and the Middle East, copies may be ordered from
American Psychological Association
3 Henrietta Street
Covent Garden, London
WC2E 8LU England

Typeset in Goudy by EPS Group Inc., Easton, MD

Printer: Edward Brothers, Ann Arbor, MI
Cover Designer: Watermark Design Office, Alexandria, VA
Production Editor: Kristine Enderle

The opinions and statements published are the responsibility of the authors, and such opinions and statements do not necessarily represent the policies of the APA.

Library of Congress Cataloging-in-Publication Data
Cognitive-behavioral group therapy for specific problems and populations / edited by John R. White, Arthur S. Freeman.—1st ed.
    p. cm.
    Includes bibliographical references and index.
    ISBN 1-55798-690-8
    1. Cognitive therapy.   2. Group psychotherapy.   I. White, John R., 1953–   .
II. Freeman, Arthur S.

    RC489.C63.C627 2000
    616.89′152—dc21

                                                                        00-027405

British Library Cataloguing-in-Publication Data
A CIP record is available from the British Library.

Printed in the United States of America
First Edition

To Ed Bourg, a natural leader of groups.

J. R. W.

CONTENTS

CONTRIBUTORS

Wayne A. Bowers, PhD, Department of Psychiatry, University of Iowa, Iowa City, Iowa

David W. Coon, PhD, Goldman Institute on Aging, San Fransisco, CA

Michelle G. Craske, PhD, Department of Psychology, University of California, Los Angeles

Arthur S. Freeman, EdD, Department of Psychology, Philadelphia College of Osteopathic Medicine

Dolores Gallagher-Thompson, PhD, ABPP, Older Adult Center, VA Palo Alto Health Care System, Menlo Park, CA and Department of Psychiatry, Stanford University School of Medicine, Standford, CA

Tom Greanias, LCSW, CADC, Behavioral and Mental Health Services, DuPage County Health Department, Wheaton, IL

M. Jane Irvine, D. Phil., York University, Faculty of Medicine, University of Toronto, and University Health Network

Joel Katz, PhD, Faculty of Medicine, University of Toronto, Toronto General Hospital, and Mt. Sinai Hospital

Ariel J. Lang, PhD, Department of Psychiatry, University of California, San Diego and San Diego VA Healthcare System

Aila Jesse McCutchen, PsyD, Department of Psychiatry, Massachusetts General Hospital, Harvard Medical School, Boston

Christine McKibbin, PhD, Department of Psychiatry, VA Medical Center and University of California, San Diego, CA

William D. Morgan, PsyD, Life Counseling Services, Paoli, PA

Kurt C. Organista, PhD, School of Social Welfare, University of California, Berkeley

David V. Powers, PhD, Department of Psychology, Loyola College, Baltimore, MD

Robert R. Radomile, M. Ed., Jerry Kear, PhD and Associates, Philadelphia, PA

Paul G. Ritvo, PhD, Ontario Cancer Institute, University Health Network, and Faculty of Medicine, University of Toronto

Brian F. Shaw, PhD, Community Health/Mental Health and Professional Services, Hospital for Sick Children, and Faculty of Medicine, University of Toronto

Sandra Siegel, MA, RN, Adler School of Professional Psychology, Chicago Medical School, Chicago, IL

Jonathan Stern, PhD, Cognitive Psychotherapy Services, New York, NY

Kellie Takagi, PhD, Older Adult Center, VA Palo Alto Health Care System, and Department of Psychiatry, Stanford University, Stanford, CA

Larry W. Thompson, PhD, Pacific Graduate School of Psychology and VA Palo Alto Health Care System, Palo Alto, CA

Susan Walen, PhD, private practice and Department of Psychiatry, Johns Hopkins School of Medicine, Baltimore, MD

John R. White, PhD, California School of Professional Psychology–Alameda and Department of Education, Stanford University, Stanford, CA

Amy S. Witt-Browder, MA, The Reading Hospital and Medical Center, Reading, PA

Janet L. Wolfe, PhD, Albert Ellis Institute for Rational–Emotive Behavior Therapy, New York, NY

PREFACE

As psychologists working in graduate and hospital training settings, we have observed a growing demand for qualified therapists skillful in conducting group therapy. Drawing on the existing cognitive–behavioral therapy (CBT) group literature, we have supervised doctoral and postdoctoral students in various CBT group therapy programs. This approach seems to have produced a consistently positive response from the clients served and offered particular advantages for applying the CBT model. In these group therapy settings, conditional beliefs naturally rose to the surface, providing multiple opportunities to identify, test, and revise those underlying rules that govern social behavior. There was immediate activation of automatic thoughts without having to resort to "out of group experience" to find clinically relevant material. The single best advantage of CBT delivered in group settings seems to be the fundamental fact that it is the group itself that generates its own adaptive response. Members gain immeasurably in acquiring this skill through social modeling with each other. First they learn to make an adaptive response together, and then they are prepared to apply the same process on their own. We have seen over and over that a group's capacity for adaptive response usually exceeds the ability of those same individuals to undertake adaptation while by themselves.

Through our contact with colleagues at other training centers, we became aware that a number of them were also developing and implementing group therapy programs based on principles similar to ours. What was notable was the remarkable range of clinical populations being treated in these various settings using group CBT methods. Of necessity, then, these colleagues have refined specialty techniques for working within this diagnostic diversity. This has led to a significant extension beyond the existing CBT literature, resulting in a second generation of group techniques and methods. Our recognition of these developments became the origin of the present volume as we have attempted to shed light on this advancement as it is occurring. Because these approaches are neither monolithic nor monochromatic, we selected the title *Cognitive–Behavioral Group Therapy for Specific Problems and Populations* to reflect their true plurality.

We have endeavored to produce a practical text that will assist clinicians in developing and providing CBT group therapy. It has been our good fortune to obtain the support and authorship of many of the leading CBT group therapists across North America. Because of the practical emphasis of this text as well as the stature of the contributing authors, we offer this collected work as "best practices" of contemporary group CBT. Obviously, this is not an exhaustive list of the prominent CBT therapists who are developing group therapy models. One of our hopes with the publication of the present work is to extend this clinical dialogue to include other accomplished therapists who are working with their own specific populations while refining relevant innovations in group CBT methods. An unexpected outcome of this process was the "group" that was formed by the group therapists who contributed. We would now like to extend those membership boundaries.

We asked each of the authors to prepare a detailed description of their work that would serve for all practical purposes as a flexible protocol, enabling another clinician to implement similar methods. Protocol, in this sense, is interpreted in light of its Greek origin *proto kollon*, which means "a table of contents crafted from sheets of papyrus glued together." These chapters provide essentially a table of contents of the substance and sequence of the best practices in group CBT. The resulting protocols are deemed flexible in acknowledging the complex demands when offering a simultaneous treatment experience to a variety of separate human beings. Accordingly, each protocol must be able to adjust to individual differences within a common syndrome, including diverse symptom profiles and ideographic problem lists. Flexibility also means that in dealing within clinical populations there should be due recognition of the different stages of development as each individual works through his or her adaptation to the syndrome. For example, within a CBT group therapy for depression, there may be clients for whom this is a first episode, others who have had a long-term low-grade depression with recent exacerbation, and others who present a chronic course of repeated major episodes. No rigid or lock-step protocol will come close to accommodating the needs of these individuals. It is precisely this complex clinical thought process that the authors in this book seek to illuminate, in essence providing a series of detailed clinical algorithms as to how these expert therapists arrive at their decisions in the various phases of group therapy.

These chapters are offered to the reader in the time-honored mode of clinical supervision. We all recognize from our therapy training that a good clinical supervisor puts forward plenty of practical advice, especially in forecasting those common problems that arise in therapy and helping to figure the best ways out. Because modeling is one of the most effective methods of learning, a clinical supervisor will typically teach by example and show what he or she really does in session. For example, in the text several authors address the specifics of what they actually say and do when dealing with potential dropouts, always a thorny issue for group therapists. And a good supervisor starts at the skill level the clinician possesses and builds from there. Accordingly, these chapters assume that some readers will come to the present discussion with a background in CBT, others may originate from their work in group therapy, whereas others begin at their specialty knowledge of the clinical population discussed in any particular chapter. Acknowledging this range of backgrounds, the authors, as good clinical supervisors, endeavor to develop each reader's own knowledge and proficiency to conduct group therapy according that individual's distinctive style.

In composing these chapters, the authors were asked to address what we considered the two defining variables of CBT group therapy. There is nothing more important in an ongoing group therapy than *cohesiveness*, defined as the degree of personal interest of the members for each other. Cohesiveness is high when people want to attend the group and look forward to relating to each other. They spontaneously think about each other between sessions. When there exists compassion and members feel concern for the suffering of other members, the group has achieved cohesiveness. It is this social force within a group that permits members to tolerate differences and disagreements. When there exists sufficient cohesiveness, these differences do not threaten the basic integrity of the group. There is opportunity to express diversity of experience and opinion with the confidence that the group will not fall apart and individuals will not be harmed. For example, members will typically not begin to engage in a process of constructive conflict until there first exists a feeling of safety that originates from cohesiveness. We asked our authors to address the many ways that they facilitate a sense of cohesiveness in the group and how they intervene when inevitable forces within the group seek to overturn cohesiveness.

The other essential variable in CBT group therapy is *task focus*. CBT is a focused therapy that seeks problem resolution. Each member usually has goals that he or she wants to attain over the course of treatment. This often involves learning and practicing specific skills that help the client to better deal with the issues at hand. If clients were to experience this focus on task as controlling or impersonal, it would certainly fail and probably bring the entire group down with it. Each CBT therapist must determine his or her own best methods of achieving task focus that convey a full sense of empathy and concern. For example, the process of checking in with homework is a good gauge of the therapist's skills in task focus. Does the therapist follow up on homework every time it is agreed to? When clients do not do homework, is there a discussion that brings the opposing factors to light (without dissolving to a power struggle or exercise in shame)? Are clients able to regard unexpected outcomes not as failures but as opportunities to learn? Is follow-up homework composed with input from all members? Do clients really feel that the homework they have agreed to do can actually help them? When there is sufficient task focus, the therapist is facilitating the group to make optimal use of its constructive energy.

In some clinical circles, the variables of cohesiveness and task focus are seen to be at odds. These critics would argue that when a group maintains high cohesiveness, it necessarily diverts from a specific task focus. "The group is too soft to work hard." Alternatively, if the group were to operate with high task focus, it could do so only at the expense of strong positive feelings between members. No real cohesiveness would exist. Sadly, there is no way to succeed on behalf of patients in this either–or dilemma. By virtue of assuming an inverse relationship, cohesiveness must be sacrificed to task focus, or vice versa. These chapters dispute the entire notion of sacrifice and argue a fundamental premise that cohesiveness and task focus are actually orthogonal (see Figure A.1). Consider cohesiveness as presented on an x-axis and task focus appearing on a y-axis. The best

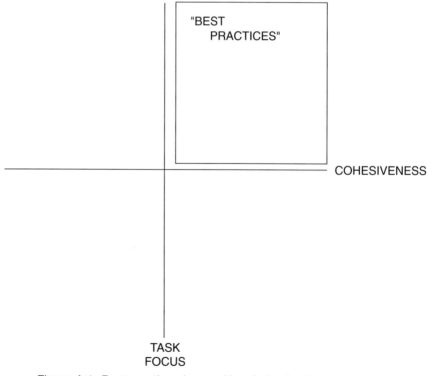

Figure A.1. Best practices in cognitive–behavioral group therapy.

practices of this text advocate clinical work that is experienced by the group as both highly cohesive *and* highly task focused. Indeed, if a problem arises in the group, these authors propose a clinical algorithm that seeks to reinforce both cohesiveness and task focus. For example, the therapist's skill in guiding the group to generate a meaningful agenda not only identifies a topic that everyone can personally relate to, but over the course of the session leads to sufficient resolution to arrive at an adaptive response satisfactory to all. How much stronger is this process than if a topic were to be pushed by the therapist or arose randomly from the first member who happens to speak up? Obviously this approach is fundamentally different from clinicians who assume that cohesiveness and task focus are diametrically opposite, and then practice in such a way that substantiates the assumption. Although it is not always easy for a therapist to conduct therapy in ways that support cohesiveness and task focus, we think that it is unfair and unnecessary to ask our clients to settle for less.

Because of the practical emphasis of this project, we specifically asked authors to limit their theoretical references and discussions. This does not mean there is neither a theoretical basis to the work nor theoretical implications to the ideas discussed. A downstream consequence of this project has been the early emergence of new thought regarding a model of CBT group therapy. Because of the practical nature of this project, the emerging theory is built inductively from the data of actual day-to-day clinical practice rather than derived deductively from a set of general principles. From these inductive origins, there seem to be promising implications for a CBT group theory that would draw on the burgeoning fields of cognitive psychology and general systems. To name a few, such features of this dual citizenship would include feedback and feed-forward loops, nonlinear and reciprocal cause-and-effect, and complex processes of change and homeostasis. The group, from a slightly surreal perspective, could be viewed as containing the distributed intelligence of the members—not unlike an out-of-skull brain with each of the participants as a distinct lobe. Down the road there might also be interesting theoretical applications of such work to nonclinical groups as well, such as in employment, family, politics, and community.

Just as the text itself is deliberately integrative, so we specified to our authors that its clinical orientation would take precedence over a research perspective. Yet the majority of these same authors are also clinical researchers, and this collective background is unmistakable in the manner these chapters are presented. The authors naturally incorporate a writing style significantly influenced by their research methodology, often including outcome measures as well as operationally defined treatment conditions. The research mindset of this project reinforces the clinical intent of a CBT treatment modality. Clients learn to test their hypotheses about themselves and the world while making behavioral experiments to gather fresh data from their own life. It is hoped that the present work will serve as a catalyst for related clinical research. Not only can these flexible protocols be tested in various clinical settings, but also they can be revised with alternative methods and populations. Research methods from a group tradition would be welcomed to better capture the complex phenomenon of evaluating a CBT treatment experience shared by some number of people simultaneously rather than one person at a time.

The interest in CBT group therapies demonstrated by the chapter authors and readers reflects a much larger tidal shift under way in the field of mental health treatment. Nick Cummings, long a respected source forecasting the emerging trends in our profession, has observed,

> The therapy of the future will be characterized by time-limited empirically derived, condition specific protocols. Of these, only 25% will involve patients in individual psychotherapy, another 25% will involve patients in group therapy, while 50% of our patients will receive psychoeductional group therapy (Cummings, as cited in White, 1995, p. 3).

If these predictions are as accurate as the others in Cummings's long and distinguished career, the therapy methods discussed in this text will be directly in line with half to as much as three quarters of mental health treatment of the future. The therapist with interest and skills in CBT group therapy will likely find opportunity and growth as these transitions unfold. We feel honored to be able to assist in the development of those therapists and look forward to all they will teach us in the years to come.

REFERENCE

White, J. (1995). *Overcoming depression and loss: A personal workbook for cognitive group therapy*. Palo Alto, CA: Mind Garden.

cognitive–behavioral

group

therapy

FOR SPECIFIC PROBLEMS AND POPULATIONS

1

INTRODUCTION

JOHN R. WHITE

This introduction to cognitive–behavioral therapy (CBT) with groups presents an overview of the basic concepts underlying this model of practice and offers the reader a quick entry into the terms commonly used by those practicing CBT. In my chapter on depression, chapter 2, I also outline some of the common process characteristics of CBT groups that should be applicable and congruent with the description of group process in all of the succeeding chapters. Over the 40-year history of this approach, there has naturally developed a language to describe its clinical methods. This chapter provides a working glossary of the main CBT terms that relate to group therapy. In addition to basic definitions, I give verbatim descriptions of how I relay these terms to my clients. I also discuss various benefits deriving from these techniques as well as specific ideas of how to troubleshoot should problems arise. This is in keeping with the practical orientation throughout this book showing the reader how to apply these methods in day-to-day clinical work. From my sample descriptions, I suggest that the reader make actual interventions modified according to his or her own therapeutic style of relating to clients.

The literature of CBT is vast, and no one source can provide an authoritative account of all the important terms. This primer chapter pursues the more modest goal to assist the reader in becoming familiar with the basic clinical language of CBT. If the chapter succeeds, the reader should then feel competent when exploring the subsequent chapters applying CBT in group treatment with various populations. Should there be further interest, the reader is encouraged to dig more deeply into the CBT literature. To this end I cite original source material from the CBT corpus, to which the reader is referred for further study.

When specific CBT terms are defined, they will be identified in italics. If those same terms appear elsewhere in the chapter, they will be noted with an asterisk to indicate that a more complete definition can be located earlier or later in the chapter.

A COGNITIVE MODEL FOR GROUP THERAPY

Fundamental to a CBT approach is an understanding of the *cognitive model* (A. T. Beck, 1976). This is a theory that focuses on the interaction of thoughts, feelings, and behaviors. *Thoughts*, in simplest terms, are the moment-to-moment mental content experienced by an individual, usually represented in words or images. For example, thoughts commonly associated with depression include "I'm no good" and "I can't do anything to make my situation better." The *feeling* aspect of the cognitive model refers to the individual's ongoing emotional experience (such as love, sadness, fear, or anger). *Behaviors* are the observable actions taken by an individual ranging from the micro (e.g., how one draws in a breath) to the macro (say, riding a bicycle in a race). Essential to life are ongoing streams of thoughts, feelings, and behaviors.

Following is a verbatim discussion that I have used to help a therapy group begin to see the value of the cognitive model:

> To gain a better understanding of yourselves, we want to be able to track your ongoing thoughts, feelings, and behaviors. This is what's called using the cognitive model. The more you are able to recognize these immediate reactions on your part, your experience will probably make more sense to you and you'll be able to determine where you want to make changes.

The automatic thought record* is one practical means of teaching clients to catch hold of their thoughts, feelings, and behaviors.

When I introduce the cognitive model into therapy, I make the point that thoughts, feelings, and behaviors are interrelated and multidirectional

> Sometimes thoughts cause feelings, which then cause behaviors. Other times, it may be feelings that cause behaviors that subsequently lead

to thoughts. Or, behaviors may engender whole sets of feelings and thoughts, which subsequently influence each other (Lazarus, 1997).

Some CBT therapists prefer a more linear approach that focuses first on thoughts, which are then seen as causing feelings, which in turn determine behaviors. I have seen good clinical results obtained both ways. The reader is encouraged to explore in his or her own clinical experience which approach (i.e., multidirectional or linear) has worked better and to experiment in various therapeutic situations to see what he or she prefers.

A significant implication of the cognitive model is that CBT is a fundamentally *phenomenological* approach (Mahoney, 1991). Clients and therapist are seeking to track the moment-by-moment personal experience of each individual. *Phenomenological* refers to how the phenomena of an experience register with an individual, rather an approach that would try to see the universal nature of an event as it would be agreed upon by most or all people. By mutual understanding, there is a steady focus on the unfolding present. Does this mean that past and future are somehow deemed unimportant? Hardly. But the past and future are seen to be constantly filtered through the present moment. So, with appropriate clinical timing, the CBT therapist might say, "What immediate thoughts were triggered when you just touched on that memory of . . . [an old trauma]?" or "Tell me all your feelings when you became aware right now of . . . [a threat in the future]?" The essence of this phenomenological approach of the CBT therapist is captured in A. T. Beck's (1976) favorite clinical question, which he called the *cognitive probe*: "What is going through your mind right now?"

Underlying the immediate thoughts, feelings, and behaviors are the individual's *conditional beliefs* (J. S. Beck, 1995). These are the if-then statements by which a person makes sense of cause-and-effect relations in the world. Some conditional beliefs are obvious. "If I walk out in the street without looking, then I may get hit by a car." Such are the basic conditions of people's lives. Other conditional beliefs are more distinctive of each individual. For example, one person may have learned, "If I speak up for myself, then my ideas will usually be listened to." Another person may have developed the expectation that "If I take a stand for something that matters to me, then I will be criticized or humiliated." Obviously, the conditional beliefs of the first individual would lead him or her to be assertive and confident; those of the latter person would influence him or her to be meek and passive. The cognitive model holds that everyone has an array of conditional beliefs that have been learned and accumulated over a lifetime. These beliefs constitute essentially a program for living or a set of rules attempting to make sense of the world.

Group therapy is a superb setting to explore conditional beliefs because multiple people are working together to reveal the underlying rules of each person's life. I explain to clients,

You are likely to be aware of some of your conditional beliefs and where you learned them. Others probably operate outside your awareness. You assume them to be true, but you don't really know for sure. In therapy we're looking for the kinds of conditional beliefs that cause you trouble. Maybe they are negative statements about yourself that are not helpful or true. Or perhaps they are your rules for surviving a difficult past that no longer apply in your current life. Or you may keep yourself from changing or growing because you assume that bad things will happen when there is no real basis for that kind of prediction.

Over the course of group therapy, CBT attempts to bring these conditional beliefs into the light of day and help clients *test the hypotheses* to determine which are valid and worth keeping versus which should be modified or dumped altogether (Clark, 1989). All those small predictions that clients make on a day-to-day basis are referred to by CBT as hypotheses. Group therapy seeks to help clients be aware of hypotheses they are forming and then determining which are true according to how accurately they predict future events. A client can test a hypothesis by deliberately setting up a situation to determine whether the hypothesis is proved to be valid. For example, a shy client believed that if he opened up he would be ignored by the people around him. With the support of the other clients he decided to test that hypothesis in group by speaking up and assessing the reactions he received. Contrary to his expectation, he found that people were interested in what he had to say and demonstrated their warmth and concern. Thus by testing the hypothesis that opening up would result in his being ignored, he was able to make an alternate hypothesis that in certain supportive settings (such as the therapy group) he could hope for a more positive response. Still in place, however, was the expectation that outside the therapy group nobody would really listen to him. This became his next area of testing the hypothesis by selecting situations and relationships in his day-to-day life where he could experiment with opening up as he had initiated in the group. He then discovered that there were two acquaintances who were more interested in him than he had predicted and their positive reactions opened the possibility of developing actual friendships with them. In this step-by-step process, the client identified his old hypotheses, put them to test, recognized what was proved false, and modified his subsequent predictions according to the new information. The resulting hypotheses led to more fulfilling experiences for him and a more adaptive approach to his interpersonal world.

Beneath these conditional beliefs, the cognitive model locates what are called the *core beliefs*. These are the fundamental ways that an individual regards himself or herself. They are seen to cluster in two areas: "To what extent is the individual capable of being loved?" and "How competent is the individual in facing the challenges of life?" These core beliefs derive from the accumulation of life experience and how each individual makes sense of what has happened. For example, a depressed client's core beliefs may indicate "I am not lovable because I have always been abandoned." Naturally this belief would darken the client's day-to-day experience as well as strain his or her current relationships. An anxious client may have a core belief that "I can't deal with threats in the future," reinforcing the pattern of avoidance commonly seen in anxiety (Burns, 1980).

Individuals usually hold a combination of positive and negative core beliefs as to their lovability and competence. If consistent with the goals of treatment, CBT explores the core beliefs as they are influential in each client's current life. This follows the downward arrow from immediate thoughts, feelings, and behaviors to conditional beliefs to core beliefs (J. S. Beck, 1995). In following the downward arrow method, the CBT therapist helps to explore the assumptions underlying a given belief. For example, a client found herself paralyzed with anxiety about making a presentation to an audience at work and the downward arrow method revealed her conditional belief "If I make a mistake in front of people, then they will think I am stupid." Then it came to light that she believed if one person in her audience had a single impression that she might have said something wrong, the thought would completely overrule all the positive reactions from everyone else. Exploring still further brought to the surface her own core beliefs about her incompetence that had developed in childhood and persisted despite her highly successful professional career. By using the downward arrow to illuminate the linkages of these beliefs, therapy could integrate methods to help her immediately with feeling more comfortable with her presentation while at the same time addressing her deep feelings of incompetence. It is usually not possible to completely remove negative beliefs. They likely had their origins in key events of the individual's life and show an indelible mark on the person's current identity. Contributing significantly to the distinctive qualities of the individual, these core beliefs ought not be eliminated, even if that were possible.

However, therapy can assist with *cognitive restructuring* (Meichenbaum, 1974). This involves helping a client to modify the constellation of beliefs that define her and her world to herself. In the process the individual typically leaves behind certain old beliefs that prove to be no longer valid or useful. There is more flexibility in being able to hold a variety of different beliefs about oneself in different situations, rather than adhering to certain rigid (and usually negative) beliefs that narrowly define the person. For example, a rigid belief that "I never know what to say to people" might be restructured to say "I may be quiet until I get to know somebody, but when I am comfortable I have a pretty good sense of humor." The therapeutic process of restructuring beliefs gives the client a firsthand experience of the positive results so that she learns to sustain this on her own after the therapy is finished. The process of examining and modifying beliefs is ongoing. A person can exercise choice over which beliefs are strongest and those that support the kinds of feelings and behaviors he or she desires. Psychological distress and symptoms almost always mean that negative core beliefs have gained ascendancy. Group CBT helps the members reduce the impact of the negative beliefs and develop current life experiences that are more rewarding. In the process, there can be creation of positive beliefs based on actual experiences of feeling loved and being competent.

TEN COMMONLY USED METHODS

Following are 10 methods commonly used in group CBT. This is not intended to be an exhaustive list but is offered instead as a serviceable introduction. For greater depth, readers are strongly encouraged to go to original source material in the CBT literature as well as to learn from practitioners who regularly use these methods. I engage in both pursuits myself.

Automatic Thought Record

The *automatic thought record* refers to a written exercise that guides clients in a process identifying thoughts, feelings, and behaviors* at a given moment, usually when they are experiencing some distress. Sometimes called a *dysfunctional thought record* or simply a *thought record*, this is one of the most frequently used clinical tools in CBT. It begins by providing clients the means of gaining awareness to see specifically what is being triggered in an immediate situation. Because awareness properly focused tends to lead to adaptive response,* the automatic thought record itself becomes a method of clinical intervention of *focusing and refocusing*. By gaining greater ability to focus and refocus, clients generally experience an enhanced sense of self-regulation, compared to when troubling situations and disturbing thoughts seemed to dominate their focus allowing no personal influence upon their own minds. In focusing, clients learn to gain perspective when viewing what is happening in their personal experience. From this vantage point, in refocusing, they are better able to see constructive responses to their triggering situations, as well as to begin modifying the dysfunctional thoughts themselves.

The group therapist typically teaches clients to complete the automatic thought record during session. This is an exercise of skills building and reflects the psychoeducational nature of CBT. I explain to clients,

> The thought record is something akin to a photograph of your mind at a moment in time. It helps us capture your immediate thoughts, feelings, and behaviors as relate to a given situation. There is not a right or wrong way to complete a thought record. But the more practice

you have, you will likely notice a greater understanding of your own reactions and you can see how to guide the experience in a favorable direction.

Members typically use thought records to deal with their day-to-day issues as well as to record new experiences during homework* between sessions. In group therapy, thought records offer certain unique advantages. When checking in at the beginning of the group session, members can share selectively from their thought records as a vivid means to relate an experience from outside of the group. I find that these reports are typically fresh and immediate, and lead to lively group exchange. Also, the thought record teaches members a common clinical language that facilitates their understanding and communication (especially valuable when time in the group may be limited).

The thought record originated in the work of Aaron Beck (A. T. Beck, Rush, Shaw, & Emery, 1979) and remains a hallmark of his approach. One of the best sources of teaching a client how to complete a thought record is provided by Greenberger and Padesky (1995), who explain the process step by step with plenty of clinical examples. Their client manual can be used as a workbook in therapy for clients to record their automatic thought process and work toward alternative or balanced thinking.

Challenging the Thoughts

CBT guides clients in a process of challenging their thoughts, particularly those that are associated with clinical symptoms and maladaptive behaviors. I will tell clients in a group,

> Once we have identified what you think or believe, now we get to see how true it is. What is the evidence* for and against? Are there other ways of looking at the same situation? Is this the only conclusion that can be drawn? By challenging your thoughts, you get to see those that may be outdated and need to be replaced. You can also see what thoughts and beliefs of yours stand up to challenge and consequently where you have a stronger and more confident sense of yourself.

This method of challenging one's own thinking harkens back to Socratic questioning* in which inductive analysis brings to the surface underlying assumptions and tests them against competing assumptions.

The process of challenging thoughts usually brings to awareness various *cognitive distortions* that have been supporting the maladaptive beliefs. These distortions are persistent patterns of thought containing idiosyncratic meanings and faulty rules of logic. For example, *dichotomous thinking* produces a narrow range of conclusions, typically at total odds with each other and expressed only in the most extreme terms: "Regardless of how she tries to explain her feelings about me, I know that she either com-

pletely loves me or totally hates me—those are the only two possibilities."
CBT challenges these extremes to alter the cognitive structure and produce
a balanced perspective that flexibly integrates a range of strong opinions
with a more objective view of the evidence (A. T. Beck, Freeman, &
Associates, 1990).

Obviously, the therapist needs to have a sufficient collaborative relationship* with clients so that the challenges are not taken to be critical
or negating. Empathy is crucial, both to know when and when not to
challenge. At the early stages of therapy, the therapist takes the lead in
challenging, but over the course of treatment clients learn more and more
how to do it on their own—in and out of session.

J. S. Beck (1995) provided a detailed explanation of this process in
her chapter 8, titled "Evaluating Automatic Thoughts." Albert Ellis described a similar method as *disputation*, in which he teaches the client to
challenge his or her irrational thinking (see Walen, DiGiuseppe, & Dryden,
1992). As opposed to identifying thoughts as good or bad (and falling into
the trap of dichotomous thinking), CBT challenges group members to reflect on the advantages and disadvantages of particular assumptions compared with others.

Mood Monitoring

This a simple behavioral method in which clients are asked to regularly rate their moods (sometimes called a *mood check*). Most often this
is used with clients who are experiencing depression, although it can also
be used for clients with anxious and manic moods (McKay, Davis, & Fanning, 1997). I explain to clients,

> Each day I would like you to rate your mood on a scale of 0 to 100:
> 100 is the most intense depression you've ever experienced, and 0 is
> the complete absence of depression. Give one score that would be your
> overall impression of the day. Write down the scores each day and
> bring the results to therapy with you.

This method gives clients and therapist alike an overview of the client's moods and longer term trends. It also helps to identify anomalous
events that stand out from the general pattern. Because clients with a mood
disorder tend to be both global and negative about their moods, the formal
act of mood monitoring can help them see subtle changes and points of
progress. Small improvements are brought into view. Results of mood monitoring can contribute to the process of outcome studies as measures of pre-
and postfunctioning to determine therapeutic effect. Clients learn to assess
their *continuum of experience,* noting slight shifts of day-to-day mood compared with dichotomous thinking* characterized by only a crude sense that
"I feel good" or "I feel bad." After the termination of therapy, continued

mood monitoring provides early warning signs of potential danger and re-inforces relapse prevention.*

The most complete means of mood monitoring in CBT is the Beck Depression Inventory (BDI; A. T. Beck & Steer, 1987).[1] The BDI permits clients to compare their scores with extensive normative samples as well as to assess their depression by multiple assessments over the course of therapy. Letting clients have direct access to actual research measures of their moods reinforces the sense of *shared empiricism* in the collaborative relationship of therapy. BDI scores, reviewed by the members of the group, encourage the group as a whole to reckon with how it is doing in reducing the depression of everyone involved. To think empirically means to ap-proach a situation as though it were an experiment. Members of the group learn to collaborate as though they are scientists who are interested in setting up favorable circumstances to experiment with their own therapeu-tic growth.

Arousal Hierarchy

This is a core CBT method in treating anxiety. In my opinion, the principle of an arousal hierarchy has been more broadly applied in general therapeutic work than any other CBT technique. Clients are guided to identify the various stimuli that cause them to feel anxious and to rank them from least to most threatening. I explain to clients,

> I want to you to think about all the different situations that cause you anxiety. Be as specific as possible. We will ask each other questions to clarify the exact nature of the threat.

Clients in group write their own description of anxious *triggers*. They then read this material to each other not only to share their personal fears with the other members but also to refine and specify exactly the nature of each trigger. The more explicit the better (Barlow, 1993).

Once the anxious items are recorded, I say to clients,

> Now, for each item I want you to write down the amount of anxiety you think you would experience when directly confronting that trigger. Use a scale of 0 to 100. I suggest you go with your first impression and not worry how that relates to any other scores you've given.

I urge clients to remain aware of their physical reactions during this exercise as an additional means to gauge their anxiety. If clients start to obsess about this number or that, I tell them that the ratings are only their impression at the moment, and they may be different 5 minutes in the past or 5 minutes in the future. If so, we can adjust the ratings then.

When the triggers and the anxiety ratings are complete, I ask the

---

[1]The BDI can be ordered from the Psychological Corporation, San Antonio, Texas.

clients to list the items from most to least threatening. A rich clinical picture of each individual's experience of perceived threat begins to emerge in hierarchical form. I suggest clients see what they can observe from their process of ordering. What is surprising? What would they choose to change? This may constitute a small breakthrough for clients, especially those who experience chronic anxiety. There can actually be a "more" and "less" to what troubles them. Prior to the beginning of treatment, clients probably felt their anxiety to be not only uniformly overwhelming but also capricious and unpredictable. With the hierarchy, we are beginning to introduce order.

And with order, *graded exposure* can begin. This is where clients determine which items in the lower regions of the hierarchy they are willing to confront, for the purpose of overriding their characteristically anxious reactions. Prolonged contact with the trigger brings a gradual lessening of the anxious reaction by *systematic desensitization*. Clients learn to tolerate being present in the situation to *decondition* their learned anxiety. As they gain confidence at the lower levels of the hierarchy, they can use the same skills to move higher. The group itself can be an excellent setting by which to experiment with exposure to anxiety-provoking situations. For example, clients may experience strong anxiety in response to speaking up, or intermember conflict, or hearing about the anxiety of other people. Successfully managing these stimuli in the group environment then sets the stage for *in vivo exposure* in real-life situations.

By consciously exposing themselves to these anxiety triggers and not letting themselves run away or be overwhelmed, therapy group members are developing the early stages of mastery.* Adaptation at the higher reaches of the arousal hierarchy eventually include *preventing safety behaviors* and *thought stopping* (Barlow, 1988). Anxiety is usually reinforced by a number of safety behaviors that give the client the impression of relieving anxiety, such as checking to make sure things are okay or steering clear of situations that might be threatening. Unfortunately, these safety behaviors usually serve to reinforce anxiety because by depending upon them the client manages to avoid dealing with the anxiety directly. The sense of threat, then, remains high. Therapy urges the client to prevent the safety behavior and use more productive means of confronting and reducing the anxiety. CBT teaches clients to stop their repetitive thoughts associated with their anxiety and redirect to a more pleasant thought content.

Activity Monitoring

In active monitoring, clients write down the activities of a given period of time, often a week. I explain to them,

> We want to get a sense how your time is spent. I'd like you to jot down in a few words the main activities you've done on an hour-by-hour basis. It's best to do this ongoing throughout the day so your recall is fresh rather than waiting too long.

Almost always, there are some surprises on the part of clients as to where their time actually goes (Bourne, 1995). Not only is this a tool to bring greater awareness on a day-by-day basis, but it serves as a baseline for each member to determine where and how to make changes. Activity monitoring naturally leads to *activity planning*, in which the client can make goals for himself or herself to spend time in ways that are more beneficial. Progress is not immediate and usually involves a process of *shaping* and *successive approximation*. When helping a client develop a therapeutic response, shaping refers to the response profile drawn on a graph that progressively takes the configuration of the desired outcome. A client rarely learns this response all at once, but more likely by successive approximation where each trial builds upon what has worked before and adds a new attempt to solve what has not yet worked. I find the most value in this exercise comes from asking clients to make assessments of their *mastery* and *pleasure* in the hour-to-hour activities during the day. I explain to clients,

> On the same sheet of paper where you have described your activities, I'd like you to make a quick judgment of how much mastery you experienced during that hour and how much pleasure. Mastery is the sense that you knew what you were doing and felt competent to deal with the situation. Pleasure is how much you enjoyed a given activity. Use a scale of 0 to 10 to make a mastery rating and a pleasure rating for each hour during the day.

This record can be fascinating to examine during therapy. What exactly are clients' experiences of high pleasure and mastery? How effective are members at planning the kinds of activities likely to lead to a sense of mastery and pleasure?

As an extension of this exercise, I will sometimes suggest that clients start each day by making a goal* for a high-mastery experience and a high-pleasure experience. There may be initial disappointment and frustration as clients fall short of their expectations, but the therapist can be helpful by continuing to support small and attainable goals. Therapy can be used to better understand what interferes with these goals (both internal and external factors) and planning how to get positive results. Group provides learning by means of *modeling*, in which members view the mastery and pleasure experiences of each other to reduce the trial and error of each individual figuring this out on his or her own.

Persons (1989) described in further depth the methods of activity monitoring. Of particular interest, she addressed a complaint sometimes expressed by clients or therapists that this exercise may appear "trivial." If there is concern that the activities of daily life are somehow superficial, I think it is by understanding the actual experience of these familiar activities that serves as the pathways to true psychological depth. I find that dealing with the real events of clients' lives through activity monitoring brings a quality of richness and nuance that these same clients had not realized when they were simply talking about their problems in stereotyped or redundant ways. Before a therapist can effectively urge a client to try activity monitoring, the therapist might consider engaging in the same in his or her day-to-day life. I would be surprised if some unexpected results do not occur. I would recommend putting forth the extra effort to make hourly assessments of mastery and pleasure. Does this lead to reassessment of how these judgments are made? What about modifying those activities that are low pleasure or low mastery so they yield better results? If the therapist experiences personal benefit from these exercises, the therapist will feel better about urging that his or her clients can gain from doing the same.

Problem Solving

Clients are likely to believe that their own capacity for problem solving is defective, whether this is actually true or not. Such a belief seems especially entrenched among anxious individuals. Group CBT wants to give clients a constructive experience in addressing problems in their day-to-day lives and figuring out solutions. I explain to clients,

> As part of the agenda for today I suggest we identify the kinds of problems that members are facing in their daily experience. We'll determine which problems seem to be strongest for the greatest number of people and that's where we'll start.

In the initial stages of the group, members tend to assume that their problems are somehow different from those of other people in the group. The development of *cohesiveness* signals the recognition that members struggle with many of the same issues.

The therapist facilitates a process whereby the group generates *adaptive responses* to the problems at hand. To *adapt* means "to gain a better fit with the environment" (Bandura, 1997, p. 24). The group seeks to revise those old behaviors of its members that are no longer working and determine what responses would achieve a better fit. Although the goal* of problem solving also applies in individual treatment, I think that group CBT is unusually well suited to generate adaptive responses. The interaction of group members is more likely to stir the consideration of alternatives, whereas the lone individual in one-to-one treatment probably takes more time to reach this stage. Members model for each other how to generate possible solutions and take steps to see what works. Drawing on role play and rehearsal, the group can generate experiential learning rather than simply talking about ideas.

I usually give a cautionary note as the group begins problem solving:

The point here is not to find the *right* answer, because human problems rarely have one and only one ultimate solution. When you first try something, don't expect it to work perfectly. Instead, see what you can learn from these new experiences. You often gain the most from what didn't work out just the way you expected. Take what you figure out, plan a follow-up solution, and see how it goes.

D'Zurilla and Goldfried (1971) developed a problem-solving approach that is easy to teach group clients. It provides five steps that members can practice together. I find a side benefit accrues from group problem solving. After a little practice, clients usually realize that they possess more natural problem-solving ability than they initially gave themselves credit for. These new successes in therapy provide an opportunity to reexamine their old core beliefs* about incompetence. Rather than now letting their prevailing anxiety dictate their feeling somehow insecure about taking care of problems, they are better able to accept new evidence* that they actually manage these matters fairly well. Group members usually graduate beyond the structured problem-solving methods and engage more liberally in adaptive responses in group. Therapy achieves its purpose when members generalize* these practices in their individual lives.

Relaxation

A basic assumption of CBT is that therapy would be overly limited if it stayed only in the realm of talking. Because many clients experience physical tension as a component of their psychological distress, CBT therapists teach relaxation as a clinical skill. In my own practice with groups I explain to clients,

As part of therapy, you will learn the ability to relax yourself and reduce the stress in your body. We will start by doing this in session, and then you will practice on your own.

Many clients have preconceived ideas about relaxation, sometimes negative in nature, and these need to be addressed. They may think that relaxation is simply "doing nothing," but it is useful to know that it is actually a learned skill to override the physical stress that has taken hold of their bodies. Or, because their tension may act as a long-standing barrier against the world, there needs to be a gradual development of safety in the therapeutic milieu so these clients can tolerate turning loose of their tension and experiencing more contact with other people. For this reason, before I introduce relaxation, I usually have several sessions for members to develop comfort with the group and for me to assess who might have strong resistance to relaxation.

The classic work in relaxation has been done by Benson (1975) with development of a broad range of techniques. I believe in the value of relaxation for my clients as a direct means for them to reduce their physical stress. It takes practice, but almost everyone can make progress if they want to. A more subtle benefit of relaxation is its positive effect on the therapy itself. Time and again I have observed that clients are more open to therapeutic work as they make progress in physical relaxation. It does not seem a radical notion that rigidity of the body is accompanied by rigidity in psychological realms. I find that the verbal part of therapy often moves ahead when the individual experiences greater physical relaxation.

Recognizing that relaxation is an integral aspect of CBT establishes a clinical rationale for related physical interventions as well. Various group CBT treatments use meditation, hypnosis, exercise, and biofeedback. Of particular interest, in my opinion, is the application of these principles with *imagery* (Lazarus, 1981). Only a portion of an individual's mental processes are encoded via language. Much of the content of perception and memory are stored in visual form. CBT brings this material into therapy by questions such as, "What imagery is associated with that memory?" or "Are you aware of any pictures in your mind immediately before you had that feeling of hopelessness?" Therapeutic use of imagery allows the client to gain access to relevant mental experience not available through language alone.

Risk Assessment

At any moment, an individual is making a whole series of determinations about the relative threat or safety that he or she is facing at that time. During anxiety or panic, an individual has a tendency to catastrophize and see immediate danger in extreme terms (A. T. Beck, 1976). Often these assessments of risk occur outside the awareness of the individual. I explain to group members,

> You may sometimes find that you feel threatened but are not be able to identify the source of risk. This can be upsetting, especially if you feel threatened much of the time while there seems to be no good reason for such a reaction on your part. In risk assessment, we want to do the detective work to figure out where the actual threat is coming from.

The therapist can provide important reassurance to clients by undertaking this risk assessment with the certainty that there exists some definable trigger. Clients have often been told in their past, "Oh, it's nothing —don't worry," and they probably try to make themselves believe this dismissal. It does not work, of course, because there remains the unrecognized source of threat that has not been properly dealt with. So clients do not really feel better in the process, and they judge themselves harshly because they are having a reaction that does not make sense to them or to anyone else.

Risk assessment helps group clients and the therapist to see what the origins of threat really are. It also provides a reading of the clients' resources to deal with the risks, producing a *risk-to-resources ratio* (A. T. Beck, Emery, & Greenberg, 1985). Risk is defined as a threat subjectively perceived by the individual. In the eyes of that person, she experiences some type of danger, such as to her self-esteem, her physical well being, or her relationships with loved ones. Other people may assess her risk differently, and this can make for useful discussion in a therapy group; ultimately it is the individual's sense of her own risk that matters. *Resources* refer to the psychological qualities that a person uses to deal with the risk. For example, this might include her self-confidence, her communication skills in conflictual situations, or her optimistic outlook. In many clinical situations, the clients' sense of risk is high, whereas their assessment of their own resources to deal with it is low. This formula of high risk/low resource is a cornerstone of the cognitive model* of anxiety. Over the course of therapy, clients examine the actual evidence of their lives to gain a truer sense of risk and resources. They gain in their appraisal of personal resources while reducing their assessment of current risk. Thereafter, when considering the odds for future challenges, they are more likely to arrive at a favorable (and more accurate) risk-to-resource ratio. For example, a client who is a very capable and assertive manager always felt intimidated in the presence of her mother and was not able to use the assertive skills that she had mastered in other areas of her life. Her therapy involved restructuring* her beliefs so that she could say no to her mother when appropriate. As this began to happen, there was a positive shift in her risk-to-resource ratio in the direction of being better able to handle the threats that she felt with her mother.

Assessment of risk and resources can be an illuminating method applied in CBT group therapy. When self-defeating views are expressed to the group by an individual, other members can share alternative views of the risks and resources based upon their more balanced view of the individual. It becomes evident that there are a number of ways of looking at a given situation. Care is taken, obviously, that the member does not feel invalidated or overruled by the group. There is a psychological reality to even the most negative of risk-to-resource ratios, and this needs to be respectfully acknowledged. Besides, it is ultimately up to the individual what, if any, alternative views to take in, so a CBT group supports the exploration of different perspectives about risk and resources with responsibility residing with each individual what to do about it.

Treatment Protocols

Given the empirical basis of CBT, there is an ongoing interest to find the clinical methods that produce the best results. Therapists are testing their approaches to determine what is most helpful to clients. Over time certain methods have demonstrated themselves to produce consistently positive results in dealing with specific problems. This primer chapter of CBT discusses a number of these empirically validated methods, including automatic thought records,* arousal hierarchy,* and relaxation.*

The next logical step from these empirically validated methods is an integrated therapeutic approach that includes all the key elements proven to be useful. Building from parts to the whole, this approach is called a *treatment protocol*. It typically draws together a core set of clinical skills that guides the therapist and clients in developing these abilities. There is typically a progression of the treatment, and the protocol addresses separate issues associated with the beginning, the middle, and the ending of therapy. In recognition of its empirical origins, the protocol usually provides on-going measurement of group clients to focus the work as well as to determine progress. The protocol may be a guide designed for the therapist's use or a workbook that clients use as homework* and then bring to session for review.

For a treatment protocol to be genuinely useful, there must still be a collaborative relationship* between client and therapist—which is fundamental to any CBT work. The protocol does not substitute for the fact that clients need to feel that the therapist is empathic and genuinely cares about positive results for the client. In some quarters, there is concern that a protocol would lead to a rigid or impersonal therapy. Obviously if this were true it would be counterproductive and a misuse of the therapeutic relationship.

One of the earliest protocols was Beck's seminal work (see A. T. Beck et al., 1979) on CBT treatment of depression. There have been subsequent developments for special techniques for various populations. Linehan (1993) developed a workbook and protocol for treatment of clients with borderline personality disorder that uses both group and individual treatment. For treatment of anxiety, protocols are available from White (1999) that incorporates the State–Trait Anxiety Inventory (Spielberger, 1983) and from Craske, Barlow, and O'Leary (1992). The use of protocols in treatment derives from a tradition in CBT drawing on a wide range of written materials to assist clients outside of session in the form of *bibliotherapy*. Bibliotherapy integrates the therapeutic work done in session with related reading undertaken by the client. This practice can deepen the experience of therapy, help the client be more involved with the therapeutic process outside of session, and bring in ideas that were discovered in the outside reading. Of course not all clients are inclined to read as part of their therapy and this must be assessed on a case-by-case basis.

Relapse Prevention

CBT recognizes that many of the problems treated in therapy have a tendency to recur over the course of a person's life. Based partly on physiological predisposition as well as deeply ingrained patterns of old learning, symptoms of anxiety and depression show a higher likelihood to return— particularly at times of crisis. Accordingly, the CBT therapist approaches these problems with intent to give clients a robust set of life skills to manage them rather than to aim for cure (which I do not think is feasible or practical). I explain to group clients,

> By learning these therapeutic skills you will have greater ability to deal with the triggers and the patterns that have caused you problems. Part of treatment, particularly in the final stages, is reinforcing these skills so the members will continue to use them on their own and stay on top of the old tendencies.

This is called *relapse prevention* and is an essential part of terminating therapy (J. S. Beck, 1995).

Clients successfully finishing CBT group can be seen to have achieved recovery from the problems that initiated treatment in the first place. It is in their best interest to establish a strong program for themselves that carries forward what they learned during group. I explain,

> When group is finished, you should be alert to old patterns and triggers that may signal your tendency to relapse. If this occurs, don't think of it as a failure of yourself or treatment. Instead, focus your efforts on doing everything necessary to regain the upper hand on the problem. You can steer yourself back into a solid recovery from the problems.

By initiating their own interventions early in the cycle, clients are able to avoid full relapse (A. T. Beck, Wright, Newman, & Liese, 1993).

Relapse prevention can be further reinforced by scheduling *booster sessions* in which the group meets for occasional sessions in the future. This often gives clients a target date so they will keep up on their therapeutic focus even when not meeting regularly. Obviously, the enjoyment of reconnecting with members is also a positive reinforcement to stay on track. For these reasons, booster sessions are seen as a good use of therapeutic resources in a time-limited treatment model (Cummings, 1995).

ELEMENTS OF A COLLABORATIVE RELATIONSHIP

A *collaborative relationship* means that the therapist and group clients are working together to get the best possible results (J. S. Beck, 1995). The word *collaborate* derives from the Latin word meaning "to labor together." This is CBT's means of achieving a therapeutic alliance. Clients need to feel heard and understood and must be able to believe that their therapist is genuinely interested in helping. Because this is a partnership, clients should feel free to ask wide-ranging questions about the treatment. These methods are useful only to the extent that clients fully understand what is intended. In issues of disagreement it is vital that group members feel comfortable to speak up.

Following are what I call the elements of the collaborative relationship. These are the practices of the CBT therapist that promote the development of collaboration. The therapist who is truly comfortable with the CBT approach draws together these elements in a flexible and even creative manner. Practice is required, as with anything else, but the reader is advised to picture this as a smoothly integrated approach that conveys the therapist's interest and ability to help.

Agenda

Most CBT treatment, either group or individual, involves the setting of an agenda for the session (Wright, Thase, Beck, & Ludgate, 1993). Typically, this is a consensus process including the clients and therapist, and so it hinges on the collaboration of everyone involved. Certain benefits of agenda are obvious. It permits a more effective use of time and helps assure that everyone in the group receives adequate attention. Additional advantages result from an agenda process because members often have not had the experience of cooperating with others to plan the use of shared time. To do so in a group setting requires skills of being assertive, listening, waiting one's turn, and seeking what is best for everyone. These are valuable qualities to learn and generalize* to everyday life.

Feedback

CBT is a feedback-rich therapeutic approach. The therapist actively encourages direct feedback from members, through verbal communication and sometimes by writing as well. This enables the therapist to adjust his or her methods and approach according to what is working best for clients. It also models ways of accepting feedback that have a constructive outcome (J. S. Beck, 1995).

Feedback between clients is generally guided by what is relevant according to each member's treatment goals.* For example, a timid individual in an anxiety group could benefit from constructive feedback about how her reticence comes across to other members. This would be particularly important if she is attempting to use the group experience to try being more assertive or open. Because most CBT groups are goal specific and time limited, there is usually not encouragement of feedback between clients that is open ended and personally based. For example, most CBT group cultures would not promote feedback such as "I hate you," "You remind me of my mother," or "I wonder if you are sexually attracted to me?"

Goal Setting

Most CBT group therapies involve the setting of goals to determine the direction of therapeutic movement. Clients often feel themselves to be stuck at first and have difficulty determining specific ways that they want to change. It becomes important to plan *positive contingencies* of change. For example, if a group member is depressed and has trouble getting to work on time, he might plan that five punctual arrivals means that he can go to a concert on the weekend. Change is more likely to be successful if it results in a reward for the individual. When therapeutic change involves adjustments that are necessary but intrinsically rewarding, such as getting to work on time, it helps to introduce extrinsic rewards like going to the concert. The client learns to motivate himself by establishing his own reward system. One of the initial steps of individuals coming together as a therapy group involves the members putting into words what they hope to get from the therapeutic experience. These individual goals then set the direction for the group as a whole. Clarity about goals proves crucial in determining in later sessions what is relevant for discussion in group and what is not. If potential issues do not relate to the goals set by members, then there is probably more useful material to be dealt with. Naturally goals are reviewed and modified over the course of therapy. Rehearsal reinforces the strength of the goals. An important aspect of terminating the group is assessing how individuals did with their goals and what issues remain after therapy is over (A. T. Beck et al., 1990).

The therapist guides the discussion of goals, but the goals originate from the group members themselves. That the therapist takes seriously the goals of the members, reinforces the nature of the therapeutic relationship. Depending on the group environment, I will sometimes voice my own goals, partly to clarify my position as well as to model the goal-setting process for members. In various groups, I have identified the following goals for myself:

- "I want to learn something new in each session."
- "I would like everyone to speak up at least at some point in the course of our therapy."
- "I hope that everyone feels they are better off than when they started."
- "Whatever differences arise, I hope we can deal with them so that no one feels they have to drop out."

Homework

Most CBT involves homework of some sort. Although there is an unlimited range of what CBT therapists use for homework experiences, what the homework has in common is a sense of *behavioral experimentation*. Clients are generating new hypotheses, putting them to test in real-life experiences, and determining the outcome of what proves helpful and true (Persons, 1989).

I think homework is one of the reasons for the favorable outcomes of CBT treatment. The more frequently a person practices a musical instrument, or rehearses a new physical skill, or speaks a different language, the more that person will gain mastery of the skill. But if group members feel that in therapy they are forced to do homework, the homework will fail, and they may break off therapy altogether. One of the arts of CBT is guiding people to find homework they feel good about doing.

In group, CBT members are typically encouraged, but not required, to do homework. Because everyone can learn from the homework experiences of each other, the more members who participate the better. There is usually not much tolerance among group members for repeated excuses, because other members somehow managed to do the work. The group therapist needs to follow up on homework with each individual because this conveys the therapist's priorities that homework is important. If members cannot or will not do the homework, it is important to explore the real reasons why—without making it a matter of shame or blame. I let it be known that I have had members in my group who, for a variety of different reasons, did not do any homework and still benefited from the group and made a contribution to other people. But on the whole, the people who get the most out of group are the ones who put the most into it—and that includes homework.

Socratic Questioning

Socratic questioning seeks to illuminate an individual's underlying assumptions. For example, a woman who is afraid of experiencing panic at work reveals that she has always felt like an outsider there and a panic attack would be the final humiliation. Therapy needs to address both her panic disorder and her feelings of alienation at work (and perhaps in other settings). Over the course of therapy a client learns how to initiate this type of Socratic questioning herself and determine the assumptions and beliefs that underlie her immediate experience. The CBT therapist guides the group members in a process to become aware of underlying assumptions and implicit predictions of how future events will unfold. By this inductive method, clients begin to discover the origins of their thinking and how they reach their conclusions. Over time, group members learn to inquire of each other with these open-ended and probing questions. If there is to be lasting benefit to group CBT treatment, individuals will have acquired the practice of self-questioning to be aware of the assumptions that affect mood and behavior (Young, 1990). It is in the context of a collaborative therapeutic relationship that the CBT techniques and methods reviewed in this chapter can be effective.

CONCLUSION

Having gained a preliminary grasp of these CBT terms, the reader is now ready to move forward to the chapters describing CBT group therapy. It will be evident that the authors have taken these basic CBT principles and techniques, and applied them in distinctive manner. Chapter topics were selected to address a range of clinical problems that are effectively treated in group venue. Further attention was directed to treatment in a variety of settings, such as outpatient, partial hospital, and inpatient. Benefit from group intervention was recognized to extend beyond traditional diagnostic categories, to also include groups for women's sexuality and parent training. Application to diverse populations is reflected in particular group approaches for Latinos and older adults. In the process of surveying the range of CBT group therapy, this book provides description of some treatment applications not frequently addressed in CBT texts—such as obesity, parenting, and partial hospitalization. It is the intent of this approach to promote the effective use of CBT group therapy and to support clinicians in a process of developing and testing further application of CBT in group settings.

REFERENCES

Bandura, A. (1997). *Self-efficacy: The exercise of control*. New York: Freeman.

Barlow, D. H. (1988). *Anxiety and its disorders: The nature and treatment of anxiety and panic*. New York: Guilford Press.

Barlow, D. H. (Ed.). (1993). *Clinical handbook of psychological disorders: A step-by-step treatment manual* (2nd ed.). New York: Guilford Press.

Beck, A. T. (1976). *Cognitive therapy and the emotional disorders*. New York: International Universities Press.

Beck, A. T., Emery, G., & Greenberg, R. (1985). *Anxiety disorders and phobias*. New York: Basic Books.

Beck, A. T., Freeman, A., & Associates. (1990). *Cognitive therapy of personality disorders*. New York: Guilford Press.

Beck, A. T., Rush, A. J., Shaw, B. F., & Emery, G. (1979). *Cognitive therapy of depression*. New York: Guilford Press.

Beck, A. T., & Steer, R. A. (1987). *Manual for the Revised Beck Depression Inventory*. San Antonio, TX: Psychological Corporation.

Beck, A. T., Wright, F. W., Newman, C. F., & Liese, B. (1993). *Cognitive therapy of substance abuse*. New York: Guilford Press.

Beck, J. S. (1995). *Cognitive therapy: Basics and beyond*. New York: Guilford Press.

Benson, H. (1975). *The relaxation response*. New York: Morrow.

Bourne, E. J. (1995). *The anxiety and phobia workbook* (2nd ed.). Oakland, CA: New Harbinger.

Burns, D. D. (1980). *Feeling good: The new mood therapy*. New York: William Morrow.

Clark, D. (1989). Anxiety states. In K. Hawton, P. M. Salkovskis, J. Kirk, & D. Clark (Eds.), *Cognitive behavior therapy for psychiatric problems* (pp. 52–96). Oxford, England: Oxford University Press.

Craske, M. G., Barlow, D. H., & O'Leary, T. A. (1992). *Mastery of your anxiety and worry: Client workbook*. San Antonio, TX: Graywind.

Cummings, N. (1995). *Focused psychotherapy*. New York: Brunner/Mazel.

D'Zurilla, T. J., & Goldfried, M. R. (1971). Problem solving and behavior modification. *Journal of Abnormal Psychology, 78*, 107–126.

Greenberger, D., & Padesky, C. (1995). *Mind over mood: Change how you feel by changing the way you think*. New York: Guilford Press.

Lazarus, A. A. (1981). *The practice of multimodal therapy: Systematic, comprehensive, and effective therapy*. New York: McGraw-Hill.

Lazarus, A. A. (1997). *Brief but comprehensive psychotherapy: The multimodal way*. New York: Springer.

Linehan, M. M. (1993). *Skills training manual for treatment of borderline personality disorder*. New York: Guilford Press.

Mahoney, M. (1991). *Human change processes: The scientific foundations of psychotherapy*. New York: Basic Books.

McKay, M., Davis, M., & Fanning, P. (1997). *Thoughts and feelings: Taking control of your moods and your life*. Oakland, CA: New Harbinger.

Meichenbaum, D. (1974). *Cognitive–behavior modification: An integrative approach*. New York: Plenum Press.

Persons, J. (1989). *Cognitive therapy in practice: A case formulation approach*. New York: Norton.

Spielberger, C. D. (1983). *State–Trait Anxiety Inventory*. Palo Alto, CA: Mind Garden.

Walen, S. R., DiGiuseppe, R., & Dryden, W. (1992). *A practitioner's guide to rational–emotive therapy* (2nd ed.). New York: Oxford University Press.

White, J. (1999). *Overcoming generalized anxiety disorder: Therapist protocol.* Oakland, CA: New Harbinger.

Wright, J. H., Thase, M. E., Beck, A. T., & Ludgate, J. W. (Eds.). (1993). *Cognitive therapy with inpatients: Developing a cognitive milieu.* New York: Guilford.

Young, J. (1990). *Cognitive therapy for personality disorders: A schema-focused approach.* Sarasota, FL: Professional Resource Exchange.

I

COGNITIVE–BEHAVIORAL GROUP THERAPY FOR SPECIFIC PROBLEMS

2

DEPRESSION

JOHN R. WHITE

Psychological depression is the most prevalent problem addressed by psychological treatment. The National Comorbidity Survey determined a prevalence estimate of 17.1% for lifetime major depression (Blazer, Kessler, McConagle, & Swartz, 1994). According to the National Institute of Mental Health, an estimated 17.4 million adult Americans experience some form of depression (major depression, bipolar disorder, or dysthymia) during any 1-year period (M. Strock, personal communication, April 17, 1998; see also American Psychological Association, 1996).

On the basis of his early research predicting suicidal risk, Aaron Beck (1964) developed cognitive therapy for treatment of depression as a structured, short-term, present-oriented method, directed toward solving current problems by means of modifying dysfunctional thinking and behavior. The key to Beck's understanding of depression was his focus on the prevailing experiences of helplessness and hopelessness—cognitive belief structures that are quite responsive to the cognitive therapy proposed by A. Beck, Rush, Shaw, and Emery (1979). Controlled studies have consistently demonstrated its efficacy in the treatment of major depressive disorder (see Dobson, 1989, for a meta-analysis). Cognitive therapy as developed by Beck has become one of the major contemporary approaches to psychotherapy and has broadened to include cognitive–behavioral therapy (CBT) with the contributions of Albert Ellis's (1962) rational–emotive therapy, Donald Meichenbaum's (1977) cognitive–behavioral modification, and Arnold Lazarus's (1976) multimodal therapy.

The first published report of group desensitization appeared in Lazarus (1961), who also authored a chapter on group behavioral therapy (Lazarus, 1968). The earliest description of cognitive group therapy was provided by Hollon and Shaw (1979). Freeman (1983) edited the first CBT text that dealt exclusively with treatment of couples and groups, an extension of theory and practice from CBT's origins working in individual therapy. Lewinsohn, Munoz, Youngren, and Zeiss (1986) developed a treatment protocol specifically for group treatment of depression that included teaching members specific skills, such as relaxation, planning pleasant activities, and social assertiveness. Miranda, Schreckengost, and Heine (1992) created a structured week-by-week group treatment for outpatients with depression in a hospital setting. Freeman, Schrodt, Gilson, and Ludgate (1993) provided an overview of the variety of CBT group therapy approaches in inpatient settings, and Brabender and Fallon (1993) compared an inpatient CBT group method with other models.

Contemporary group therapy literature demonstrates the utility of group therapy in current mental health settings (Cummings & Sayama, 1995). Addressing issues of time-managed group work (MacKenzie, 1997) and effective use of groups in managed care (MacKenzie, 1995), MacKenzie found that there is greater common ground with topics that have been the traditional domain of CBT, such as relapse prevention and goal setting. It is recognized that with certain populations the therapist's role and the group structure are adjusted significantly, again consistent with CBT's empirical orientation to modify clinical technique according to the specific needs of the people to be served.

A seminal contribution to the development of this CBT group method for treatment of depression was provided in the work of Yalom (1983), in which he addressed the unique requirements of delivering group therapy in inpatient settings. Given the shortening of hospital stays that was under way at the time and has continued since, Yalom (1983) observed that patient turnover demanded a fundamental shift in the group treatment.

> Inpatient group therapists cannot work within a longitudinal time frame; instead, *they must consider the life of the group to last a single session*. [italics added] This necessity suggests that they must attempt to do as much effective work as possible for as many patients as possible during each group session. The single-session time frame dictates that inpatient group therapists strive for efficiency. They have no time to build the group, no time to let things develop, no time for gradual working through. Whatever they are going to do, they must do in one session, and they must do it quickly. These considerations demand a *high level of activity* [italics added]—far higher than is common or ap-

propriate in long-term outpatient group psychotherapy. Inpatient group therapists must structure and activate the group; they must call on members; they must actively support members; they must interact personally with patients. There is no place in inpatient group therapy for the passive, inactive therapist. (p. 84)

What Yalom was describing in inpatient settings in 1983 has become endemic in mental health treatment in the 21st century, particularly for group therapy. Most settings do not provide the opportunity for a completely intact group of people to work together for an extended period of time. It is far more common that there will be treatment of shorter duration and that people will be joining and leaving the group on an ongoing basis. Therefore, this approach to CBT group therapy strongly endorses Yalom's principle of the single-session time frame. Make the session complete unto itself, including the resolution of problem to the extent possible, because there can be no assumption that the same group of people will ever meet together again. Obviously, there will be cumulative benefit from session to session for certain members who have continuity with each other, but that does not alter the fact that the therapist operates for maximum effect in the single session at hand. With this in mind, the present method has been used (and adapted) effectively in settings in which a cohort of patients begins and finishes therapy together, usually 8–16 sessions altogether, or in which patients join an ongoing group with a minimum commitment of attendance, commonly 8 consecutive sessions.

A separate influence in the development of this model of CBT group therapy derives from organizational literature and the healthy functioning of a working team. To the extent that people join together to form an effective therapy group, they are also succeeding as a work team whose purpose is to reduce the depression of all the people involved. Senge (1990), in his influential text in organizational development, used general systems theory to develop a model for what he called the *learning organization*, which paralleled the higher goals of the therapy group. It is "where people continually expand their capacity to create the results they truly desire, where new and expansive patterns of thinking are nurtured, where collective aspiration is set free, and where people are continually learning how to learn to together" (Senge, 1990, p. 3). Bennis and Biederman (1997), eschewing the antiquated "great man" theory of leadership, provided a case study method of six "great groups" that changed the course of 20th-century life by virtue of their creative collaboration. "None of us is as smart as all of us" (Bennis & Biederman, 1997, p. 1). In a lyrical treatment of leadership, DePree (1989) described the optimal bond between people at work, but much the same could be said to apply within the therapy group, when he stated, "covenantal relationships fill deep needs, enable work to have meaning and to be fulfilling. They make possible relationships that can manage conflict and change" (p. 15).

The present model for CBT group therapy of depression was developed in association with Dr. Aaron T. Beck. I was retained by a national psychiatric hospital system to design and implement a unified group treatment for depression in inpatient, partial hospital, and outpatient settings. Beck served as consultant to the project and provided onsite training. The method presented here is fundamentally consistent with Beck's formulation of cognitive therapy and would not have been possible without his generous support. For the sake of consistency in this chapter, all of the applications and clinical examples focus on outpatient group therapy for depression, although with slight modifications the approach can also be used in inpatient and partial hospital settings.

CBT GROUP PRINCIPLES

Cohesiveness

Cohesiveness is a central focus of the group therapy literature; it reflects the degree of personal interest of the group members for each other. Cohesiveness is high when people want to attend the group and look forward to relating to each other. They spontaneously think about each other between sessions. It is the social force in a group that permits members to tolerate differences and disagreements. When there exists sufficient cohesiveness, these differences do not threaten the basic integrity of the group. There is the opportunity to express diversity of experience and opinion with the confidence that the group will not fall apart and individuals will not be harmed. When there exists compassion and members feel concern for the suffering of other members, the group has achieved cohesiveness. Unless there is cohesiveness, there is not a group that has formed, only a collection of people who happen to occupy the same time and space.

The group therapist's fundamental task is to build cohesiveness in the therapy group. It serves to guide the therapist in selecting prospective members who are capable of developing cohesive relations with other people. The therapist will explicitly describe and reinforce cohesiveness as a vital component of the therapy group as it is forming. When inevitable challenges and obstacles to cohesiveness arise, the therapist will provide guidance to the group so it can work through the issues and develop greater strength of connection between members. Because cohesiveness defines a fluid and complex set of relationships between a number of people, it exists in no permanent or perfect state. Rather, it is a matter of balance. The therapist is mindful when a group tips in the direction of too much cohesiveness—recognizable when the group becomes overbearing, does not tolerate individual differences, or undercuts autonomy and independence.

By the same token, the therapist becomes aware if there is too little cohesiveness and members feel lonely, isolated, or cold. It is not long before poor attendance and dropouts develop. A skillful group therapist, in addition to managing all of his or her other therapy work, will always keep a finger on the pulse of the group's cohesiveness and be ready to gently steer as adjustments need to be made.

Task Focus

CBT is a focused therapy that seeks problem resolution. The group CBT therapist seeks to bring to the group therapy a strategy that builds cohesiveness *and* task focus. In the minds of some people, these would appear to be contradictory goals. They would argue that for members to maintain a good feeling of connection with others would push resolution of problems out of the way, or that to focus on the work of cognitive therapy would mean no group feeling has developed and "it's every man for himself." To assume that cohesiveness and task focus are antagonistic manifests the cognitive distortion of dichotomous thinking and would lead to an unbalanced and incomplete approach to leading a CBT group.

In fact, cohesiveness and task focus can be mutually enhancing, and the therapist seeks to facilitate movement from one to the other. When, for example, there has been an emotional group experience that reinforces the empathic connection between members, the therapist might ask, "How does this closer feeling help people make progress in dealing with your depression and moving ahead with your therapeutic goals?" Or, when a group has developed a new stage of task focus and achieved an important piece of problem resolution, the therapist might ask at time of wrap up to that session, "If this is a new level of group mastery, does it lead to a closer feeling between members?" The therapist is also monitoring when the group gets sidetracked and stuck on issues of cohesiveness or task focus. Oftentimes the means to help the group get unstuck is to turn attention to the underrepresented goal. For example, a group that is struggling to develop its group focus may be assisted by the therapist redirecting and asking, "What feelings are members getting from each other in this group?" There are likely to be undiscovered tasks that are overshadowed by the emotional tone being expressed. The therapist remains attuned when certain members find themselves in rigid roles, representing only task focus or only cohesiveness, and attempts to facilitate a more integrated participation for those people. If a member spends disproportionate time trying to smooth conflicts and make people happy, hoping for absolute cohesiveness, the therapist might ask, "How do you feel about your own progress in the group and what you are getting from it?"

THERAPIST ROLE AND SELECTION OF MEMBERS

Therapist Role

By his or her conduct in the group, the therapist models active participation and collaboration. The therapist is involved with members in building agenda, generating adaptive responses, designing homework, and teaching skills. He or she seeks a high level of involvement of all members, and it is the unusual session when everyone does not speak up in some significant way. The therapist helps to establish a group atmosphere that tolerates individual differences and encourages people to speak openly. By personal example, the therapist takes responsibility for his or her own experience and likewise urges members to do the same. The therapist's primary mode of communication is Socratic inquiry, which draws people into group discussion by asking probing questions that attempt to stimulate thinking in new ways (see chapter 1). For example, questions to a depressed man recently unemployed might ask, "In what ways do you see yourself differently now that you've been laid off from your job?" or "What are your best and worst views of your personal future?" More often than not the answers to Socratic questions lead to new levels of questioning, a process that becomes an important skill for members to acquire in their own self-exploration outside of the group.

As the exploration of automatic thoughts (see chapter 1) moves into the deeper levels of belief, usually common themes emerge that approach the scope of universal experience. Who could not, for instance, acknowledge feelings related to core beliefs of being unloved or identify with the sense of feeling incompetent? In this process, the CBT group therapist is more likely to refer "us" and "our" issues rather than to "you" members with "your" problems. Whereas obviously the therapist does not disclose personal history inappropriately, the therapist is willing to convey his or her familiarity with the therapeutic struggle and personal knowledge of dealing with depression. Such is the true nature of the collaborative relationship that is central to CBT. It is not uncommon for members to wonder aloud whether the therapist uses CBT methods in his or her personal life. After all, because the therapist is urging members to do thought records (discussed in chapter 1) on a regular basis to deal with triggering events, would it not be sensible for the therapist to make use of the same? Any therapist gains solid credibility when it is evident the therapist lives the way that he or she practices.

I have chosen to think of the role of CBT therapist as akin to the director of a film or the conductor of an orchestra. Similar to the director and the conductor in these artistic venues, the therapist guides a creative process produced by other people. In these roles, the therapist seeks to elicit from the actors or the musicians their best performances, but with the notable paradox that the film director appears exclusively off camera and the orchestra director is the only one on stage who does not play a note. The therapist's best contribution occurs when members are creating their own therapy. It is usually not the words of the therapist that are the most memorable over the course of a group treatment.

The role of director can be enhanced in the therapy group if the therapist chooses to do the group from a standing position. Although entirely optional, there is the obvious benefit to the therapist in being able to write group notes on an upright board (the joke about the cognitive therapist who could not talk if he could not write seems to be true). There is a more subtle advantage owing to the fact that a roomful of people with depression tends to be low in energy. The therapist who stands and moves can bring physical activity into the group milieu that encourages members to expand their own energy level. As the therapist steps forward to elicit a statement from an individual in the group, then turns to write those comments on the board, then moves laterally to talk with another individual, he or she can better guide the pace and direction of dialogue (again, as a director might). Not all therapists would be comfortable standing and moving during therapy group, but it might be worth experimenting with this limited aspect of charismatic leadership.

Selection

In selecting people to join a CBT group therapy, the therapist's intent is to bring in those who would benefit from this mode of treatment and who would make a contribution to the experience of other members in the group. It is recommended that there be at least one evaluation session in which the prospective member meets individually with a clinician to determine if group therapy would be a good fit. This evaluation would assess the extent of clinical depression and, most importantly, determine if there is active suicidal ideation. If present, that individual would need to be treated on an urgent basis, with evaluation for crisis intervention, medication, or psychiatric hospitalization. It would obviously be inappropriate to refer an actively suicidal person to an outpatient group therapy. This is a crucial determination for the safety of all individuals involved and so requires one-on-one evaluation with a clinician prior to referring to group. Clinical systems that perform only a telephone screening to refer to a depression group or simply publicize the beginning of a group and have people present themselves are failing this clinical and legal responsibility. It is debatable whether these alternative referral practices would be suitable for diagnostic categories other than depression, but it is certainly not for this population given that suicidal potential is a perennial danger.

Active suicidal ideation is the primary exclusion criterion of CBT outpatient group therapy. Others include current and untreated chemical dependency or current psychosis. Given the nature of these clinical problems, they require immediate attention before treatment of depression can begin. It would be a disservice to the individual to confound his or her treatment by beginning group therapy for depression without first addressing the more urgent needs. It would be an equal disservice to the members of a depression group to admit a member whose active chemical dependency or active psychosis was going to disrupt the cohesiveness or the task focus of the group. Depending on the skill level of the therapist and the nature of the how the group is composed, it is possible to consider inclusion of members who have past suicidal ideation, chemical dependency, or psychosis, as long as these issues have been properly treated and do not constitute a current problem. There can be good value and positive mutual influence, for example, for a member who is participating in the CBT group treatment for depression who is also active in his or her recovery from substance abuse. There are a number of parallels between CBT and treatment of addictions, including identifying triggers, determining the chain of thought that permits impulsive action, and taking active steps for relapse prevention (Beck, Wright, Newman, & Liese, 1993).

The process of determining who will be given the opportunity to join CBT group therapy for depression comprises only half of the selection process. No less important is whether the appropriate individuals elect to join group treatment once it has been offered to them. When the clinician makes a determination that an individual would be a good fit for group, a prime factor determining whether that person elects to join the group depends on the influence of the clinician. Can the clinician speak with firsthand knowledge about the effectiveness of group therapy? Can the clinician knowledgeably address questions or concerns about group treatment that might be raised by a prospective member? Does the clinician actually lead groups himself or herself and convey a positive belief in this work? These are all factors that influence whether the person who could benefit from group therapy actually chooses to be in group therapy. It is obviously preferred if a prospective member is not "forced" into group therapy as the only treatment available. Otherwise there would be referrals of inappropriate cases (such as people who are actively suicidal, chemically dependent, or psychotic). And people who might be appropriate could rightfully resent that they are given no choice as to the type of treatment they receive, thereby undercutting the benefit they would accept from therapy. While the referring clinician may recommend group treatment (perhaps, even strongly), the final decision ought to remain with the individual client. It is on this basis that a solid group therapy program can be built that works hard to maintain the voluntary participation of all individuals involved.

When members drop out of group, it usually results from a failure of selection, or treatment, or both. This approach to CBT group therapy for depression seeks to reduce dropouts to a minimum. When even one member drops out of group, that individual probably had a negative therapeutic experience and will be less likely to seek alternative treatment for his or her depression. The group suffers, too, when cohesiveness is broken with the member's departure and there is no opportunity to resolve the rupture. This is why a ground rule for CBT group therapy asks any member to speak up when he or she is not satisfied with the group or is thinking of dropping out. It is hoped that such a discussion could resolve the individual's difficulties with the group, which likely mirror the dissatisfactions experienced by other members that have not yet been voiced.

If a member misses a session without prior notification, the therapist makes a policy to contact the individual. Although it remains that person's choice whether to drop out, the therapist would prefer to discuss the issues to see if they can be settled in the group or at least to determine whether alternative treatments would be more appropriate. If the decision is to drop out, and with that individual's permission, the therapist conveys to the group at the next session the reasons for the dropout because this is rightly a group issue and should be open to discussion, usually brief. The members typically want to know if the person who dropped out is okay and whether he or she is in some other type of therapy. Responding to these questions helps the remaining members gain closure with the individual who has left the group and reestablish a sense of cohesiveness.

STRUCTURE AND CONTENT OF GROUP SESSIONS

Session Part 1: Check-In

At the beginning of each session, group members check in by sharing significant developments of the week, reporting on changes in their depression and recovery, and relating what was interesting from their homework experiences (see chapter 1). Members are typically pleased to see each other, and this segment serves to reestablish cohesiveness of the group as carried forward from the previous week. Homework design will be described in detail below, but this check-in is essential in making sure that homework experience on one's own is brought back to the members and becomes part of the ongoing group discussion. The check-in occupies about 20 minutes, and the therapist monitors the session to ensure that everyone has an opportunity to speak.

Session Part 2: Agenda

The practice of CBT recognizes that wise use of time is vital in therapy as well as in life. Most individual CBT treatment protocols involve the patient and the therapist collaborating to establish a flexible agenda for each session (see chapter 1). The same is true for group CBT treatment of depression as the therapist guides members to determine for themselves what is going to be the best use of available time. Skillful development of agenda facilitates the feeling of cohesiveness as members collaborate to determine what is most important to talk about. As much as possible, these decisions are made by consensus. Members gain in a sense of power as they determine the content of their group and learn skills of setting an agenda in their own lives and joining with other people to do the same. The agenda process, as detailed in the example below, occupies approximately 20 minutes, but it typically takes less time over the course of treatment as members become familiar with each other and the process itself.

Clinical Vignette: Generating the Agenda

In an early session of group therapy, members were guided in their first experience developing an agenda to determine what they were going to work on that day. The therapist explained, "I'd like to begin by getting a sense of the kinds of automatic thoughts that are troubling to the people here. Let's build a list of at least one automatic thought for each person, and then we'll determine which one is strongest for the greatest number of people, and that will be the focus of our therapy today." The therapist then asked the members to review aloud what they had learned about automatic thoughts. Various members responded: "They are statements we make to ourselves about ourselves, our world, or our future." "Strong automatic thoughts go with strong feelings." "They tend to be outside our awareness, like hiding in the shadows or behind the curtain." "Automatic thoughts just seem to pop into my head." "They go really fast, more than 90 miles an hour." "Once you recognize it, you realize you've had that thought ten thousand times before." Periodic rehearsal of CBT terms helps reinforce these ideas in the minds of members and puts the material in the domain of group experience and language more effectively than would a therapist's lecture on the same topic.

The therapist initiated the agenda process by saying, "We are going to use a democratic vote to determine which of these thoughts we will work with today. In a moment we will go around the room for each automatic thought, and I'll ask people to raise their hands if they can personally relate to it. You may vote for one of the thoughts, or some of them, or all of them." The therapist recorded the vote count beside each written thought. The minimum was two votes (in fact, it is rare for a thought to have fewer than two votes). The highest vote count was an item that was endorsed by all members of the group: "I will never be normal." This became the target thought of the group's focus for the remainder of the session. Every member had a strong personal stake in working through this thought; no one was an outsider. An agenda properly generated by the members transcends a group model of serial individual therapy with spectators, which is not group therapy in the true sense. From this point forward in the session, there was a discernible increase in cohesiveness because the members were joined together by what they experienced in common. Although each individual obviously carried personal history and meaning to "I will never be normal," the group could now focus on a target thought that belonged to everyone. The next stage of the clinical narrative is presented below, after discussion of the adaptive response.

Session Part 3: Adaptive Response

Generating the adaptive response is the primary therapeutic mechanism of CBT (see chapter 1). It is a psychological process by which an individual who has been trapped in a pattern of one's own thoughts and feelings begins to sense that there are real choices and opportunities. The individual starts to feel able to take action when none seemed possible before. This therapeutic process is particularly important in depression because it is a condition that seems to dictate that there are no options at all. The combination of helplessness and hopelessness, which characterize depression, paralyzes a person from making an adaptive response. The more protracted the failure of adaptive response, the worse the sense of helplessness and hopelessness. It is the immediate experience of adaptive response in taking small tangible steps that begins the process of recovery from depression. There is a natural tendency for a depressed individual to say, "If I were able to feel less depressed, *then* I would be able to make the adaptive response." A CBT therapist would answer, "As long as you are not able to make adaptive response, you are likely to go on feeling depressed. It is the responsibility of this therapy to help you first make changes in how you act and adapt, with the reasonable expectation that you will then begin to feel better."

There seems to be less of a tendency in a CBT group setting for members to rely on the therapist to be the one who is responsible for making the adaptive response happen. It has been observed repeatedly that, when participating in CBT group therapy for their depression, the same individuals who in one-on-one treatment felt themselves unable to generate an adaptive response and took a passive role in their treatment became more active and involved in generating the adaptive response. There seems to be reduced tendency in the CBT group setting for the illusion that an authority figure will step in to make the necessary changes.

Given CBT's emphasis on adaptive response, it is then recognized that asking for or giving advice in the group setting is generally countertherapeutic. To do so would undermine individual responsibility and predispose a person to a group role of "the help-rejecting complainer" (Frank,

1992). The CBT group therapist models the practice of not giving advice and addresses the issue when it arises between members as follows: "We're not really here to be in the business of giving advice to each other. It is far more important for us to support each person in determining what he or she needs to do. After all, we're all grown ups here, and it's not going to be terribly useful for people to be trying to tell other people how to live their lives, even with the best of intentions." It usually makes sense to members why individual responsibility is preferred over advice giving, although at certain stressful times in the group when feelings of helplessness are freshly triggered, the therapist can be most effective by identifying the negative thoughts that are coming to the surface in the form of asking for or offering advice. The therapist can keep the group on track by helping members generate adaptive responses to that immediate sense of helplessness. "What do individuals need to do right now in this session to address their own sense of being helpless?" "What is getting in the way of people being able to take responsibility for themselves?" "How does what is being triggered right now relate to your general sense of depression?" The ability to generate an adaptive response in the session is the best way for an individual to gain confidence in being able to do the same in his or her day-to-day life.

Clinical Vignette: Progressing Toward the Adaptive Response

After developing the agenda as described in the previous narrative, the therapist asked the group what were the consequences of believing the target thought "I will never be normal." Members responded variously, "Sometimes I quit trying to get better." "I feel hopeless." "I don't tell regular people anything personal about me." "I look for others to take care of me." "I feel sorry for myself." "I compare myself with other people." "I become critical of myself." Members saw firsthand that the target thought, which they all had in common, led to a broad range of thoughts, feelings, and actions. To recognize that there are multiple pathways leading from a single target thought suggests the possibility that members are not forced to be trapped in the one habitual pathway they experience, but could perhaps guide the alternative pathways they prefer to follow. CBT group therapy tries to show its members that practically any thought has consequences, and to gain awareness of this ongoing process is also to gain influence on it.

The therapist then asked group members what would be useful in their feeling less troubled by the automatic thought. This was the quiet beginning of generating the adaptive response. The therapist's remarks were deliberately low key as he or she guided members to draw on their previous life experiences. There is an implicit assumption in CBT that members possess in their repertoire of behaviors much of what they need to know to help themselves. Therapy enables the individual to connect the right response to the right situation while feeling ready to give it an honest try. If the group therapist were to approach the adaptive response as a "big deal," it would probably intimidate members and mislead them to think the process was more complicated than it really needs to be.

The therapist made clear that members were not expected to perform the items that they suggested, nor would the group critique whether or not the response would work. No one was asking for or receiving advice. Instead, it was a process that generated possibilities, and then it was the responsibility of each individual to determine which to apply in one's own personal situation. In the present clinical narrative, the group generated the following adaptive responses and the therapist wrote verbatim on the board: "I remind myself that many other people struggle with depression. I am not alone." "Feeling better is a whole lot more important than being normal." "My worry about whether I'll ever be normal originates from my fear that I'll relapse to depression. While that would not make me happy, I could deal with it. Relapse doesn't mean failure." "Who wants to be normal? I've never been completely mainstream, anyway." "I've found people I feel close to. They're probably not normal either." When there is a proper climate for members to expect that collectively they can begin to make an adaptive response in the face of the depression, their efforts are often remarkable in their simplicity and good sense.

In concluding this therapy session by collaborative design of personal homework, the therapist asked if members would be willing to select one of these adaptive responses and practice it during the week. Whenever the thought occurs, "I will never be normal," the member would put into action the adaptive response he or she had selected. The therapist explained that the point of this homework was to learn what works and does not work while in the process of responding to automatic thoughts. It is not expected that anyone would achieve a complete resolution. The benefit of the experience for the group is for members to generate a number of the possibilities, test them in real-life situations, and share the results with each other in the next session. From this discussion, members can gain a deeper understanding of adaptive responses and refine their methods for subsequent weeks. By the time members had progressed from generating adaptive responses to designing homework, the mood of the group had shifted from somber to feeling hopeful as it faced a challenge that now seemed manageable.

Session Part 4: Homework

Therapeutic homework attempts to put into action what was discussed in session. It seeks to integrate therapy and regular life, thereby making therapy more practical and one's life more amenable to the positive influences of treatment. CBT recognizes that therapeutic progress requires both talking and doing. Each member in the group designs homework that will be relevant to his or her progress in therapy and what needs to be practiced and learned next. Most frequently, homework arises from an individual selecting some aspect of adaptive response generated by the group and deciding how to apply it in his or her personal life in the ensuing week. The therapist and the other members can provide feedback when homework is initially discussed, but the final design and follow-through for homework rests fundamentally with the individual. The group is a good place to explore "negatives" that might emerge in the midst of homework and problem solve ahead of time during session so these factors do not undermine or derail the work.

Homework is particularly valuable in a group setting because of the opportunity to learn from the experience of a variety of people. Sometimes it seems that members learn as much, if not more so, from the homework experience of other people than with their own. If homework is to be used in CBT, it is crucial to check up on the homework in the next session. By this method, the results of homework are integrated back into the group experience and signals to each individual that the homework is sufficiently important to follow up on it. The discussion of homework usually involves what worked, what did not, what can be learned from the experience, and what could be done next. The purpose of homework is to learn from new experience, not to perform any given task "correctly." One probably learns more from what turns out in unexpected fashion. If all homework turns out exactly as planned, it probably means that the homework was too easy or too safe.

Homework in CBT group therapy for depression is encouraged but not required. Because homework is successful to the extent that it is designed and carried out by the individual, to make it an issue of control or compliance would violate the principle of autonomy. Homework is encouraged on the basis that it helps people get better sooner and because members often learn a considerable amount from the homework experiences of other people. A certain positive momentum develops in a group when members generate homework at the end of one session, encourage each other to follow through during the week, and then check in on the experience in the following session. Homework models a self-initiative and healthy discipline, both of which are often lacking in the midst of a clinical depression. Part of the reason for the favorable outcome measures of CBT may derive from the simple fact that in doing homework individuals are putting more effort into their therapy, and, as in most endeavors, harder work usually yields better results.

Practically all CBT therapies teach individuals how to complete an automatic thought record, a one-page structured inquiry to determine the key elements of the thoughts, feelings, and actions at a given moment in time. It is the written equivalent of what Beck called the *cognitive probe* (Beck, 1976): "What is going through your mind right now?" (see chapter 1). This approach to CBT group therapy teaches members the automatic thought record in the second session and uses it regularly in homework for the duration of treatment. It proves to be helpful when members are facing troubling thoughts or feelings during the week and want to gain a greater understanding of what has been triggered. It becomes a written record that can be useful in reconstructing the internal details of what happened, such as during check-in of the next session. The other application of the thought record in group therapy is for members to use it while attempting new adaptive responses in order to pay close attention to one's cognitive process while putting into action this different experience. Practicing self-reflection during the process of change deepens what one can learn about the adaptive response.

This approach to CBT group also suggests as part of homework that members use a mastery and pleasure record (see chapter 1). In this one-page sheet, the individual is asked to generate a 1-day mastery goal, a pleasure goal, and then to evaluate what has been the high and low experiences of mastery and pleasure during that day. There is obvious value in members planning such activities on a daily basis and then paying close attention to what happens with their experience of mastery and pleasure. Not surprisingly, depression often undermines the sense of mastery, pleasure, or both regardless of what the individual has done. The more this tendency to undermine oneself is brought into plain view, as recorded in daily mastery and pleasure records, the more negative effects of the depression can begin to be challenged and turned aside. There could hardly be a better predictor of long-term mental health than a rich ongoing experience of mastery and pleasure, as defined on one's own terms.

Clinical Vignette: "Resisting" Homework

In the fourth session of the group, while checking in on homework completed from the week before, two members indicated they had not done the homework. Each person was willing to discuss and explore the reasons, understanding they would not be grilled. The therapist asked, "At one of the moments when you considered doing the homework and decided not to, what were your underlying thoughts at the time?" The first member, Mike, responded, "I didn't feel it would do any good." Asked for his definition of good, he answered, "To *feel* good, significantly better than when I started." The therapist then asked Mike to explore the downstream consequences in his thoughts and actions for the pattern he had described. "Well, I didn't do the homework, and I felt the same, not better and not worse. Being in the session now and listening to other people talk about what they learned from their homework experience, I get the feeling that I'm being left behind. They're getting ahead and I'm not. I feel a little out of it." Mike was then asked what would happen if this trend continued. "I'd probably drop out. I'd feel I failed and I had lost an opportunity."

The therapist addressed the other group members to determine who else could relate to the automatic thought, "The homework won't do any good." The majority of members indicated that they, too, had experienced the same thought at some point during the week. Asked how they responded to it at the time, they provided various answers: "I figured I'd try it anyway, I didn't have anything to lose." "Because the therapist said it would be helpful to me, I would do it and see how I felt later on." "I know that my depression makes me negative to practically everything. If I don't do something different, I'll stay depressed." Once the topic had been broached, most of the members experienced at least transient doubts whether homework would make them feel better. Those who were able to complete the homework found ways not to be immobilized by their doubts. The doubts themselves were not the problem, rather how one responded to the doubts. Mike concluded, "I'm not as weird as I thought I was. Other people can relate to my negative thoughts, and I don't feel as left behind as I did at first."

The group was asked to generate adaptive responses for occasions when members of the group may experience significant doubts about future homework. "I'll try to do a thought record when I find myself thinking, 'the homework won't do any good.'" "I'll focus on alternative beliefs that I can get something valuable from the homework. It helps if I review the evidence of what I've learned in the past." "I'll adjust my homework to smaller and more manageable tasks. I don't have to accomplish everything all at once." "I'll downsize how much improvement I expect. It will take a while before I'm well." "I'll call other members of the group during the week when I feel doubts to get support and encouragement in attempting my homework." The group members wrote down these adaptive responses and agreed to try them when they encountered doubts about the homework. Members also agreed to remain honest in being candid about their doubts rather than keeping quiet and giving the false illusion that nobody had any such questions. Mike responded that he felt more positive about trying homework as well as being reconnected with people in the group.

The second member who had not completed homework, Diane, was asked about her underlying thoughts at one of the moments when she considered giving it a try. She responded, "I don't like the therapist telling me what to do. The therapist is trying to make me do homework. It feels demeaning, I resent it. I am not a child." She said that the consequences of these beliefs were that she did not attempt the homework, and she dreaded coming to the session. "I'm going to get called on. The therapist is going to try to criticize me and guilt trip me." Further consequences would be, "I would probably drop out of the group and avoid future therapy. I'm not to that point yet, but I can feel it coming on if things don't change."

No members experienced those exact thoughts about the homework during this group, but they agreed with having similar reactions in situations in which they felt forced to do things against their wills. The therapist responded to Diane, "I'm sorry if I gave you the impression that I was forcing you to do homework, or anything else for that matter. I would certainly not want to be treated that way. My approach is that we're all fundamentally responsible for ourselves in here, and people need to decide on their own terms what they will do and what they won't do. As your therapist, I think it is my job to try to work with each of you to help create homework that feels useful to you and that you want to do. But the decision is ultimately yours. Please tell me when I seem to be forcing or controlling, OK?" Diane indicated she felt better about the issue and would tell the therapist if she felt forced. The group was asked about adaptive responses in this situation. "In the future I won't do homework I don't want to do." "I'll confront the issue if I feel I'm being controlled." "I'll check out with other members how they would feel if I don't do homework." "I'll remind myself there is no right answer when it comes to homework, and nobody does it perfectly." "I'm willing to say what I learn from other people's homework and will welcome hearing what they learn from mine."

Diane seemed to have deeper issues about feeling controlled and expressed a distinct sense of resentment in declaring "I'm not a child." During this session, Diane took no initiative to discuss the personal nature of her reactions to the homework, and the therapist chose not to explore these issues at this time. There needed to be first a clarification that Diane's concerns were legitimate and no one would be forced to do homework. To have tried to sidestep this issue and move into discussing her individual history would be ill timed and perhaps be seen as manipulative. Cohesiveness suffers when a valid group concern is neglected. As long as the first priority of proper group culture is developed and maintained, individuals will then bring up their personal issues and benefit from the therapeutic influence of the group. The therapist made a silent mental note of Diane's issues of control and feelings of resentment and looked for opportunities to advance this work in subsequent sessions.

Throughout the Phases of Therapy: Goal Setting

People who are experiencing depression typically do not feel that goal setting is a pleasant or productive activity. Either they cannot generate goals and so have a difficult time initiating action or they tend to create goals that are so overwhelming that there is no chance of being able to satisfy them. They fall short in one of the fundamental aspects of psychological health—the ability to generate goals and build hope. This CBT group for treatment of depression seeks to guide the members in the experience of successful goal setting. This is a deficit skill for most people with depression, and group is an especially good venue to practice the new approach and put it to use. In the early stages of forming a group, the therapist explains how each individual can develop goals that are specific, observable, and lead to completed action. Members who feel more confident to discuss goals provide a good model for others who are frightened. In the group discussion about goals, there is a combination of encouragement and constructive suggestions about how to make the goals more attainable. As the cohesiveness of the group grows, the personal goals of individual members develop into the goals for the group. At mid-course in therapy, it is important for each member to assess progress toward goals. Is the therapy on course for reaching one's goals? Is it off course? Do goals need to be adjusted or added? Members can provide a useful perspective in observing how they each stand in relation to each one's goals. This view of each other is one of the benefits of group treatment, especially for individuals with depression who are likely to have distortions or blind spots in how they assess themselves. When the conclusion of therapy has been reached, it is important to determine which goals were fulfilled and what new feelings and behaviors developed as a result. It is equally important to determine which goals were not fulfilled and to reckon with feelings of disappointment and discouragement. How did the members, the therapist, and the group fall short of the goals, and what can be learned from the experience? On what goals should members keep trying, and which goals should be let go?

When the members of the group have a good sense of their own goals, group sessions are more likely to remain focused on the necessary therapeutic work that will attain the goals. There is less likelihood of incidental and unnecessary conflict that does not bear directly on members attaining their goals. There is less small talk or social discourse because to do so would be a distraction. When there is a clear sense of individual goals in the group, there is a stronger basis for the therapist to address and confront an individual who insists on dominating the sessions. All members need the opportunity to participate in each session in support of everyone making headway on their goals. This method of confronting does not need to be used often, but is usually effective because goal setting has been established as such a strong priority in the CBT therapy group. The group's skillful use of goals reinforces not only the task focus but also the cohesiveness.

Weekly: Outcomes Measures

Because CBT is an empirical method (see chapter 1), it involves regular clinical measurement in the form of therapeutic outcome measures. This model of CBT group therapy for depression uses the Beck Depression Inventory, or BDI (Beck & Steer, 1987) as described in chapter 1, although there are other good assessment tools available. Members are asked to complete a BDI each week prior to attending the session. The BDI is usually provided in the waiting room. In the initial group meeting, the therapist discusses the BDI results in some detail so members know what their scores mean and understand the various symptoms that compose a diagnosis of depression. In subsequent weeks, members may elect to mention notable BDI responses, particularly if there have been significant changes from the previous session. Members are provided with a graph to chart their weekly scores to show trends over the course of therapy. Because of its normative sampling, the BDI provides an objective measure of severity of depression that the individual can compare with his or her subjective sense of his or her condition. Weekly assessment can reveal subtle improvements, which can be encouraging for this population because people with depression tend to underestimate their progress in therapy unless they have some objective comparison of where they started. A BDI item specifically inquires about suicidal intent, and another item regarding hopelessness also correlates positively with suicidal risk. These data sources, in addition to verbal statements in group, provide another means to assess suicidal risk (always an issue with a population with depression) and provide the therapist with some peace of mind that each member has answered this vital query each week. BDI results, with the permission of members, provide a good means to summarize treatment status to referral sources, to assess the ongoing effectiveness of the group, and to conduct outcome research.

COMMON THEMES IN GROUP TREATMENT OF DEPRESSION

Certain themes emerge regularly in CBT group treatment for depression: loss, anger, suicidal ideation, and guilt. The following is a discussion how CBT conceptualizes each problem and provides group methods for treatment, as illustrated by selected case narratives.

Loss

Personal loss is a prominent feature of depression. There are, of course, numerous losses experienced by a person with depression, including loss of energy, of appetite for food, of social contact, of interest in sex, and of concentration. These losses are seen as a consequence of the depression and constitute several of the items on the BDI.

Equally important are the types of personal losses that cause or lead to the development of depression. These are vital resources of the self that are missing, and, in this frame of mind, there seems to be no way to make up the loss. It is a state of protracted grief in which the individual is not able to properly mourn or to recover. A first step in the therapeutic process is to determine specifically per each individual what exactly has been lost. For example, three people might have experienced the death of their spouses, but the precise meaning of that loss would be different for each individual. For one, it might be the loss of love and no longer feeling deeply connected with anyone else. For another, it might be the loss of personal support and feeling that there is no one to call on in time of crisis. For a third, the death could mean the loss of companionship and missing shared experiences of pleasure. Obviously these categories are not mutually exclusive, but the losses will take on separate and distinct qualities for each individual. Consider, with the loss of a job, one person experiences the loss of financial security, another the loss of friendship at work, and a third might be the loss of opportunity to learn new things. When a depressed person gains sufficient clarity to know exactly what has been lost according to his or her terms, the depression becomes less confusing and more comprehensible. A CBT therapist would say, "We now understand what the loss has meant to you and how your reactions make sense." As the cognitive aspects of the loss are clarified, this becomes a starting point for change.

When the experience of loss has developed into depression, there is commonly a suppression of feeling. People with depression often describe their emotional reactions to the loss as being characterized as empty, numb, dead, or feeling nothing at all. If depression is regarded as the absence of feeling, recovery involves the return of feeling. Group therapy for depression provides an optimal means to bring about the restoration of affect. Consider that funeral customs in most cultures involve a group of people who come together to mourn, to remember, to share feelings, and to prepare to move on. There seems to be a similar emotional passage for people with depression in a therapy group. In the process of mourning, remembering, and sharing, they are enacting a social ritual that addresses loss. Members make personal gains as they offer empathy to other members of the group regarding their various losses. Recovery from depression means being able to care again, not infrequently directed toward other members of the group before one is ready to care for oneself again. If the group has not spontaneously introduced loss as an agenda item by the halfway point in the course of group treatment, it is advised that the therapist raise the topic for discussion. To wait longer would likely confound the working through of loss with the termination of the group (see chapter 1), itself a significant loss.

Clinical Vignette: Loss

Following a session in which members discussed at length their various types of loss, the therapist posed the following question: "What automatic thoughts surface when you feel depressed and unable to move ahead in you life beyond the loss?" Members generated a list of the following thoughts: "My feelings are overwhelming to me." "That relationship was my best chance for happiness; now it's over." "I'm too old." "Circumstances are out of my control." "Other people don't understand what I've lost." "I don't know what to do next." "I'm scared to try again." "It feels that a part of me is gone." Hopelessness was a pervasive theme, demonstrating why the compounding effects of loss eventually lead to the loss of hope.

Members were then guided in a democratic agenda process to determine which of the negative thoughts about loss was the strongest for the group. There were equal votes for "Other people don't understand what I've lost" and "It feels that a part of me is gone," and so the consensus decision was made to work with both. The therapist asked the group to examine advantages and disadvantages for holding these beliefs. The disadvantages were readily apparent: "I stay depressed and alone" and "I'm unable to do anything." The advantages required more uncovering: "I don't have to try to get better," "I won't let people forget what I have lost," "If I hoped for more I might fail or be disappointed; I couldn't handle it," and "I might look foolish." If people are having a difficult time getting over loss, it only stands to reason there are strong underlying beliefs and predictions that compel them not to change. Members were asked to identify which one of these underlying beliefs they wanted to change, and they selected "Better able to deal with disappointment." The therapist explained that one of the reasons a person with depression has trouble generating hope is that the person fears that he or she could not handle the feelings of disappointment if he or she failed to get what is hoped for.

The therapist probed the group to generate adaptive responses to disappointment and recorded the following thoughts from the members: "If I try lots of little things, one disappointment is going to be less overwhelming to me." "I'm better able to get over disappointment if I share it with other people." "I try to figure out why my attempt was worthwhile even if it didn't turn out the way I had hoped." "If I can learn from a disappointment it feels less likely that I'll have to repeat it." "Feelings of disappointment are natural. They don't last forever." For the following week's homework, members were asked to plan one new activity that related to their recovery from their loss. For example, one member who was depressed having lost a job and feeling too demoralized to start looking for a new position stated that she would try to spend an hour reading a technical magazine in her field. As were the other members, she was then asked to select from the list generated by the group the adaptive response that she would use to deal with feelings of disappointment that might arise in this exposure to her field of work. She chose "I'm better able to get over disappointment if I share it with other people," and she planned to contact her best friend if her feelings became overwhelming. When members feel more confident that they can deal with disappointment, they will be more willing to undertake risk to make life changes following loss. Each member described to the group his or her plan for taking an attainable risk, members offered each other constructive feedback, and a master list was prepared by which to check in on results of the homework in the subsequent session.

Anger

Most people who are depressed experience problems dealing with anger. They may be anger phobic and feel afraid or guilty that people will get hurt, they may lose control and go into rages followed by contrition, or they may experience a low-grade irritability most of the time. CBT attempts to help people with depression distinguish between constructive and destructive anger. Most anger problems are manifestations of what would be considered destructive anger: fighting to hurt each other, overpowering, blaming, holding a grudge, and never really settling the issue. By contrast, constructive anger is defined as providing the strength to stand one's ground for the people and principles one cares about, and it is hoped that includes oneself.

Constructive anger is a key feature of many adaptive responses when the individual refuses to accept the status quo and resolves to make serious changes in old patterns. The therapist might ask when the group is stuck, "How would you respond to this situation if you had the skills and confidence to use your constructive anger for the good of the people involved?" These strategies could include increasing one's power, establishing level footing with someone who has been overbearing, or verbalizing one's resistance to inappropriate use of force. It is the means by which people establish and maintain limits, and disengage from destructive relationships and reengage when they improve. As constructive anger starts to emerge, it is wise for the therapist to explore among members any negative reactions. There is often a backlash of guilt or anxiety, which can be explored and challenged by using CBT methods.

This model of CBT group therapy for depression is designed to keep interpersonal conflict inside the group to a minimum. Because it is a time-limited treatment, there is usually not sufficient opportunity to work through conflicts that might arise between members. A group atmosphere that is rife with conflict is likely to feel unsafe to individuals who are fragile by reason of their depression. Conflict, particularly in a depression group, generally does not further the goals that drew people into therapy in the first place. Working on a consensus model reduces the incidence of conflict. Members determine agenda by democratic vote that makes for a decision process everyone can understand and support. Because the giving or the receiving of advice is discouraged, it is less likely that members will feel controlled or criticized—two of the biggest triggers for conflict in a therapy group.

In this model of group treatment, a conflict that does occur may be directed toward the therapist. Members sometimes object that CBT uses an agenda (rather than being free flowing), moves toward adaptive response each session (rather than waiting for problems to be fixed), and urges homework (rather than expecting nothing of members outside of group). These are legitimate issues to discuss in the group, and the therapist can demonstrate good methods of conflict resolution to settle the issue in the group and to provide a model for dealing with conflict outside of group in everyday life. When significant anger mixes with depression, suicidal risk needs to be assessed. Anger brings psychological energy to perhaps act upon self-destructive tendencies. Risk increases to the extent that an individual uses suicidal means to express her anger or she becomes so angry that she doesn't care about the consequences of her destructive actions. When these developments are evident, the therapist must determine the relative safety and danger of the individual, and consider steps to de-escalate the anger.

Clinical Vignette: Suicidal Ideation

It seems inevitable that the issue of suicidal thoughts will surface at some point in a group therapy for people dealing with depression. One indication of the felt level of safety and honesty in the group is whether members take the opportunity to discuss suicide. A typical clinical exchange occurred when an individual indicated that her troubling automatic thought was "There's no point to living. I feel like ending it now." She understood the ground rule regarding no self-harm and was bringing this thought to the attention of the group and therapist so as not to act on it. Once she had broken the ice with this candid statement, enough other members could relate to suicidal thoughts that the group determined to make it the agenda topic for that session.

The therapist called on an underlying principle of cognitive therapy that there are at least two sides to virtually any issue, including suicide. She proposed that members examine the advantages and disadvantages of suicide and encouraged personal reactions from the members (see chapter 1). Several expressed they were rather shocked and dismayed that the group would explore the apparent advantages of suicide. "Wouldn't that make it more likely that people would do it?" Others responded that a discussion alone would be unlikely to trigger suicidal actions. The therapist added that if at some point in the discussion individuals needed take a time-out, they could do so. It proved unnecessary. As for advantages to suicide, members variously stated the following: "It is an end to pain." "Sometimes the world doesn't feel worth continuing to live for." "If things are never going to get better, why not end it now?" "It will teach a lesson to all those people in my life who didn't believe how bad it really was." "I don't deserve to live." "I've been a burden to loved ones around me." There was a nervous energy in the group as members shared these opinions. They were taking permission to voice a taboo and breaking through traditional shame and phobic avoidance about suicide. The stated disadvantages regarding suicide were recorded, too, but had less emotional power (such as, "I wouldn't want to hurt my family," which is not a reason to live, simply a reason not to die).

Each member of the group was asked to select one of the advantages of suicide and explore another way of satisfying that advantage without killing oneself. For example, one member addressed "If things are never going to get better, why not end it now?" in the following manner: "How is it possible to predict that things will never get better? When have I been that completely accurate in my predictions? Furthermore, I know when I'm depressed I have a negative view of the future, which ignores or distorts anything positive. Because I can't be sure that things will not get better, it makes sense for me to keep trying and see what happens." As these responses to the suicide advantages accumulated in the group, the nervous energy shifted to a more relaxed and confident feeling. Not only were they breaking through a significant taboo, but also they were finding effective ways to respond that showed that the suicidal thoughts were neither overpowering to individuals nor contagious in the group. An empathic openness to these vulnerable topics strengthens the cohesiveness of the group and its confidence in being able to handle the challenge.

It was significant in this exchange that the therapist did not take a position of trying to urge members away from suicidal thoughts or actions. To do so would have been counterproductive, for it would have communicated her doubts about the group's capacity to handle this material as a group and eventually make an adaptive response. Instead, she was more effective using Socratic questioning to uncover hidden strengths of the group to address difficult topics and work through them. Her approach of active probing is not to be confused with a passive or laissez-faire style, which would have not served the group in reaching a good resolution. Thus, she needed to actively assess whether all members were prepared to keep discussing this topic. She pressed for the adaptive response in the same session in which the issues surfaced and achieved closure rather than letting the issue drift unfinished into the future. The therapist will have a stronger confidence for favorable outcome when prospective members have been initially screened for suicidal potential and found to be safe, and when group members support the ground rule of no self-harm.

Guilt

Guilt originates from standards and beliefs individuals hold for themselves as to what they are responsible for, what they should attain, what they are deserve, and what they must do. When individuals conclude that they are falling short of these standards, there is commonly an affective experience of guilt. This feeling state is accompanied by self-condemnations of being wrong, bad, dirty, or a failure. When the guilt cycle continues unabated, it leads to a widening circle of clinical depression.

CBT, which can be viewed as a psychology of belief, provides a foundation with which to analyze the standards and beliefs underlying guilt. These standards maintain power, as well as the capacity to perpetuate depression, by remaining in the cognitive shadows. They are cloaked in authority and tradition, thereby resisting direct examination by those identified as guilty. In a group setting, there is both recognition and relief in hearing other members divulge their own expectations for themselves and how they feel they are falling short. The depressed individual usually thinks he or she is quite alone in his or her guilt, when actually there is notable commonality with other members. Simply bringing these judgments out into the light of day makes them less overwhelming, and sharing them with other people breaks the loneliness.

Guilty self-judgments associated with depression usually derive from distorted views of the evidence of one's life. The negative is inadvertently magnified, whereas anything positive is diminished, often colored by unresolved guilt and punishment from the past. Other members can help the individual begin to challenge the guilty judgments (to determine what is distorted and what is not) as well as contribute their own views of the individual, which are probably more balanced and complete (challenge and distortions are both described in chapter 1). The longer term recovery from depression involves a restructuring of one's standards and beliefs to ones more congruent with what is currently meaningful and fulfilling in one's life.

Clinical Vignette: Guilt

When members were checking in with homework and discussing mastery and pleasure experiences, the therapist asked an open-ended question whether anyone experienced guilt in these situations. The majority of members answered yes, although they were rather sheepish and puzzled by their reaction. One member said, "I haven't done anything wrong. Why should I be feeling guilty?" Others added that guilt seemed to lessen their experience of mastery and pleasure and sometimes eliminated it altogether. The therapist suggested the group pursue this topic during the agenda portion of the session.

The group identified feelings of guilt as a common experience shared by all members and set out to identify the automatic thoughts that accompanied them. At first members felt stymied, but there were nods of agreement when an individual said, "I feel I don't deserve the mastery or pleasure." Other automatic thoughts followed. "I've made other people suffer, why should I feel good?" "I'm only being self-centered and that's bad." "I'm not supposed to be happy." "I should be punished." "It's my fault." These judgments are typically harsh, uncompromising, and quite effective in making the individual suffer.

The therapist directed the group toward adaptive response by asking, "What kind of challenge can you make to these old voices of guilt? Is it possible to stand your ground and not cave in to the negative judgment?" The therapist suggested that to facilitate a dialogue the group divide itself in half; one side was asked to forcefully present the guilty automatic thoughts, whereas the other half was asked to speak with equal force on behalf of the adaptive response of challenge and standing one's ground. The therapist asked someone to volunteer a personal experience of pleasure and the resulting guilt as the focus for an internal dialogue between the guilty voice and the adaptive response. The exchange was lively with a good deal of laughter and mock vehemence, both favorable antidotes to the guilt-laden affect experienced earlier in the session. Those arguing for the adaptive response stated, "My feeling good doesn't hurt other people." "I *do* deserve to have nice things happen." "Punishment doesn't do anything any good." "Yes, I'll accept part responsibility for what goes wrong. But I won't feel guilty for the whole thing." "My pleasure is good for the people I care about." "Strange as it sounds, I've worked hard to have this pleasure, and I won't let anyone take it away from me." After a discussion of approximately 10 minutes, the therapist reversed the roles of the two groups and suggested a dialogue about an example of personal mastery experience and resulting guilt.

In the discussion following this exercise, members shared how good it felt to hear a strong challenge to judgments of self-guilt. It was quite a contrast to feeling powerless and helpless in the face of negative judgments. And when the guilty judgments are pulled out in the light of day for discussion, their harshness and distortions become more apparent. One member raised concern that this approach was a "new age racket to eliminate any feelings of guilt and let people off the hook no matter what they did. That would be dangerous and self-deceptive." The therapist asked the other members if they agreed. A member responded, "This is about challenging guilt and telling the difference between reasonable and unreasonable guilt." There followed a discussion that people needed to learn from reasonable guilt to stop doing what they are doing. But the guilt that stops people from feeling mastery or pleasure is unreasonable and leads to depression. The member who raised the initial objection agreed with this distinction.

The therapist suggested that members analyze their cumulative thought records and mastery and pleasure records to determine to what extent guilt was present. Most people with depression seem to find a considerable amount of guilty content in these written records. Members were then asked to determine how their standards had influenced the development of guilt. "When you challenge your own guilty judgments, do you reexamine your beliefs about yourself? When you have a more balanced view of the evidence, do you feel less guilty?" Members were encouraged to share these insights in the subsequent session. One of the distinctive benefits of a group treatment is the opportunity for members to weigh the evidence (see chapter 1) of what they perceive, believe, and feel. When a number of people share the effort to analyze the assumptions underlying how they relate to the world, there can be a multifaceted discussion. Members gain in their ability to incorporate various points of view and develop a more sophisticated perspective that builds on the additional ways of looking. To be able to incorporate various vantage points is an important skill in general, but particularly so when making adaptive response to guilt. With support provided by the group, members can get beyond acting guilty or punishing themselves.

CONCLUDING TREATMENT

Drawing a time-limited group therapy (see chapter 1) to a good conclusion is arguably the most multifaceted skill of the therapist. In the metaphor of therapist as director or conductor, this constitutes the final act of therapy. The therapist seeks to assist members to consolidate their learning and gains in the group. Recurrent themes are brought forward for a final review, especially helplessness and hopelessness—twin towers of depression (Beck, Rush, Shaw, & Emery, 1979) twin towers of depression), as will be addressed below. Members assess themselves in the status of their depression and determine where they stand relative to their goals and expectations from the beginning of the group. For the majority of members, this will be the conclusion of treatment and they will be saying goodbye to other members, the therapist, and this regular venue to join with other people. There is the hope that the cohesiveness that developed in the group can be transferred and developed in other areas of life. Some members may elect to pursue additional treatment after the conclusion of the depression group therapy, and the therapist needs to orchestrate this process as well.

Sometimes the conclusion of group therapy for depression means that, although the depression has resolved, other areas of psychological distress seem to emerge in stronger manner. Depression, with its decrease of energy, inhibition of feeling, and social withdrawal, can mask the presence of other types of problems. In such cases, successful treatment of the depression brings a return of energy and feeling and reengagement in relationships that can lift heretofore masked problems into plain view. Anxiety is the most frequent condition that exists comorbidly with depression and, once the depression is treated, anxiety may emerge as a more prominent issue (Clark, 1989). For example, a member who successfully completed the depression group feeling more active and hopeful found herself also worrying anew about recent opportunities she was undertaking. As long as her depression had restricted what she felt she could take on, there was not much to feel anxious about. This member recognized her lifelong tendency toward anxiety and elected to join a CBT group for anxiety on completion of her work with depression.

In similar fashion, there will likely be a subset of members who complete treatment for their depression and would benefit then from group therapy for their comorbid anxiety. Given the fact that these members know the CBT methodology and have already experienced therapeutic gains in their depression, they are good candidates to take a strong and successful role in anxiety group. It is useful for the therapist to facilitate discussion about the emergence of these other psychological issues over the course of the depression group therapy so members do not feel completely strange if this occurs to them. If evaluation and referral to another group therapy is to occur after the depression group is finished, the therapist should arrange individual contact with the member outside of group.

Another type of follow-up group therapy is for treatment of schema issues (Young, 1990). These are the deepest patterns in a person's life, integrating one's history, family of origin, beliefs about oneself, and one's most powerful emotions (both expressed and unexpressed). Young's work has identified approximately 18 schemas, such as self-sacrifice or unrelenting standards, and has developed CBT treatment modalities that address the recurrent and dysfunctional nature of these recurrent patterns. Related to the development of group CBT for depression, comparable methods have been adapted for group treatment of schema issues. These include members identifying their own and each other's schema, determining schema triggers and alternative responses, understanding the adaptive intent in early schema experience, reducing the damage and duration of schema activation, and finding life circumstances and relationships that cultivate the more functional aspects of the schema. Members who have completed CBT depression group and are feeling better may use these psychological gains to address their deeper life patterns in a CBT schema group. These possibilities may be mentioned in the CBT depression group, but if members are to engage in a serious evaluation and referral, this should happen outside of group time.

Helplessness

It is the pervasive sense of helplessness that was likely to have been one of the stronger motivations for members to seek treatment for their depression. Because their attempts to improve their situation on their own have likely failed, they decided that it was time to seek professional help. CBT group treatment is generally regarded as a practical approach that offers tangible help, and the discussion in this chapter demonstrates that the help comes in the form of members generating their own agenda, developing their own adaptive response, and designing and checking in with their own homework. In other words, the help is produced by the very people who feel helpless. The explanation for this paradox lies in the nature of the group process itself. By establishing a genuine cohesiveness with each other and maintaining a reliable task focus, members create what could be thought of as a "group mind." This mind is the cumulative product of all the agendas, adaptive responses, and homework experiences that have transpired over the life of the group. Members sometimes verbalize that they can find the inner resources to cope during their day-to-day life by "listening" to the voice of the group that they carry inside them. Bringing a good conclusion to therapy means consolidating the gains experienced by each individual. When confidence that one can reasonably adapt to future life changes outweighs the sense of helplessness, the depression has been largely resolved.

Hopelessness

If CBT has truly helped members over the course of group treatment, they are departing group with a greater sense of hope than when they entered. This would suggest that they had resolved issues of loss sufficiently that they could generate a sense of positive expectation for their lives. Treatment gains resulted when members supported each other in generating goals, assessing their progress, and redirecting as necessary. In preparing for life after therapy, members are urged to continue the practice of making goals. This is one of the primary means to avert hopelessness, because the formations of goals and of hope are fundamentally related. An optimal plan for relapse prevention would include the consolidation of therapeutic learning (as described above) while at the same time the individual directs himself or herself in ongoing goals of his or her choosing. The CBT group, which sought to organize the best adaptive efforts of the constituent members, fulfills that purpose when people have learned how to do the same on their own.

Clinical Vignette: Termination

In the next to the final session of a group, the therapist suggested members discuss their reactions to finishing therapy. The majority of comments were favorable, and people felt that they had made good gains. These comments were consistent with members' BDI scores, which reflected a general decrease in depressive symptoms over the course of the treatment. The therapist wanted to provide the opportunity to discuss those negative reactions that individuals might experience but perhaps would find difficult to verbalize in the face of upbeat statements from the other members. She asked, "Does anyone find themselves having a negative reaction as this therapy comes to an end? Are there doubts or concerns that need to be addressed before we finish?" Socratic questioning provides a good method to explore what may be unexpressed and underneath the surface of a group. Because CBT acknowledges one can hold simultaneously a variety of thoughts, each possessing some partial truth, there can be greater freedom to explore the negative because it does not automatically cancel the positive.

Taking the therapist's questions as permission to provide feedback (see chapter 1) about less favorable reactions to termination, members shared the following automatic thoughts: "Part of me worries that I'm not any better." "Other people in the group seem to have improved more than me." "I worry that I'm going to relapse and get depressed again." "Sometimes I think I didn't learn anything." "Cognitive therapy doesn't help." "I won't remember anything I learned." "This group is concluding before I'm ready." "I didn't make serious changes in myself." "I wish I'd been in individual therapy." The mood of the group shifted during this discussion and became noticeably gloomy and anxious. The therapist discussed these concerns as a natural part of concluding group therapy and expressed confidence that this process would have a favorable outcome. Even more significant than the content of her words was her positive demeanor and affect, which conveyed she was not personally daunted by discussing these doubts.

The therapist used a democratic agenda process to determine which of these negative reactions was strongest for the greatest number of members. The vote revealed that everyone could personally relate to the fear of relapsing to depression. The therapist proposed to explore this thought by eliciting advantages and disadvantages of believing it. The disadvantages were voiced first: "It makes me feel like a failure." "I would stop thinking about what I had learned." "My view of the future would be pessimistic." "I'd give up and let the relapse happen, maybe even help it along." The advantages took longer to come to the surface: "Keeping some skepticism protects against complacency." "I'm more likely to keep using what I learned in this group." "It's more realistic. I do have a higher chance to relapse to depression. As long as I'm smart, it doesn't need to get out of control." Once again, dialogue on both sides of a difficult issue yielded a more comfortable feeling in the group.

As homework for the next session, which would be the final meeting of the group, the therapist suggested that members determine at least one thing they had learned over the course of the group. They were asked in particular to think how that discovery had helped them deal with their personal sense of depression. The ensuing discussion turned into a review of the best parts of the group and provided members a tangible way to consolidate what they had learned. The therapist suggested that members consider taking notes, and most people did so. At the conclusion of this review, the therapist again raised the group's concern about relapse as first voiced the previous week. It seemed that the worry was less strong this session and that the discussion of the advantages and disadvantages had less emotional charge. Moreover, the consolidation of what had been learned over the course of the group helped members prepare for relapse prevention.

CBT group treatment for depression seeks to enhance the sense of cohesiveness among group members as well as increase their task focus in practical ways of overcoming their problems. By developing cohesiveness members experience a therapeutic environment where they can share and identify with each other, enjoy the favorable effects of being cared for, and develop a general sense of belonging. The therapist reinforces group behaviors that favor cohesiveness, such as finding themes and agenda that the majority of members can relate to and encouraging regular participation from everyone. Task focus involves members taking specific steps for therapeutic gains, such as using thought records to identify triggers for depressive reactions and goal-setting to initiate regular activity. This chapter has demonstrated that effective CBT therapy needs to be flexible in developing cohesiveness and task focus. In this therapeutic process, depressed people learn what it feels like to work together for the mutual improvement of each other.

REFERENCES

American Psychological Association. (1996). *How therapy helps people recover from depression.* Available: http://www.helping.apa.org/depress.html

Beck, A. (1964). Thinking and depression: II. Theory and therapy. *Archives of General Psychiatry, 10,* 561–571.

Beck, A. T. (1976). Cognitive therapy and the emotional disorders. New York: International Universities Press.

Beck, A., Rush, A., Shaw, B., & Emery, G. (1979). *Cognitive therapy of depression.* New York: Guilford Press.

Beck, A., & Steer, R. (1987). *Manual for the Revised Beck Depression Inventory*. San Antonio, TX: Psychological Corporation.

Beck, A., Wright, F., Newman, C., & Liese, B. (1993). *Cognitive therapy of substance abuse*. New York: Guilford Press.

Bennis, W., & Biederman, P. (1997). *Organizing genius: The secrets of creative collaboration*. Reading, MA: Addison-Wesley.

Blazer, D., Kessler, R., McConagle, K., & Swartz, M. (1994). The prevalence and distribution of major depression in a national community sample: The National Comorbidity Survey. *American Journal of Psychiatry, 151,* 979–986.

Brabender, V., & Fallon, A. (1993). *Models of inpatient group psychotherapy*. Washington, DC: American Psychological Association.

Clark, D. (1989). Anxiety states: Panic and generalized anxiety. In K. Hawton, P. Salkovskis, J. Kirk, & D. Clark (Eds.), *Cognitive–behavior therapy for psychiatric problems: A practical guide* (pp. 52–96). New York: Oxford University Press.

Cummings, N., & Sayama, M. (1995). *Focused psychotherapy: A casebook of brief, intermittent psychotherapy throughout the life cycle*. New York: Brunner/Mazel.

DePree, M. (1989). *Leadership is an art*. New York: Dell.

Dobson, K. (1989). A meta-analysis of the efficacy of cognitive therapy for depression. *Journal of Consulting and Clinical Psychology, 57,* 414–419.

Ellis, A. (1962). *Reason and emotion in psychotherapy*. New York: Lyle Stuart.

Hollon, S., & Shaw, B. (1979). Group cognitive therapy for depressed patients. In A. Beck, A. Rush, B. Shaw, & G. Emery (Eds.), *Cognitive therapy of depression* (pp. 328–353). New York: Guilford Press.

Frank, J. (1992). Some determinants, manifestations, and effects of cohesiveness in therapy groups. In R. MacKenzie (Ed.), *Classics in group psychotherapy* (pp. 154–165). New York: Guilford Press.

Freeman, A. (1983). (Ed.). *Cognitive therapy with couples and groups*. New York: Plenum Press.

Freeman, A., Schrodt, R., Gilson, M., & Ludgate, J. (1993). Group cognitive therapy with inpatients. In J. Wright, M. Thase, A. Beck, & J. Ludgate (Eds.), *Cognitive therapy with inpatients* (pp. 121–153). New York: Guilford Press.

Lazarus, A. (1961). Group therapy of phobic disorders by systematic densensitization. *Journal of Abnormal and Social Psychology, 63,* 505–510.

Lazarus, A. (1968). Behavioral group therapy. In G. Gazda (Ed.), *Basic approaches to group psychotherapy and group counseling* (pp. 124–155). New York: Charles C. Thomas.

Lazarus, A. (1976). *Multimodal behavioral therapy*. New York: Springer.

Lewinsohn, P., Munoz, R., Youngren, M., & Zeiss, A. (1986). *Control your depression*. New York: Simon & Schuster.

MacKenzie, R. (Ed.). (1995). *Effective use of group therapy in managed care*. Washington, DC: American Psychiatric Press.

MacKenzie, R. (1997). *Time-managed group psychotherapy: Effective clinical applications*. Washington, DC: American Psychiatric Press.

Meichenbaum, D. (1977). *Cognitive–behavioral modification: An integrative approach*. New York: Plenum Press.

Miranda, J., Schreckengost, J., & Heine, L. (1992). Cognitive–behavioral group treatment for depression. In M. McKay & K. Peleg (Eds.), *Focal group psychotherapy* (pp. 135–162). Oakland, CA: New Harbinger.

Senge, P. (1990). *The fifth discipline: The art and practice of the learning organization*. New York: Doubleday.

Yalom, I. (1983). *Inpatient group psychotherapy*. New York: Basic Books.

Young, J. (1990). *Cognitive therapy for personality disorders: A schema focused approach*. Sarasota, FL: Professional Resources Exchange.

3

PANIC AND PHOBIA

ARIEL J. LANG AND MICHELLE G. CRASKE

Significant advances have been made in recent years with respect to cognitive–behavioral treatment of anxiety disorders, including panic disorder with and without agoraphobia. Twenty independently conducted and controlled studies of treatment for panic that reported rates of zero panic attacks suggest that after 11 sessions of treatment, an average of 76% of treatment completers are free of panic, as are 78% at follow-up (up to 2 years).[1] The more stringent criteria of being free of panic and excessive anxiety were met by 52% at posttreatment and 66% at follow-up. Two points are noteworthy from these data. First, more success is achieved initially in terms of panic than anxiety about panic. Second, status maintains or continues to improve over the follow-up interval, after active treatment

---

[1]These 20 studies are as follows: Arntz and van den Hout (1996); Barlow, Craske, Cerny, and Klosko (1989); Beck, Sokol, Clark, Berchick, and Wright (1992); Beck, Stanley, Baldwin, Deagle, and Averill (1994); Black, Wesner, Bowers, and Gabel (1993); Bouchard et al. (1996); Clark et al. (1994); Cote, Gauthier, Laberge, Cormier, and Plamondon (1994); Craske, Maidenberg, and Bystritsky (1995); Gould and Clum (1995); Gould, Clum, and Shapiro (1993); Hecker, Losee, Fritzler, and Fink (1996); Klosko, Barlow, Tassinari, and Cerny (1990); Laberge, Gauthier, Cote, Plamondon, and Cormier (1993); Lidren et al. (1994); Margraf, Gobel, and Schneider (1989); Öst (1988); Öst and Westling (1995); Shear, Pilkonis, Cloitre, and Leon (1994); Williams and Falbo (1996).

is terminated. Thirteen studies that targeted agoraphobia and panic with agoraphobia and reported responder rates indicate that after 12 sessions 50% show substantial improvement (i.e., achieving normative levels of functioning or mild or less distress across a variety of measures), as do 59% at follow-up.[2] Comparison with the former data set suggests that panic attacks are alleviated sooner, whereas agoraphobia and its pervasive effects may require longer treatment. Ongoing research is addressing the best way to combine panic control and agoraphobia treatments.

These treatment developments are particularly important given the frequency with which anxiety and phobias are experienced. The most recent epidemiological data show that almost 17% of the U.S. population is currently experiencing an anxiety disorder, and that figure excludes obsessive–compulsive disorder and posttraumatic stress disorder (Kessler et al., 1994). Furthermore, untreated anxiety disorders tend to be chronic, with relatively low rates of remission (e.g., Goisman et al., 1994; Wittchen, 1988). Untreated anxiety results in serious medical, social, and financial repercussions and is associated with additional psychiatric disorders, including substance abuse, depression, and suicidality (e.g., Markowitz, Weissman, Ouellette, Lish, & Klerman, 1989; Rice & Miller, 1993; Wittchen, 1988; Zaubler & Katon, 1996).

Despite the serious consequences of untreated anxiety, between 60% and 92% of afflicted individuals (Angst & Dobler-Mikola, 1985; Pollard, Henderson, Frank, & Margolis, 1989; Thompson et al., 1988) do not receive treatment, perhaps as a result of the high financial cost of psychological intervention. Furthermore, treatment that is obtained is not necessarily effective. For example, of 562 clients with panic or agoraphobia, or both, followed for 1 year, only 15% received behavior therapy, and 16% received cognitive therapy (both of which have demonstrated efficacy for panic disorder), whereas 33% received psychodynamic therapy (a therapy with little demonstrated efficacy for panic disorder; Goisman et al., 1994). This may reflect limited availability of mental health professionals trained specifically in psychological treatments shown to be effective for anxiety disorders, such as cognitive–behavioral therapy (CBT). Group treatments are generally less costly and enable the dissemination of empirically supported treatments to a larger number of clients. This chapter describes the cognitive–behavioral approach to the group treatment of anxiety and phobias, with emphasis on panic disorder and agoraphobia.

---

[2]These 13 studies are as follows: Cerny, Barlow, Craske, and Himadi (1987); Craske, Rowe, Lewin, and Noriega-Dimitri (1997); Craske, Street, and Barlow (1989); Evans, Holt, and Oei (1991); Feigenbaum (1988); Hoffart (1995); Jansson, Jerremalm, and Öst (1986); Marks et al. (1993); Mavissakalian and Michelson (1986); Michelson, Mavissakalian, and Marchione (1985); Michelson, Marchione, Marchione, Testa, and Mavissakalian (1988); Schulte, Kuenzel, Pepping, and Schulte-Bahrenberg (1992); Telch et al. (1993).

COGNITIVE–BEHAVIORAL MODEL OF PANIC DISORDER AND AGORAPHOBIA

Originally, panic attacks were viewed as occurring without specific triggering cues. Consequently, most theoretical and treatment attention was directed toward agoraphobic symptoms. However, a specific conceptualization now exists for panic attacks and panic disorder that emphasizes fears of bodily sensations (Barlow, 1988; Clark et al., 1988; Ehlers & Margraf, 1989). The treatment described in this chapter is based on this conceptualization, and thus we begin with a brief description of this theory.

Panic disorder is thought to be driven by a cycle of "fear of fear," which is hypothesized to develop in psychologically and biologically vulnerable individuals (Barlow, 1988). Psychological vulnerability is hypothesized to include danger-laden beliefs about bodily sensations such as "I feel out of control when my heart races" (e.g., Reiss, Peterson, Gursky, & McNally, 1986) and about uncontrollability of events and emotions in general (Barlow, 1988). Biological vulnerability is the topic of much research and probably accounts for the strong familial concordance for panic disorder (e.g., Moran & Andrews, 1985).

The cycle begins with an initial event in which the body's autonomic fear response is triggered in a situation that does not represent actual danger to the individual. Often, such an event happens at a time of stress or under circumstances that intensify arousal or are perceived as threatening (Craske & Rowe, 1997). As a result of this initial episode, the individual develops fear of the associated bodily sensations (e.g., racing heart, dizziness, and parasthesias). Fear of sensations is believed to develop as a result of misappraisals of bodily sensations as signs of imminent death, loss of control, and so on and of interoceptive conditioning (Barlow, 1988; Clark et al., 1988; Ehlers & Margraf, 1989). *Interoceptive conditioning* (Razran, 1961) refers to learned fear of internal states as a result of aversive associations. In this case, panic attacks create an aversive association between certain bodily sensations and feelings of terror, resulting in subsequent fear of sensations that signal the possibility of another panic attack. For this reason, activities that produce bodily sensations similar to the sensations of panic sometimes trigger panic attacks. Such activities include exercise, sexual arousal, anger, humidity, and caffeine ingestion.

Several features distinguish fear of bodily sensations from fears of external stimuli. First, autonomic arousal generated by fear of sensations in turn intensifies the sensations that are feared, thus creating a vicious circle. The cycle is sustained until the physiological arousal is exhausted or perceptions of safety are achieved. In contrast, fears of external stimuli do not intensify the object of fear. For example, fears of dogs do not make dogs grow larger. Second, cues that trigger panic attacks (i.e., internal bodily sensations) are not always immediately obvious to the individual, thus generating the perception of being unexpected or "out of the blue" (Barlow, 1988). In this model, all panic attacks are triggered by specific, although sometimes subtle, stimuli, despite their apparent spontaneous nature on occasion.

A third feature that distinguishes fear of fear from fear of external stimuli is that bodily sensations that cue panic attacks tend to be less predictable than external stimuli. Fourth, bodily sensations generally are more difficult to control than external objects; that is, sensations are relatively uncontrollable. Unpredictability and uncontrollability have been shown to elevate general anxiety about upcoming aversive events (e.g., DeCola & Rosellini, 1990; Maier, Laudenslager, & Ryan, 1985; Weinberg & Levine, 1980) and panic attacks (Craske, Glover, & DeCola, 1994). Consequently, the unpredictable or uncontrollable nature of panic is believed to contribute to high levels of chronic anxious apprehension (Barlow, 1988) and to maintain anticipatory anxiety about the recurrence of panic (Rachman & Levitt, 1985). In turn, anxious apprehension increases the likelihood of panic by increasing physical tension and, therefore, the availability of sensations that have become triggers for panic, as well as by increasing attentional vigilance for these bodily cues. Thus, a continual cycle of panic and anxious apprehension develops.

Finally, agoraphobic avoidance is viewed as one method of coping with the anticipation of panic. Individuals with agoraphobia who seek treatment almost always report a history of panic that preceded the development of their avoidance (e.g., Noyes et al., 1986; Pollard, Bronson, & Kenney, 1989). Not all people who panic, however, develop agoraphobic avoidance, and the extent of avoidance that does emerge is highly variable. The reasons for these individual differences are not clear; agoraphobic avoidance is not related to age of onset, panic symptom profiles, different types of attacks, or frequency of panic (Craske & Barlow, 1988). Gender, however, is significantly related to agoraphobia, with women increasingly predominating as avoidance becomes more severe (e.g., Thyer, Himle, Curtis, Cameron, & Nesse, 1985). Low masculinity scores are even more predictive of agoraphobia (Chambless & Mason, 1986). In contrast, men are more likely to use alcohol or drugs in anticipation of panic (Barlow, 1988). Thus, agoraphobic avoidance is viewed as one style of coping with the anticipation of panic that may be influenced by gender roles and expectations. The cognitive–behavioral model of panic disorder is depicted in Figure 3.1.

Evidence for this model is accruing. For example, individuals with panic disorder have strong beliefs and fears of physical or mental harm arising from bodily sensations that are associated with panic attacks (Chambless, Caputo, Bright, & Gallagher, 1984; Clark et al., 1988; van den Hout, Van der Molen, Griez, & Lousberg, 1987). In addition, such individuals fear procedures that induce bodily sensations similar to the ones

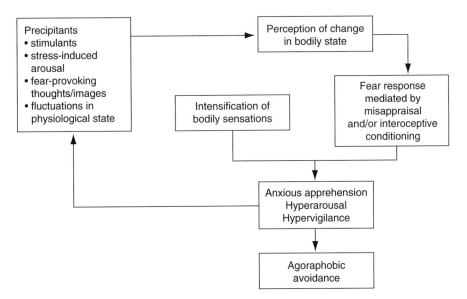

Figure 3.1. Cognitive–behavioral model of panic disorder. Reprinted from "An Integrated Treatment Approach to Panic Disorder" by M. G. Craske, 1996, in *Bulletin of the Menninger Clinic, 60* (Suppl. A), A87–A104. Copyright 1996 by the Menninger Clinic. Reprinted with permission.

experienced during panic attacks (Barlow, 1988), including benign cardiovascular, respiratory, and audiovestibular exercises (Zarate, Rapee, Craske, & Barlow, 1988). Not only is misappraisal associated with fearfulness, but reappraisal has been found to lessen fear. For example, people with panic disorder report significantly less fear and panic during laboratory-based panic provocation procedures when they perceive the procedure as safe and controllable (Craske, 1998; Rapee, Mattick, & Murrell, 1986; Sanderson, Rapee, & Barlow, 1989). Furthermore, there is some evidence for heightened awareness of or ability to detect bodily sensations of arousal in these individuals (Ehlers & Breuer, 1995; Ehlers & Margraf, 1989).

Given this conceptualization, cognitive–behavioral treatment targets fear of bodily sensations, anxious apprehension over the recurrence of panic, and agoraphobic avoidance. This contrasts with earlier behavioral treatments that targeted avoidance of agoraphobic situations and either ignored panic or assumed that panic would diminish as agoraphobia reduced. Before detailing the treatment procedures, their efficacy is briefly reviewed.

EFFICACY OF GROUP TREATMENTS FOR PANIC DISORDER AND AGORAPHOBIA

Several of the studies described in the introduction to this chapter used group treatments (Cerny et al., 1987; Craske et al., 1989, 1997; Evans et al., 1991; Feigenbaum, 1988; Hoffart, 1995; Lidren et al., 1994; Telch et al., 1993). The fact that their outcomes were generally consistent with the summary statistics obtained from mostly individual treatments suggests that group treatment is as effective as individual therapy. Only one study has directly compared the efficacy of group versus individual treatments with respect to panic disorder and agoraphobia. Neron, Lacroix, and Chaput (1995) compared 12–14 weekly sessions of individual or group CBT ($N = 20$), although the group condition received two additional 1-hour individual sessions. The two conditions were equally effective for panic and agoraphobia measures at posttreatment and 6-month follow-up. However, the individual format resulted in superior alleviation of generalized anxiety and depressive symptoms by the follow-up point. Another study (Lidren et al., 1994) found that group treatment and individually conducted self-help treatment were equally effective. Obviously, there is need for more investigation of the efficacy of group treatments relative to individual therapy, but extant data suggest that the groups are generally effective for targeted symptoms of panic and agoraphobia.

Various other features of group treatments have been examined. Barlow, O'Brien, and Last (1984) compared group treatments for agoraphobia that either fully incorporated partners in every treatment session or excluded partners from treatment. Although it is obvious that these findings are limited to clients with partners who are willing to be involved in treatment, groups that incorporated partners achieved superior outcomes. This finding was even stronger 2 years after treatment completion (Cerny et al., 1987). Carter, Turovsky, Sbrocco, and Meadows (1995) examined predictors of attrition from group treatment for panic disorder and agoraphobia that included partners. Completers and noncompleters did not differ in terms of pretreatment severity, although it is interesting to note that partners of noncompleters rated themselves as less communicative about panic-related issues. This suggests that communication between couples facilitates couples group treatments. Finally, Bowen, South, Fischer, and Looman (1994) found that depression and mastery, as well as number of group sessions attended, predicted outcome from group treatment that combined behavioral and medication approaches within a community treatment setting.

GROUP TREATMENT FOR PANIC AND AGORAPHOBIA

Described herein is our most recent group treatment approach for panic disorder with agoraphobia (Craske & Lewin, 1994). The treatment incorporates panic control treatment and an additional component specifically targeting agoraphobic avoidance. These are available in detailed manuals for clients and therapists, including *Mastery of Your Anxiety and*

TABLE 3.1
Brief Outline of Session Content

Session	Topics
1	Education about anxiety
2	Model of panic, hyperventilation, and breathing retraining
3	Breathing retraining, cognitive restructuring I—overestimates of danger
4	Breathing retraining, cognitive restructuring II—evaluation of consequences
5	Symptom induction testing, interoceptive exposure
6	Hypothesis testing, interoceptive exposure
7	Causal analysis, interoceptive exposure to activities
8	Management of intense anxiety, processing of worst panic, interoceptive exposure to activities
9	Introduction—concept of agoraphobia
10	Identification and challenging of thoughts in agoraphobic situations
11	Introduction to in vivo exposure
12	Review of in vivo exposure and common procedural difficulties
13	Review of in vivo practices, design of new practices I
14	Review of in vivo practices, design of new practices II
15	Review of in vivo practices, design of new practices III
16	Review of in vivo practices, maintenance of treatment gains

Note. From *Panic Disorder and Agoraphobia Treatment*, by M. G. Craske and M. Lewin, 1994 [unpublished treatment manual].

Panic (3rd ed.; Barlow & Craske, 1999), *Agoraphobia Supplement to Mastery of Your Anxiety and Panic* (3rd ed.; Craske & Barlow, 1999a), and *Therapists Guide to Mastery of Your Anxiety and Panic* (3rd ed.; Craske & Barlow, 1999b). Treatment normally takes place over 16 weekly sessions, each lasting 1.5–2 hours. The treatment is manualized to ensure adherence by therapists and maximal delivery to clients. A brief outline of session content is presented in Table 3.1. Issues specific to group formats are mentioned throughout the following description and are revisited following the treatment description.

The first phase of treatment, or the first 8 weeks, targets panic attacks. The goal of this phase is to influence directly the cognitive and misinterpretational aspect of panic attacks and anxiety, the hyperventilatory response, and conditioned reactions to physical cues. Panic control incorporates four components: (a) education about the fear response, (b) cognitive restructuring, (c) breathing retraining, and (d) interoceptive exposure (i.e., exposure to internal sensations).

Education

The first two sessions of treatment are dedicated to education about anxiety, fear, and panic. As described previously, panic disorder is conceptualized as fear of fear, particularly fear of the bodily sensations that are characteristic of panic. These include accelerated heart rate, shortness of breath, chest pain or discomfort, feeling of choking, sweating, trembling, numbness, abdominal distress, dizziness, and feelings of unreality.

> Steve, age 43, developed panic disorder shortly after a friend died of a heart attack. The death of this friend, who was Steve's age, left him feeling that anyone could die very suddenly. Steve began making repeated visits to the emergency room and medical specialists on noticing inexplicable accelerations in his heart rate. No problems with his heart were detected. Nonetheless, Steve continued to fear that he was having a heart attack whenever he noticed symptoms of racing heart, chest tightness, and numbness in the hands.

Steve was clearly focused on the cardiovascular changes that he experienced during panic. Although this is a common presentation, individuals differ in which symptom is the most noticeable or distressing.

> Stephanie, age 20 and a college junior, described her first panic attack as occurring in the classroom. She had been late that day, so she ran to get to class on time. It was the first meeting of the class, so students were asked to introduce themselves. Stephanie was still out of breath when the instructor asked her to introduce herself. She felt herself blush, became worried about how she looked to the rest of the class, and experienced a panic attack. After that, she became very concerned about feeling warm or flushed. She began to avoid crowded situations and was careful to dress in layers that could be easily removed to prevent sensations of overheating and flushing.

Like Steve, Stephanie became very fearful about experiencing bodily sensations. Her fear, however, focused on feeling warm and flushed.

The Nature of Fear

Fear is described as a natural and protective emotion, elicited by perceptions of imminent threat. Anxiety is conceptualized as the preparatory state when danger is expected to occur sometime in the future, whereas fear or panic represents the escape or alarm state when danger appears imminent. Observed across a wide variety of species from humans to sea slugs, the fear response activates the organism to deal with threat. As such, the goal of treatment is not to remove all fear and anxiety but to control its inappropriate expression. We emphasize that fear and panic are reactions to stimuli that are perceived as threatening, despite the common misperception that panic occurs from out of the blue. First, clients are taught to describe their emotions in terms of three major components: physiology, cognitions, and behaviors. In other words, each panic attack and episode of heightened anxiety is described in terms of what a person thinks, does, and feels. The following example illustrates the therapist's role in this task.

Therapist:	Tell me about your most recent panic attack and see if you can identify what you thought, felt, and did.
Client:	Well, it hit me very suddenly as I was driving to work this morning.
Therapist:	What was the panic attack like? What were the sensations that you noticed?
Client:	I felt like I was going to crawl out of my skin. My heart was racing, and I was sweating. I felt like I had to get out of there.
Therapist:	OK, so let's put that in terms of "think, feel, and do." You described a couple of physical sensations, a racing heart and sweating. There was also a thought—that you had to get out of there. What did you do?
Client:	I couldn't do anything. I just had to sit there because I was stuck in the traffic. But I remember rolling down the window and turning up the music very loud, trying to distract myself. I was also watching for openings in the traffic so that I could get off the road.
Therapist:	So you did do something; you tried to distract yourself, and you started looking for exits. So in this example, we can isolate all three systems.

Not only does this approach begin to engender a personal scientist model, it fits nicely with the treatment rationale, given that treatment incorporates strategies to deal with each component: the thoughts, physical feelings, and behaviors. Next, we give special emphasis to the way in which those three systems interact with each other. For example, when sensations are cognitively misinterpreted as dangerous, they may intensify (because fearful arousal elicits stronger sensations), which in turn provides further confirmation for the perception of danger and an urgency to escape the situation. Urgency to escape a situation is likely to contribute to accelerating arousal, and so on.

In addition, we help clients identify the various triggers to their panic and anxiety. We call this *causal analysis*. Causal analysis is helpful because understanding precipitants removes anxiety associated with uncertainty and helps to decrease the tendency to search for irrational reasons (e.g., "I must be going to have a heart attack"). Also, causal analysis contributes to a sense of personal control. Application of causal analysis is illustrated in the following example.

Client:	I was doing very well on my trip. I made it through the flight, and I was having a great time. Then, all of a sudden on the third day I had a panic attack for no reason. After

that, I panicked a couple more times. I feel like I'm not any better after all.

Therapist: So you felt like the panic happened for no reason. Let's see if we can figure out what might have led to a panic in that situation. Tell me what was going on at the time.

Client: That's the thing; I was just walking around a museum, looking at the paintings.

Therapist: What were your thoughts?

Client: Nothing really, we were just talking about the art.

Therapist: How long had you been there?

Client: Oh, just a few minutes. We had just walked in.

Therapist: What did you do just before coming into the museum?

Client: We had taken a bus from our hotel. We got off in front of the museum and walked up the stairs and into the museum.

Therapist: How many stairs were there?

Client: I don't know. There's a big staircase both outside and inside.

Therapist: So, I bet we have found the trigger. What do you think of this scenario? You walked up all of those stairs without really thinking about it because you and your friend were talking. Next thing, you were in the museum, and you noticed some sensations from the climb. Not thinking about the stairs, you didn't come up with a good explanation for the feelings, and your immediate association was panic.

Physiology

The second segment of the educational component explains the physiology of fear and anxiety. The goals are to normalize fear and anxiety, provide a realistic explanation for physiological sensations of panic, and recognize the time-limited nature of the response. Fear triggers the "fight-or-flight" response, which is the body's reaction to impending threat. The changes that take place during this response serve the goal of harm avoidance. The body prepares itself to be able to move quickly, to use brain resources, and to minimize the immediate impact of wounds. A listing of fear-related somatic changes is presented in Table 3.2. The fear response is controlled by the autonomic nervous system (ANS). The ANS has two branches: the sympathetic nervous system (SNS) and the parasympathetic nervous system (PNS). The SNS is a catabolic system; that is, it is re-

TABLE 3.2
Physiological Changes During the Fear Response

Change	Result
Increased rate and strength of the heart beat	Rapid mobilization of oxygen
Contraction of the spleen	Release of red blood cells to carry oxygen
Release of stored sugar from the liver	Provides energy for muscles
Redistribution of blood to the brain and muscles from the skin and viscera	Readies the body for action
Deepening of respiration and dilation of bronchi	Increases oxygen intake
Dilation of the pupils	Increases visual efficiency
Release of coagulants and lymphocytes	Readies the body to seal wounds and repair tissue damage

Note. From *The Psychology of Fear and Stress,* by J. A. Gray, 1988, pp. 55–56. Copyright 1988 by Cambridge University Press. Adapted with permission.

sponsible for expending energy. The PNS, on the other hand, is anabolic, or responsible for energy storage (e.g., digestion and rest). The fear response primarily is controlled by the SNS and release of adrenaline and noradrenaline (also known as epinephrine and norepinephrine) by the adrenal gland (Gray, 1988). Because threat (e.g., attack by a predator) is normally short-lived, activation of the SNS typically is short-lived. Adrenaline and noradrenaline break down over time, and the body returns to a parasympathetically controlled state of energy storage and rest. Thus, although clients often feel that their panic could go on forever, this is actually not the case. A main premise of this educational component is that sensations experienced during panic attacks are based on protective physiological mechanisms. That is, the physiological changes that occur during panic attacks all have an adaptive value (a concept that is obviously in direct contrast with the panic client's misinterpretations of symptoms as dangerous). For example, heart rate and breathing acceleration speed the flow of oxygen to the muscles that are gearing up to run or fight. Blood flow is redirected away from the periphery and toward the central organs, resulting in cooling of temperature in the extremities. The digestive system is suppressed, often resulting in diarrhea as the body attempts to rid itself of all matter that may absorb energy. Pupils dilate to allow more sensitivity of vision (i.e., to detect signs of danger), resulting in various visual symptoms. Thus, panic attack symptoms represent "side effects" of these protective physiological changes.

Model of Panic

The theoretical model of panic, as described previously, is presented to clients. There are two parts to the model: (a) fear of sensations and (b)

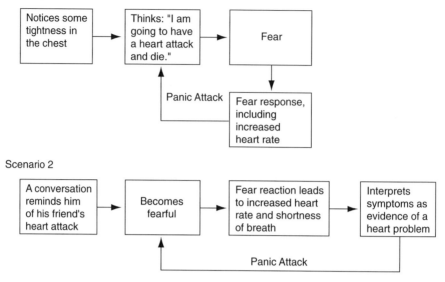

Scenario 1

Notices some tightness in the chest → Thinks: "I am going to have a heart attack and die." → Fear

Fear → Fear response, including increased heart rate

Panic Attack

Scenario 2

A conversation reminds him of his friend's heart attack → Becomes fearful → Fear reaction leads to increased heart rate and shortness of breath → Interprets symptoms as evidence of a heart problem

Panic Attack

Figure 3.2. Panic attack cycle for Steve.

awareness or occurrence of sensations. Panic is rooted in fear of physical sensations, caused by misinterpretations of sensations as dangerous and conditioned fear from repeated pairings between sensations and the feelings of panic. Figure 3.2 presents two possible scenarios for Steve's panic attacks. As these scenarios demonstrate, the initial trigger for a panic attack may be a sensation or a thought. Once the cycle of panic begins, however, thoughts and sensations interact to escalate fear and arousal.

Several factors increase the likelihood of the occurrence of such bodily sensations. First, clients tend to be hypervigilant for bodily sensations, which increases the likelihood of noticing changes. Also, many sensations occur because of natural fluctuations in physiology. In addition, sensations may be increased by activity (e.g., exercise and moving quickly), environmental factors (e.g., humidity and bright lights), substances (e.g., caffeine, alcohol, and medications), and irregular breathing patterns.

Myths

The final goal of the educational component is to address some commonly held myths about panic. Here are some examples.

Myth 1: "These panic attacks mean I am going crazy." Many clients fear that panic attacks are an early sign of a major mental disorder, such as schizophrenia. We explain the different symptoms and pattern of onset associated with the two.

Myth 2: "I am going to lose control of myself when I have a panic attack." Although panic produces very strong feelings, it is very unlikely that someone will either be unable to control himself or herself or be totally paralyzed by panic. The purpose of the fight-or-flight response is self-protection, and losing control works against that aim. We ask group members to think about their own experience with panic attacks. Even though they fear losing control and may even interpret past behaviors as indicative of loss of control, closer examination usually reveals that they have maintained goal directedness and functioning.

Myth 3: "Panic attacks must be bad for me" or "My nerves may wear out." The fear response is not harmful and has a shutoff system to protect the body. Whereas sustained stress has been shown to have long-term negative consequences, the same has not been shown for panic attacks.

Myth 4: "I'm going to have a heart attack." The most common symptoms of heart disease are chest pain and breathlessness, and the symptoms are most often directly related to effort. Panic attacks, on the other hand, can occur during exercise or rest and normally include many more symptoms. Heart disease also generally produces cardiac changes, which are detectable by an EKG. We certainly encourage consultation with a physician if a client is concerned about heart disease and has not had a recent medical evaluation. Most often, however, clients have been to the medical emergency room, to specialists, or both, all of whom have been unable to detect any problem. If this is the case, we ask clients to hypothesize that their cardiac symptoms are related to anxiety and to test this hypothesis over the course of treatment.

Myth 5: "I am going to pass out." Fainting is highly unlikely during a panic attack because panic is associated with accelerated sympathetic nervous system activity, which is physiologically incompatible with fainting. Previous fainting tends to be a good predictor of future fainting.

As mentioned, this educational component generally takes two treatment sessions, involving much didactic presentation by therapists as well as encouragement for group members to relate the information to their own experiences. Thus, group members are asked for personal examples for each major discussion point. The group format enables comparison between group members regarding their thoughts, sensations, and behaviors. Most often, awareness of similarities serves to provide reassurance and to reduce fears of being different. Sometimes the group is the first place in which clients learn that others experience the same feelings. Therefore, the sharing of information during the early sessions helps to build group cohesion.

Occasionally, group members express fear over "contagion"—that they will acquire specific fears expressed by other group members. In our experience, this type of contagion effect is rare, and when it does occur, is short-lived, dissipating as soon as active skill instruction begins. Notably, the same effect sometimes occurs with self-monitoring. That is, clients are asked to log their daily experiences with panic, anxiety, and other relevant variables, throughout the entire treatment. (Examples of these monitoring forms are provided in Exhibits 3.1 and 3.2.) On occasion, such monitoring initially elicits more anxiety, particularly for individuals whose major coping strategy is distraction. Self-monitoring becomes less anxiety provoking over time, as with exposure procedures in general.

Given the amount of information to be presented in the first two sessions, it is important to keep group discussions focused. In fact, group focus is essential throughout the entire treatment. Members who raise issues not directly relevant to the ongoing discussion are invited to speak with the therapist about those issues outside of group time. Therapists attempt to redirect discussion that goes off task in session, particularly in light of evidence for stronger efficacy from focused versus nonfocused treatments (e.g., Schulte et al., 1992). Furthermore, therapists make an effort to equalize group participation by soliciting involvement from the more reticent group members.

EXHIBIT 3.1
Panic Attack Record

Panic Attack Record

Date: _____ Time: _____ Duration: _____ (minutes)

With: Partner _____ Friend _____ Stranger _____ Alone _____

Stressful situation: Yes/No   Expected: Yes/No

Maximum Anxiety (Circle):   0-----1-----2-----3-----4-----5-----6-----7-----8
                            none   moderate   extreme

Sensation (Rate 0–8)

Pounding heart ____	Sweating ____	Hot/cold flashes ____
Tight/painful chest ____	Choking ____	Fear of dying ____
Breathlessness ____	Nausea ____	Fear of going crazy ____
Dizziness ____	Unreality ____	Fear of losing control ____
Trembling ____	Numbness/tingling ____	

Note. From *Mastery of Your Anxiety and Panic II*, by M. G. Craske, E. Meadows, and D. H. Barlow, 1994, Figure 6.3. Copyright 1994 by Graywind Publications, Inc. Reprinted with permission of publisher, The Psychological Corporation.

EXHIBIT 3.2
Weekly Record of Anxiety and Depression

Each evening before you go to bed, please rate your *average* level of anxiety (taking all things into consideration) throughout the day, the *maximum* level of anxiety that you experienced that day, your *average* level of depression throughout the day, and your average feeling of pleasantness throughout the day. Use the scale below. Next, please list the dosages and amounts of any medication you took. Finally, please rate, using the scale below, how worried or frightened you were, on the average, about the possibility of having a panic attack throughout the day.

```
0----------1----------2----------3----------4----------5----------6----------7---------8
none          slight          moderate          a lot          extreme
```

Date	Average Anxiety	Maximum Anxiety	Average Depression	Average Pleasantness	Medication	Fear of Panic Attack

Note. From *Mastery of Your Anxiety and Panic II*, by M. G. Craske, E. Meadows, and D. H. Barlow, 1994, Figure 6.3. Copyright 1994 by Graywind Publications, Inc. Reproduced with permission of publisher, The Psychological Corporation. All rights reserved.

Cognitive Restructuring

At Session 3, we introduce cognitive restructuring, beginning with a description of cognitive principles along the lines described by Beck and Emery (1985). The main point is that the way events are interpreted determines the nature of ensuing emotional reactions. Frequently, anxious individuals misattribute their anxiety to external factors, for example, "The shopping mall made me anxious" or "The humid weather makes me panic." We stress interpretations: "Your interpretation of being trapped and suffocating in the mall leads you to feel anxious" or "Your fear of feeling hot and suffocated leads you to panic." According to Beck and Emery, maladaptive cognitions are automatic and involve specific predictions about or interpretations of a given situation. Thus, the first step is to help clients identify specific, maladaptive cognitions.

Errors in thinking are divided into two types: (a) overestimation of probability and (b) catastrophic estimation of consequence. Anxious individuals tend to overestimate the likelihood that an aversive event will occur, particularly to themselves (Butler & Mathews, 1983). Clients are taught to question and challenge their assumptions and beliefs by looking at realistic probabilities, gathering evidence, exploring alternative interpretations, and considering realistic consequences and ways of managing events should they occur. The cognitive monitoring homework form, which is presented in Exhibit 3.3, is used for at-home practice of identifying and challenging faulty cognitions. The following example demonstrates a discussion that occurred in group after a client recorded panicking while in traffic the week before.

Client: ... and if I hadn't taken my medication, I don't know what would have happened.

Therapist: What possibilities did you imagine?

Client: I don't know. I don't think that I could have stayed in control of the car. I might have caused an accident.

Therapist: What do you think is the likelihood of losing control and causing an accident?

Client: I don't know. It felt pretty likely at the time. Maybe 50/50.

Therapist: So you think that there was a 50% chance that you would lose control of the car and cause an accident. Let's think about that. How many times have you had panic attacks in the car?

Client: Oh, hundreds, I'm sure.

Therapist: And of those, let's say, 200 panics, how many times have you felt like you would lose control of the car?

Client: All of them.

Therapist: And how many times have you actually lost control of the car?

Client: Well, never.

Therapist: But based on your estimate, you should have lost control of the car and caused an accident 100 times. So, it sounds like your estimate is an overestimate. In fact, you are probably more careful and pay more attention to your driving when you feel anxious in comparison with when you feel relaxed.

EXHIBIT 3.3
An Example of Cognitive Monitoring Homework

Triggering Situation	Initial Thought	Realistic Probability	Alternative Thought
Going to work, driving on freeway	I thought that I might get a panic attack and worried that I would not be able to breathe.	80/1	I have felt like this, and I have panicked before, but I have never not been able to breathe.
Came home to an empty house	I might lose control, and no one could help me.	0	I have never actually lost control, and even if I did someone would probably help me.
In a movie theater	There will be a fire or something, and I won't be able to get to an exit in this crowd.	2	I have gone to the movies many times, and nothing has ever happened to me. Fires in theaters are rare.

As can be seen in this example, it is important to differentiate how likely something feels at the time from realistic likelihood. It is the nature of panic that doom nearly always feels imminent.

The second type of error, catastrophization (Craske, Meadows, & Barlow, 1994), involves expecting the worst possible outcome of an event. To decatastrophize, clients learn that worst outcomes are usually relatively unlikely, anxiety and its effects are time limited and manageable, and even the worst outcomes are manageable.

Client 1: I don't like to be in a crowd because if I panic I might faint, and I don't know what would happen to me then.

Therapist: What do you imagine?

Client 1: I'd pass out and fall. I can see my body lying there, and nobody would help me.

Therapist: Wow. That does sound pretty bad. [To other group members]: Has anyone ever seen someone pass out or fall in a crowd?

Client 2: I did one time.

Therapist: What did the people in the area do?

Client 2: Someone called 911, the paramedics came, and they took the guy to the hospital.

Therapist: So, does it seem pretty catastrophic to think that you'd fall, and people would just step over you and leave you there?

The questioning and challenging techniques are extended through *hypothesis testing*, which refers to behavioral experiments designed to test predictions and gather more data to disconfirm fearful predictions. For example, an individual may predict falling in the absence of a wall to rest against when feeling anxious. The hypothesis-testing experiment would involve standing away from walls the next time they felt anxious to test whether falling is a true outcome. Similarly, for fears of being ridiculed, clients may test the reactions of others by disclosing their feelings of panic and anxiety.

Doubts commonly arise as fearful assumptions are being challenged, and each doubt is based on another cognitive distortion. For example, "Even though I have never fainted before, it could still happen" (which reflects distorted possibilities), or "Even though I've never fainted before, it's only because I've managed to get to safety in time" (which reflects false attribution of safety to escape behavior), or "Even though I've never fainted before, the next time the sensations could become worse than ever and then I will faint" (which reflects false association between intensity of sensations and risk level). Also, doubts arise from reliance on selective information to support fearful appraisals. A typical example is history of psychosis in the extended family (e.g., second cousin), which is used as evidence for the likelihood of going crazy if panic attacks continue. Sometimes fears are couched within the context of perceived consequences of avoidance behavior. For example, "I am most afraid of becoming so anxious that I'd leave the classroom and never return." In this case, it is helpful to identify and challenge thoughts that generate the motivation to leave (e.g., "I'll go crazy and scream if I don't escape"). Finally, individuals often report that they do not have specific thoughts, but rather that they "can't stand the feelings" of panic. In most cases, careful questioning identifies specific thoughts, such as "I cannot function if I have these feelings" or "These feelings will get progressively worse." Cognitive restructuring is continued throughout the remainder of the treatment program.

Several issues are relevant to group implementation of cognitive restructuring. First, although group members are asked to keep records of all panic episodes, we usually take just one example from each member's cognitive monitoring forms, for the purpose of reviewing their efforts at cognitive restructuring over the previous week. In contrast, an individual therapist may review the entire form. Second, observing others identify and restructure cognitions obviously provides excellent opportunities for learning vicariously. After the group is fully familiar with the cognitive approach (perhaps by Session 6), we encourage them to help each other identify and challenge anxious cognitions. Sometimes the challenging and restructuring offered by other group members is more effective than by the therapist, given the tendency for group members to affiliate more with people who have experienced similar feelings. In addition, helping other group members with restructuring contributes to the development of an objective perspective, or a personal scientist model. Finally, the group can be a great resource for hypothesis testing or gathering of evidence. For example, the group draws on collective experience or role plays fearful scenarios, such as one client laying on the floor, as if he or she had fainted, and other group members respond to this event in the same way that they would respond if it occurred naturally. This becomes valuable for purposes of decatastrophizing, because by acting out a feared event, clients learn that it is not as bad as they first thought and that there are ways of coping.

Breathing Retraining

Also at Session 3, we introduce breathing retraining. Several researchers have examined the efficacy of breathing retraining for panic disorder, given that 50% to 60% of clients describe hyperventilatory symptoms as being very similar to their panic attack symptoms (e.g., Holt & Andrews, 1989). However, it is noteworthy that recent research indicates that hyperventilatory symptoms do not necessarily represent actual hyperventilatory physiology (Holt & Andrews, 1989). Nevertheless, breathing retraining has been shown to be helpful, even if it does not correct habitual breathing patterns. The purposes of breathing retraining are to decrease symptoms of acute hyperventilation that sometimes occur during panic, reduce vulnerability to such symptoms, and develop a self-control technique.

Breathing retraining begins with a demonstration hyperventilation exercise, in which clients are asked to stand and breath deeply and fast for up to 90 seconds. We usually have the entire group, including therapists, do this exercise together. We emphasize that individuals differ in their response to this exercise to minimize group pressure for each member to continue as long as other members. Obviously, this exercise requires medical clearance from conditions such as pregnancy, neurological disorder, and some cardiovascular disorders. Most often, clients do not endure for the 90 seconds because they become fearful of the sensations produced by hyperventilation. Following this demonstration exercise and an assessment of the degree of similarity between induced sensations and those experienced during panic attacks, education is provided about the nature of hyperventilation. The educational information serves to correct fear-based interpretations (e.g., "I cannot breathe" or "I will suffocate").

The main points conveyed are as follows:

- It is natural to overbreathe when one is anxious or panicky as the body searches for more energy in the form of oxygen in preparation for dealing with danger.
- If the oxygen is not used at the rate at which its consumed, a state of hyperventilation can ensue.
- Hyperventilation refers to a lowering of the proportion of carbon dioxide to oxygen in the blood, which in turn increases alkalinity of the blood, oxygen stickiness of hemoglobin, and constriction of the blood vessels.
- All of these changes lead to slightly less oxygen getting to the tissues and the resultant sensations of lightheadedness, dizziness, depersonalization, and parasthesias.
- These effects are not dangerous.

The next step is to teach "correct" breathing. Clients are taught to breathe from the diaphragm as opposed to the chest, because chest breathing is believed to contribute to hyperventilation. In addition, they are instructed to concentrate by counting during inhalation (e.g., "one, two . . .") and thinking the word *relax* during exhalation, proceeding up to 10 and back down to 1 in a continuous cycle. The group practices this form of breathing in session, and then practices at least two times a day, approximately 10 minutes each time, for the next week. There is no attempt to slow the breathing at this point. Sometimes individuals encounter difficulties breathing diaphragmatically. One aid to diaphragmatic breathing is to lie on one's back on the floor with one hand on the sternum and the other under the ribcage. The hand below the ribcage will move more if the person is breathing from the diaphragm. Once the "feeling" of diaphragmatic breathing is experienced in this position, practice can continue in a sitting position, concentrating on filling the lower part of the lungs as if slowly filling a balloon.

After 1 week of practice, slowed breathing is approximated, by gradually reaching a 6-second cycle (3 seconds inhalation, 3 seconds exhalation). After another week of slow diaphragmatic breathing practice, practice takes place in distracting environments, such as at work or in the car. The last step is to apply slow breathing as a coping strategy at times of anxiety or panic, which is usually achieved by around Session 6.

One difficulty that can arise with breathing retraining is an overreliance on breathing exercises. The provision of a concrete exercise, particularly one that slows symptoms of arousal, is particularly appealing. Frustration and "desperation" can arise from drastic attempts to use the breathing exercise "at all costs" for fear that if breathing is not slowed, then dreaded events such as fainting or death would actually occur. The most effective use of breathing retraining is in combination with cognitive restructuring principles. Another problem is the experience of dizziness or other feared symptoms during slowed breathing exercises.

> Diane paged her therapist a couple of days after the breathing retraining exercise had first been introduced. She complained that she had been trying the exercise and that she was now unable to breathe normally. She felt that she was not getting enough air. She said that her chest hurt from the effort of breathing and that she was exhausted from being unable to sleep.

> Therapist: It does sound like you are expending a lot of effort breathing. It sounds also like you are feeling very anxious about this.

> Diane: Well, yes. I'm not getting enough air.

> Therapist: That's a scary thought. Let's test it out as a hypothesis. What evidence do you have for that idea?

> Diane: I don't know, it really feels like I can't get enough air. And my chest really hurts.

> Therapist: So, they are some feelings that you have. What about objective evidence? For example, a good sign that you are actually not getting enough air is passing out or turning blue. Have either of those happened?

> Diane: No.

> Therapist: So, can you think of another possible explanation for those sensations?

> Diane: Well, I guess anxiety.

Thus, symptoms can arise from fear caused by misappraisals of danger. In addition, chronic hyperventilation may render individuals vulnerable to exacerbation of symptomatology when breathing patterns are disrupted, even though the disruption is in the form of breathing retraining exercises. However, symptoms are likely to subside with practice.

Others have used applied relaxation in place of breathing retraining. This involves training in progressive muscle relaxation and cue-controlled relaxation that is applied to practice items from a hierarchy of anxiety-provoking tasks (Öst, 1988).

Interoceptive Exposure

The purpose of interoceptive exposure (as in the case of exposure to external phobic stimuli) is to disrupt or weaken associations between specific bodily cues and panic reactions. The theoretical basis for interoceptive exposure is fear extinction, given the conceptualization of panic attacks as conditioned or learned alarm reactions to salient bodily cues. Interoceptive exposure is conducted through procedures that induce paniclike sensations reliably, such as cardiovascular exercise. The exposure is conducted using a graduated format and proceeds from simulated exercises in the clinic setting to more naturalistic activities in the home environment. Provision of a credible rationale for interoceptive exposure is essential, given the apparent conflict between earlier strategies that emphasized decreasing sensations (through cognitive restructuring and breathing control) and this more confrontational procedure. In addition, a rationale is important for clients who fear inducing the sensations of panic. We emphasize the value of exposure by eliciting examples of situations or objects that clients themselves learned to become less fearful of as a result of practice and experience (e.g., bike riding, skiing, and public speaking). Clients sometimes express doubts because their fear of sensations has not reduced despite their daily occurrence. We emphasize that in contrast to their current experience of sensations, this exposure entails systematic and controlled exposures to sensations and, in contrast to their current attempts to eliminate the sensations as soon as they arise, this exposure entails progressive toleration of sensations.

We begin this segment of treatment at Session 5 with a series of exercises that produce sensations similar to the ones that occur during panic (these are listed in Table 3.3). Over the next several sessions, exposure to individually relevant sensation-induction exercises is repeated, for clients to learn that feared aversive consequences do not occur. A

TABLE 3.3
Induction Exercises for Interoceptive Exposure

Exercise	Sensations	Intensity of Sensation (0–8)	Intensity of Anxiety (0–8)	Similarity to Panic (0–8)
Shake head side to side (30 seconds)				
Head between legs (30 seconds), sit up quickly				
Run in place (1 minute)				
Hold breath				
Muscle tension (1 minute)				
Spin (1 minute)				
Hyperventilation (1 minute)				
Breathe through a straw (2 minutes)				
Stare at a light (1 minute) then read				

hierarchy is established in order of anxiety level associated with each exercise. Repeated exposure begins with lower anxiety level items. Each item is practiced enough times until the maximum amount of anxiety during the exercise is no more than mild. With each practice, clients are instructed to experience the sensations as fully as possible and to tolerate them for a period of time before terminating the exercise. For example, they may be asked to hyperventilate until they feel sensations of light headedness or dizziness and then to continue to hyperventilate for at least 30 seconds longer. By so doing, they have an opportunity to correct their natural tendencies to avert the sensations as soon as possible and also to learn that feared outcomes do not occur. With each repetition, clients are encouraged to apply cognitive and breathing strategies after inducing and tolerating the sensations.

In addition to within-session practices, the exercises are practiced between sessions. Not only does homework practice consolidate learning, but it also facilitates generalizations to conditions in which the therapist is not present as a safety signal. After completing the simulated exercises, the clients identify naturalistic exposure activities, listed in a hierarchy and practiced in the same way. Naturalistic interoceptive exercises include activities such as aerobic exercise or running up flights of stairs, taking steamy showers or saunas, watching suspenseful movies, and drinking caffeine. These are activities that inherently generate sensations. Although interoceptive exposure is the major treatment focus for Sessions 5 through 8, it is continued when necessary throughout the remainder of treatment.

Interoceptive exposure works well within a group setting, partly because of the camaraderie and group support offered for each member to confront his or her most feared sensations. We conduct the initial symptom induction exercises as a group, but, as with the hyperventilation demonstration, emphasize individual differences in tolerability of each exercise. Individual members use their own ratings of each exercise to generate their own hierarchy. For the purposes of repeated exposure to each interoceptive exercise, group members form pairs. One member of the pair completes the exercise, whereas the other rates levels of anxiety, informs the first person when to stop the exercise, and prompts the use of breathing and cognitive strategies when the induction is over. Then, they switch roles. Therapists spend some time with each pair, giving feedback when necessary. We have found this type of pairing to be very effective. Furthermore, we often incorporate naturalistic interoceptive exposure exercises for the entire group, such as by providing coffee and chocolate (i.e., stimulants that produce sensations) for all group members to partake in throughout a group session.

In Vivo Exposure

The second 8 weeks of treatment incorporate panic control into in vivo exposure, or confrontation with agoraphobic situations. We begin by having each group member list a number of situations that he or she fears or avoids, which are ranked from the least to the most anxiety provoking. We explain that agoraphobia is maintained by fears of panicking or experiencing certain bodily sensations. Therefore, learning that took place in the first phase of treatment—that bodily sensations of panic are not actually dangerous—is central to overcoming agoraphobia. However, direct confrontation with agoraphobic situations is equally important. First, this is achieved by identifying and challenging the thoughts that maintain fear about certain situations. Second, by repeated confrontation with each item from their hierarchy, clients learn that the situations are manageable and the expected catastrophic consequences do not occur.

For the duration of the second phase of treatment, clients are asked to practice in vivo exposure at least three times per week, starting with the least anxiety-provoking item on their hierarchy. Included among the more challenging items should be situations associated with the very first panic or a very bad panic attack. The difficulty of exposure can be further increased by including exercises to elicit feared sensations, and we generally encourage clients to combine interoceptive exercises with their in vivo exposure to feared agoraphobic situations. As an example of this,

> Christie had her first panic attack at the track at her school. Bolstered by her ability to manage other situations, she decided that she wanted to return to the track, where she had not been in over a year. She began by simply going to the track and watching people. The next step was to begin walking and then to jog. Finally, she jogged around the track while intentionally looking down to elicit a dizzy sensation that was similar to the sensations that she experienced during her first panic attack.

During every exposure exercise, clients are asked to identify and challenge negative cognitions and to apply breathing retraining when appropriate. In addition, we attempt to correct commonly used but maladaptive methods of coping with agoraphobic situations. The first is the use of safety signals, such as other people (who would help in the event of a panic) or objects (e.g., telephones or phone numbers, money, medications). Safety signals result in maintenance of the erroneous belief of danger (e.g., "I would have gone crazy if my husband had not been there to help me" or "I might have fainted if it hadn't been for the knowledge that the medication was in my pocket"). Thus, safety signals are gradually weaned. A second negative coping strategy is "holding on for dear life coping," which refers to taking unnecessary precautions (e.g., sitting in the aisle in a movie theater so faster escape is possible, tightly gripping the steering wheel to prevent losing control of the car). Mastery behavior is encouraged in place of these unnecessary precautions (e.g., sitting in the middle of the row at a movie theater, loosening the grip on the steering wheel). A third strategy is distraction (e.g., pretending to be elsewhere, using music or games to keep one's mind occupied), which tends to alleviate anxiety in the short term but may not be effective in the long term. Thus, clients are encouraged to maintain an objective focus on the situation and their feelings (e.g., "OK, I am in the elevator, the doors are closing and I can feel it moving, my hands are sweaty, and I would judge my anxiety to be about 3 on the 0–8 scale"). Note that an objective focus is very different from subjective focus, which tends to be negative and fear provoking (e.g., "OK, I am in the elevator and it feels as if I can't breathe—the doors may get jammed shut, and I would be stuck in here forever.").

In vivo exposure can be challenging. To maximize the benefit of exposure, we plan and rehearse practices within the group setting. That is, each session is devoted to reviewing exposure practices over the preceding week for each group member, learning from those experiences, and planning new exposures for the coming week. Group members are encouraged to become fully involved in evaluation of past and planning of future exposure for themselves as well as for others in the group. For example, planning involves consideration of situational factors (e.g., how many people are likely to be there, how much traffic will there be), and sensations that are likely to occur and how they will be managed. Also, rehearsal is given to the negative cognitions that are likely to occur and how they can be countered. The group setting provides an excellent opportunity for input from everyone regarding management of anxiety in an upcoming exposure task. In addition, the group provides reinforcement for each other's accomplishments, offsetting the tendencies for clients to minimize their successes and magnify their failures. We encourage reinforcement of behavioral accomplishments regardless of level of anxiety experienced.

In addition, the group can be incorporated directly into in vivo exposures by conducting exercises within sessions. These might include role plays of situations, much in the same way that was described previously for hypothesis testing. For example, the group may be arranged in seating positions that simulate a flight, with one group member expressing and managing fear and other members responding as if in the real situation, and also responding by providing examples of cognitive restructuring for the fearful person. In addition, certain exposures can be practiced in vivo as a group, such as exposure to elevators, heights, stores, walking, and other situations that are in close proximity of the clinical setting. Obviously, when conducting group exposures, some members will be more anxious than others. The less fearful members provide excellent models for the more fearful members.

Problems with compliance with in vivo exposure are addressed directly in the group. From the start, we attempt to avoid such problems by selecting exercises that are feasible (e.g., not costly, not requiring a good deal of travel). Sometimes, there are complaints about finding the time to complete the homework. Throughout treatment, we emphasize the importance of homework. In regard to the in vivo exposures, we remind group members that the treatment is time limited and explain the importance of practicing while they have the opportunity to come back to the group with any difficulties that they encounter. In many cases, noncompletion of exposure exercises is a function of fear. Thus, therapists and other group members elicit thoughts about the avoided task and help the client through cognitive restructuring. Finally, it may be necessary to work up to a given task gradually, as described below.

> Jessica wanted to have her eyelashes dyed. She began by covering her eyes and sitting in the dark for 30 seconds and worked up to the 5 minutes required for the dyeing process. She scheduled her appointment but found herself unable to stay. With some discussion, it was established that she felt that when she covered her own eyes she could always uncover them but felt that she would be too embarrassed to ask someone else to uncover her eyes, meaning that she would be trapped.

We completed cognitive restructuring around the embarrassed and trapped feelings. We also added new exercises by involving her roommate in blindfolding and locking her in a dark room to give her practice with being in someone else's control.

GROUP STRUCTURE AND SELECTION

Our groups normally have 3–5 members. The group size is small to allow for sufficient individual attention. We believe that whereas didactic presentation is feasible in larger groups (e.g., 10–12 clients), cognitive restructuring and exposure exercises are most effective when they are tailored to each individual, in which case a smaller group is necessary. This is consistent with a finding in the area of social phobia treatment: the results from one study that did not achieve the usual rate of effectiveness of CBT (Gelernter et al., 1991) were attributed to large group sizes (Hope, Heimberg, & Bruch, 1995). In addition, we have two therapists per group, ideally one female and one male. The availability of two therapists enhances role plays, demonstration exercises and division of responsibility for different components of the treatment.

We require that group members have a principal diagnosis of panic disorder, that is, panic disorders is currently the most disturbing or most disabling condition. The diagnosis is established by use of a semistructured interview (e.g., Anxiety Disorders Interview Schedule for the 4th edition of the *Diagnostic and Statistical Manual of Mental Disorders*; Brown, Di Nardo, & Barlow, 1994). To increase objectivity in the assessment, the interview is not conducted by the treating clinician, but this is not always feasible in clinical settings. This is a demanding treatment. In addition to attending weekly meetings, group members are expected to complete daily homework. Motivation to engage in treatment is therefore important, and motivation may be diminished if panic disorder is not the primary concern. Furthermore, as seen from the above description, the treatment is not a general anxiety management program but instead is focused on fears of bodily sensations and agoraphobic situations. Thus, it would not adequately address the primary concerns of individuals for whom panic disorder is not the principal diagnosis. It is interesting, however, that our research shows that additional diagnoses tend to diminish substantially after treatment for panic disorder. For example, in addition to a principal diagnosis of panic disorder, the majority of clients have additional diagnoses of generalized anxiety, social phobia, specific phobia, and depression. After treatment, those additional diagnoses commonly subside in intensity, even to the point of being no longer diagnosable (e.g., Tsao, Lewin, & Craske, 1998).

Although the majority of clients have additional diagnoses that do not exclude them from group participation, there are some additional diagnoses that are reason for exclusion. These include current psychosis, suicidality, and substance abuse or dependence, given their likely interruption of the group process and of engagement in the treatment. In addition, we require a medical examination before beginning treatment to ensure that there is no medical contraindication to interoceptive symptom induction or fearful arousal in general (e.g., cardiovascular disease, respiratory conditions, and pregnancy). In the case of medical comorbidity, the treatment can be conducted with the supervision of a physician and with modifications to lessen the intensity of symptom induction and fear arousal, perhaps in combination with ongoing monitoring of certain physiological parameters (such as by using ambulatory blood pressure cuffs).

Medication status is another important issue. As many as 50% of our clients take anxiolytic or antidepressant medication or both when they first enter our clinic. The interaction between medications and CBT for panic and agoraphobia is a complicated issue and is in need of further investigation (see Craske, 1996, for a review). For those who come to us on medication, we work with them and their physicians either to stabilize medications at a regular dosage during treatment or to withdraw medications. We generally discourage use of medication on an as-needed basis (most commonly benzodiazepines). We believe that use of as-needed medications works against the principles of treatment. We teach that the fear response is harmless, manageable, and time limited and that bodily sensations will come and go and need not be avoided. As-needed medications deprive the individual of learning these principles. Furthermore, as-needed medications lead to attributions of control and safety to medications as opposed to oneself. Attributions of improvements to medications predict relapse (e.g., Basoglu, Marks, Kilic, Brewin, & Swinson, 1994). On the other hand, cognitive–behavioral treatments for panic improve the rate of successful withdrawal from medications (e.g., Otto, Pollack, Meltzer-Brody, & Rosenbaum, 1992) and, thus, clients who use medications throughout our treatment frequently successfully discontinue their medications once the treatment is complete.

SUMMARY

In summary, it appears that group treatments for anxiety disorders are strongly justified for several reasons. First, their cost-effectiveness results in increased availability of treatment to individuals experiencing anxiety disorders who would not otherwise receive treatment because of financial limitations or availability of therapists. Second, group formats may be conducive to the development of anxiety management skills and overcoming fears of particular situations, given the modeling, reinforcement, and opportunities for simulated or in vivo exposure provided by group members.

Third, the data, albeit limited, suggest that on average, group treatments are as effective as individual therapies in the case of cognitive–behavioral approaches for anxiety disorders. It is hoped that future investigation will elucidate the optimal parameters under which group treatment should take place (e.g., frequency and schedule of meetings, number of members) as well as characteristics of individuals who are better suited for group as opposed to individual treatment.

REFERENCES

Angst, J., & Dobler-Mikola, A. (1985). The Zurich Study: V. Anxiety and phobia in young adults. *European Archives of Psychiatry and Neurological Sciences, 235,* 171–178.

Arntz, A., & van den Hout, M. (1996). Psychological treatments of panic disorder without agoraphobia: Cognitive therapy versus applied relaxation. *Behaviour Research and Therapy, 34,* 113–121.

Barlow, D. H. (1988). *Anxiety and its disorders: The nature and treatment of anxiety and panic.* New York: Guilford Press.

Barlow, D. H., & Craske, M. G. (1999). *Mastery of your anxiety and panic* (3rd ed.). San Antonio, TX: Harcourt Brace.

Barlow, D. H., Craske, M. G., Cerny, J. A., & Klosko, J. S. (1989). Behavioral treatment of panic disorder. *Behavior Therapy, 20,* 261–282.

Barlow, D. H., O'Brien, G. T., & Last, C. G. (1984). Couples treatment of agoraphobia. *Behavior Therapy, 15,* 41–58.

Basoglu, M., Marks, I. M., Kilic, C., Brewin, C. R., & Swinson, R. P. (1994). Alprazolam and exposure for panic disorder with agoraphobia attribution of improvement to medication predicts subsequent relapse. *British Journal of Psychiatry, 164,* 652–659.

Beck, A. T., & Emery, G. (1985). *Anxiety disorders and phobias: A cognitive perspective.* New York: Basic Books.

Beck, A. T., Sokol, L., Clark, D. A., Berchick, R., & Wright, F. (1992). A crossover study of focused cognitive therapy for panic disorder. *American Journal of Psychiatry, 149,* 778–783.

Beck, J. G., Stanley, M. A., Baldwin, L. E., Deagle, E. A., & Averill, P. M. (1994). Comparison of cognitive therapy and relaxation training for panic disorder. *Journal of Consulting and Clinical Psychology, 62,* 818–826.

Black, D. W., Wesner, R., Bowers, W., & Gabel, J. (1993). A comparison of fluvoxamine, cognitive therapy, and placebo in the treatment of panic disorder. *Archives of General Psychiatry, 50,* 44–50.

Bouchard, S., Gauthier, J., Laberge, B., French, D., Pelletier, M.-H., & Godbout, C. (1996). Exposure versus cognitive restructuring in the treatment of panic disorder with agoraphobia. *Behaviour Research and Therapy, 34,* 213–224.

Bowen, R., South, M., Fischer, D., & Looman, T. (1994). Depression, mastery, and number of group sessions attended predict outcome of patients with panic and agoraphobia in a behavioral/medication program. *Canadian Journal of Psychiatry, 39,* 283–288.

Brown, T. A., Di Nardo, P. A., & Barlow, D. H. (1994). *Anxiety Disorders Interview Schedule for DSM-IV.* San Antonio, TX: Psychological Corporation.

Butler, G., & Mathews, A. (1983). Cognitive processes in anxiety. *Advances in Behaviour Research and Therapy, 5,* 51–62.

Carter, M. M., Turovsky, J., Sbrocco, T., & Meadows, E. A. (1995). Patient dropout from a couples' group treatment for panic disorder with agoraphobia. *Professional Psychology: Research and Practice, 26,* 626–628.

Cerny, J. A., Barlow, D. H., Craske, M. G., & Himadi, W. G. (1987). Couples treatment of agoraphobia: A two-year follow-up. *Behavior Therapy, 18,* 401–415.

Chambless, D. L., Caputo, G., Bright, P., & Gallagher, R. (1984). Assessment of fear in agoraphobics: The Body Sensations Questionnaire and the Agoraphobic Cognitions Questionnaire. *Journal of Consulting and Clinical Psychology, 52,* 1090–1097.

Chambless, D. L., & Mason, J. (1986). Sex, sex-role stereotyping and agoraphobia. *Behaviour Research and Therapy, 24,* 231–235.

Clark, D. M., Salkovskis, P., Gelder, M., Koehler, C., Martin, M., Anastasiades, P., Hackmann, A., Middleton, H., & Jeavons, A. (1988). Tests of a cognitive theory of panic. In I. Hand & H. Wittchen (Eds.), *Panic and phobias: Treatments and variables affecting course and outcome* (pp. 71–90). Berlin: Springer-Verlag.

Clark, D. M., Salkovskis, P. M., Hackmann, A., Middleton, H., Anastasiades, P., & Gelder, M. (1994). A comparison of cognitive therapy, applied relaxation and imipramine in the treatment of panic disorder. *British Journal of Psychiatry, 164,* 759–769.

Cote, G., Gauthier, J. G., Laberge, B., Cormier, H., & Plamondon, J. (1994). Reduced therapist contact in the cognitive–behavioral treatment of panic disorder. *Behavior Therapy, 25,* 123–145.

Craske, M. G. (1996). An integrated treatment approach to panic disorder. *Bulletin of the Menninger Clinic, 60*(Suppl. A), A87–A104.

Craske, M. G. (1998). *Anxiety disorders: Psychological approaches to theory and treatment.* Boulder, CO: Westview Press/Harper Collins.

Craske, M. G., & Barlow, D. H. (1988). A review of the relationship between panic and avoidance. *Clinical Psychology Review, 8,* 667–685.

Craske, M. G., & Barlow, D. H. (1999a). *Agoraphobia supplement to mastery of your anxiety and panic* (3rd ed.). New York: Graywind.

Craske, M. G., & Barlow, D. H. (1999b). *Therapists guide to mastery of your anxiety and panic.* (3rd ed.). New York: Graywind.

Craske, M. G., Glover, D., & DeCola, J. (1994). Predicted versus unpredicted panic attacks: Acute versus general distress. *Journal of Abnormal Psychology, 104,* 214–223.

Craske, M. G., & Lewin, M. (1994). *Panic disorder and agoraphobia treatment.* Unpublished treatment manual.

Craske, M. G., Maidenberg, E., & Bystritsky, A. (1995). Brief cognitive–behavioral versus nondirective therapy for panic disorder. *Journal of Behavior Therapy and Experimental Psychiatry, 26,* 113–120.

Craske, M. G., Meadows, E., & Barlow, D. H. (1994). *Mastery of your anxiety and panic (II): Therapist guide.* New York: Graywind.

Craske, M. G., & Rowe, M. (1997). Nocturnal panic. *Clinical Psychology: Science and Practice, 4,* 153–174.

Craske, M. G., Rowe, M., Lewin, M., & Noriega-Dimitri, R. (1997). Interoceptive exposure versus breathing retraining within cognitive–behavioural therapy for panic disorder with agoraphobia. *British Journal of Clinical Psychology, 36,* 85–99.

Craske, M. G., Street, L., & Barlow, D. H. (1989). Instructions to focus upon or distract from internal cues during exposure treatment for agoraphobic avoidance. *Behaviour Research and Therapy, 27,* 663–672.

DeCola, J. P., & Rosellini, R. A. (1990). Unpredictable/uncontrollable stress proactively interferes with appetitive Pavlovian conditioning. *Learning and Motivation, 21,* 137–152.

Ehlers, A., & Breuer, P. (1995). Selective attention to physical threat in subjects with panic attacks and specific phobias. *Journal of Anxiety Disorders, 9,* 11–31.

Ehlers, A., & Margraf, J. (1989). The psychophysiological model of panic attacks. In P. M. G. Emmelkamp, W. T. Everaerd, F. W. Kraaimaat, & M. J. Van Son (Eds.), *Fresh perspectives on anxiety disorders* (pp. 1–29). Lisse, The Netherlands: Swets & Zeitlinger.

Evans, L., Holt, C., & Oei, T. (1991). Long term follow-up of agoraphobics treated by brief intensive group cognitive behavioural therapy. *Australian and New Zealand Journal of Psychiatry, 25,* 343–349.

Feigenbaum, W. (1988). Long-term efficacy of ungraded versus graded massed exposure in agoraphobics. In I. Hand & H. Wittchen (Eds.), *Panic and phobias: Treatments and variables affecting course and outcome* (pp. 149–158). Berlin: Springer-Verlag.

Gelernter, C. S., Uhde, T. W., Cimbolic, P., Arnkoff, D. B., Vittone, B. J., Tancer, M. E., & Bartko, J. J. (1991). Cognitive–behavioral and pharmacological treatments of social phobia: A controlled study. *Archives of General Psychiatry, 48,* 938–945.

Goisman, R. M., Warshaw, M. G., Peterson, L. G., Rogers, M. P., Cuneo, P., Hunt, M. F., Tomlin-Albanese, J. M., Kazim, A., Gollan, J. K., Epstein-Kaye, T., Reich, J. H., & Keller, M. B. (1994). Panic, agoraphobia, and panic disorder with agoraphobia: Data from a 4 percent multicenter anxiety disorders study. *Journal of Nervous and Mental Disease, 182,* 72–79.

Gould, R. A., & Clum, G. A. (1995). Self-help plus minimal therapist contact in the treatment of panic disorder: A replication and extension. *Behavior Therapy, 26,* 533–546.

Gould, R. A., Clum, G. A., & Shapiro, D. (1993). The use of bibliotherapy in the treatment of panic: A preliminary investigation. *Behavior Therapy, 24,* 241–252.

Gray, J. A. (1988). *The psychology of fear and stress.* New York: Cambridge University Press.

Hecker, J. E., Losee, M. C., Friztler, B. K., & Fink, C. M. (1996). Self-directed versus therapist-directed cognitive behavioral treatment for panic disorder. *Journal of Anxiety Disorders, 10,* 253–265.

Hoffart, A. (1995). A comparison of cognitive and guided mastery therapy of agoraphobia. *Behaviour Research and Therapy, 33,* 423–434.

Holt, P., & Andrews, G. (1989). Hyperventilation and anxiety in panic disorder, agoraphobia, and generalized anxiety disorder. *Behaviour Research and Therapy, 27,* 453–460.

Hope, D. A., Heimberg, R. G., & Bruch, M. A. (1995). Dismantling cognitive–behavioral group therapy for social phobia. *Behaviour Research and Therapy, 33,* 637–650.

Jansson, L., Jerremalm, A., & Öst, L.-G. (1986). Follow-up of agoraphobic patients treated with exposure in vivo or applied relaxation. *British Journal of Psychiatry, 149,* 486–490.

Kessler, R. C., McGonagle, K. A., Zhao, S., Nelson, C. B., Hughes, M., Eshleman, S., Wittchen, H.-U., & Kendler, K. S. (1994). Lifetime and 12-month prevalence of *DSM–III–R* psychiatric disorders in the United States: Results from the National Comorbidity Survey. *Archives of General Psychiatry, 51,* 8–19.

Klosko, J. S., Barlow, D. H., Tassinari, R., & Cerny, J. A. (1990). A comparison of alprazolam and behavior therapy in treatment of panic disorder. *Journal of Consulting and Clinical Psychology, 58,* 77–84.

Laberge, B., Gauthier, J. G., Cote, G., Plamondon, J., & Cormier, H. J. (1993). Cognitive–behavioral therapy of panic disorder with secondary major depression: A preliminary investigation. *Journal of Consulting and Clinical Psychology, 61,* 1028–1037.

Lidren, D., Watkins, P., Gould, R., Clum, G., Asterino, M., & Tulloch, H. L. (1994). A comparison of bibliotherapy and group therapy in the treatment of panic disorder. *Journal of Consulting and Clinical Psychology, 62,* 865–869.

Maier, S. F., Laudenslager, M. L., & Ryan, S. M. (1985). Stressor controllability, immune function and endogenous opiates. In F. R. Brush & J. B. Overmeier (Eds.), *Affect, conditioning and cognition: Essays on the determinants of behavior* (pp. 183–201). Hillsdale, NJ: Erlbaum.

Margraf, J., Gobel, M., & Schneider, S. (1989). Cognitive–behavioral treatments for panic disorder. In H. Zapotoczsky & T. Wenzel (Eds.), *The scientific dialogue: From basic research to clinical intervention. Annual series of European research in behavior therapy* (Vol. 5, pp. 149–155). Lisse, The Netherlands: Swets & Zeitlinger.

Markowitz, J. S., Weissman, M. M., Ouellette, R., Lish, J. D., & Klerman, G. L. (1989). Quality of life in panic disorder. *Archives of General Psychiatry, 46,* 984–992.

Marks, I. M., Swinson, R. P., Basoglu, M., Kuch, K., Noshirvani, H., O'Sullivan, G., Lelliot, P. T., Kirby, M., McNamee, G., Sengun, S., & Wickwire, K. (1993). Alprazolam and exposure alone and combined in panic disorder with agoraphobia: A controlled study in London and Toronto. *British Journal of Psychiatry, 162,* 776–787.

Mavissakalian, M., & Michelson, L. (1986). Two-year follow-up of exposure and imipramine treatment of agoraphobia. *American Journal of Psychiatry, 143,* 1106–1112.

Michelson, L., Marchione, K., Marchione, N., Testa, S., & Mavissakalian, M. (1988). Cognitive correlates and outcome of cognitive, behavioral and physiological treatments of agoraphobia. *Psychological Reports, 63,* 999–1004.

Michelson, L., Mavissakalian, M. Y., & Marchione, K. (1985). Cognitive and behavioral treatments of agoraphobia: Clinical, behavioral, and psychophysiological outcomes. *Journal of Consulting and Clinical Psychology, 53,* 913–925.

Moran, C., & Andrews, G. (1985). The familial occurrence of agoraphobia. *British Journal of Psychiatry, 146,* 262–267.

Neron, S., Lacroix, D., & Chaput, Y. (1995). Group vs. individual cognitive behavior therapy in panic disorder: An open clinical trial with a six month follow-up. *Canadian Journal of Behavioural Science, 27,* 379–392.

Noyes, R., Crowe, R. R., Harris, E. L., Hamra, B. J., McChesney, C. M., & Chaudry, D. R. (1986). Relationship between panic disorder and agoraphobia: A family study. *Archives of General Psychiatry, 43,* 227–232.

Öst, L.-G. (1988). Applied relaxation vs. progressive relaxation in the treatment of panic disorder. *Behaviour Research and Therapy, 26,* 13–22.

Öst, L.-G., & Westling, B. E. (1995). Applied relaxation vs. cognitive–behavior therapy in the treatment of panic disorder. *Behaviour Research and Therapy, 33,* 145–158.

Otto, M. W., Pollack, M. H., Meltzer-Brody, S., & Rosenbaum, J. (1992). Cognitive–behavioral therapy for benzodiazepine discontinuation in panic disorder patients. *Psychopharmacology Bulletin, 28,* 123–130.

Pollard, C. A., Bronson, S. S., & Kenney, M. R. (1989). Prevalence of agoraphobia without panic in clinical settings. *American Journal of Psychiatry, 146,* 559.

Pollard, C. A., Henderson, J. G., Frank, M., & Margolis, R. B. (1989). Help-seeking patterns of anxiety-disordered individuals in the general population. *Journal of Anxiety Disorders, 3,* 131–138.

Rachman, S., & Levitt, K. (1985). Panics and their consequences. *Behaviour Research and Therapy, 23,* 585–600.

Rapee, R. M., Mattick, R., & Murrell, E. (1986). Cognitive mediation in the affective component of spontaneous panic attacks. *Journal of Behavior Therapy and Experimental Psychiatry, 17,* 245–253.

Razran, G. (1961). The observable unconscious and the inferable conscious in current soviet psychophysiology: Interoceptive conditioning, semantic conditioning, and the orienting reflex. *Psychological Review, 68,* 81–147.

Reiss, S., Peterson, R., Gursky, D., & McNally, R. (1986). Anxiety sensitivity, anxiety frequency, and the prediction of fearfulness. *Behaviour Research and Therapy, 24,* 1–8.

Rice, D. P., & Miller, L. S. (1993). The economic burden of mental disorders. *Advances in Health Economics and Health Services Research, 14,* 37–53.

Sanderson, W. S., Rapee, R. M., & Barlow, D. H. (1989). The influence of an illusion of control on panic attacks induced via inhalation of 5.5 percent carbon dioxide enriched air. *Archives of General Psychiatry, 48,* 157–162.

Schulte, D., Kuenzel, R., Pepping, G., & Schulte-Bahrenberg, T. (1992). Tailor-made versus standardized therapy of phobic patients. *Advances in Behaviour Research and Therapy, 14*(2), 67–92.

Shear, M. K., Pilkonis, P. A., Cloitre, M., & Leon, A. C. (1994). Cognitive–behavioral treatment compared with nonprescriptive treatment of panic disorder. *Archives of General Psychiatry, 51,* 395–401.

Telch, M. J., Lucas, J. A., Schmidt, N. B., Hanna, H. H., LaNae Jaimez, T., & Lucas, R. A. (1993). Group cognitive–behavioral treatment of panic disorder. *Behaviour Research and Therapy, 31,* 279–287.

Thompson, J. W., Burns, B. J., Bartko, J. J., Boyd, J. H., Taube, C. A., & Bourdon, K. H. (1988). The use of ambulatory services by persons with and without phobia. *Medical Care, 26,* 183–198.

Thyer, B. A., Himle, J., Curtis, G. C., Cameron, O. G., & Nesse, R. M. (1985). A comparison of panic disorder and agoraphobia with panic attacks. *Comprehensive Psychiatry, 26,* 208–214.

Tsao, J. C. I., Lewin, M. R., & Craske, M. G. (1998). The effects of cognitive–behavior therapy for panic disorder on comorbid conditions. *Journal of Anxiety Disorders, 12,* 357–371.

Van den Hout, M., Van der Molen, G. M., Griez, E., & Lousberg, G. (1987). Specificity of interoceptive fear to panic disorders. *Journal of Psychopathology and Behavioral Assessment, 9,* 99–109.

Weinberg, J., & Levine, S. (1980). Psychobiology of coping in animals: The effect of predictability. In S. Levine & H. Ursin (Eds.), *Coping and health* (pp. 39–59). New York: Plenum Press.

Williams, S. L., & Falbo, J. (1996) Cognitive and performance-based treatments for panic attacks in people with varying degrees of agoraphobic disability. *Behaviour Research Therapy, 34,* 253–264.

Wittchen, H.-U. (1988). Natural course and spontaneous remissions of untreated anxiety disorder: Results of the Munich Follow-Up Study (MFS). In H. Hand & H. Wittchen (Eds.), *Panic and phobias: Treatments and variables affecting course and outcome* (pp. 3–17). Berlin: Springer-Verlag.

Zarate, R., Rapee, R. M., Craske, M. G., & Barlow, D. H. (1988, November). *Response norms for symptom induction procedures.* Poster presented at 22nd Annual Convention of the Association for the Advancement of Behavior Therapy, New York, NY.

Zaubler, T. S., & Katon, W. (1996). Panic disorder and medical comorbidity: A review of the medical and psychiatric literature. *Bulletin of the Menninger Clinic, 60*(2, Suppl. A), A12–A38.

4

OBESITY

ROBERT R. RADOMILE

Americans today are obsessed with weight loss. Commercial and medical approaches are ubiquitous, many promising easy, rapid, permanent weight loss that will turn one's life around. Yet, despite this preoccupation with weight loss and the preponderance of weight-loss programs, 24% of men and 27% of women are obese, that is, 20% or more above ideal weight (Kuczmarski, 1992). Moreover, despite all the dieting and weight-loss programs, the incidence of obesity remains on the rise, having doubled since the early 1900s despite stable or even declining caloric intake (Marston & Raper, 1987). Decreased physical activity, diets high in fat, and changed eating patterns (specifically increased snacking and eating out) would seem to explain the dramatic increase.

Although many would seem motivated to lose weight for cosmetic reasons, the serious health implications of obesity cannot be denied. Increased risk of hypertension, diabetes, and cardiovascular disease has been associated with obesity (Bray, 1986; Pi-Snyder, 1991), and higher levels of fat intake have been related to greater risk for cardiovascular disease and cancer (National Academy of Sciences, 1989; U.S. Department of Heath and Human Services, 1988).

Despite the contribution of diet and lifestyle changes to the increased incidence of obesity, it should not be assumed that all obesity is caused by diet and lack of exercise and that an altered lifestyle can always correct obesity. Researchers have determined conclusively that genetics play a substantial role in obesity (Bouchard et al., 1990; Price, 1987; Stunkard et al., 1986), and numerous studies have found no significant difference in the caloric intake of obese and nonobese participants (Garrow, 1974; Klesges, Hanson, Eck, & Duff, 1988; Liebel & Hirsch, 1984; Wooley, Wooley, & Dyrenforth, 1979). It should be noted, however, that the accuracy of these and similar studies has come into question as more recent studies have demonstrated that obese participants significantly underreport caloric intake in such studies compared with nonobese participants (Mertz et al., 1991; Schoeller, 1988). The implications of these findings are significant for weight-loss programs, especially as they relate to the self-monitoring of food intake.

Pursuit of the "ideal body" or "ideal weight" in the treatment of obesity has been widely condemned by both researchers and practitioners. In addition to the significant role genetics play in both body weight and shape, there is also ample evidence that dieting to achieve the ideal weight simply does not work. In fact, it has been determined that as high as 95% of people who achieve significant weight loss fail to keep the weight off and return to or near their starting weight (Garner & Wooley, 1991). It is not actually known, in other words, whether there are in fact long-term health and psychological benefits from losing and sustaining significant weight loss over a long period of time.

What is also not known and probably impossible to single out is the negative psychological effect that repeated failure to lose and sustain significant weight loss has on obese individuals. Weight-loss programs by their very nature reinforce the stereotype that an individual's weight is in fact under his or her control. Failure to achieve and maintain "goal weight" carries with it the full burden of shame and guilt associated with presumed traits of laziness, lack of pride, and lack of discipline commonly attributed to obese people. It is critical, therefore, that any weight-loss program be particularly sensitive to the potentially damaging effects that failure may have on its participants and be especially cautious when it comes to setting treatment and weight-loss goals.

Although there is significant evidence that striving for the ideal weight when working with people who are obese is doomed to failure, much evidence exists supporting the feasibility and benefits of more modest weight loss. It was found, for example, that the blood pressure of participants with obesity and hypertension could be normalized with weight losses of as little as 10% of body weight (Blackburn & Kanders, 1987). Most losses were found to have long-term benefits for people with Type II diabetes (Wing, Marcus, Epstein, & Jawad, 1991). Other studies also support the significant positive effects of modest weight loss on blood pressure and cardiovascular risk factors (Brownell & Wadden, 1991).

The psychological benefits of modest weight loss have been less extensively studied, but what research exists suggests that improved self-image, improved body image, and decreased depression are associated with modest weight loss (Prochaska, DiClemente, & Norcross, 1992; Wadden & Stunkard, 1985).

This chapter describes a time-limited cognitive–behavioral group treatment for obesity that works through education, targeted behavioral change, and cognitive restructuring, with a goal of modest, attainable, and sustainable weight loss. Each of these components is present throughout the 20-week treatment, with education stressed more in the earlier group sessions and behavior change and cognitive restructuring being predominant in the middle and later group sessions. Research has shown that a number of characteristics are common to effective weight-loss programs, and these are emphasized throughout the group sessions. The chapter begins with a review of these characteristics and then proceeds to describe the group's structure and process and the cognitive–behavioral techniques that are used.

TEN CHARACTERISTICS OF AN EFFECTIVE WEIGHT-LOSS PROGRAM

1. Set Modest Goals

As previously stated, clients should be encouraged to set modest weight-loss goals (around 10% of body weight). Clients may be resistant to a low target at first, especially because of the great emphasis placed on thinness and ideal weight in American society. However, through education and cognitive restructuring, clients should be able to accept the more modest weight-loss goal as positive rather than negative, beneficial both physically and psychologically, realistic to achieve, and potentially a first step toward greater weight loss if desired.

2. Understand Eating Behavior

A client should have an increased awareness of and ability to understand his or her own eating behavior (Kirschenbaum, 1987). As noted earlier, obese individuals tend to significantly underestimate and underreport food intake. This is undoubtedly a result of the shame that they feel about themselves, their weight, and their eating behavior. This shame can be identified and its effects brought to light through guided discovery and Socratic questioning. Through cognitive restructuring, clients can become aware that honest, accurate record-keeping is the cornerstone of successful behavior change, the starting point of success rather than a cause for shame.

3. Use Stimulus Control

Stimulus control (Schacter & Rodin, 1974) refers to minimizing or eliminating the cues that can lead to overeating and unhealthy eating. This includes practices such as keeping only low-fat snacks in the house or, if that is not possible, making sure any high-fat snacks are out of sight and making sure that all food is wrapped and put away. Some amount of assertiveness training may be necessary to help clients effectively communicate their need for cooperation in this area to family and friends.

4. Exercise

Numerous studies have demonstrated that regular aerobic exercise contributes to initial weight loss and the successful maintenance of weight loss (Pavlou, Krey, Steffee, 1989; Racette, Schoeller, Kushner, & Neil, 1995). These and other studies have found that sustained regular exercise contributes to long-term weight loss in a variety of ways. Long-term aerobic exercise raises the metabolic rate, an essential element of weight loss. Furthermore, it encourages the body to burn fat, builds muscle, and reduces the appetite. Participants committed to regular aerobic exercise during weight loss tend to be more successful at losing weight initially, more likely to maintain weight loss over the long term, and more compliant with treatment than those who do not.

Positive psychological effects have also been noted even when the level of exercise is below that which would have a physiological impact (Brownell & Wadden, 1992). This points to the value not only of programmed exercise (e.g., aerobics, racquetball, and treadmill) but also lifestyle exercises (e.g., gardening and walking the dog) in a weight-loss program.

5. Practice Cognitive Restructuring

Obese individuals exhibit cognitive distortions, including overgeneralization and arbitrary inference (Kramer & Stalker, 1989). *Overgeneralization* refers to extrapolating an all-encompassing rule about life from one or a few incidents. For example, a participant who fails to lose any weight after 1 week of following a weight-loss program might conclude "I'll never lose any weight. I'm just meant to be fat." *Arbitrary inference* refers to coming to a conclusion—usually an extreme, negative conclusion—despite the absence of any supporting evidence. For example, despite being enthusiastically welcomed at a social gathering, an overweight person might conclude "They think I'm lazy and fat and obnoxious, and they really don't want me here."

Other cognitive distortions include catastrophizing and dichotomous thinking. In *catastrophizing*, a negative occurrence is projected in a given situation, the damaging impact of which is thought of as insurmountable. For example, an individual trying to lose weight looks ahead to an upcoming holiday meal, imagines himself not being able to exercise any self-control, and concludes that his weight-loss efforts will be irreversibly destroyed, rather than at worse temporarily sidetracked. *Dichotomous thinking* is all-or-nothing thinking in which there is only absolute success or total failure, no in-between. For example, a program participant might consider weight loss hopeless and herself a complete failure after one "slip" in the program.

Identifying and correcting such self-defeating cognitive distortions is critical to successful treatment. The ability to reframe past and present setbacks as a normal part of the change process and valuable as learning opportunities can be the difference between an individual continuing to work at weight loss or one giving up in frustration and disgust. Cognitive–behavior therapy (CBT) has been found to be effective in treating all aspects of eating disorders, including correcting abnormal attitudes about weight and body shape and promoting normal cognitive and behavioral coping skills to resist the urge to binge (Wilson & Fairburn, 1993).

6. Reduce or Eliminate Binge Eating

Binge eating, as defined in the *Diagnostic and Statistical Manual of Mental Disorders* (4th ed.; American Psychiatric Association, 1994), involves the consumption of a large amount of food in a discrete period of time (e.g., 1 hour, 2 hours) and a feeling of being out of control over what is eaten during the episode. Binge eating has been found to be a problem for nearly half of the participants studied in hospital and university-based weight-control programs (Marcus, Wing, & Hopkins, 1988; Marcus, Wing, & Lamparski, 1985; Spitzer et al., 1991; Telch, Agras, & Rossiter, 1988). Binges and the out-of-control feeling experienced during binges reinforce for the individual the familiar feelings of hopelessness and worthlessness. Binges can prompt people to purge, try starving themselves, or give up altogether. The reduction of binge eating has been shown to correlate to both decreased depression (Telch, Agras, Rossiter, Wilfley, & Kenardy, 1990) and greater weight loss (Agras et al., 1994; Smith, Marcus, & Kaye, 1992). CBT has been shown to be effective in reducing the frequency of binge eating (Smith, Marcus, & Kaye, 1992; Telch et al., 1990).

7. Adopt a Low-Fat Diet

Several studies have shown that reduced fat intake promotes weight loss (Kendall, Levitsky, Strupp, & Lissner, 1991; Prewitt et al., 1991). Several studies have also shown that more body fat is gained by eating fats than by eating the same number of calories from carbohydrates or proteins.

8. Use Short-Term Reachable Goals

Clients can be taught to use short-term reachable goals (Racette et al., 1995). These may be daily or even morning, afternoon, and evening goals (Dubbert & Wilson, 1984). These goals should be defined in terms of new behaviors and cognitions rather than in terms of weight loss. They should be specific, such as replacing a snack of higher fat content with one of lower fat content or adding one additional exercise period to a weekly routine. Such goals are reachable and repeatable and when added together equate to substantial and sustainable long-term change.

9. Foster Change in Eating Behavior

Fostering change in eating behavior includes eating at a slower pace; never eating while doing something else, (e.g., watching television); and developing pleasurable, nurturing alternatives to eating (e.g., taking a walk or calling a friend). Interrupting the compulsive and habitual eating routines can be beneficial. Even getting into the habit of doing something, no matter how mundane (like straightening up the living room, paying bills, or reading the newspaper) before engaging in compulsive, nonnutritive eating can sometimes be enough to allow the urge to pass or to give the individual time enough to think of a lower fat, more nutritive alternative.

10. Develop Social Support

Social support has proved to have a powerful impact on behavior change and health (Cohen & Syme, 1985) and on weight-loss maintenance (Kayman, Bruvold, & Stern, 1990; Wing et al., 1991). Both the family and the therapy group can be invaluable as support systems and conversely disastrous to the treatment process if experienced as shaming and judgmental. A successful treatment program will maximize the supportive potential of group and family by fostering a supportive and sensitive environment in the therapy group and by developing adaptive responses to friends and family through assertiveness training and cognitive restructuring.

More extensive treatment has been found to be more effective than treatment of a shorter duration. Treatment that runs for 20 to 25 weeks has been seen to produce better, longer lasting results than treatment lasting the more traditional 8 to 12 weeks (Brownell & Wadden, 1992).

GROUP PROTOCOLS AND FORMAT

The CBT group for the treatment of obesity should be relatively small (6–8 members), should last 1–1.5 hours, and should extend for about 20 weekly sessions. Participants should be mildly to moderately obese (20% to 60% over ideal body weight), screened for more serious psychopathology (discussed under the Assessment section below), cleared by a physician to participate in some level of regular aerobic exercises, and capable of carrying out the required homework assignments.

Although the goal of the group is weight loss, the greater emphasis will be on cognitive and behavior changes that are conducive to weight loss and a lifetime of healthier eating and living. The purpose of this approach is to steer away from the "diet" and "quick weight-loss" mentality and to emphasize substantive cognitive and lifestyle changes. As is the case in all CBT, the goal is not merely short-term symptom relief (i.e., weight loss) but the fundamental modification of behaviors, automatic thoughts, and the underlying schemas that have proved to be problematic for the individual. Thus, the goal is to identify the dysfunctional cognitions and behaviors and replace them with more adaptive ones.

The process by which these cognitions and behaviors are identified and changed is essentially no different from any other CBT process. Agenda setting, record-keeping, homework assignments, and goal setting are staples of the group therapy process, along with the use of Socratic questioning and guided discovery.

A typical therapy session will begin with setting the agenda, at which time the group members and the therapist will

- identify issues and topics to be covered in the session
- address any reactions or feedback relating to the previous session
- review clients' status and their past week
- review homework from the last session
- focus on main agenda items
- develop new homework
- solicit feedback regarding the current session.

Because the focus is on behavior change and cognitive restructuring, clients will agree to weigh themselves only one time a week and always at the same time. This is to discourage obsession with weight loss and to avoid promoting still more experiences of shame and failure if the pounds are not seen to be falling away as expected. For those who so choose, weighing oneself can be omitted altogether.

Active participation will be expected of each group member, as well as consistent attendance, punctuality, and adherence to strict confidentiality. Clients will be expected to give constructive feedback in the group, assist in the implementation of cognitive techniques, and have input in the development of helpful lists to be used by the group. Interaction by members outside the therapy sessions may be included as part of the treatment process, but only if it does not pose a threat to confidentiality or in some other way undermine the treatment process. This will be up to the therapist's judgment and is discussed later in the Treatment Process section.

ASSESSMENT

The first step in forming the therapy group will be to meet with each prospective member individually. The purpose of the individual sessions is to assess whether the client's weight-loss goals are compatible with those of the therapy group (i.e., moderate, paced weight loss vs. rapid, significant weight loss), to obtain a weight history (the Stanford Eating Disorders Questionnaire [Agras et al., 1976] can be used), to determine whether there is psychopathology present for which treatment should be provided concurrent with participation in the therapy group, and to assess the client's ability and willingness to do what will be required in the treatment process (e.g., record-keeping and exercise). If the candidate is currently in psychotherapy, obtaining permission to confer with the candidate's therapist to determine the client's appropriateness for the group would be in order. An individual with a major psychopathology, such as major depression, a severe anxiety disorder, personality pathology, or any form of psychosis, would not be suitable for the group and should be referred for appropriate treatment. The Beck Depression Inventory (BDI; Beck, Ward, Mendelson, Mock, & Erbaugh, 1961) can be used to determine the presence and degree of depression.

It is also helpful to determine as much as possible the likelihood that the prospective group member will reliably and consistently attend group sessions. Current or previous attendance in either group or individual therapy can be a valuable indicator.

This is also when clients can become acquainted with some of the record-keeping instruments, the treatment process, fees, and group norms (e.g., confidentiality, active participation, and mutual supportiveness). The assessment process can take one to three sessions, depending on familiarity with the client and the client's level of appropriateness for the group.

Assessment does not end with the initial assessment process. The BDI can be used as an ongoing evaluation tool to both correlate treatment gains with reduction of depressive symptoms and uncover emerging or increasing depressive symptoms that might otherwise go undetected.

THE TREATMENT PROCESS

As discussed in chapter 1, CBT is first and foremost a collaborative effort between therapist and client. As such, the treatment process does not take the form of a didactic presentation by the therapist or a predetermined treatment regimen. Rather, it is a dynamic process shaped by the unique priorities, needs, and personality of each particular group and the treatment decisions made by the therapist.

The direction and focus of each session is established during agenda setting. The agenda should relate, at least in part, to the ongoing records being kept by the group. The agenda is determined by the group as a whole (including the therapist) in the first 10 minutes of each session. Items for the agenda are suggested by the participants and discussed. Ideally, they are agreed on by the therapist and the group. There may be times, however, when the therapist has to include or omit items unilaterally, on the basis of the group's needs as perceived by the therapist at that time. This may include introducing 1 of the 10 essential aspects to effective weight-loss treatment noted earlier, such as exercise or the importance of a low-fat diet.

For the therapist, one of the primary goals of group therapy is to facilitate the development of the group into a supportive, effective change agent unto itself. As such, the therapist is always looking for opportunities to allow the group to guide participants toward more functional behaviors, cognitions, and adaptations. Early in treatment, when the emphasis is educational, essential lists of healthy snacks, healthy foods, alternative activities to eating, and so forth are developed with client input. As the treatment process progresses and the group members become more attuned to dysfunctional behaviors and cognitions, more aware of more adaptive alternatives, and more adept at cognitive techniques, they can be looked to more often to take the "therapist role." In guiding another group member through cognitive techniques such as decatastrophizing or reattribution, clients will experience a powerful reinforcement of what they have learned. In this way, all of the members will benefit from having a chance to exercise their newly acquired expertise, and each person will be making an active investment in the success of every other member and in the group as a whole, thus building group support and cohesiveness.

Once all agenda items have been addressed, homework assignments can be agreed on for the next session. The homework assignment may simply be to continue the record-keeping that will be an ongoing part of treatment (discussed in detail in the First Session section below). Homework may also include specific tasks to be completed over the upcoming week. Like agenda setting, homework assignments are decided on collaboratively by the group members and the therapist. Finally, attention is paid to tying up any loose ends from the session.

Although the format of each session will be basically the same, the focus and goals of each session will be different at various times during the treatment process. The 20-week treatment process can be seen as consisting of five phases: First Session, Early Sessions, Middle Sessions, Later Sessions, and Final Session. Each phase has a particular set of priorities, although it should be remembered that any issue can arise and warrant attention at any time. The goals and content focus of each treatment phase are summarized here and are developed in detail a bit later in the chapter.

First Session

In this session, clients meet and get to know a little about each other. They are introduced to the treatment format and at least one of the two record-keeping instruments to be kept daily. The group goals are reintroduced (they were first introduced during the assessment interviews), and some of the basic principles of CBT are presented.

Early Sessions

The focus in the early sessions is primarily educational. Participants are taught the basic principles and techniques of CBT. Helpful lists of healthy foods, snacks, behaviors, and activities are developed. Close attention is also paid to the refinement of self-observation and record-keeping skills during this phase.

Middle Sessions

During this period, particular cognitive and behavioral problem areas are identified and addressed. With most, if not all, of the educational pieces in place, the work of therapy is taken up in earnest. The difficult but critical task of eliminating binge eating is taken up in this phase, and the identification as well as modification of schemas is begun.

Later Sessions

Further emphasis is placed on schema work at this time. Change strategies are expanded, relapses (which are bound to have occurred by this point) are addressed, future relapses are anticipated, and attention is paid to preventing future relapses.

Final Session

In the final session, any loose ends are tied up, the effectiveness of the group is discussed, and concerns about facing the future without the group are addressed. In this session also, the possibilities for follow-up treatment are discussed.

GROUP DYNAMICS

Throughout the treatment process, attention is paid to the group's dynamics. Providing a safe environment for all members and promoting healthy interactions between them is as critical here as it is in any form of group therapy. As such, the importance of confidentiality should be stressed at the outset and reiterated throughout. Clients should also be instructed in giving constructive feedback. This includes asking if feedback is wanted before giving it, being specific when giving feedback, and making "I" statements wherever possible.

The therapist must be on alert for statements that might be shaming or blaming and help both the client making the statement and the one receiving it reframe the message when necessary. The following is an example:

Client: Boy, it sounds like you really pigged-out last night.

Therapist: Is "pigged-out" another way of saying "binged"?

Client: Yes.

Therapist: Is that how you talk to yourself when you've binged?

Client: Yes.

Therapist: Do you find that kind of self-talk helpful?

Client: No, it just makes me feel worse.

Therapist: What could you say to yourself after a binge that might be more helpful?

Client: I don't know, something like, "Something must have been going on emotionally or physically that led to bingeing."

Therapist: Good. Now, can you say something along those lines to _____ [another group member]?

Client: Yeah, I guess. "What do you think was going on emotionally or physically that led to a binge?"

Therapist: Very good.

Here, Socratic questioning helped modify both the client's self-talk and delivery of feedback. In the process, a shaming statement was reworked into a helpful one. This is just one example of how attention must be paid to making the group safe and the interactions healthy. Such concerns must remain a permanent fixture atop the therapist's priority list.

The group also has the potential to provide members with support and to reinforce learning beyond the confines of the therapy session itself. Telephone calls between sessions and getting together for planned exercise sessions, meals, and the like can go a long way toward fostering change and the achievement of treatment goals. The therapist must be keenly tuned in to the group's level of trust, cohesiveness, and interpersonal comfort, however, before such steps can be taken. Not all individuals or groups will be comfortable with such increased levels of contact and intimacy. If such extra-group therapy interaction is desired by the group, the nature of that interaction should be clearly defined and circumscribed by the therapist and the group so that the interaction remains supportive and therapeutically productive. The rules of confidentiality must be strictly adhered to in such cases, meaning no discussion of the group or group members is permissible outside the group.

FIRST SESSION

In the first session, clients will be asked to introduce themselves, discuss their weight-loss goals, share with the group (to the extent that they are comfortable) what their previous attempts at weight loss have been like, and begin to identify some individual problem areas with which they have struggled (e.g., late-night snacking, sticking with an exercise regimen, and lack of support). It is here that the initial work of identifying and labeling self-defeating negative thoughts can begin. Statements such as "At this point I figured since I'd eaten one cookie, I might as well eat the rest" can be pointed out, labeled (dichotomous thinking or overgeneralization), and examined for accuracy, for example, "Is it true that there is no difference between eating one cookie and eating the whole bag?"

The Daily Food-Intake Record (DFIR), adapted from Kramer and Stalker (1989), is introduced in the first session, and clients are instructed in its completion (see page 122 at the end of the chapter.) (A binder is supplied for holding the various record-keeping and information sheets.) Attention is paid to identifying feelings and thoughts associated with each meal or snack. For example, after eating far more than planned, an individual might record thinking, "I'll never be able to lose weight. It never fails, I always screw up!" And the client might record feeling depressed and hopeless. How thoughts influence feelings and behavior will be demonstrated in the course of treatment, and ways to refute and change those thoughts will be developed. At this point, however, emphasis is placed on accurate and timely record-keeping as one of the fundamental key elements of the treatment process. To promote compliance and reliable record-keeping, the therapist assures the group that no one but the individual members themselves will see their DFIR and that they are invited to share as much or as little information from it in the group as they so choose. Keeping the DFIR is the first assignment of the treatment process and will be maintained throughout the course of treatment.

Finally, the group is introduced to the format that will be followed in each session: the basic treatment format of CBT, as noted earlier. The session ends after a closing summary of the session by the therapist and final comments and questions from the group.

EARLY SESSIONS

With the DFIR as a database, individuals are helped to identify dysfunctional cognitions and problematic eating behaviors and situations. The DFIR, along with the agreed-on agenda items, serve as the starting points for the treatment process. Here the therapist must cull the most important and relevant areas to focus on at that time. These decisions are made on the basis of the therapist's awareness of what is essential to focus on early in treatment and the agenda priorities of the group. For example, the importance of exercise and a low-fat diet are necessary to introduce early in treatment. However, for treatment to be truly collaborative, these cannot be discussed to the exclusion of what the clients find important. For the most part, these critical aspects of weight loss can be arrived at through guided discovery based on the DFIR. For example,

Therapist: So what, if anything, jumps out at you when you review your DFIR?

Client: That 90% of my problem is late-night snacking.

Therapist: Would you mind sharing with the group the kinds of snacks you find yourself eating at night?

Client: Cookies, ice cream, potato chips, you know, junk.

Therapist: Were those the only kind of snacks you ate? In other words, was there ever a time when you ate what you would consider a less fattening snack?

Client: Well, one night I ate some pretzels, which aren't very fattening.

Therapist: Would late-night snacking be as much of a problem if you ate pretzels instead of the other kinds of snacks?

Client: Well, no, but I still see it as a problem.

Therapist:	Is there any kind of late-night snacking you could do that you would not consider a problem?
Client:	Well, yeah, if I could just eat a reasonable amount of low-fat snacks.
Therapist:	Such as?
Client:	Well, pretzels as I said. Maybe cereal, yogurt.
Therapist:	Any others?
Client:	None that I can think of offhand.
Therapist:	Do you think it would help if you had say, 10–20 options rather than just 3?
Client:	Yeah, I guess.
Therapist:	Okay. [To the group] How about if we come up with a list of low-fat snack options to help out everyone in the group who's struggling with late-night snacking.

At that point, the group would offer suggestions for the list, and the list would be checked by a dietary consultant (if necessary), typed, and added to each person's binder.

Note that at this stage of therapy, the therapist chose to go in the direction of developing a list of low-fat snacks rather than, say, exploring possible alternatives to snacking. This direction is both appropriate for the situation and preferable early in treatment to begin to generate some low-fat food options for the group. This is an example of how the therapist using guided discovery can subtly steer treatment in the necessary direction without diminishing the collaborative quality of the process.

Lists to be developed early in treatment include the following:

- healthy snacks
- healthy foods
- programmed exercises (walking, running, weight training, etc.)
- lifestyle exercises (gardening, walking the dog, doing housework, etc.)
- alternative activities to eating
- helpful changes in eating behavior
- ways to reduce eating cues.

The lists are typed and added to each person's binder.

Along with the DFIR, clients will maintain a second record, the Daily Record of Physical Activity (see page 122 at the end of the chapter). This instrument should be introduced no later than the third session. Again, emphasis is on the automatic thoughts and feelings associated with each activity. Particular attention is paid to modifying negative automatic thoughts. For example,

> Client: As far as exercise goes, I went out walking twice this past week.
>
> Therapist: How long did you walk?
>
> Client: About a half hour each time.
>
> Therapist: Did you record your thoughts and feelings about the exercise?
>
> Client: Yes. And both times my thoughts were really positive. I wrote, "This is easier than I thought. I'm really getting somewhere. I can do this four to five times a week." And I was really happy with myself.
>
> Therapist: Were there any other thoughts about your exercising?
>
> Client: Yeah. Now I'm thinking I failed again because I didn't walk four to five times; I only walked the two times.
>
> Therapist: Is it true that you failed because you only walked twice?
>
> Client: It feels that way.
>
> Therapist: Can you identify any positives in having walked two times last week?
>
> Client: Well, yes. I'd been trying to get myself to walk forever, and I did finally get out there.
>
> Therapist: Anything else?
>
> Client: Well, yes. I found the best time for me to walk was right after work. Up to now I'd always thought I should get up early and walk before work, but I never could.
>
> Therapist: And from the thoughts and feelings you wrote down it sounds like you enjoyed walking and felt good about yourself when you did it.
>
> Client: Yeah, that's true. I guess on balance it really was more positive than negative.

Challenging dichotomous thinking, as in this case, and other cognitive interventions will be used throughout therapy and increasingly become the focus as therapy moves on. In the early sessions, the emphasis is on establishing the treatment format, keeping accurate records, developing informational lists, targeting problem behaviors, and identifying new and more desirable behaviors.

The middle sessions are devoted largely to pinpointing specific dysfunctional behaviors and cognitions and using the full arsenal of CBT techniques to bring about substantive change. Binge eating; problem foods and situations; and difficult parts of the day, week, month, and year are targeted. Schema work is also begun in this phase and carried through the rest of the treatment process. Most, if not all, of the necessary information has been disseminated, and the clients are well skilled at record-keeping and have a working knowledge of CBT techniques. At this time, long-standing problems in the areas of eating habits, lifestyle, maladaptive coping techniques, automatic thoughts, and underlying beliefs are identified and modified. The goal of treatment is lifelong change, and this is when that process truly begins. The approach consists of targeting and changing specific problem areas and replacing them with new, healthier, more adaptive cognitions and behaviors. It is through the steady integration of small, specific, positive changes into one's daily life that sustained, long-term weight loss and healthier living is achieved.

The DFIR and the Daily Record of Physical Activity will reveal many of the problem areas that need to be addressed. These areas include the following:

- problem or binge foods, such as cakes, breads, and ice cream
- problem times during the day
- thoughts, feelings, and situations that lead to giving up
- thoughts, feelings, and situations that lead to binge eating
- the lack of viable alternatives to eating
- the lack of physical activity.

Certain cognitive and behavioral techniques will be most applicable to these problems and to this population in general. Examples of those techniques are presented next.

Cognitive Techniques

Challenging Absolutes

      Client: I'll never be able to stop bingeing. When I think about it, it's hard to remember a time when I haven't binged. I just can't fight the urge.

  Therapist: Does your DFIR show that you've binged every day?

      Client: Well, no.

Therapist:	About how often are you binge eating according to your DFIR?
Client:	About twice a week.
Therapist:	Would you say that you are bingeing at about the same rate as when you started treatment?
Client:	No, not nearly that much.
Therapist:	How have you managed to reduce it?
Client:	You know, by using what we've been talking about in here, like keeping low-fat snacks in the house, doing something else first when I feel the urge to binge, thinking about how I'll feel if I do binge and how I'll feel if I don't. You know, that sort of thing.
Therapist:	It doesn't sound as completely hopeless after all, does it?
Client:	No, I guess not. It just always feels that way when I screw up.

Reattribution

Client:	Well, I can't believe I blew it again. Last night I sat down and ate half of a chocolate cake. I just have absolutely no willpower.
Therapist:	I thought you had been doing pretty well at staying away from cakes and pastries.
Client:	Yeah, until last night.
Therapist:	Where'd the cake come from?
Client:	My wife made it. She said I was doing so well that she thought I deserved a reward.
Therapist:	Did you want a reward?
Client:	No way. I knew it would be trouble. But she was trying to do something nice, and I wanted to show her that I appreciated it. I intended to eat just one piece, which I did at first. But of course, all I could think of the rest of the night was that cake sitting there until finally I had to scarf down half of it. God, I'm pathetic.
Therapist:	You seem to hold yourself totally responsible for this slip.
Client:	It's no one's fault but mine.
Therapist:	What about your wife. Is it her fault at all? Even just a little bit?
Client:	Well, I guess a little. I have asked her not to make any more cakes.

Therapist: Is there any other way your wife can reward you that you'd enjoy?

Client: Yeah, plenty of ways.

Turning Adversity to Advantage

Client: I'm totally disgusted. I can't believe with all the work I've done I actually *gained* two pounds.

Therapist: That's got to be very disheartening. Have you been doing anything different over the past couple of weeks?

Client: Foodwise I've been doing pretty well. The only thing I haven't been doing the same is exercising. I've just been too busy.

Therapist: Did you think not exercising would make that much of a difference?

Client: No, I really didn't, but I sure know it now.

Therapist: It sounds like you really learned something important through this.

Client: Yeah, I sure did. I absolutely cannot afford not to exercise.

Externalization of Voices

In this, the therapist and client role play the client's internal struggle. The therapist may have to play the positive voice first to model for the client effective responses to the negative voice. As group members become more adept at such cognitive interventions, one of them can play the therapist's role.

Therapist: [As negative voice] Boy, you screwed up again. You're never going to be able to change and lose weight.

Client: I may have slipped this time, but it doesn't mean I won't succeed. I've already had a lot of successes and will have more. Nobody's perfect.

Therapist: Yeah, but you always start out good, then before you know it you're back to your old ways and heavier than ever.

Client: That happened because there were things I didn't know then that I'm learning now. It's going to take time, and I will have setbacks, but I will be able to change my lifestyle to maintain weight loss even though I'll never be perfect.

Decatastrophizing

Client: I can't possibly go to my mother-in-law's for Thanksgiving and eat moderately the way I'd like to. It would be so out of character.

Therapist: And what would happen if you did?

Client: My husband's family would be teasing me the whole time, probably saying things like they're going to call the doctor because I must be sick.

Therapist: And what feelings would you have if that happened?

Client: Upset, embarrassed.

Therapist: Would it be the most upset and embarrassed you've ever felt?

Client: No, but it would be uncomfortable.

Therapist: Would it still be possible to enjoy the day to some extent?

Client: Well, yeah, I guess so, once the teasing died down.

Therapist: When do you think the teasing would die down?

Client: Probably once dinner's over.

Therapist: And how would you feel after dinner when you've eaten sensibly the way you wanted to?

Client: I'd be ecstatic. It would be an unbelievable accomplishment.

Behavioral Techniques

Graded-Task Assignments

This is an invaluable behavioral technique in the treatment of weight loss. Clients are often overwhelmed by the perceived immensity of the task of losing weight and can become easily discouraged. By breaking the process down into small, manageable tasks, the client experiences both success and the realization that the overriding goal of weight loss is actually made up of a number of small steps. An individual, for example, may find it nearly impossible to spend 20 minutes on an exercise machine but may find using the same machine for 5 minutes no problem. The 5-minute segments can be done a number of times a day or may gradually be expanded to 20 minutes.

Activity Scheduling

This is another invaluable technique in the treatment of obesity. For the compulsive overeater, unstructured time is often filled with food. Activity scheduling has two uses here: (a) planning noneating activities (such as writing letters, making telephone calls, walking, and cleaning) and (b) meal planning. Meal planning is among the most helpful and necessary lifestyle modifications the obese individual can make. By planning meals the day before, the individual is making food decisions rationally rather than on the basis of impulses, feelings, and the like on the spur of the moment. Meal planning is best used at specific target times at first, rather than over the whole day (i.e., like a graded-task assignment). A particular meal or snack time is singled out and planned. Once the technique is mastered in one time slot, it can be expanded to others.

Assertiveness Training

Assertiveness training may be important for clients as it pertains to boundary setting involving food. Saying no without sounding mean or nasty will be a critical skill, especially for someone who is overly concerned with offending others. Assertiveness training also comes into play when it comes to making one's needs or feelings known to others. It may be necessary, for example, to tell family members in an assertive way not to leave food out, buy certain foods, or say hurtful things about the client's weight. Other behavioral techniques that will be useful include behavioral rehearsal, relaxation and breathing exercises, behavioral experiments, fixed role therapy, and role rehearsal. Together the cognitive and behavioral techniques shown here will be the dominant treatment interventions in this phase.

The identification and modification of schemas also begins in the middle sessions. The cognitive distortions revealed in the DFIRs are manifestations of the faulty underlying beliefs, or schemas, held by most overweight people. These dysfunctional beliefs are accessed through Socratic questioning and guided discovery. Underlying the cognitive distortion of "It's hopeless, I'll never lose weight," for example, may be the dysfunctional belief that "I've always been fat, I'll always be fat, and nothing can change it." Such self-defeating, dysfunctional schemas must be recognized, refuted, and modified for clients to maintain hopefulness and progress, rather than succumb to the ponderous power of relapse and despair.

The negative underlying beliefs of overweight people can be extremely deep-seated and resilient. They will not be transformed easily, and the therapist can anticipate ongoing, often repetitive work in this area. The importance of this work, however, cannot be overstated. Invalid, self-defeating schemas are at the core of the cognitive distortions that lead to quick-fix attempts to lose weight (pills, dieting, etc.), the identification of one's worth with one's weight, and the obsession with weight and weight loss that dominate the lives of so many obese people.

The new, more adaptive schemas to be developed include beliefs that meaningful change will come as a result of numerous, small lifestyle changes developed and sustained over a lifetime; that over time other sources of gratification can be developed to replace the maladaptive use of food; and that most obesity is the result of faulty learning and dysfunctional habits rather than laziness, worthlessness, lack of character, and so on. Positive, accurate, progress-producing new schemas such as these will serve clients through a lifetime of greater mental and physical health.

In the middle sessions, the critical work of eliminating or reducing binge eating is begun. The answers to three key questions regarding binge eating are supplied by the DFIR:

1. What was eaten?
2. When was it eaten?
3. What thoughts and feelings preceded the binge?

Typically, patterns of binge eating will emerge, and these patterns can be anticipated and changed. Binge foods can be avoided, potential binge times can be filled with other activities, and new responses to binge-producing thoughts and feelings can be developed. This is when the development of new, alternative forms of gratification is critical. Learning to respond differently to feelings of loneliness, boredom, anxiety and emptiness, and thoughts of worthlessness and hopelessness will be essential to overcoming this demoralizing problem. Like schema work, binge elimination or reduction takes time. Establishing a repertoire of healthy, adaptive forms of gratification to replace food will take the length of the treatment process and beyond. Alternative activities (reading, walking, talking on the telephone, writing letters, and so on) will be viable alternatives to bingeing only after they have become an established, reliable part of everyday life.

LATER SESSIONS

In the later sessions, treatment focuses more on the modification of schemas. One critical schema to identify and modify is "If I stop berating and shaming myself for overeating and being fat, I'll just eat everything in sight and get as big as a house." The underlying belief here is that self-shaming is good—that it is necessary for keeping one's impulses in check.

Two questions to the client are usually sufficient to uncover the inaccuracy of this belief:

1. "How long have you shamed yourself for overeating and being fat?" The answer will typically be along the lines of "For as long as I can remember."

2. "Has it worked?" The answer of course is no. People are not overweight because they are lazy, stupid, or have no self-pride. As we have seen, some people are genetically predisposed to obesity. For others, it is a matter of having too high an amount of fat and calorie intake for their amount of caloric expenditure. The body's adaptation to a high-fat diet, the habit of inactivity, and the cognitive distortions that prompt individuals to give up when they meet with some disappointment and failure are the reasons people are overweight.

Food also provides quick, easy gratification. There will be times when eating will be the pleasure-producing activity of choice in nearly everyone's life. Problems arise when other pleasure-producing options have not been developed, and eating is too often seen as the only choice.

A more adaptive schema is "I am overweight because I've gotten into the habit of too often eating for nonnutritive reasons, and I need to develop a wider range of exercise, activity, and interpersonal options to meet my needs." With this schema replacing the dysfunctional, shame-based schema, the individual can view lapses as opportunities for learning and insight about an overweight problem rather than an occasion for self-deprecation. This more adaptive schema promotes constructive work and change rather than destructive self-loathing and dichotomous thinking.

Problem areas that have proved to be more intractable are concentrated on in this phase. These can be either individual or groupwide issues and involve any aspect of change or weight loss.

The application of change strategies such as meal planning is expanded in this phase, encompassing whole days and weeks rather than just one meal or time period. This is an extension of the graded-task skills already developed. Failures in this area would indicate that the client is simply not yet ready to extend those skills into new areas but might well be able to in the future.

Finally, toward the end of therapy, attention must be paid to relapses and relapse prevention. Clients' self-talk regarding relapses should be monitored to make sure it is not self-shaming and the relapse is not catastrophized. Relapses are to be expected. Situations that could be stress producing and trigger a relapse (such as holidays) should be anticipated and discussed, as should the expected fluctuations in diet and exercise that are bound to occur. The coping skills that have been developed in therapy will serve the purpose for relapse prevention and should be reinforced. These would include activity scheduling, assertiveness training, behavioral rehearsal, thinking it through, and others. Again, slips or relapses should be viewed as a normal part of the change process.

FINAL SESSION

In the final session, overall progress by the group and individuals is reviewed, and the effectiveness of treatment discussed. Did therapy meet expectations? Were individual goals achieved? Do the participants feel prepared to face the future? Certain individuals may feel a need for some form of continuation or follow-up. Is there an interest in subsequent individual sessions, or would the group like to schedule follow-up group sessions, say every 3 months? The therapist should also be available for future check-ins when necessary. Follow-up studies should be carried out using mailed questionnaires to assess the long-term treatment effects.

This is a time for reinforcing both individual and group gains. It is also worth reiterating that the 20-week treatment process represents the start, not the end, of the change process. With more practice, the treatment gains will become more generalized and solidified, and the skills and knowledge acquired will serve a lifetime.

Finally, any lingering doubts, problems, or questions should be addressed, and any further future concerns should be discussed.

SUMMARY

The problem of obesity has become all too pervasive in recent years. It causes or contributes to serious and even life-threatening conditions, psychopathology, and intense emotional suffering. The causes of obesity are complex, and for the most part, the struggle with obesity is life long. CBT has proven to be effective both short and long term in the treatment of obesity. When combined with the therapeutic power and invaluable support of group therapy, CBT can effect positive, life-long changes in the obese individual. CBT can be tailored to bring about short- and long-term cognitive and behavioral change and adapted to individual needs to provide the kind of support that has proven to be beneficial, if not essential to ultimate success.

APPENDIX

EXHIBIT 4.1
Daily Food-Intake Record

Date/Time	Food	Place	Feelings	Thoughts

EXHIBIT 4.2
Daily Record of Physical Activity

Date/Time	Programmed Exercise	Lifestyle Exercise	Feelings	Thoughts

REFERENCES

Agras, W. S., Fergususon, J. M., Greaves, C., Qualls, B., Rand, C. S. W., Ruby, J., Stunkard, A. J., Taylor, C. B., Werne, J., & Wright, C. (1976). A clinical and research questionnaire for obese patients. In B. J. Williams, S. Martin, & J. P. Foreyt (Eds.), *Obesity: Behavioral approaches to dietary management* (pp. 168–176). New York: Brunner/Mazel.

Agras, W. S., Telch, C. F., Arnow, B., Eldredge, K., Wilfley, D. E., Raeburn, S. D., Henderson, J., & Marnell, M. (1994). Weight loss, cognitive–behavioral, and desippramine treatments in binge eating disorder, an additive design. *Behavior Therapy, 25,* 225–238.

American Psychiatric Association. (1994). *Diagnostic and statistical manual of mental disorders* (4th ed.). Washington, DC: Author.

Beck, A. T., Ward, C. M., Mendelson, M., Mock, J., & Erbaugh, J. (1961). An inventory for measuring depression. *Archives of General Psychiatry, 4,* 561–571.

Blackburn, G. F., & Kanders, B. S. (1987). Medical evaluation of treatment of the obese patient with cardiovascular disease. *American Journal of Cardiology, 60,* 55–58.

Bouchard, C., Tremblay, A., Després, J., Nadeau, A., Lupien, P., Thériault, G., Dussault, J., Moorjani, S., Pinault, S., & Fournier, G. (1990). The response to long-term overfeeding in identical twins. *New England Journal of Medicine, 322,* 1477–1482.

Bray, G. A. (1986). Effects of obesity on health and happiness. In K. D. Brownell & J. P. Foreyt (Eds.), *Handbook of eating disorders: Physiology, psychology, and treatment of obesity, anorexia, and bulimia* (pp. 3–44). New York: Basic Books.

Brownell, K. D., & Wadden, T. A. (1991). The heterogeneity of obesity: Fitting treatment to individuals. *Behavior Therapy, 22,* 153–177.

Brownell, K. D., & Wadden, T. A. (1992). Etiology and treatment of obesity: Understanding a serious, prevalent, and refractory disorder. *Journal of Consulting and Clinical Psychology, 60*(4), 505–517.

Cohen, S., & Syme, S. F. (1985). *Social support and health.* New York: Academic Press.

Dubbert, P. M., & Wilson, G. T. (1984). Goal setting and spouse involvement in the treatment of obesity. *Behaviour Therapy and Research, 22,* 227–242.

Garner, D. M., & Wooley, S. C. (1991). Confronting the failure of behavioral and dietary treatment for obesity. *Clinical Psychology Review, 11,* 729–780.

Garrow, J. S. (1974). *Energy balance and obesity in man.* New York: Elsevier Science.

Kayman, S., Bruvold, W., & Stern, J. S. (1990). Maintenance and relapse after weight loss in women: Behavioral aspects. *American Journal of Clinical Nutrition, 52,* 800–807.

Kendall, A., Levitsky, D. A., Strupp, B. J., & Lissner, L. (1991). Weight loss on a low-fat diet: Consequence of the imprecision of the control of food intake in humans. *American Journal of Clinical Nutrition, 53,* 1124–1129.

Kirschenbaum, D. S. (1987). Self-regulatory failure: A review with clinical implications. *Clinical Psychology Review, 7*, 77–104.

Klesges, R. C., Hanson, C. F., Eck, L. H., & Duff, A. C. (1988). Accuracy of self-reports of food intake in obese and normal-weight individuals: Effects of parental obesity on reports of children's dietary intake. *American Journal of Clinical Nutrition, 48*, 1252–1256.

Kramer, F. M., & Stalker, L. A. (1989). Treatment of obesity. In A. Freeman, K. Simon, L. E. Beutler, & H. Arkowitz (Eds.), *Comprehensive handbook of cognitive therapy* (pp. 385–401). New York: Plenum Press.

Kuczmarski, R. J. (1992). Prevalence of overweight and weight gain in the U.S. *American Journal of Clinical Nutrition, 55*(Suppl.), 495S–502S.

Leibel, R. L., & Hirsch, J. (1984). Diminished energy requirements in reduced obese patients. *Metabolism, 33*, 164–170.

Marcus, M. D., Wing, R. R., & Hopkins, J. (1988). Obese binge eaters: Affect, cognitions, and response to behavioral weight control. *Journal of Consulting and Clinical Psychology, 56*, 433–439.

Marcus, M. D., Wing, R. R., & Lamparski, D. M. (1985). Binge eating and dietary restraint in obese patients. *Addictive Behaviors, 10*, 163–168.

Marston, R., & Raper, N. (1987, Winter/Spring). Nutrient content of the U.S. food supply. *National Food Review, 36*, 1392–1398.

Mertz, W., Tsui, J. C., Judd, J. T., Reiser, S., Hallfrisch, J., Morris, E. R., Steele, P. D., & Lashley, E. (1991). What are people really eating? *American Journal of Clinical Nutrition, 54*, 291–295.

National Academy of Sciences, National Research Council. (1989). *Diet and health: Implications for reducing chronic disease risk.* Washington, DC: National Academy Press.

Pavlou, K. N., Krey, S., & Steffee, W. P. (1989). Exercise as an adjunct to weight loss and maintenance in moderately obese subjects. *American Journal of Clinical Nutrition, 49*, 1115–1123.

Pi-Snyder, F. X. (1991). Health implications of obesity. *American Journal of Clinical Nutrition, 53*(Suppl.), 1595S–1603S.

Prewitt, T. E., Schmeisser, D., Bowen, P. E., Aye, P., Dolecek, T. A., Langenberg, P., Cole, T., & Brace, L. (1991). Changes in body weight, body composition, and energy intake in women fed high- and low-fat diets. *American Journal of Clinical Nutrition, 54*, 304–310.

Price, R. A. (1987). Genetics of human obesity. *Annals of Behavioral Medicine, 9*, 9–14.

Prochaska, J. O., DiClemente, C. C., & Norcross, J. C. (1992). In search of how people change. *American Psychologist, 47*, 1102–1114.

Racette, S. B., Schoeller, D. A., Kushner, R., & Neil, K. M. (1995). Exercise enhances dietary compliance during moderate energy restriction in obese women. *American Journal of Clinical Nutrition, 62*, 345–349.

Schacter, S., & Rodin, J. (1974). *Obese humans and rats.* Washington, DC: Erlbaum/Wiley.

Schoeller, D. A. (1988). Measurement of energy expenditure in free-living humans by using doubly labeled water. *Journal of Nutrition, 118,* 1278–1289.

Smith, D. E., Marcus, M. D., & Kaye, W. (1992). Cognitive-behavioral treatment of obese binge eaters. *International Journal of Eating Disorders, 12,* 257–262.

Spitzer, R. L., Devlin, M., Walsh, B. T., Hasin, D., Wing, R., Marcus, M., Stunkard, A. J., Wadden, T., Yanovski, S., Agras, W. S., Mitchell, J., & Nonas, C. (1991). Binge eating disorder: To be or not to be in *DSM–IV. International Journal of Eating Disorders, 10,* 627–630.

Stunkard, A. J., Sorenson, T. I. A., Hanis, C., Teasdale, T. W., Chakraborty, R., Schull, W. J., & Schulsinger, F. (1986). An adoption study of human obesity. *New England Journal of Medicine, 314,* 193–198.

Telch, C. F., Agras, W. S., & Rossiter, E. M. (1988). Binge eating increases with increasing adiposity. *International Journal of Eating Disorders, 7,* 115–119.

Telch, C. F., Agras, W. S., Rossiter, E. M., Wilfley, D., & Kenardy, J. (1990). Group cognitive behavioral treatment for the nonpurging bulimic: An initial evaluation. *Journal of Consulting and Clinical Psychology, 58,* 629–635.

U.S. Department of Health and Human Services. (1988). *The Surgeon General's report on nutrition and health* (DHHS Publication No. 88-50210). Washington, DC: U.S. Government Printing Office.

Wadden, T. A., & Stunkard, A. J. (1985). Social and psychological consequences of obesity. *Annals of Internal Medicine, 103,* 1062–1067.

Wilson, G. T., & Fairburn, G. C. (1993). Cognitive treatments for eating disorders. *Journal of Consulting and Clinical Psychology, 61,* 261–269.

Wing, R. R., Marcus, M. D., Epstein, L. H., & Jawad, A. (1991). A "family-based" approach to the treatment of obese Type II diabetic patients. *Journal of Consulting and Clinical Psychology, 59,* 156–162.

Wooley, S. C., Wooley, O. W., & Dyrenforth, S. R. (1979). Theoretical, practical and social issues in behavioral treatment of obesity. *Journal of Applied Behavior Analysis, 12,* 3–25.

5

EATING DISORDERS

WAYNE A. BOWERS

Treatment of eating disorders has typically used three treatment modalities—family, individual, and group therapy, either singly or in combination. Early treatment of eating disorders relied on individual therapy that focused on long-term treatment from a psychodynamic perspective. In the 1970s, treatment of eating disorders focused primarily at anorexia nervosa. At this time, bulimia was seen as a variant of anorexia nervosa rather than as a separate disorder. In the 1980s, the emphasis on treatment began to shift. Bulimia nervosa became a distinct diagnosis that brought into play greater interest in the research and treatment of both disorders. In the same decade, there was a greater emphasis on the treatment of bulimia over anorexia nervosa. Along with this shift, more emphasis also was given to the use of group interventions, with more specific and organized research that followed (Hall, 1985; Johnson, Connor, & Stucky, 1983; Kirkley, Schneider, Agras, & Bachman, 1985; Mitchell et al., 1985; Polivy & Federoff, 1997; Roy-Byrne, Lee-Benner, & Yager, 1984; Schneider & Agras, 1985; Stevens & Salisbury, 1984; White & Boskind-White, 1981). In the ensuing years, the major focus of research was on treatment of bulimia nervosa that left research regarding anorexia nervosa in the shadows (Bowers & Andersen 1994).

With group psychotherapy gaining support as a primary intervention in the treatment of eating disorders, researchers found that the group provides the opportunity to incorporate a wide array of therapeutic techniques within one format. For example, Fairburn (1981) used experiential and social learning methods as well as a sociocultural orientation to help alleviate symptoms of bulimia and effect changes in self-acceptance, social presence, self-control, and body image. Besides targeting reduction in symptoms, Fairburn examined more adaptive changes in attitudes toward food, body shape, and weight.

The power of the therapeutic group to provide a forum for discussing, sharing, and support has been harnessed by practitioners from different theoretical orientations, including psychodynamic (Bruch, 1982; Goodsitt, 1997; Harper-Guiffre, Mackenzie, and Sivitilli, 1992; Polivy & Federoff, 1997), behavioral (Laessle & Pirke, 1987; Rosen & Leitenberg, 1982, 1985), and cognitive–behavioral (Garfinkel & Garner, 1982; Garner, 1985; Garner & Bemis, 1982; Garner, Vitousek, & Pike, 1997; Wilson, Fairburn, & Agras, 1997). These groups have been conducted in intensive outpatient settings, including extended hours and marathon group settings (Johnson et al., 1983; Lee & Rush, 1986; Schneider & Agras, 1985; Wilson & Fairburn, 1993; Wooley & Kearney-Cooke, 1986), day treatment settings (Piran, Langdon, Kaplan, & Garfinkel, 1987), and inpatient settings (Bowers, Evans, & Andersen, 1997).

The use of cognitive–behavioral therapy (CBT) as part of the general treatment for eating disorders has been recommended in the American Psychiatric Association's (2000) practice guidelines. Like most other recent writings on treatment of eating disorders, these guidelines have been primarily oriented toward bulimia nervosa. Group therapy has also been recommended for bulimia nervosa (Kirkley et al., 1985; Lee & Rush, 1986; Merrial, Mines, & Starkey, 1987), as it has been found valuable in reducing binge–purge behavior as well as modifying dysfunctional beliefs about weight, shape, size, and eating patterns. Fairburn's work (Fairburn, 1985; Wilson et al., 1997) has set the stage for manualized interventions and shows consistent results in the treatment of bulimia.

Long-term follow-up using CBT in a group format indicates good maintenance of change at 6- and 12-month follow-up (Fairburn, Jones, Peveler, Hope, & O'Conner, 1993). Additionally, in the treatment of bulimia nervosa, results show that at posttreatment times of 5.8 years, abstinence rates of 48% are maintained (Fairburn et al., 1995; Wilson et al., 1997). The focus of this chapter is on the use of a cognitive therapy format to treat eating disorders. This approach does not distinguish between diagnostic groups and is appropriate for all eating disorders.

COGNITIVE MODEL OF EATING DISORDERS

Cognitive therapists working with eating disorders generally view the disorder as "multidetermined" (Garfinkel & Garner, 1982; Garner, 1985;

Garner & Garfinkel, 1980). From this standpoint, eating disorder symptoms are based on the interaction of sociocultural, individual, and familial factors (Garner, 1997). The interaction of these factors leads to the development of an eating disorder even though the specific nature of this interaction is not fully understood. What is certain, however, is that the effects of starvation, chaotic eating, and distorted cognitions play a prominent role in maintaining an eating disorder while simultaneously having profound psychological, emotional, and physical consequences.

The cognitive–behavioral model conceptualizes eating disorders in a developmental framework, with primacy on cognition mediating distressed emotion and resulting abnormal behavior (Garfinkel & Garner, 1982; Garner, 1985, Garner & Bemis, 1982; Garner et al., 1997; Wilson et al., 1997). The model also views biology as an important part of the disorder, similar to other disorders such as depression.

A cognitive model conceptualizes eating disorders as involving certain personality characteristics of vulnerable individuals, such as introversion, sensitivity, and tendency to interpersonal isolation. These vulnerabilities combine with certain life experiences to produce specific dysfunctional ideas (known as *schemas*) regarding the self, the world, and the future. Anorexia nervosa, for example, has been hypothesized to develop from these vulnerable characteristics in combination with the schema that weight loss will magically alleviate distress and dysphoria in adolescence (Bowers & Andersen, 1994; Garfinkel & Garner, 1982; Garner & Bemis, 1982, 1985). Brunch (1982) noted negative cognitive factors influenced development and maintenance of anorexia nervosa.

Most investigators would accept that at some point, causal factors converge at the point in which this sensitive individual's central belief is that "it is absolutely essential that I be thin." This fixed idea can result in a set of core beliefs, attitudes, and assumptions about the meaning of body weight, shape, personal competency, as well as other aspects of the individual's life. These variables are posited to both cause and maintain the eating disorder.

Over time, dieting, weight loss, and attaining thinness become factors these individuals manipulate in an attempt to exercise control over their internal and external environments (Garner & Bemis 1982, 1985). Additionally, thinness is often reinforced by the positive compliments of others and an enjoyable sense of success within the individual. At first, the individual decreases food intake and is reinforced for weight loss. Continued weight loss, however, may lead to social criticism, which reinforces the person's propensity to social isolation from family and friends. This isolation, in turn, deprives the individual of feedback that would contradict the already distorted cognitions and maladaptive behaviors related to the eating disorder.

Decreased affective expression or the complete denial of feelings often accompanies and maintains anorexia nervosa. Individuals may be unable to identify what they are feeling in a given situation and may be highly resistant to admitting that they are experiencing emotional reactions in any given situation. Even if they are aware of affective arousal, they may be unable to differentiate between emotions, such as anxiety and anger, or to identify their source (e.g., a recent interpersonal interaction).

CBT of eating disorder therefore places a high value on working with the client's affective states. Increased awareness of emotions is generally achieved through therapy by assisting the client to observe inconsistencies, incongruities, and inappropriate emotional reactions from the client's everyday events. Confirmation and reinforcement of emotions that are a genuine part of the client's past and present experience are essential. A number of specific strategies can be used to achieve this goal. Analogies, hypothetical situations, and Socratic questioning may be used to help the client see that reactions in specific situations are distorted. The client can recognize that, in a hypothetical sense, emotion is acceptable, but only for other people, not themselves. The client is encouraged to express all emotions, especially "unacceptable" emotions. With the therapist serving as a model for expression of emotion, the client can learn that open expression of emotions does not lead to rejection (Garfinkel & Garner, 1982) or out-of-control behavior.

Cognitive therapy can address the lack of trust in and the fear of feelings or expression of emotions (Garfinkel & Garner, 1982). Individual CBT can facilitate the client's identification of internal experiences and help overcome the distorted beliefs that inhibit his or her appropriate expression. To accomplish this, the therapist must confirm genuine expressions of inner feelings, while labeling misperceptions and errors in the client's thinking. Denial or absence of seemingly appropriate affect should be explored in greater detail. It is critical to progress slowly and let the clients learn to identify their emotions. Another crucial component of CBT is assisting the client with identifying his or her affective states as well as promoting a sense of acceptance of these feelings as being real.

In summary, CBT of eating disorders relies on active techniques to change schemas and core beliefs (Beck, 1995; Freeman, 1993). It also places a high value on identifying, understanding, and appropriately labeling emotions. This work will be increasingly successful as weight is gradually restored to 85%–90% of healthy goal weight.

Cognitive therapy also focuses on helping the client recognize and change the rigid standards used to determine self-worth. CBT reinforces the gradual discovery of personal interests and gently challenges performance based on others' expectations. A message that needs to be communicated is that positive self-evaluation can be developed from success in small, personal activities and not simply from exceptional or perfect performances. Competence by way of reasonable standards (emphasizing adequacy, not perfection), as well as learning and accepting "in-betweens," is very important. The client can learn that uniform excellence is not the requirement for self-acceptance. Self-acceptance, despite personal shortcomings from unrealistic standards, is a fundamental goal for the therapist working with a client with an eating disorder. Helplessness and incompetence can be decreased by encouraging efforts at mastery in areas that have been avoided because of fear of failure (Garfinkel & Garner, 1982).

Because CBT has been shown to be effective in the treatment of bulimia nervosa (Wilson & Fairburn, 1993; Wilson et al., 1997), many of those strategies can be applied to treatment of anorexia nervosa. Shared goals between the two disorders include decreased illness-driven eating patterns and the substitution of healthy behavior. Because anorexia nervosa and bulimia nervosa share symptoms (overemphasis on body shape and weight, rigid dietary habits), CBT seems well suited for the treatment of both types of eating disorders (Bowers, 1993; Eckert & Mitchell, 1989; Fairburn & Cooper, 1989; Wilson & Fairburn, 1993).

A cognitive model also acknowledges that clinical differences do exist between the two diagnostic categories (anorexia nervosa and bulimia nervosa) and attempts to approach treatment with this in mind. On the basis of clinical experience, differences between the two disorders mainly revolve around issues of control. On the one hand, individuals with anorexia develop symptoms (extreme weight loss, limited diets, compulsive exercise, etc.) as a way to exercise control over their otherwise chaotic lives. They also seem to be more preoccupied with intense family relationships. On the other hand, individuals with bulimia are very concerned about being socially accepted and about their relationships with significant others and people in general. People with bulimia frequently hold the misperception that food and eating control them and often feel powerless to effect change. An episode of bingeing, overeating, and purging is either preceded or accompanied by a profound sense of loss of control, guilt, and self-disgust. Bulimic behaviors are used to enhance a sense of control. However, the self-deprecating thoughts eventually leave them vulnerable to losing control.

It is very important that before beginning a group with this population, the therapist has a good grounding in all aspects of eating orders. This includes medical, nutritional, and psychological aspects of starvation, potential outcomes of such behavior as use of laxatives, diuretics, and restriction of calories. The therapist must also understand basic treatment of such disorders as depression, anxiety, and obsessive–compulsive disorder. Even more important is the consultation and supervision by an individual who is skilled in treating these disorders. Without this assistance, even the most skilled group or cognitive therapist can become frustrated and discouraged when conducting cognitive group therapy.

COGNITIVE GROUP THERAPY WITH EATING DISORDERS

Cognitive group therapy combines Beck's (1995) theory and interventions in a process-oriented framework (Bowers & Andersen, 1994). Group therapy in the treatment of eating disorders is increasingly recognized as an important, effective, economical, and psychotherapeutic tool (Bowers & Andersen, 1994; Hall, 1985). As a basic approach, a blend of process orientation (Yalom, 1995) and cognitive–behavioral principles (Bowers & Andersen, 1994; Lee & Rush, 1986) appears to be clinically effective. Blending these two models gives the group latitude to deal with personal and interpersonal issues. The curative factors of group (Yalom, 1995) and cognitive therapy principles create a focus on cognitive and developmental factors involved with eating disorders. These factors are the sociocultural, individual, and familial events that have influenced the world of the person with an eating disorder and have created the schemas and core beliefs that sustain the eating disorder. The group therapy also influences the perceptions of the clients and permits clients to assist in each other's recovery. The group creates an environment for change through self-disclosure and confrontation of symptomatic behavior, distorted ideas, and negative attitudes.

Cognitive group therapy for eating disorders blends cognitive conceptualization, cognitive interventions, and process orientation. The group emphasis is on interactions within the group itself as well as the thoughts, feelings, and behaviors of each member between group sessions. This dual focus leads to an understanding that the behavior within the group represents how each client functions in the outside world. This also allows the client to identify various cognitive distortions, automatic thoughts, schemas, and core beliefs during the group. The group creates an atmosphere for members to increase their awareness of various cognitive ideas in a here-and-now setting. Additionally, this group provides a fertile ground for clients to practice identifying cognitive distortions, automatic thoughts, schemas, and core beliefs for other clients as they occur within the group.

Curative factors as defined by Yalom (1995) are elements of the group process itself that become tools to promote change. According to Yalom, the therapeutic group provides an environment in which these curative factors take place. These factors include an instillation of hope, feelings of universality, an opportunity for altruism and interpersonal learning, the imparting of information, and the development of socializing techniques. For example, people who struggle with an eating disorder frequently are not aware that there are many others who also experience such difficulties. Being with similar others allows individuals to overcome feelings of shame and secrecy and to begin to express their feelings of frustration or helplessness about their relationship with food. A central factor for instilling a sense of hope is to show that it is possible to confront and change these seemingly unresolvable issues surrounding food and weight (Lee & Rush, 1986; Yalom, 1995). The power to help others, frequently unnoticed among those who see themselves as struggling, can allow a member to move away from being self-centered and begin to experience a sense of altruistic self-worth. Thus, the group provides the opportunity both to observe and to contribute to solving others' problems, as well as to understand the self (Yalom, 1995). Additionally, as many individuals with an eating disorder have had unsatisfactory childhood experiences in their families, they can bring those experiences into a group setting. Members in a group (especially when there are male and female cotherapists) can resemble a family in structure. Because of this influence, members can interact with leaders and other members in modes resembling their past interactions with parents and siblings. The family "ground rules" that have been established over time can be identified. With this new awareness, an opportunity is created to challenge existing maladaptive thought and actions and to encourage new thoughts, feelings, and behaviors. Additionally, working with a group and the cotherapists, members can develop specific homework assignments related to family or significant others in their lives. Many group members look back on their experience in group and credit the comments on their automatic thoughts and cognitive distortions as important in making both personal and interpersonal changes. The comments and support of others are seen as a key to learning about themselves and in the identification of schemas and core beliefs. Thus, the group provides the opportunity to both observe and contribute to being aware of negative automatic thoughts, maladaptive schemas, and negative core beliefs as well as increasing members' ability in solving others' problems.

Group composition is a somewhat controversial subject. Research on group therapy with eating disorders has focused on homogeneous groups and suggests that this may be a better way to address the issues needed to create change (Garner & Garfinkel, 1997). Size of the group is dependent on the type of group offered. However, when working with a eating disorders group, an optimal size for group is 5–8 members. It has also been suggested that the more optimal group size is 4–5 members when working with clients with anorexia (Polivy & Federoff, 1997). From clinical experience, there does not seem to be any clear evidence regarding what type of client mix is optimal for a group. Blended groups—individuals with anorexia and those with bulimia—allow both to interact and learn from each other. Also, blended groups bring more pressure to each diagnostic group regarding their distortions, especially when looking at issues of body image, weight, and need for control. Often, individuals with an eating disorder are capable of making good distinctions about the weight and shape of those around them. However, they frequently fail to understand how they really look (i.e., they see themselves as too fat when they are actually at normal weight or extremely thin). In a blended group, the group members' confrontation regarding the cognitive distortions of other members can carry more importance than a group leader. Confrontations can lead members to be aware of the need to challenge their own cognitive distortions. Also, it can increase the awareness of the group member making the confrontation to assess his or her distortions regarding weight and body image.

BLENDED GROUPING: TWO DIAGNOSTIC GROUPS

Investigations (Garfinkel & Garner, 1982; Stolz, 1984) have shown that persons most likely to develop problems with eating disorders make up a relatively homogeneous population. The literature indicates that women are primarily affected by eating disorders (95% women vs. 5% men; American Psychiatric Association, 1994). However, both men and women are subject to the same factors that can contribute to an eating disorder. Among the variables that may lead to extreme methods to control weight are cultural aspects, such as the preoccupation with fatness in the United States. Also, American culture places an extremely high value on beauty and being slender and often portrays role models (male and female) with overly slim physiques that are impossible to maintain. A strong concern regarding one's appearance often predates the onset of an eating disorder (Garner, 1997). Thus, groups that are effective for anorexia nervosa and bulimia nervosa frequently revolve around elements common to both of these disorders.

There are few criteria that would exclude a person from this type of group. One criterion would be group members' inability to commit to change. This would include a commitment to active weight restoration for clients with anorexia nervosa and cessation of bingeing and purging for clients with bulimia nervosa. Without this type of commitment, even the best therapy would have little effect. Outside of this factor, essentially all individuals would be welcome in the group.

Despite their physical size, most individuals with eating disorders rarely perceive themselves accurately. Rather, they have a morbid fear of becoming fat, coupled with an obsessive desire to be thin. In focusing much of their attention on how they hate their bodies, these individuals seem to separate intellectual or emotional aspects from their physical selves. This, in turn, leads to a distortion of how they actually look. The disgust with which they view their bodies seems to mirror how they feel about themselves.

Group treatment, including individuals with anorexia nervosa and bulimia nervosa within the same therapy group, can provide an opportunity in which to challenge common, irrational concerns about body shape, weight, and emotional issues. For example, most members are clearly able to see that others in the group are not grossly overweight and, in fact, are attractive. Slightly overweight members are confronted with the extremely thin or underweight members who feel as overweight, as worthless, and as unlovable as they do.

In preparing a client for a group, the therapist must, for example, state the existing norms such as confidentiality and being on time. Silent norms, such as the avoidance of direct expression of feelings, are explored and discouraged, whereas open and honest communication is encouraged. Expectations or fears of new members can thus be openly addressed. However, the common themes of both types of eating disorders blend the otherwise diverse population into a psychologically homogeneous group by emphasizing the common features.

A didactic format can be built into the group. Information about cognitive therapy principles can be presented in minilessons at the start of a session, especially when it enhances an ongoing issue. When this type of information is taught at the start of the group, each member is asked to be aware of that particular concept and to identify it during the session. Concepts such as cognitive distortions, automatic thoughts, schemas, and core beliefs are reinforced in a setting that uses situations that have happened during that day or between sessions. Additionally, material that comes from the group itself is available to show how the ideas of cognitive therapy are ever present with clients. It is also an opportunity for more skilled members of the group to assist newer group members in initially identifying automatic thoughts, schemas, and core beliefs. At any point during a group session, a coleader or advanced member can take time to help other members understand the ideas associated with cognitive therapy. This type of "minilecture" can be very valuable when it is attached to a here-and-now situation and can make the concepts of cognitive therapy more realistic and personal.

Group cognitive therapy relies heavily on the use of both cognitive and behavioral interventions. Within the group itself, it is often advantageous to have a blackboard or some type of board so that automatic thoughts can be worked through during the session. For example, when specific automatic thoughts are identified during group, one member could write and keep track of those thoughts for the other member or members of the group. Later in the session, the member or members could then challenge those thoughts and work to reframe them, perhaps using a daily record of dysfunctional thoughts. This acts as a vehicle to help group members be more aware of their own and others' automatic thoughts. Also, thought records from a pervious situation or session can be worked with during the group session. The material discussed is an integral part of the group therapy and potentially creates homework assignments. Suggestions for individual members can come from group leaders, and, depending on the circumstances, homework assignments can be given to the whole group by the leaders or by an individual within the group. Material given as homework assignments is then set up as agenda items for the next group. Homework assignments are always integrated into the next session.

A hallmark of an eating disorder is the individual's distortion of how the individual sees himself or herself. Group cognitive therapy focuses on helping clients understand their body distortions and how these distortions affect their lives and sustain the eating disorder. Changing the distorted body perception is one of the most difficult aspects of the illness. What is often seen is that the distortion usually does not completely resolve. However, through group work, the clients learn to diminish the impact of these thoughts and begin to put them into proper perspective. The cognitive therapy group is extremely valuable for adjusting distorted body images. Clients are supportive yet confrontational with one another, helping each other face their distortions and bringing their cognitions into the realm of reality. The cognitive therapy group is effective in challenging clients' belief systems, realizing their lack of validity, and creating alternative views of their body image. Additionally, it is often found that these clients have not thought through how they came to believe these distortions. When the clients are challenged to provide a rationale to support their distortions, they are frequently surprised to find that they cannot offer any validation.

When working on body image issues in group, clients are told they cannot trust their perceptions of how they appear to themselves and others. In each session, clients share their thoughts and how they feel about changes their bodies are undergoing during treatment. It is an accepted fact in the group that the clients' body sizes are changing and this change is a frightening experience for them. Trust and self-disclosure are paramount, and clients are encouraged to openly and honestly express feelings concerning body perceptions. Additionally, there is a fact-versus-fiction discussion regarding distorted body image. Clients need to discover that to feel positive about their bodies, they must rely on facts, not their distorted perceptions. They are advised to identify, challenge, and reframe automatic thoughts to feel differently about their bodies.

Working in the CBT group format increases awareness about the interaction of thoughts and feelings. Clients learn that when they experience negative thoughts about their bodies, there is an underlying emotional issue. Clients are guided to understand that when they are feeling emotionally out of control, they rely on other strategies to deal with their fears. One strategy used to control that fear is to focus on control over their physical body (e.g., control of food, weight, and appearance). An expression of this phenomenon is their stating, "I feel fat." This statement is corrected by the therapist stating that "fat is not a feeling." Clients then explore what the feeling is they are experiencing and the thoughts or issues that are underlying the emotion. Next, they are then taught the steps to understand their feelings by identifying their automatic thoughts, challenging them, and reframing their distorted perceptions about their body. This process creates a base for change in a core symptom of the disorder —distorted body image. The group allows members to apply the CBT skills to specific symptom of the eating disorder and to assist others in the same type of work. An example follows from an inpatient group session:

Therapist 1: You've been awfully quiet today (to Client 1). What is happening?

Client 1: Nothing, I'm just tired I guess.

Client 2: How come it has taken you so long to eat your last two meals? You're going home in 3 days.

Client 1: I've been afraid of being out of control since I learned what my weight was 3 days ago.

Client 3: What about knowing your weight makes you uncomfortable? You know that your weight is healthy.

Client 1: I know, but if I continue to eat I'll blow up like a balloon.

Client 2: What kind of statement did you just make?

Client 1: I know, I know, it's an automatic thought. But I'm afraid I'll be out of control.

Therapist 2: What is usually said when members start talking about food or weight or start to focus on food or weight?

Client 4: Well, usually that means there is some other problem. Something else is going on. What's really going on [to Client 1]?

Client 1: I guess I am trying to numb out my feelings. I'm afraid that no one will miss me or remember me after I'm gone.

Client 3: I'm hurt and angry at that remark.

Therapist 2: What goes on when you start to not express your emotions?

Client 1: Well, I'm afraid of what people might think if I show them, especially if I cry or tell someone I care.

Client 4: Client 1, when does that type of thinking occur and how did that concern get started?

Client 1: I know I get that way when I have strong feelings around my family, especially my parents.

Client 4: Do you think that might be happening right now and for the past few days?

Client 1:	I suppose what might be going on is a schema. I feel uncomfortable about my feelings and instead of talking about it I start taking it out on food. I know that this is how I have acted when I was at home and felt my emotions were not by accepted by my parents.
Therapist 1:	What makes you think that others would not remember you or miss you?
Client 1:	Well, I have been real distant to people lately. I've pissed them off with my behavior. They have had to miss activities while I sat and finished my breakfast or lunch.
Client 2:	What meaning do you attach to those actions?
Client 1:	I don't deserve for others to like me. You should feel glad that I'm gone.
Therapist 1:	We "should" feel glad that you are gone.
Client 1:	I know! "Should" statement, cognitive distortion. But I just don't feel worthy of someone's positive feelings to me. I don't deserve that.
Client 4:	Client 1, what does that statement sound like to you, "You are not worthy of others' good feelings?"
Client 1:	It is one of my core beliefs. I know that, but it is still hard to change when my emotions are strong.
Client 2:	Sounds like you still have some work to do during your outpatient care. I hope that you can make changes in the belief.
Client 1:	Let us help you by writing and we want you to keep in touch with us.

A CBT group challenges the view of the world that the clients have established through their distorted cognitions. Much of the group work lends itself toward helping the clients understand how their cognitions affect their mood and consequent behaviors. Another healing factor is the ability of group members to easily identify in others the ramifications of their own eating disorder. As clients help each other identify and change negative cognitions, they also improve their own, often coming to resolution of their issues as reflected in others.

Cognitive group therapy focuses on the view of the world that the clients have established through their cognitions. Through group participation, clients begin to understand how the eating disorder has been a strategy to cope with their world and can explore alternative methods of meeting their needs. This exploration focuses on the creation of adaptive responses, particularly in areas regarding nutrition, body image, social, and interpersonal interactions. Clients can see how their behavior in group parallels how they react outside of the group. The cognitive distortions, automatic thoughts, schemas, and core beliefs that appear in group are similar to those in their day-to-day living. When these are identified, group members can work to change them and develop plans to generalize those changes to the outside world. Frequently, interpersonal issues among group members are translated into actions with peers and family members. Plans and homework about how members interact with each other in group can be suggested and tested outside of the group.

In group therapy with eating disorders, use of male and female cotherapists is preferred (when possible) to either a single therapist or same-sex cotherapists. The presence of male and female therapists in our group expanded the range of possible reactions by group members and thus enhanced the opportunity for group process. The female therapist could alternately be viewed as the figure of authority, as another woman to compete with, as the maternal figure, or as the understanding teacher or older sibling. Similarly, the male therapist could be viewed as the establishment authority figure, as the paternal figure, as the male to be pleased, or as the understanding teacher or older sibling. Because the interpersonal aspects of eating disorders have been increasingly recognized (Schwartz, Barrett, & Saba, 1985), the skilled therapist can use group interactions to illustrate a wide range of relationships. Some authors (e.g., White & Boskind-White, 1981), however, have cautioned against using a male therapist only, to reduce competition for his attention especially for a female-dominant group. However, male and female cotherapists can provide strong role models for how to interact with members of the opposite sex in nonsexual, nonaggressive, yet assertive ways.

Feedback is very important in a group for eating disorders. Because the group has an emphasis on schemas and core beliefs, expression of emotion and feedback within the group increases the clients' affective arousal. The group setting also becomes a place to practice the identification and challenging of automatic thoughts. Groups with ongoing feedback can point out when automatic thoughts have been stated and challenge the client who holds those thoughts. Feedback can also address obvious cognitive distortions and dispute misinformation. Because there is an attempt to raise the awareness of how emotions interact with thoughts and behaviors, feedback is one tool that can keep this awareness in the front of the group.

Feedback can be valuable, yet it also can be destructive. Fortunately, the group setting not only encourages members to be open but also monitors that openness. Confrontation can inhibit expression of thoughts and feelings, especially when confrontations turn into personal attacks. It is not unusual for individuals with an eating disorder to have had a history of others telling them what they feel and how they think, as well as stating clearly what is right and wrong. In the group, coleaders monitor the type and intensity of feedback and step in when it is deemed unhealthy or unhelpful. The interventions may be as simple as asking for the reason behind the confrontation and checking whether personal schema material has been triggered. Coleaders may also meditate the confrontation between various members or direct members to use the confrontation and the emotion that is attached to it as a catalyst for their self-understanding. When necessary, one or both of the coleaders will intervene and bring the feedback or confrontation to a halt. When that happens, the leaders will explain the reasons behind the intervention and then assess what reactions (thoughts and feelings) each member is experiencing.

Contact outside the group is not encouraged or discouraged. It is a topic for discussion when it does happen and a group issue for ongoing discussion. It is important for the group and the group leaders to remain aware that what happens to members outside of group is only an extension of the group itself. It is made clear to all group members that although they can be helpful to each other with their struggle, the disorder they share can also impair and interfere with change and growth. An attempt is made to use outside group support only when necessary to prevent becoming involved in eating disorder behavior. It is equally important to let clients know that they must also create a support system of individuals who are not engaged in the disorder.

Conflict is an important part of group. Although is can be distracting, conflict in group is similar to conflict in life in that each person needs to construct a framework for coping with this conflict. Often individuals with an eating disorder have gone to great lengths to avoid conflict and are often "people-pleasers." What is needed is to make conflict something that is then addressed from a problem-solving standpoint. Also conflict can be useful in identifying and beginning to change schema and core beliefs. Conflict is monitored by the group leaders and is discouraged when members begin to become negative or "mean spirited" in their use of feedback or working with the group in an open expression of emotion.

Self-disclosure is one aspect of group that is encouraged by all members, including the group leaders. Group leaders can use their own experience as a platform for change among members and be a tool that models the use of expression of emotion in minimal and high-intensity situations. Therapists take a more active role in a cognitive group to make certain that the ideas (automatic thoughts, schema, and core beliefs) of the cognitive model are clearly understood. When possible, female and male cotherapists will be a more effective treatment team. The female and male coleaders help create role models for interactions between sexes, displaying how differences of opinion can be worked out between two individuals.

Additionally, it can reproduce situations that are similar to the primary family unit (Yalom, 1995).

Cohesiveness is developed by building on the shared aspects of the eating disorder between clients. The similarities within the disorders (concerns about weight, shape, food, control, independence) are addressed as both precursors of the disorder and maintaining factors for the disorder. These issues can be addressed within a psychoeducational group or brought into a more open-ended group by pointing out the similarities of symptoms between group members when they arise. In an open-ended group, more experienced members can heighten cohesiveness by telling newer clients the advantages of not engaging in the eating disorder. They also can share how their lives have become better by using other methods besides the eating disorder to express their concerns.

GROUP FORMAT

Group sessions are generally started by one of the group members; rarely does a group leader start the session. Each member is responsible for his or her agenda, and often members will ask for some discussion time during a group. Group leaders will model opening a group by asking if there is anything that needs to be discussed. More often than not the leaders remain silent until one of the group members begins. The pressure of silence will most often get members at least talking about the lack of discussion. The goal is to create an interactive session with little emphasis on individual use of time. The group is meant to avoid doing individual therapy in a group setting. The role of a group leader is to help members discuss the issues related to change. When group members appear to stay away from important issues (expression of feeling, confrontation, and people pleasing), the group leader focuses attention on these issues to prompt discussion from group members.

Keeping a group interactive is one of the more difficult tasks for co-leaders of a group. One of the best ways is for group leaders to model interactive behavior. This can be accomplished by group leaders making an effort to talk to all members in the group sessions if possible. Another way to keep a group interactive is to have cotherapists talk between themselves during groups. Having cotherapists talk to each other about group process interactions or observations about a specific group member or members and the interactions can model communications across the group. Additionally, group leaders can ask members what they think or how they feel about what is going on in the group or if they have similar experiences and ask them to share them. This creates a norm that discussion and open communication are important. Another approach is to have the members of the group assume the role of coleaders. This approach has been successful in getting all members thinking about assisting fellow members to join in the group. One final suggestion may be to have members develop topics or agendas that are agreed on by the group with the expectation that all members share their thoughts and feelings about that topic. Creativity among group leaders in this group is key in getting all members to be involved.

The goals of a group working with an eating disorder are varied; some are extremely explicit and others more personal. Explicit goals in this type of group include changes within disordered eating (bingeing, purging, restriction of dietary intake, and overexercise), whereas others are more subtle (expression of emotion and overcoming fear of interpersonal relationships). The group itself has a goal of creating change, and it is obvious when members in the group are making progress. Additionally, each member is aware what the others are working on, and it is built into the group to discuss and challenge other members regarding their goals. When clients start the group, they are expected to have developed a set of written goals to work on during the group. When a new member enters the group, their goals are shared with other group members. Periodically these goals are reviewed and new ones are generated with input of the group. Often each member's goals are directly related to an aspect of each group. For example, groups have a focus on being open and discussing their emotions along with being aware of their cognitive distortions, automatic thoughts, schemas, and core beliefs. This group focus brings to the surface many subtle goals while helping all members to be aware of the cognitive theoretical aspects of the disorder.

Consistent with the cognitive model of an eating disorder, food and weight are not direct issues and are seldom pursued during a group session. At best food and weight are surface strategies or a smoke screen to avoid more intense issues. These emotionally intense concerns are related to thoughts of being out of control or fears of maturity. Additionally, schematic material related to social interactions, or core beliefs regarding not being lovable, or having personal worth or value can be triggered. When these issues do arise, they are quickly translated into more intense issues and worked with on that level to identify, challenge, and change various thoughts, feelings, and behaviors.

Groups with eating disorders have a here-and-now emphasis that uses historical material to address and understand how the current problems were created. Historical material is viewed through the concepts of schemas and core beliefs and addressed by looking at more immediate interventions such as identifying automatic thoughts and basic assumptions. When working in group, clients often have mood shifts or react to events that are occurring in the group. It is not unusual that the intensity of the emotional shift is not proportional to the event being observed. When this type of intense emotion occurs, it is a good time to assess if the group member is reacting to a schema that has been triggered or specifically to an event in group. The member is asked if there have been other situations in his or her life that are similar to what is currently happening. If the member can access a historical event, then he or she is asked to remember to the best of his or her ability the emotions that occurred during that event. It is also suggested that the member's reaction may be part of a schema that has not been adaptive. The group member is then asked to explore how he or she handled that event and what he or she would prefer to have done differently.

If the member identifies automatic thoughts or cognitive distortions, he or she is asked to challenge them and develop alternative way of seeing the situation. When the member has worked on the earlier situation, he or she is then asked to use the same methods in the here-and-now situation. Once that intervention has taken place, the member is asked if the current situation is more understandable and if the intensity of the emotional response has been reduced. The member is also asked to reframe his or her thoughts and search for another way of dealing with that situation. Additionally, the group member is encouraged to be more aware of how the current situation triggered the schema. He or she is then asked to be aware of similar situations and create a plan to deal with those situations when they occur. The member is also asked to increase his or her awareness of how he or she can actively change the schema and that he or she does not automatically need to respond to schema material.

While a particular member is working with his or her schema material, all other group members are encouraged to engage in the same process. In this way, they assist other members in understanding their reactions; support each other; and share their thoughts, feelings, and behavior. Members are also encouraged to discuss their schema material and to ask fellow members if they might be working with trigger schemas when they notice changes in emotions during the group. There is a blend of using the present group experience to identify automatic thoughts that signal more complex materials brought up in these automatic thoughts, such as schemas and core beliefs. Depending on the setting, the use of more immediate interactions are worked with. Group therapy in an inpatient setting will work much more closely with the actions and interactions of clients in the milieu while more traditional outpatient group settings will have a more historical focus on those events that have taken place in the past week.

Consistent with the use of cognitive therapy and similar to work with personality disorders, group cognitive therapy focuses on the expression and understanding of emotions. The interaction of thoughts, feelings, and behaviors is highlighted as in other client groups. However, there is a greater focus on identification, understanding, and expression of emotion than might occur in a group setting for depression or anxiety disorders. This greater focus brings to awareness specific triggers for clients with eating disorders to engage in their behavior (e.g., bingeing and restricting calories), and it also is used as a way to identify both the schemas and core beliefs that contribute and maintain the disorder.

There is a greater focus on emotional expression when working with clients with eating disorders than with patients with depression or an anxiety disorder. This is related to a core belief that clients with an eating disorder have an inability to accurately identify and respond to their emotions and internal sensations. These clients have often been told that what they feel is wrong and that they should not feel a certain way. This is different from clients with depression, who have more problems with the content of their thoughts yet seem more accurate in the understanding and expression of their emotions. Confusion regarding internal states creates uncertainty about the validity and reliability of their thoughts, feelings, and behaviors leading to a reduced sense of confidence in their ability to see the world. This poor confidence contributes to difficulty in the expression of emotions that is then seen as fanatic self-monitoring and rigid approaches to the world.

Conducting group therapy with individuals with eating disorders will push the limits of the skill of the therapist working with this population. It will challenge the therapists' understanding of group process, their mastery of cognitive therapy interventions, and their creativity in blending the two. Also, group therapy with eating disorders is not conducting individual cognitive therapy in a group setting.

CONCLUSION

What is the essence of a cognitive group for eating disorders? It is not, like some descriptions of group cognitive therapy, individual work with clients who are in group for a common problem (Freeman, 1983, Wessler & Hankin Wessler, 1989). A cognitive group therapy for eating disorders uses intervention of cognitive therapy and the cognitive conceptualization to make changes in the group and each member in the group to function in a way to understand the interaction of thoughts, feelings, and behavior. Clients learn to use these strategies not only in their own lives but translating that knowledge to each member in the group, the group as a single entity, and to the broader world view. Group cognitive therapy blends more immediate interventions (challenging automatic thoughts, identifying cognitive distortions) in a way that group members practice these skills by listening and assisting other group members. Simultaneously members increase their own awareness of these interventions. The group is a blending of emotional intensity with awareness of the schemas and core beliefs that drive their disorder. Additionally, the group's here-and-now focus and process orientation present opportunities for each member to deal more effectively with their own emotions. This approach to cognitive group therapy creates an environment for each member to be aware of his or her own role in the maintenance of the disorder and offers an opportunity for change.

REFERENCES

American Psychiatric Association. (2000). Practice guidelines for eating disorders. *American Journal of Psychiatry, 157,* 1–39.

American Psychiatric Association. (1994). *Diagnostic and statistical manual of mental disorders* (4th ed.). Washington, DC: Author.

Beck, J. S. (1995). *Cognitive therapy: Basics and beyond.* New York: Guilford Press.

Bowers, W. A. (1993). Cognitive therapy for eating disorders. In J. H. Wright, M. E., Thase, A. T. Beck, & J. W. Ludgate (Eds.), *Cognitive therapy with inpatients: Developing a cognitive therapy milieu* (pp. 337–356). New York: Guilford Press.

Bowers, W. A., & Andersen, A. E. (1994). Inpatient treatment of anorexia nervous: Review and recommendations. *Harvard Review of Psychiatry, 2,* 193–203.

Bowers, W. A., Evans, K., & Andersen, A. E. (1997). Inpatient treatment of eating disorders: A cognitive therapy milieu. *Cognitive and Behavioral Practice, 4,* 291–323.

Bruch, H. (1982). Anorexia nervosa: Therapy and theory. *American Journal of Psychiatry, 139,* 1531–1538.

Eckert, E. D., & Mitchell, J. E. (1989). An overview of the treatment of anorexia nervosa. *Psychiatric Medicine, 7,* 293–315.

Fairburn, C. G. (1981). A cognitive behavioral approach to the management of bulimia. *Psychological Medicine, 11,* 707–711.

Fairburn, C. G. (1985). A cognitive behavioral approach to the treatment of bulimia. In D. M. Garner & P. E. Garfinkel (Eds.), *Handbook of psychotherapy for anorexia nervosa and bulimia* (pp. 160–191). New York: Guilford Press.

Fairburn, C. G., & Cooper, P. J. (1989). Eating disorders. In K. Hawton, P. M. Salkovskis, J. Kirk, & D. M. Clark (Eds.), *Cognitive behavioral therapies for psychiatric problems* (pp. 277–314). New York: Oxford University Press.

Fairburn, C. G., Jones, R., Peveler, R. C., Hope, R. A., & O'Conner, M. E. (1993). Psychotherapy and bulimia nervosa: The longer-term effects of interpersonal psychotherapy, behavior therapy, and cognitive behavior therapy. *Archives of General Psychiatry, 50,* 419–428.

Fairburn, C. G., Norman, P. S., Welch, S. L., O'Connor, M. E., Doll, H. A., & Peveler, R. C. (1995). A prospective study of outcome in bulimia nervosa and the long-term effects of three psychological treatments. *Archives of General Psychiatry, 52,* 304–312.

Freeman, A. (1983). *Cognitive therapy with couples and groups.* New York: Plenum Press.

Freeman, A. (1993). A psychosocial approach to conceptualizing schematic development for cognitive therapy. In K. T. Kuehlwein & H. Rosen (Eds.), *Cognitive therapies in action* (pp. 54–87). San Francisco: Jossey-Bass.

Garfinkel, P. E., & Garner D. M. (1982). *Anorexia nervosa: A multidimensional perspective*. New York: Brunner/Mazel.

Garner, D. M. (1985). Individual psychotherapy for anorexia nervosa. *Journal of Psychiatry Research, 19*, 423–433.

Garner, D. M. (1997). Psychoeducational principles in treatment. In D. M. Garner & P. E. Garfinkel (Eds.), *Handbook of treatment for eating disorders* (2nd ed., pp. 145–177). New York: Guilford Press.

Garner, D. M., & Bemis, K. M. (1982). A cognitive behavioral approach to anorexia nervosa. *Cognitive Therapy and Research, 6*, 1–27.

Garner, D. M., & Bemis, K. M. (1985). Cognitive therapy for anorexia nervosa. In D. M. Garner & P. E. Garfinkel (Eds.), *Handbook of psychotherapy for anorexia nervosa and bulimia* (pp. 107–146). New York: Guilford Press.

Garner, D. M., & Garfinkel, P. E. (1980). Socio-cultural factors in the development of anorexia nervosa. *Psychological Medicine, 10*, 647–656.

Garner, D. M., & Garfinkel, P. E. (1997). *Handbook of treatment for eating disorders* (2nd ed.). New York: Guilford Press.

Garner, D. M., Vitousek, K. M., & Pike, K. M. (1997). Cognitive–behavioral therapy for anorexia nervosa. In D. M. Garner & P. E. Garfinkel (Eds.), *Handbook of treatment for eating disorders* (2nd ed., pp. 67–93). New York: Guilford Press.

Goodsitt, A. (1997). Eating disorders: A self-psychological perspective. In D. M. Garner & P. E. Garfinkel (Eds.), *Handbook of treatment for eating disorders* (2nd ed., pp. 205–228). New York: Guilford Press.

Hall, A. (1985). Group psychotherapy for anorexia nervosa. In D. M. Garner & P. E. Garfinkel (Eds.), *Handbook of psychotherapy for anorexia nervosa and bulimia* (pp. 213–239). New York: Guilford Press.

Harper-Guiffre, H., Mackenzie, K. R., & Sivitilli, D. (1992). Interpersonal group psychotherapy. In H. Harper-Guiffre & K. R. Mackenzie (Eds.), *Group psychotherapy for eating disorders* (pp. 280–310). Washington, DC: American Psychiatric Press.

Johnson, C., Connor, M., & Stucky, M. (1983). Short-term group treatment or bulimia: A preliminary report. *International Journal of Eating Disorders, 2*, 199–208.

Kirkley, B. G., Schneider, J. A., Agras, W. S., & Bachman, J. A. (1985). Comparison of two group treatments for bulimia. *Journal of Consulting and Clinical Psychology, 53*, 43–48.

Laessle, R. G., & Pirke, K. M. (1987). A structured behaviorally oriented group treatment for bulimia nervosa. *Psychotherapy and Psychosomatic, 48*, 141–145.

Lee, N. F., & Rush, A. J. (1986). Cognitive–behavioral group therapy for bulimia. *International Journal of Eating Disorders, 5*, 599–615.

Merrial, C. A., Mines, R. A., & Starkey, R. (1987). The premature dropout in the group treatment of bulimia. *International Journal of Eating Disorders, 6,* 293–300.

Mitchell, J. E., Hatsukami, D., Goff, G., Pyle, R. L., Eckert, E. D., & Davis, L. E. (1985). Intensive outpatient group treatment for bulimia. In D. M. Garner & P. E. Garfinkel (Eds.), *Handbook of psychotherapy for anorexia nervosa and bulimia* (pp. 240–253). New York: Guilford Press.

Piran, N., Langdon, L., Kaplan, A., & Garfinkel, P. E. (1987). Evaluation of a day hospital program for eating disorders. *International Journal of Eating Disorders, 8,* 523–532.

Polivy, J., & Federoff, I. (1997). Group psychotherapy. In D. M. Garner & P. E. Garfinkel (Eds.), *Handbook of treatment for eating disorders* (2nd ed., pp. 462–475). New York: Guilford Press.

Rosen, J. C., & Leitenberg, H. (1982). Bulimia nervosa: Treatment with exposure and response prevention. *Behavior Therapy, 13,* 117–124.

Rosen, J. C., & Leitenberg, H. (1985). Exposure plus response prevention treatment of bulimia nervosa. In D. M. Garner & P. E. Garfinkel (Eds.), *Handbook of psychotherapy for anorexia nervosa and bulimia* (pp. 193–209). New York: Guilford Press.

Roy-Byrne, P., Lee-Benner, K., & Yager, J. (1984). Group therapy for bulimia: A one year experience. *International Journal of Eating Disorders, 3,* 97–116.

Schneider, J. A., & Agras, W. S. (1985). A cognitive behavioral group treatment for bulimia. *British Journal of Psychiatry, 146,* 66–69.

Schwartz, R. C., Barrett, M. J., & Saba, G. (1985). Family therapy for bulimia. In D. M. Garner & P. E. Garfinkel (Eds.), *Handbook of psychotherapy for anorexia nervosa and bulimia* (pp. 280–310). New York: Guilford Press.

Stevens, E. V., & Salisbury, J. D. (1984). Group therapy for bulimic adults. *American Journal of Orthopsychiatry, 54,* 156–161.

Stolz, S. G. (1984). Recovering from foodaholism. *Journal for Specialists in Group Work, 9*(1), 51–61.

Wessler, R. L., & Hankin Wessler, S. (1989). Cognitive group therapy. In A. Freeman, K. M. Simon, L. E. Beutler, & H. Arkowitz (Eds.), *Comprehensive handbook of cognitive therapy* (pp. 559–582). New York: Plenum Press.

White, W. C., & Boskind-White, M. (1981). An experiential–behavioral approach to the treatment of bulimiarexia. *Psychotherapy: Theory, Research, and Practice, 18,* 501–507.

Wilson, G. T., & Fairburn, C. G. (1993). Cognitive treatments for eating disorders. *Journal of Consulting and Clinical Psychology, 61,* 261–269.

Wilson, G. T., Fairburn, C. G., & Agras, W. S. (1997). Cognitive–behavioral therapy for bulimia nervosa. In D. M. Garner & P. E. Garfinkel (Eds.), *Handbook of treatment for eating disorders* (2nd ed., pp. 67–93). New York: Guilford Press.

Wooley, S. C., & Kearney-Cooke, A. (1986). Intensive treatment of bulimia and body image disturbance. In K. Brownell & J. Foreyt (Eds.), *Handbook of eating disorders: Physiology, psychology, and the treatment of obesity, anorexia and bulimia* (pp. 476–502). New York: Basic Books.

Yalom, I. (1995). *The theory and practice of group psychotherapy* (4th ed.). New York: Basic Books.

6

DUAL DIAGNOSES

TOM GREANIAS AND SANDRA SIEGEL

C.W. is a young African American man who grew up in a large inner-city housing project. He did well in high school and was once ranked as the best high school basketball player in the nation. In his first year of college, he had a schizophrenic break, which began a cycle of hospitalizations and incarcerations. He was never able to realize his dreams. After his first hospitalization, he began using drugs and alcohol on a regular basis.

Nick, a 37-year-old man, was first diagnosed with paranoid schizophrenia at age 22. He was also dependent on alcohol and marijuana, and for many years used cocaine whenever he could obtain it. Over the 14 years from age 22 to 36, he was hospitalized in excess of 50 times for both psychosis and substance abuse.

These are typical stories of clients seen daily at community mental health centers throughout the United States. They are dually diagnosed, or mentally ill substance abuser (MISA), clients. Since deinstitutionalization in the early 1960s, seriously mentally ill individuals have been diverted away from state institutions into the community at large, usually the poorest, most disorganized communities with the fewest resources. They are exposed to, and affected by, the problems of the larger society: a struggling economy with dwindling funds and resources, increased competition for jobs and for safe low-income housing, and widespread drug and alcohol abuse. Added to these problems is a pervasive atmosphere of racism, fear, and discrimination. Although deinstitutionalization was meant to give chronically mentally ill patients increased opportunities, in many cases it has failed and left them abandoned.

MISA clients have a major mental illness diagnosis or a serious personality disorder or both, plus a substance abuse or dependence disorder. They often have overlying depression with high levels of hopelessness. Many are involved in the penal system, have histories of aggressive behavior, and are considered not only "mad" but "bad." They have recurring hospitalizations and are likely to have failed in multiple mental health and substance abuse treatment programs. Their support systems are limited, and they are frequently homeless and in "nothing-to-lose" situations (for review, see Brown, Ridgely, Pepper, Levine, & Ryglewicz, 1989; Evans & Sullivan, 1990; N. Miller, 1994).

Many therapists view MISA clients as difficult or impossible to treat. Very few therapists are trained in both mental illness and drug abuse treatments, and without a systematic approach to the client's multiple problems, the therapist can become overwhelmed and discouraged. On the one hand, when clients with substance abuse problems present at mental health facilities, clinicians often minimize the mental illness, believing it to be secondary, deny responsibility, and reject the individual. If these clients are accepted for treatment of their mental illness, the substance abuse problem is frequently minimized or ignored. On the other hand, MISA clients who present at drug treatment settings may not be accepted because of a mental illness diagnosis or because they are on psychiatric medications. This atmosphere of "this client is yours, not mine" can add to a cycle of hopelessness (Cohen & Levy, 1992): The client comes in feeling hopeless, therapists view them as difficult and unmotivated, therefore believing there is nothing that can be done, and the clients in turn feel even more discouraged and unmotivated (Goldsmith, 1992; Goldsmith & Miller, 1994; N. Miller, 1994).

Currently there is no definitive etiology of either mental illness or substance abuse. Both disorders present heterogeneously, with a wide variety of symptoms, severities, and outcomes (Kaplan & Sadock, 1991; Weiss, Mirin, & Frances, 1992). There is a high prevalence rate for the comorbidity of a psychiatric disorder and addictive disorder in psychiatric settings (N. Miller, 1994). According to the National Institute of Mental Health's Epidemiological Catchment Area study, having a psychiatric disorder triples the risk of having an alcohol or drug problem (Regier et al., 1990). To complicate things further, an addictive disorder can produce symptoms that are difficult to distinguish from a psychiatric disorder (Kaufman & McNaul, 1992; N. Miller, Erickson, & Owley, 1994). Do psychiatric disorders lead to drug abuse? Does drug abuse cause psychiatric disorders?

What are the most effective means of treatment? The answers to these questions are largely unknown.

Some empirical studies have demonstrated the efficacy of psychotherapy in the treatment of substance abuse disorders and have indicated that when there are moderate to severe psychiatric symptoms associated with the substance abuse, psychotherapy is superior to traditional drug counseling. It was also found that the best results were obtained by therapists who adhered to their theoretical beliefs and had positive relationships with their clients. These findings suggest the need for mental health professionals to be involved in the treatment of substance abuse disorders with moderate to severe psychiatric symptoms (Kaufman & McNaul, 1992). Given this complicated picture of uncertain etiologies, comorbid relationships, and heterogeneous presentations of both mental illness and substance abuse disorders, an individualized, structured approach that addresses the person holistically offers greater possibilities for the effective treatment of dually diagnosed clients. A collaborative therapeutic relationship is also essential. Recognizing these special needs of dually diagnosed clients, we present in this chapter a cognitive–behavioral model currently being used successfully in two diverse community mental health centers: one in an inner-city environment and the other a suburban setting.

SETTING AND PURPOSE OF THE GROUP

The cognitive model of an outpatient therapy group described here is designed to help clients understand and accept their dual diagnoses and to motivate them to engage in treatment and recovery from their multiple disorders. This "Engagement and Motivation Group" is the third of four phases of treatment of our dually diagnosed clients. The remaining three phases are briefly described in this chapter to give the reader a context of the progression of clients through the different phases and interventions. The therapy group described here is one phase of a multistage integrated outpatient treatment program for dually diagnosed clients that has been developed and implemented in a community mental health center. The center provides a variety of services, including individual therapy, group therapy, family therapy, case management, psychiatric services, medication management, psychosocial day treatment, and home visiting. The staff operate from a multidisciplinary team approach and are comfortable with a collaborative style of interacting with each other and clients. All clients have a primary therapist and psychiatrist with whom they work, and treatment planning and scheduling is done cooperatively between the client and therapist. Clients are involved at their level of function and desire and can move in and out of various modes or types of treatment according to their needs, abilities, and willingness. The milieu is one of acceptance and encouragement and serves as a secure base for clients to move forward from.

CLIENT CRITERIA AND MIX

Clients are at least 18 years of age and must either definitely or provisionally meet the criteria for both a substance abuse or dependency diagnosis, as well as another Axis I disorder. Diagnosis is determined by a biopsychosocial mental health assessment and a multidisciplinary staffing. Much has been written about the difficulties in accurately diagnosing such clients (Cohen & Levy, 1992; Evans & Sullivan, 1990; Lehman, 1996). In this model of treatment, such accuracy is not as critical, as the suspicion of dual diagnoses is enough to begin the collaborative exploration in group.

Clients are invariably extremely heterogeneous in their presentation, diagnosis, psychosocial history, and life circumstances. There is no "typical" client or client group. Clients in the same group can be both male and female and range from the severity of illness of C.W. and Nick, discussed in the beginning of the chapter, to Jack, a 45-year-old with obsessive–compulsive disorder and cannabis dependence, who is fully employed as a travel agent; to Sue, a 29-year-old single mother of two who lives with her family and suffers from Bipolar I disorder and alcohol and cocaine dependence as well as borderline personality; to Sam, a 60-year-old retired union worker living with a companion and battling with alcohol dependence and severe depression.

Although the cognitive–behavioral model is flexible and can accommodate a wide range of functioning clients, the client must be alert and attentive enough to be able to participate and benefit from group activity and be able to sufficiently follow instructions and conform to group rules (Kalmus, 1996). Abstinence is *not* a criteria for group participation; however, the client must agree not to attend group while under the influence of alcohol or drugs, and in fact will not be allowed to attend group if under the influence.

TRANSFERENCE AND COUNTERTRANSFERENCE ISSUES

The client–therapist relationship may present many problems, particularly when substance abuse and personality disorders are involved. Such clients may well have been involved in illegal and antisocial behavior. Their behavior is often inconsistent and offensive, ranging from manipulative, abusive, angry, grandiose, aggressive, or intimidating to dependent, suicidal, or seductive (Kalmus, 1996). The therapist may have negative views about substance abusers or certain personality traits, or feel incompetent to treat a persons with such high-risk problems. A therapist must challenge his or her own beliefs about working with these clients and avoid taking a position of either negativity or overpermissiveness.

The therapist's role is proactive, or that of guide and teacher, not judge or savior. Keeping the group focused and on task requires diligence and commitment on the part of the therapist. The tendency of client to sidetrack the group and go off on tangents is often matched only by the therapist losing track of the purpose of the group and trying to address issues or "fix" clients before they are ready to change. By having a good understanding of how each client sees the world, keeping the relationships collaborative, and ensuring the therapy is goal oriented, the therapist will encounter fewer transference or countertransference issues. If a therapist has strong negative beliefs or feelings about an individual client, or a type of client that cannot be resolved through supervision or self-reflection, the therapist should refrain from working with these clients (Beck, Freeman, & Associates, 1990; Beck, Wright, Newman, & Liese, 1993; Goldsmith, 1992).

CONCEPTUALIZATION

The dually diagnosed client is seen as suffering from two coexisting disorders: mental illness and substance abuse or dependency. Although there are often clearly interactive effects between these disorders, each must be attended to (Drake, Muesser, Clark, & Wallach, 1996; Weiss et al., 1992). It is not sufficient to treat one disorder in hopes the other will clear on its own or as an effect of treatment of whatever is viewed as the primary diagnosis. Both the mental illness and substance disorders are seen as bio-psycho-social-spiritual disorders with symptoms that can be treated and brought into remission. Each of these areas must be addressed to bring about change. It is not that this model ignores the physiological, biological, and environmental components of the disorders, but it focuses on the client's cognitive perceptions of internal and environmental stimuli (Marlatt, 1985). Once the client is medically and psychiatrically stabilized, emphasis in the early phases of treatment is on the cognitive processes that perpetuate the progression of the disorders and are, often, typically the major hurdle to the client's willingness, or even ability, to change. While often labeled as resistance, these cognitive processes are a part of the client, often beyond his or her awareness.

Beck, Wright, Newman, and Liese (1993) and Marlatt (1985) classified these processes involved in substance abuse into the general areas of self-efficacy, outcome expectations, attributions of causality, and decision-making processes. This broad classification provides a useful tool for beginning to look at the client's schema and automatic thoughts related not only to his or her substance abuse but also the mental illness. It is also a useful way for organizing interventions into a coherent treatment plan. The commonalty of such processes in those with both substance disorders and mental illness makes group treatment not only effective but also the preferred method of intervention. The group can provide the identification, feedback, and support the client needs as he or she begins to contemplate change (Flores, 1988).

Although this chapter focuses on a group model for the engagement and motivation for treatment of dually diagnosed clients, it is only one phase of a complete treatment program for this client population. The complete program consists of the following phases.

Phase I: Assessment and Compliance

From one to six individual sessions are used to diagnosis and assess the client. The goal of this phase is to begin to understand and conceptualize the client's problems as definitively, or at least provisionally, stemming from both mental illness and substance use. It is not necessary, at this point, to eliminate the diagnostic uncertainty in the often complicated and confusing array of symptoms and problems these clients present and make a definitive diagnosis. This model of treatment relies on a collaborative effort between therapist and client to explore the client's problem. This collaborative approach to diagnosis and assessment avoids the pitfalls of client denial and resistance as well as the difficulties often inherent in making a dual diagnosis. The goal is to have the client be able to make a statement such as, "I am willing to work with you to explore whether or not my problems might somehow be related to both a mental illness and substance use problem."

Although the emphasis is on cognitive interventions, other techniques can also be useful in this phase. These techniques may include, individually or in combination, (a) giving clear advice, (b) identifying and removing barriers, (c) providing choices, (d) decreasing the desirability of not changing, (e) practicing empathy, (f) providing accurate feedback on the client's current situation, (g) clarifying goals, and (h) actively helping (W. Miller & Rollnick, 1991). The emphasis here is to gain the client's compliance with the next phase of treatment—education. Clients often are more willing to attend a "class" than go to "group therapy," thus presenting the next phase in such a way helps to further the collaborative alliance and attitude the therapist is trying to build.

Phase II: Psychoeducation Group

The client attends six sessions of 90 minutes, held twice each week for 3 weeks. Here the client is given a broad survey of what mental illness is; how substance use, abuse, and dependency are defined and assessed; the interactive effects of mental illness and substance use; recovery from mental illness and substance abuse; relapse prevention; and the various treatment options for both disorders. The client is also taught the concepts and vocabulary he or she will use in the next phase of treatment—the engagement and motivation group. The client is also introduced to others, some of whom will be attending this next group with the client, thus easing the transition to the new group and again helping with compliance. Upon the completion of this group, an individual session is held with the client to explain the options for the next phase of treatment. Some clients may be willing to enter intensive treatment, and appropriate referral and linkage may be made at this time. The majority of clients will likely agree to continue exploring their problems in the next phase.

Phase III: Engagement and Motivation Group

We believe the key to successful treatment outcome and continuing successful recovery from both mental illness and chemical dependency is the client's motivation for recovery and his or her engagement with treatment. For this reason, this chapter goes into great detail about how this group is structured and conducted. This group may well therefore be the foundation on which a successful treatment outcome is built. The goal is for the client to be able to identify the causes of his or her problems, establish goals for treatment as well as for his or her life, and develop and commit to a treatment plan to resolve problems and reach his or her goals. Clients refer to this as the "Identification Group" as they are see themselves involved here in identifying what their problems are and where they are coming from. Expected length of stay in this group is 6 to 12 months.

Phase IV: Intensive Treatment

Working with the client, the therapist develops an appropriate treatment plan for and committed to by the client. This may involve detoxification, inpatient treatment, residential treatment, intensive outpatient treatment, psychiatric treatment, extensive involvement with self-help, or whatever other services or combination is appropriate. Much of the emphasis in this phase is on behavioral interventions. It is behavioral changes in such areas as abstinence, medication compliance, lifestyle changes, social skills, problem solving, and coping skills that are the primary focus of this phase of treatment.

Planning the appropriate treatment, whether at the therapist's agency or through an outside referral, is crucial. Among the factors that must be considered are the extent and nature of the client's mental illness and its impact on the client's cognitive and social functioning, client resources, availability of treatment alternatives, race, culture, gender, education, socioeconomic status, time, and whether inpatient or residential treatment is deemed necessary, available, affordable, and agreeable.

Phase V: Recovery Support

The goals of this group center on relapse prevention, improved functioning, ongoing support, development of community and social support networks, and personal growth. Interventions are both cognitive and behavioral. Particular attention must also be paid to the client's affect and the ability to be able to identify and productively cope with feelings. The client will normally attend this group for 2 years.

ENGAGEMENT AND MOTIVATION GROUP

Group Philosophy and Goals

The focus in this group is primarily on the individual more than the relationship or process within the group. This group is closest to an educational model in using a rationalistic approach that assumes the client's behavior and difficulties in changing are a direct result of the client's thinking about himself or herself, the client's problems, and the client's world (Wessler & Hankin-Wessler, 1989). The therapist helps the client identify, examine, and change those beliefs and thoughts that are harmful to less problematic and more useful beliefs or thoughts that will facilitate change. The group provides feedback and support and helps to provide alternative ways of thinking for the individual client.

Although the ultimate goal of treatment is stabilization or remission of the symptoms of the mental illness, abstinence from use of substances, improved functioning, and meeting the individual goals of the client, the goal for this group is simply to motivate and engage each client in more intensive treatment designed to help the client reach the ultimate goals just mentioned. It is most often the failure of the client to fully engage, or commit himself or herself, and be motivated to treatment and recovery that causes treatment failure. This failure is often dismissed as the client "not being ready" or seen as client denial, defense, or resistance. Too often, too little attention and effort is made to work directly with the client's motivation and to fully engage the client (Drake, McHugo, & Noordsy, 1993; Osher & Kofoed, 1989). This group model is based on the premise that the greater the effort put into this phase of treatment, the better the outcome. After the client is sufficiently medically and psychiatrically stabilized, what then typically prevents the client from this engagement and motivation is the client's basic beliefs and thoughts about himself or herself and his or her problems and capacity to change (Beck et al., 1993). A cognitive approach to therapy that directly addresses the client's beliefs and thinking can be the most effective and efficient way to help the client begin the change process.

Cognitive Beliefs

The emphasis in the group work is the cognitive schema and automatic thoughts the client has that perpetuate the disorders or that prevent him or her from making changes. Beck et al. (1993) identified addictive beliefs as falling into two general categories: expectation beliefs and permission-giving beliefs. Expectation beliefs are those that relate to what the client feels are, or will be, the benefits of use. These beliefs involve ideas of pleasure seeking, problem solving, relief, and escape (Beck et al., 1993). Permission-giving beliefs relate to justification, risk taking, and entitlement (Beck et al., 1993). We believe it is useful in planning interventions to further classify these permission-giving beliefs into (a) denial-related beliefs —those that the client uses to tell himself or herself that the problem or behavior does not exist or to minimize it, and (b) rationalizing beliefs— those beliefs that admit, at least partially to the behavior, but justify, explain, entitle, attribute, or deny the connection between behavior and consequences. A beliefs inventory (Beck et al., 1993) can be used to help identify and track these beliefs and any changes that may occur as a result of treatment.

Group Organization and Rules

The group meets for 90 minutes, one time per week, with a preferred size of 6 to 10, although this may vary briefly from time to time as members prepare to terminate therapy. The group is open in that clients can enter and leave at any time. This helps to establish continuity, and newer group members can more easily understand the work to be done in the group by observing others who are ahead of them. This also gives the "older" members of the group an opportunity to help and model for the newer members. This in and of itself can be therapeutic for the older member, as this may well be the first time the client has ever been a mentor, teacher, or role model for anyone.

The group is time limited with the expectation that the client will complete the group work in 26 sessions, or 6 months. This time limit helps serve to remind the client that this is a working group and that he or she needs to do the work. Experience thus far shows that despite the work and focus of the group, clients come to feel an affinity for the group and would like to stay as long as possible. Although the 6-month time limit is important and reasonable, it is also important for the therapist to accept that because of impairment, or other valid reasons, some clients may require more time and this should be given, but in fixed increments such as 1 or 3 months. The important thing is that the client is making as sincere and honest an effort as he or she is capable of.

The only rules the therapist imposes on the group, beside those needed to ensure safety in the group, are the following: (a) Regular attendance is expected, (b) assignments are to be completed in a timely and complete manner, (c) clients are not allowed to attend group while under the influence, and (d) clients are to honestly report their alcohol or drug use during the prior week. The group members are encouraged to establish, by themselves, any other rules they may feel necessary for the group to function effectively.

It is important, again, to note that abstinence is not required at this point in the overall treatment program. Although abstinence is usually the ultimate goal, the purpose of this group is one of exploration, identification, and change in thinking. The majority of interventions are thus more cognitive than behavioral. Not insisting in abstinence serves several functions. First, it is often difficult to engage clients in treatment if abstinence is an absolute rule. Second, it seems somewhat disingenuous to insist that the client begin practicing immediately what is in effect one of the final goals or outcomes of the treatment process. Third, clients are often defended against a constant barrage of abstinence efforts from their environment. The lack of such a requirement for this group, as well as the acceptance of the client's use, is something the client is usually not used to and thus he or she may find it easier to connect with the therapist or group. Fourth, this policy of allowing use avoids confrontation and defensive maneuvers by the client and can lead to better acceptance of, and compliance with, the goals and process of the group, as well as to a more open, honest, and willing effort by the client.

Pregroup Orientation

During an individual pregroup session, the purpose and goals of the group are reviewed. The client is educated on how the group works and how to give and receive feedback. Expectations of attendance and compliance with homework assignments are explained, and the client is asked to sign a contract agreeing to accept and follow through with group requirements. Throughout, it is important to reinforce that this group is a collaborative effort at exploring and understanding the client's problems and to help develop an effective plan of treatment. The client is told that his or her use of chemicals will not prevent him or her from participating in treatment, but that the client will not be allowed to attend group while under the influence of alcohol or drugs.

Group Assignments

Each client is expected to complete a similar set of homework assignments. As the client progresses in the group, results of the Beliefs Inventory and the therapist's experience of the client in the group may lead to the development of individualized interventions to help the client deal with particularly intransigent or unique beliefs or thinking. Specialized assignments or assistance may also need to be developed to accommodate a particular client's physical or psychological needs, abilities, or limitations. For example, Barb, a client who is legally blind, required a tutor and the use of audiotape to successfully complete her assignments.

Essential to the meeting of the goals for group are the written homework exercises. These assignments help to identify and challenge the client's beliefs and thoughts about his or her substance use and mental illness. Dually diagnosed clients often have severe distortions about the extent and impact of their substance use on their lives and the course of their mental illness. We have found that clients, when verbally relating their history of substance use and mental illness, will almost invariably minimize the extent and severity of problems. They may not be purposely misrepresenting or minimizing their history, but cognitive distortions, defense mechanisms, memory problems, lack of knowledge, the effects of long-term substance use, and, often, psychotropic medication on the brain all play a role in the client's thinking about the extent, severity, and cause of his or her problems. Written assignments put the "facts" in black and white in front of the client and as such are a form of self-confrontation. Written assignments also provide the opportunity for reflection. The client is encouraged to complete the assignment as best as he or she can, then put it aside for awhile and not think about it. The client is then instructed to pick up the assignment from time to time, review it, and add to it.

Clients often protest that they are unable to remember everything the homework asks for. They are assured that this is normal, and all that is being asked is their best, most honest, and open effort. They are also given the assignment and encouraged, if possible, to ask those significant people in their history for their input. This assignment not only serves to enhance the history but also to encourage participation of the client's social and support system. Being an open group, members will hear and participate in others' assignments before doing their own and thus gain confidence in their own ability to complete the homework.

The members are not initially given a deadline for completing the assignments but are encouraged to work steadily at their own pace. They are reminded that this is a time-limited group and they are to report any problems with any assignment to the group or the group leader. If the client is not making sufficient effort or progress and the group is unable to intervene, then it is the responsibility of the group leader to intervene individually. Many clients have been through prior treatment programs and consider themselves "treatmentwise." There must be a clear message from the group and the group leader that the client will not be allowed to sit in group for 6 months without an honest effort to participate.

Repeated failure to complete assignments or cursory or incomplete efforts must be addressed, if possible, by the group and definitely by the therapist. Group norms as to the importance and meaning of the work are fragile and can be easily infected by an uncooperative or continually defiant group member. If such a case arises, and neither the group nor the therapist can gain the cooperation of the client, then the client should be discharged with a referral for other treatment and with the attitude that this was not necessarily a treatment failure but rather an inappropriate program for this client at this time.

The client presents each assignment in group for the group's feedback and support. After completion of each assignment, the group leader also needs to process, with the client and the group, what the client found of value in doing the assignment, as well as the client's feelings about it. Other group members are also encouraged to share what they got for themselves out of each presentation. From listening and participating in others' assignments, group members will often identify problems of their own or gain insight into their own past and present life.

The usual set of assignments consists of the following homework interventions.

Assignment 1: Life Goals

The majority of substance abuse treatment, and much of the treatment of serious and chronic mental illness, is "pain" or consequence-based treatment (White & Chaney, 1993). In other words, it is treatment designed to ease symptoms, alleviate pain, or reverse negative consequences. The client is trying to move away from something. If the pain or adverse effects of the mental illness or substance use are sufficiently severe, the client is, or can easily be, motivated to attempt change. The change may, however, be short lived. Once the "pain" is removed, the memory of it and the motivation to maintain changes made often quickly fade, and relapse is all too common a result. This is especially true of dually diagnosed clients, who often have been through chemical dependency programs to treat their substance abuse and mental health treatment for their mental illness but tend to relapse quickly to one or both disorders. Often these clients are not suffering the severe consequences or "pain" on which so many programs are based (Osher & Kofoed, 1989; White & Chaney, 1993). They are often unemployed, unmarried, living in some type of residential or subsidized housing or with parents, and receiving financial benefits through social security or state aid. Thus, the usual social pressures and motivations do not work (Levy, 1993; Osher & Kofoed, 1989). These clients may well be socialized to the client role, or so compensated for their mental illness and substance abuse, that they do not think of the future with any goal or direction, with any dream or fantasy, and with little hope. Thus, these clients are often not highly motivated to change. Why should they be?

This goal of this intervention is to begin to provide a reason for the client to want to change. It is designed to help the client begin to move *toward* something. The intervention consists of three parts. First, the clients are educated in group as to the nature of goals, the benefits of having goals, and how to develop goals for themselves. They are told clearly and explicitly that the purpose of this exercise is not to develop a plan for goals to work on in the group but to develop individual goals or dreams or hopes or fantasies for themselves. The concept of recovery is discussed in terms of not only "moving away" from something but in terms of the essential nature and importance to significant and long-term change of "moving toward" something.

The group members are then given the homework assignment of preparing brief written statements of their goals or direction they would like their lives to take. Each member may do this in any way he or she sees fit. One way that is suggested to the client is to think in terms of the whole-person model (Wegscheider-Cruse, 1989) that he or has become familiar with in the education group. This model is reviewed, and the members are encouraged to identify changes, goals, or direction in several or all areas of the model—physical, mental, emotional, social, volitional, and spiritual. The client is, however, free to go about this exercise in any way he or she feels comfortable. Emphasis is placed on these goals being the client's own, not those the client feels he or she "should" have or those that will please others. It should also be emphasized that these goals can be as simple or as grand as the client wants. The client is encouraged to let his or her imagination or fantasy run free. The only rule is that the goals be something the client would really want for him- or herself. When completed, the client reviews his or her homework with the group for their feedback and support.

Clients often either struggle with this assignment as they state they have never really thought about what they want for themselves or produce a list of superficial, material goals such as a new car, a job, a house, and so on. These goals are fine if they are truly what the client wants. Too often in exploring the basis for said goals, we find that these are goals the clients have been told throughout their life to have or goals they "feel" they should have. Although we agree such things would be nice, we point out to clients that having such goals does not seem to have been working for them. We point this out as possibly being one of the reasons they have not been achieved. In other words, these are someone else's goals. We feel that embedded in such goal lists can be found clues to the client's automatic thoughts and schema. We begin to try and change these by asking the client to answer the questions, "What do I truly want for myself that I'm willing to work hard and make changes for? What do I want and what am I willing to do about it?"

The third part of this intervention is to relax the client in group and to use replacement, or future, imagery (Edwards, 1989; Freeman, Pretzer, Fleming, & Simon, 1990) to help anchor the goals and make it more real to the client. Care and time should be taken to make the new images as detailed and complete as possible. The ease or difficulty each member has with establishing the new images can be a clue as to how important these goals are or how much they are truly the client's own.

Care and time should be taken with this intervention, as it can be the foundation for the client developing motivation for treatment. From our experience, client responses to this assignment and the time spent on it have generally been excellent. Positive comments include "I've never had goals for my life. I've never thought about it. This is good." or "I feel like a new person. I have something to look forward to." or "This was hard and frightening, but I'm glad I did it. It made me think about myself."

This assignment gives the client hope, purpose, and a reason to work. The client is asked to begin working for himself or herself, maybe for the first time in the client's life.

Assignment 2: Substance Use History and Impact on Life

The development of the client's alcohol and drug use history is an important element in moving the client to a change in thinking about the extent and meaning of his or her use (Beck et al., 1993). This homework assignment is done in two parts: a history of use and an examination of consequences and impact. The client is given and completes a history of use before being given the consequences and impact assignment. In the history, the client is instructed to record nothing more than the type of chemical used, the quantity, frequency, and duration of use. What is being looked at are the "facts" of use, not the explanations for the use. The therapist and client are also looking for the development of tolerance and the progression of the use, as well as the pervasiveness of use in the client's life. As the client presents this assignment in group, the therapist must be proactive in maintaining the client on task. The therapist must only allow the client to present what the assignment is asking for. There is a tendency of clients to want to tell the story of the using and the therapist gently prevents this, telling the client he or she will have a chance to describe what went on around the use in the next part of this assignment. This is done not only so that the history is a "factual look in black and white," but also to avoid reinforcing the client's beliefs relating to the justification, blaming, explanation, or even the euphoric recall of the use. Telling the story of the use also tends to fragment the history and lessen its impact.

When given this assignment, clients will often protest that they will not be able to remember all the details. They are encouraged to do the best they can. Helpful suggestions include associating use with different time periods such as high school or work, asking those close to the client how they remember the use, and working on the assignment and putting it aside from time to time and coming back to it. Group members who have already completed the assignment can share their same doubts and how they dealt with the assignment. Each member is also reminded that this is not a graded assignment, and it will not be collected or reviewed by anyone. The only purpose is for the client to gain an understanding, with the help of the group, of his or her patterns of use.

When completed, the client shares his or her assignment with group. This is not done for "confessional" reasons but so that the client can get feedback and support from the group. Members of the group, based on their own experience, will be able to tell whether the client's history and patterns of use ring true or whether the client may be minimizing or otherwise defending his or her use. The client receives feedback and support from the group while at the same time the group is often able to identify with the client and begin to feel less alone or unique in their own history of use. Processing of the client's and the group's feelings about having done the assignment and what the client learned about his or her history of use, as well as what group members may have learned about their own history, completes this intervention. This can be a powerful intervention because it focuses only on the "facts" of the using. Reactions from clients have included "I never realized how my whole life has been tied up with drugs," "I didn't know that I drank so much," and "My whole life has revolved around using."

The second part of this intervention involves the client looking at the results, consequences, and impact of his or her using on different aspects of the client's life. These areas include preoccupation, attempts to control, finances, education, work, home, social activities, emotional health, physical health and appearance, legal, sexual, spiritual, and family and relationships. Again the purpose here is to have the client look at the reality of his or her substance use. The assignment is reviewed in group and the client is asked to describe his or her thoughts about his or her use both before and after doing the assignment. The difference is often dramatic and will probably show clearly in changes in the beliefs inventory, particularly those beliefs relating to denial type: permission-giving thoughts.

This is a very powerful assignment because the affective component of using is being brought into play. The client is looking at the impact his or her substance use has had not only on the client but also those close to him or her. Feelings of guilt, shame, anger, and a whole host of others are usually evoked by this assignment. Bob, a 52-year-old "macho, nobody tells me anything" construction worker wept openly in group. He stated that was the first time he had cried in over 20 years. This is a typical reaction, and group support and feedback is key to helping the client begin to deal with these feelings. The therapist and group point out to the client that this is not an ending but can be a new beginning. Processing of the client's feelings and thoughts about completing this assignment is extremely important to assure client safety.

Assignment 3: Mental Health History and Impact on Life

Too often in dual-diagnosis programs the emphasis is on the substance abuse, and the mental illness part of the dual diagnosis is treated with medication or it is believed that it will get better with sobriety. In this group model, an attempt is made to place equal emphasis on the mental illness. Although it is difficult, if not impossible, to treat a mental illness in the face of continuing substance use, the mental illness must be examined to help clarify the diagnosis, that is, as a coexisting *Diagnosis and Statistical Manual of Mental Disorders* (4th ed., American Psychiatric Association, 1994) diagnosis or as a substance-induced disorder, so that appropriate treatment for the mental illness can be planned and, if possible, begun.

The first part of the mental health history is similar to the substance use history. It is important for the client to list all periods when he or she feels symptoms might have been present, whether or not they were diagnosed or treated. When describing symptoms, for example, depression or anxiety, many clients will state I have "felt this way all my life" or "I have felt this way since I was a teenager." This may begin to help clarify the diagnostic picture as well as possibly provide any indicators for possible personality disorders. This also helps begin to explore the possibility of the client having self-medicated symptoms, the symptoms of mental illness preceding the substance use. Conversely, there may begin to be indications of symptoms being the result of chemical use. A review of the common symptoms of thought disorders, mood disorders, and anxiety disorders from the preceding education phase may be useful. At this time, the severity of the episodes is also rated to help the client identify those periods when the mental illness might have been less severe and possibly minimized or even ignored.

The second part of this assignment, again not given until after the first is completed, looks at how the client sees the mental illness as having affected his or her life. The whole-person model is used as a simple and coherent way of examining impact. The same care and effort is expended by the client, group, and therapist on this assignment as on the substance use history and impact. The same care and support for the client's safety is equally important as the client looks at this part of his or her life.

Assignment 4: Integrating Histories

This intervention builds on the prior assignments and is designed to graphically, as in Exhibit 6.1, show the clients the connection between their substance use and mental illness. It can be a difficult assignment, and

EXHIBIT 6.1
Graph of Substance Abuse and Mental Health History

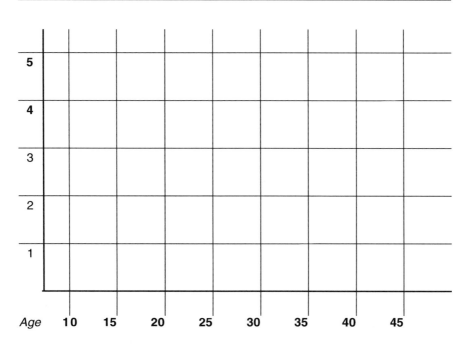

In completing the graph, please follow these instructions carefully. We suggest that you read them over once completely before beginning the assignment.

A. Go back to your substance use history and for each age you listed put a number in the margin next to that age as follows:
    1. No use of any substances
    2. Used any amount of any substance 1 time per week
    3. Used any amount of any substance 2–3 times per week
    4. Used any amount of any substance 4–5 times per week
    5. Used any amount of any substance 6–7 times per week
B. Using a colored pencil or crayon, enter the number (1–5 from the margin) on the above chart above the corresponding age.
C. Using a different colored pencil or crayon, enter the severity ratings from your mental health history above the corresponding age.
D. Please be ready to discuss with the group what you have learned from this about how your mental illness and substance use are related.

extra individual or group time may be necessary to help the clients conceptualize and carry out the assignment. Once completed, however, the graph can present a clear and vivid picture of the relationship between the client's mental illness and substance use.

The client assigns frequency-of-use values to his or her substance use history and then literally graphs the history of use and the severity of the symptoms of his or her mental illness. Frequency of use, rather than quantity, type of substance, or duration, is used for two reasons. First, clients will usually admit to use but may have trouble with quantity or significance of such use. Clients may be vague or may minimize the type of substances or quantities used, and this approach avoids confrontation and defensiveness over such issues. This method of measuring the significance of use also avoids debate as to the significance of quantity or type of substance used (e.g., "two beers never hurt anyone"). Second, many clients may be "exquisitely sensitive" to even small amounts of a substance (Evans & Sullivan, 1990). It is thus important to see the relationship of any use to any symptoms of mental illness.

When this assignment is presented in group, it is critical to evaluate the client's explanation of the correlation between his or her substance use and symptoms. If the client continues to deny a connection between use and symptoms, or offers alternative explanations or beliefs about what the chart shows, then group and therapist feedback, Socratic questioning, or possibly even direct confrontation may play an important role in helping the client confront the reality and acceptance of his or her dual diagnoses and alter any irrational thoughts the client may have about himself or herself and his or her condition.

Assignment 5: Advantages–Disadvantages Analysis

The client is told he or she now has a fairly accurate and complete picture of his or her substance use, mental illness, and the impact both have had on all aspects the client's life. The client is then assigned the task of identifying the advantages and disadvantages (Beck et al., 1993; Freeman et al., 1990) of being mentally ill and not being mentally ill as well as the advantages and disadvantages of using and not using substances. The therapist and group need pay particular attention to the client being able to identify both advantages and disadvantages in each part of the matrix. The client is asked to discuss with the group his or her overall evaluation and weighing of the value to continuing use and to treatment of symptoms.

Assignment 6: Treatment Plan

With the assistance of the therapist, alternative treatment plans are reviewed with the client. These may range from doing nothing to intensive inpatient treatment. Often by the time the clients arrive at this stage of the group, they may have already begun to make changes. Often substance use has been decreased or eliminated, symptoms may be better managed, and other life changes may be under way. Clients may at this point declare that they have "learned so much" about themselves and "become aware of things" they never realized that any further treatment is not necessary. They may believe that knowledge and will are going to be enough for them to quit using and get well. It is crucial that the therapist not allow this thinking to go unchallenged. The client has been educated on treatment and recovery, as well as relapse, and this information should be reviewed. The client is told that treatment will help with the skills to implement his or her decision and commitment to recovery and growth, improve the client's chances to get better, help prevent relapse, and most important of all help the client reach his or her own goals.

If the client is still reluctant to commit to treatment, he or she may be directed to seek others who have successfully dealt with similar problems and identify what they did and what worked or did not work for them. If the client states he does not know where to find such people, the client can, if available, be referred to former clients and is also told that such people can be found at open meetings of groups such as Dual Diagnosis Anonymous, Alcoholics Anonymous, Depressive/Manic–Depressive Association, or other similar and appropriate groups. The client is asked to attend several of these meetings with an investigative attitude and to report back to the group his or her findings.

The client then is asked to prepare a written treatment plan for what he or she is going to do next. This plan is reviewed with group for its feedback. The therapist then helps the client to terminate with the group, reviewing what the client has learned, changes in beliefs, feelings about the group, his or her experience in it, and feelings about leaving. The group also shares what it has learned from the client and their feelings, hopes, and fears about the client's leaving.

Progress Through Treatment

Group members are allowed to complete the assignments at a pace comfortable to themselves. The client is, however, reminded that this is a time-limited group and may need to be monitored and encouraged to maintain progress. As many of these clients are not used to organizing themselves or their activities, or used to meeting deadlines or keeping commitments, group or individual intervention may be needed to help keep the client on track. If the client appears to being making a sincere effort to complete the work, then extensions to the time limit may be given, preferably in discrete increments, possibly related to each assignment that needs to be completed. For most members, 6 months is sufficient time to complete the work.

It happens from time to time that individuals or the entire group begin to lag behind on completing homework assignments. A questionnaire, such as that suggested by Beck, Newman, and Liese (1993) or Burns (1993), on reasons why the client is not completing their assignment can be used with positive results. It not only helps to address the issues of not doing homework but also does so in a somewhat lighthearted way. It is useful as both an individual and a group exercise. When used in group, the questionnaire is passed out at the beginning of the group and the members are given 10 minutes or so to fill it out. The questionnaires are not collected in this case, but the answers are noted for each member and then tallied for the group. The reasons tallied will typically, we have noted, tend to cluster into a few reasons. The group can then do some problem solving or goal setting or whatever it needs to address the identified reasons for not getting homework assignments done and get back on track. Compliance almost inevitably goes up after completing this task.

It is important to track the client's progress through treatment. A useful tool for this is a beliefs inventory (Beck et al., 1993). This instrument could be filled out by the client at the beginning of treatment and at regular intervals during treatment. The results can be reviewed with the client and individual interventions developed to address any persistent maladaptive beliefs or errors in thinking. The ultimate measure of progress, of course, is whether or not the client engages in treatment and develops and is motivated to commit to the plan he or she develops for the next phase of treatment.

Structure of the Group Session

Structuring the group session is an essential element of the cognitive model. Structuring each group session allows for the maximum use of time, focuses the session on the tasks at hand, creates a working atmosphere, and helps maintain continuity from session to session (Beck et al., 1993). Although the focus and majority of the time spent in group should be used for completing the assignments, some time at the end of group can be allocated for group members to discuss any crisis or serious problems they feel they need immediate help with. This should be reserved for the end of group because substance abusers can often present large amounts of material on long-standing and ongoing problems as well as often seemingly constant and acute crisis.

> **Situation 1:** A.O., a young male client, brought to the floor a situation he had to face later in the day, which he felt he could not go through without getting high: "My baby daughter is in the hospital real sick and I have to go see her. My girlfriend's family doesn't like me, and

they will be looking at me all mean. The baby will be crying, and I have no idea what to do. The only way I can go is if I am high."

With group encouragement, he was able to identify a number of automatic thoughts associated with going: "I am a bad father because I don't work," "I have nothing to offer my daughter or girlfriend," "My girlfriend's family thinks I am a bum," and "I feel helpless when the baby cries, and there is nothing I can do for her."

The group then helped A.O. compile a list of things he could do when he went to visit: (a) offer his girlfriend some relief to take a break; (b) bring her a cup of coffee; (c) talk to the baby and softly soothe her; and (d) introduce himself to the nurse or doctor and get information on the baby's condition.

The group leader then guided him through imagining himself going sober and doing the things suggested. Next, A.O. role-played interacting with his girlfriend, her family, and the doctor with other group members. At the next meeting, he reported he had followed through with the plan and had not used drugs.

Cognitive–behavioral techniques can be learned and used to intervene between the stimulation and the craving, or between the craving and the actual using, to stop the addictive cycle. Some useful intervention techniques include using the daily thought record to monitor automatic thoughts and identify underlying beliefs (Beck et al., 1993, pp. 143–145), activity monitoring and scheduling, listing the advantages and disadvantages of using and not using, identifying and learning new ways of feeling good, role playing, and using imagery to distract or to imagine having self-control (Edwards, 1989).

> **Situation 2:** A young man, C.W., who is schizophrenic and has a serious cocaine abuse problem, is in danger of losing his current living situation at a transitional housing program if he comes in high again. He is intelligent, but uncomfortable around other people, and he usually problem-solves by himself without asking for help. He was given a homework assignment the week before to track the times and situations when he felt like using, rate how strong the craving was on a scale of 1 to 10, and identify his automatic thoughts. C.W. has been faithful about doing his assignments in the past.
>
> C.W: "I was feeling pretty good, it was Friday afternoon and I hadn't used for 2 weeks. I said to myself that I deserved to have a good time because I had been good. It was a medium craving, about a 5. I looked at my disadvantage-versus-advantage to using card, and I decided not to use because I might end up homeless, but I don't know about next time."
>
> The group explored with C.W. what other ways he could reward himself for being good. It was very hard for him to come up with any ideas, but he finally was able to identify these few things: (a) play a video game by himself; (b) buy himself some snacks if he has money; and (c) play basketball or go to the gym to work out. He wrote these

items on an index card and agreed to refer to them next time he felt like using. Further exploration revealed his underlying beliefs were, "I have never succeeded at anything and I never will" and "I am a loser." He is doing ongoing work on these mistaken beliefs.

The therapist must balance the need to use the group time for the purposes and goals of the group and to deal with those situations that truly present a danger to the client or others or that are impeding the client's ability to make progress. A suggested structure for a typical group session might be the following:

1. Client check-in	Mood check
	Status of assignments
	Substance use during week
	Time needed at end of group
2. Setting the agenda	Therapist and clients agree on session agenda
3. Homework assignments	Presentation and feedback
4. Individual's issues	As time permits or as needed
5. Summary and feedback	Both in session and group

CONCLUSION

Currently, very few truly integrated programs for dually diagnosed clients are available or funded (Kaufman & McNaul, 1992; Minkoff, 1994), and because of the chronic nature of mental illness and substance dependence, most individuals will end up in the public sector, most often in a local community mental health center, for treatment. It is therefore important for community mental health centers to develop programs that will accept rather than reject these dually diagnosed clients and treat the co-existing problems. The program should (a) have staff familiar with both mental illness and substance abuse treatments and (b) provide ongoing staff training with a specific theoretical focus that includes exploring underlying beliefs about mental illness and substance abuse.

Clients with diagnoses of mental illness and substance abuse or dependency present a complex and difficult challenge for the therapist. Difficulties in treatment and treatment failures too often result from the client not being sufficiently motivated for change and fully engaged in the treatment process. Although mental illness and substance disorders involve physical, emotional, and environmental factors that must not be minimized, it is the client's maladaptive cognitions that are often the barrier to a willingness to attempt change. The model of group therapy presented in this chapter focuses on these cognitive issues and attempts to help the client change his or her beliefs and thoughts about himself or herself, his or her world, and his or her future, and to become invested in the possibility of change and the willingness to work at it. Using cognitive–behavioral techniques in a secure group atmosphere can be an effective model that allows for maximum learning to take place that can be transferred to the larger world.

Working with the dually diagnosed client takes patience and an ability to appreciate small improvements, without being discouraged by setbacks. The cognitive–behavioral model allows for a structured focus so that improvements can be identified and measured. It is also important for the therapist to continually be aware of his or her own thoughts and underlying beliefs that affect working with these clients and to maintain a belief that dually diagnosed clients can and do heal.

REFERENCES

American Psychiatric Association. (1994). *Diagnostic and statistical manual of mental disorders* (4th ed.). Washington, DC: Author.

Beck, A. T., Freeman, A., & Associates. (Eds.). (1990). *Cognitive therapy of personality disorders.* New York: Guilford Press.

Beck, A., Wright, F., Newman, C., & Liese, B. (1993). *Cognitive therapy of substance abuse.* New York: Guilford Press.

Brown, V. B., Ridgely, M. S., Pepper, B., Levine, I. S., & Ryglewicz, H. (1989). The dual crisis: Mental illness and substance abuse. *American Psychologist, 44,* 565–569.

Burns, D. (1993). *Ten days to self-esteem.* New York: Quill William Morrow.

Cohen, J., & Levy, J. (1992). *The mentally ill chemical abuser; whose client?* New York: Lexington Books.

Drake R. E., McHugo, G. L., & Noordsy, D. L. (1993). Treatment of alcoholism among schizophrenic outpatients: 4-year outcomes. *American Journal of Psychiatry, 150,* 328–329.

Drake, R., Muesser, K., Clark, R., & Wallach, M. (1996). The course, treatment, and outcome of substance disorder in persons with severe mental illness. *American Journal of Orthopsychiatry, 66,* 42–51.

Edwards, D. (1989). Cognitive restructuring through guided imagery: Lessons from gestalt therapy. In A. Freeman, K. Simon, L. Beutler, & H. Arkowitz (Eds.), *Comprehensive handbook of cognitive therapy* (pp. 283–297). New York: Plenum Press.

Evans, K., & Sullivan, J. (1990). *Dual diagnosis.* New York: Guilford Press.

Flores, P. (1988). *Group psychotherapy with addicted populations*. New York: Haworth Press.

Freeman, A., Pretzer, J., Fleming, B., & Simon, K. (1990). *Clinical applications of cognitive therapy*. New York: Plenum Press.

Goldsmith, R. J. (1992). The essential features of alcohol and drug treatment. *Psychiatric Annals, 22,* 419–424.

Goldsmith, R. J., & Miller, N. S. (1994). Training psychiatric residents in the addictions. *Psychiatric Annals, 24,* 432–439.

Kalmus, J. (1996, March). *Dual diagnosis.* Paper presented at the annual conference of the Illinois Alcohol and Drug Abuse Professional Counselor Association, Arlington Heights, IL.

Kaplan, H. I., & Sadock, B. J. (1991). *Synopsis of psychiatry* (6th ed.). Baltimore: Williams & Williams.

Kaufman, E., & McNaul, J. P. (1992). Recent developments in understanding and treating drug abuse and dependence. *Hospital and Community Psychiatry, 43,* 223–235.

Lehman, A. (1996). Heterogeneity of person and place: Assessing co-occurring addictive and mental disorders. *American Journal of Orthopsychiatry, 66,* 32–41.

Levy, M. (1993). Psychotherapy with dual diagnosis patients: Working with denial. *Journal of Substance Abuse Treatment, 10,* 499–504.

Marlatt, G. (1985). Cognitive factors in the relapse process. In G. Marlatt & J. Gordon (Eds.), *Relapse prevention* (pp. 128–200). New York: Guilford Press

Miller, N. (1994). Prevalence and treatment models for addiction in psychiatric populations. *Psychiatric Annals, 24,* 399–406.

Miller, N., Erikson, A., & Owley, T. (1994). Psychosis and schizophrenia in alcohol and drug dependence. *Psychiatric Annals, 24,* 418–423.

Miller, W., & Rollnick, S. (1991). *Motivational interviewing: Preparing people to change addictive behavior*. New York: Guilford Press.

Minkoff, K. (1994). Models for addiction treatment in psychiatric populations. *Psychiatric Annals, 24,* 412–417.

Osher, F., & Kofoed, L. (1989). Treatment of patients with psychiatric and psychoactive substance abuse disorders. *Hospital and Community Psychiatry, 40,* 1025–1030.

Regier, D., Farmer, M., Rae, D., Locke, B., Keith, S., Judd, L., & Goodwin, F. (1990). Comorbidity of mental disorders with alcohol and other drug abuse: Results from the Epidemiologic Catchment Area (ECA) study. *Journal of the American Medical Association, 264,* 2511–2518.

Wegscheider-Cruse, S. (1989). *Another chance* (2nd ed.). Palo Alto, CA: Science and Behavior Books.

Weiss, R., Mirin, S., & Frances, R. (1992). The myth of the typical dual diagnosis patient. *Hospital and Community Psychiatry, 43,* 107–108.

Wessler, R., & Hankin Wessler, S. (1989). Cognitive group therapy. In A. Freeman, K. Simon, L. Beutler, & H. Arkowitz (Eds.), *Comprehensive handbook of cognitive therapy* (pp. 559–582). New York: Plenum Press.

White, W., & Chaney, R. (1993). *Metaphors of transformation: Feminine and masculine* [Monograph]. Bloomington, IL: Lighthouse Training Institute.

7

DISSOCIATIVE DISORDERS

AILA JESSE McCUTCHEN

Clients with dissociative disorders are a subgroup of trauma survivors that are particularity difficult to treat because of the pervasiveness of their symptoms and a world view that fixes them rigidly in dysfunctional life patterns. Dissociative clients must be helped to address the beliefs and assumptions that are problematic in their lives in addition to other aspects of treatment: symptom management, coping strategies, social skills, and medication. A major dimension in cognitive therapy is to challenge fixed, pathological beliefs and assumptions about oneself, others, and the future. A fundamental premise of this chapter is that this dimension must be an integral part of the treatment of dissociative clients, a feature that is lacking in other treatment models. If it is not, the result is likely to be treatment frustration, conflict, and even failure. Aaron T. Beck's (1979) cognitive model of treatment provides the foundation for the group approach described here. It is an approach that operates on the premise that life changes are brought about by changing beliefs.

THE CHAPTER FORMAT

Cognitive therapy is a treatment model that has proved useful in the treatment of a variety of Axis I and Axis II disorders. Its effectiveness has been shown in numerous controlled clinical trials, and it is currently probably the most researched psychotherapy model. The cognitive model of psychotherapy provides the basis for the group model described here, a group designed specifically for clients with dissociative disorders. It will be referred to in this chapter as the *Cognitive (CT) group model*. Although no formal clinical trial has been conducted with the CT group model, clients use scales and measures weekly that indicate improvement. A feedback form at termination also indicates improvement and satisfaction.

The CT group model is presented as a two-level model. Level 1 is a symptom-focused model for acute, actively dissociative inpatients, and this chapter describes its initial conceptualization and purposes. Level 2 is a second model built on the foundations of the first to allow work toward new objectives as group members' skills and abilities increase. Level 2 of the model assumes a degree of symptom control and is described in greater detail. It has more flexibility as well as higher expectations of its members.

Consistent with the basic elements of the cognitive model, this cognitive group model is helpful to clients with dissociative disorders in three basic ways:

1. The general treatment approach of the group therapy protocol is structured, systematic, measurable, and educative.
2. The protocol contains specific interventions and strategies that motivate clients to observe and assess their perceptions.
3. It teaches skills that improve clients' interpersonal connection and increase satisfaction about their own resourcefulness and competency.

Both the general structures and the specific interventions are outlined in this chapter. The rationale for these structures and interventions are given to group members and are discussed through the course of this chapter. The effects and reactions of the group members are described, and other comments, observations, and questions are raised.

To clarify why the CT group model is particularly helpful for clients with dissociative disorders, I give a description of the developmental context of this type of client. The description is a composite of childhood experiences reported by dissociative clients and provides a link to the pervasive and rigidly held beliefs and assumptions that they hold in their current lives. These beliefs and assumptions help dissociative clients make sense of the world, but in pathological ways that lock them into cycles that actually replicate the contexts from which they come. Examples of these are given throughout the chapter.

This chapter also proposes principles of treatment to serve as guidelines for the group leader. These principles were developed as a result of my reflections about, and also grappling with, the disorientation and fragmentation that can occur in treatment for both the clients and group leader. These principles are shared with the clients in developing the group culture and provide some of the rationales for specific interventions.

Thus, the following is a summary of the format of this chapter. The CT group model is described as having two levels: one for more symptomatic (acute inpatient) and the other for less symptomatic (partial or outpatient) group members. There is a description of the developmental contexts of clients with dissociative disorders that links their history to their beliefs and symptoms. I also provide an outline of therapist principles designed to help keep the treatment on course. Two major learning tools are illustrated—one for helping clients understand their perceptions, the other for indentifying patterns of perceptions. These are comments about the nature of these beliefs and assumptions underlying these patterns. Finally clinical observations are given about issues raised in the group.

COGNITIVE GROUP THERAPY: ORIGIN OF THE MODEL

I received postdoctoral training in cognitive therapy at the Center for Cognitive Therapy in Philadelphia, Pennsylvania, and used this approach as a staff psychotherapist working with trauma survivors on a specialty inpatient unit. The work involved treating individual patients daily and leading psychotherapy groups. It was here that this particular group model originated. At the time, having trauma survivors in inpatient groups was difficult for patients and group leaders, with a high probability of emotional extremes and disruptive behavior sometimes ending in the need for restraints. Groups rarely began or ended calmly. There had to be two group leaders: one to attend to whatever acuity might erupt on an individual level, and the other to try to keep the group going. In the treatment of these trauma survivors, there was ongoing staff controversy as to whether or not dissociative states were a part of the process of working through traumatic events and should be permitted because not doing so would invalidate the patients' reality. Many staff and patients felt that working within the dissociative states was beneficial, and that expecting self-control could be perceived as punitive and could not only block the healing process but also create an adversarial relationship between patients and staff. There was an ongoing tension posed by the conviction of some staff that dissociative states (which often included behavioral acting out) were part of a healing process, and the equally strong conviction among other staff that dissociation caused too much chaos and disturbance to the unit and its group program.

Having come to understand the benefits of cognitive therapy approaches involving self-observation, symptom control, and small experiments in self-improvement, I requested forming a twice-weekly group directed specifically toward helping dissociative patients (a) control symptom acuity and (b) participate (i.e. communicate verbally with each other). The group goals could be expanded once stability and participation became a part of the group's culture. This did happen over time as inpatient and partial programs became more accepting of cognitive therapy. In these later groups, patients were encouraged to look beyond the traumatic events to examine the lessons they drew from these events. This was based on the premise that it is not the events themselves, but the individual beliefs and assumptions generated by these events, that eventually interfere with the dissociative patients' functioning and the quality of their lives. In all cases, symptom stability (i.e., a minimum of dissociation) was requested of group members and was carefully monitored in each group session.

COGNITIVE GROUP THERAPY: LEVEL 1

At the beginning, as far as the unit staff was concerned, the group's purpose was to keep acutely distressed trauma patients together and in one place for 45 to 50 minutes: to keep them contained, to keep them as calm as possible, and to prevent them from harming themselves or each other. The dissociative acuity of these patients took a variety of forms: deep trance, alteration of identity, flashbacks, uniquely perceived images, lost time, unusual gestures, and self-harming activities, such as scratching, head-banging, or hitting, to name a few. The onset of a dissociative episode could be completely unpredictable. It could become violent, and it was contagious. As noted earlier, much of the individual treatment at that time consisted of working with trauma survivors in their dissociative states. It was clear, however, that the best way to accomplish the group's goal (the experience of being contained, calm, and connected) was to help these severely dissociative patients become "grounded" (focused and present in the here-and-now and not in a dissociative state) as soon as possible and to stay that way for the duration of the group. The idea of getting something of value from the group and giving something to the group ultimately became a question in the screening process. A basic premise of this first group was that only by not dissociating could members be expected to get something from and give something to each other. Another premise was that self-assessment of symptom acuity from group candidates empowered patients to speak for themselves, taught them a first step in self-observation, and also taught them a first step in the collaborative process of cooperating with other group members. Hence, this group of patients with dissociative disorders, called the "multiples" by patients (referring to the dramatic dissociative episodes experienced among this diagnostic group), had *not dissociating/being nondissociative* as the primary ground rule for membership. Dissociation was defined by the group leader to group members as a disruptive, trauma-derived symptom, which had little usefulness in the current lives of the patients and which could actually make their lives worse instead of better. It was added that dissociation prevented people from connecting with each other, and connection was something we all wanted to accomplish in the group. Group members were able to accept this rule for the purposes of this one group, despite the sense of belonging that dissociation fostered in a different way on the unit, and despite the relief from anxiety that dissociation could sometimes provide.

The group differs from many of the psychodynamically oriented groups typically found in inpatient disorder units in the following ways:

1. The leader explains the goals and process of the group.
2. The leader is directive in facilitating the group.
3. The group process is structured.
4. A dry erase board is used to diagram and link experiences.
5. Members are responsible for their own symptom assessment and control.
6. Members are expected to participate by verbal communication.
7. Psychoeducation is a part of the group process.
8. Members give feedback to each other and the leader during and at the end of the group session.

Through the gradual addition of other cognitive therapy principles and strategies to the basic group culture, the group evolved from its initial symptom-focused inpatient format to become an outpatient group whose members were able to commit to the containment of their dissociative symptoms while they addressed painful beliefs, made reference to traumatic experiences, and reported no increase in acuity between group sessions. Being able to contain symptoms freed patients up to examine their perceptions of daily events and identify patterns of beliefs that perpetuated dysfunction in their lives. Symptom containment also permitted patients to experience a degree of consistency with each other with increased confidence in their interactions.

Screening for Level 1

Screening is a simple process, often done while passing by a patient in the unit hallway. It goes as follows: "There is a group you might be interested in joining. It's for people who are dissociative. For the stability of the group, and for the benefit of other members, we ask that people who come in to the group stay present." Then the principal question was asked, "Do you feel you can make it through the group without dissociating (or leaving us, or going away from us)?" In essence, patients desiring to join the group are asked to make a decision prior to coming in as to whether or not they could be nondissociative after the group started. If they want to join the group, the options are that they can come in and try to remain nondissociative; they can leave if they have too much difficulty being non-dissociative; or they can choose not to come in. Patients are asked to make their own assessment of their level of acuity.

The group is elective; no one is required to join. Patients are discouraged from joining if, for example, they are actively self-destructive or if they report that control has been taken over by a hostile alter. If a patient feels that they have no self-control, the patient is asked to wait until they feel more stable before joining.

Group Members and Their Reasons for Joining

The patients who came to the original Level 1 group were all women, all trauma survivors, between 16 and 50 years old, with a variety of overlapping diagnoses: posttraumatic stress disorder, multiple personality disorder, dissociative disorder not otherwise specified, borderline personality disorder, eating disorders, the addictions, somatic problems, and others. Most of them exhibited some form of dissociative phenomena or what appeared to be dissociative phenomena. The manifestation of dissociative symptoms was always taken at face value. The leader did not attempt to question how real the episode was. In the beginning, this group was known as the "multiples group" because of the fact that the most symptomatic patients were referred to it, and on the trauma unit, these were women who were dissociative. Many of these women had been diagnosed or were self-reported as having multiple personality disorder. When the patients learned there was going to be a new group especially for "multiples," they wanted to join for a variety of reasons. One was that if a patient was dissociative, the patient might fit in with some of the more high-profile, interesting, and likable patients on the unit. Another was curiosity about some "special thing" going on in this group that other groups were not doing. Some patients wanted to join because they wanted to stop dissociating. Others hoped that this was a group where the "little ones" could come out and play together. Most went to the group because it was part of the inpatient therapy program, which they hoped would help. Patients joined other unit groups such as Journaling Group, Coping Group, Trauma Group, Creativity Group also to get help, even though help was of limited value if symptoms were too acute. The CT group, however, focused on the symptom, rather than on a topic or task that was constantly interrupted by the symptom. Removing dissociation from the group was a new idea, and patients were at the very least curious to see what the group was like. Once in the group, the benefits of "being an adult" and putting their daily experiences into words, as well as being responded to by other members struggling to do the same, were reinforcing and gave a sense of mastery and interpersonal connection to new members. This was not to say that the group process flowed smoothly. No group session, however, was disbanded or dissolved because of dissociative episodes.

Level 1 Session Structure

The Level 1 group model is a twice-weekly group, with new members coming in and others being discharged. The size of the group can range from 2 to 12 women and lasts for 50 minutes, with a 5-minute late stipulation. There is one group leader. Some aspects of the structure and process are consistent with other group psychotherapy models but most are quite different. The structure for this group actually follows the standard CT individual session structure:

- Introduction: welcome, rules, procedures
- Introduction of members and agenda-setting
- Group discussion
- Feedback from members
- Feedback from group leader

Because of the high turnover in the group, and because of symptom instability, no scales, measures, or feedback forms were given to members in the original Level 1 CT group.

Introduction to the Group

The group may be introduced as follows:

I want to welcome everyone to the group, which is a group for people with dissociative disorders. I am _____, and I meet with the group twice a week. I see people who have been in the group before, and some new faces. I will ask people to say their name and briefly what they hope to get from the group today. For the sake of the newcomers, and as a reminder to the older members so that we're all on the same wavelength, the purpose of the group is to address concerns any of you may have about the management of dissociative symptoms as well as any concerns you may have as to how those symptoms interfere with your lives. In order to best communicate with each other about these issues, everyone is asked to try to stay present in the group, and not dissociate. If anyone finds that too difficult, it's perfectly all right to leave and seek staff help—just let the group know why you're leaving, where you're going, and if you'll be coming back. We encourage anyone who thinks someone may be dissociating to ask the person, because sometimes it's hard to know. We also encourage anyone who is getting triggered by another member to let that person know. And lastly, although our main topic has mostly to do with problems you're having with dissociation, we also like to hear when anyone has made any breakthroughs or successes in dealing with it. We urge everyone to make some contribution, because we learn best by input and feedback from each other.

This welcome and introduction is for the purpose of letting group members watch each other and size up the group leader before having to be conspicuous or on the spot themselves. Orienting members to the group culture, providing an explanation of the group's purposes, and setting forth expectations of group members in this way was intended to be both collaborative and psychoeducational, two important components of cognitive therapy.

Introduction of Members and Agenda-Setting

Each group member is asked to introduce herself and to say what she wanted to get from the group that day. Those who say "I just want to listen" are told that it is all right to only listen but that it is important to try to participate by saying something if they can. Members are urged to use the group actively, and the group leader makes suggestions about how more reluctant members might participate based on familiarity with them, observations from the previous groups, and general themes on the unit. Patients are requested to discuss their own problems and issues and to ask for input from the group. Struggles with mental health professionals or unit staff are not seen as topics the group members can adequately address except in terms of how any individual might manage her own personal reactions appropriately. The leader does a quick triage of topics and sets priorities, first proposing what the group might address and asking if that meets with the group's approval. Any adjustments based on group member input are then addressed. These topics most frequently pertain to managing flashbacks, recognizing triggers, dealing with dangerous alters and internal alter battles, and coping with the scariness of dissociative symptoms, but there are also topics about how painful and hopeless life can be as a dissociative person. Topics felt not to be useful to the group's purposes are descriptions of traumatic experiences, personal issues with staff, or frustration with the hospital. This introduction and agenda-setting takes about 10 minutes.

The CT basis for this introduction and agenda-setting is the building of a collaborative culture that includes everyone, activates them to participate, provides some psychoeducation, and establishes an expectation that their stated needs deserve to be addressed by all members as a group.

Group Discussion

Because of the high levels of acuity, the group discussion is kept simple, concrete, and low key. Group members are encouraged to engage with each other in minimal ways. Helping them to make eye contact, nod in agreement, or take initiative by saying things such as "I agree" or "Yes, me too" requires considerable activity on the part of the group leader, who must guide members through these small steps in interpersonal outreach. Group members are encouraged to have different points of view and even to disagree—with each other and with the group leader. It is difficult to accomplish this with such variable symptom stability, but it does happen. As noted above, traumatic events should not be discussed, although for some reason in the early stages of Level 1 group formation, the reputation of the group was that you can "say anything." It may be that trying to stay nondissociated while talking about their lives in the here-and-now and tolerating affects generated in the discussions, as well as engaging in strategies of interpersonal outreach, made them feel vulnerable in a way that dissociating did not.

Because of the high propensity of members to dissociate, the topic of dissociation is alluded to frequently. In the context of the Level 1 group, dissociation is seen as a problem that gets in the way of the group's progress. If a group member appears to be dissociative, the group leader may ask if the member is still present and connected to the group. Other members are also encouraged to ask if someone is dissociating. The assumption is that dissociation can creep up and take hold suddenly, sometimes without a member's awareness. It can help to remind group members to check in with themselves. Encouraging members to do this helps them share their perceptions with each other and question these perceptions. Both the basic symptom management and perceptual verifications, as well as activating group members to collaborate with each other in the group, are based on the CT model.

Feedback and Closure From Members

Ten minutes before the group ends, the leader brings the discussion to a close, deferring unfinished portions to the next meeting. The leader asks each member to state briefly what from the group has been useful: "I'd like for each of you to say just one thing about what you got from the group today—something you learned about yourself, or someone else, or an idea or way of looking at things that hadn't occurred to you before now." The feedback statements may range from "I learned I could stay in a group" or "I said something" to "I feel closer to people when I don't dissociate" or "I used to be afraid of _____, but now I think we have a lot in common" or "I always thought when I dissociated, it was because of real danger. Now, I'm not so sure."

The CT basis for the request for feedback is to help patients learn how to participate, to give them practice in describing a positive experience, to promote the idea that perceptions can be changed, and to demonstrate that topics of discussion can contain more than one point of view.

Feedback From Group Leader

After the group member feedback, the leader makes summarizing statements about the group discussion, and then gives observations about each member and the efforts or contributions the member has made in the group. These include such tasks as trying to stay present, making an effort to connect, helping each other, and even disagreeing with the leader so that members experience being perceived not only as a working, collaborative unit but also as individuals with particular contributions for the group.

This is in keeping with the cognitive therapist's role of acknowledging strengths, encouraging effort, and promoting balance, tolerance, and consistency in the interpersonal process.

The Focus on Dissociative Symptoms

Dissociation is one of the most disturbing and disruptive symptoms that clients experience, with reports of experiences resembling mania, psychosis, and paralyzing fear, to name a few. It is generally considered by clinicians and clients to be a mechanism that permits a type of escape from intolerable events in childhood, but it can reappear in adulthood as an uncontrollable and disruptive phenomenon. At best, dissociation removes a client from feelings, physical pain, and thoughts and images evocative of previous trauma. At worst, it undermines self-efficacy, interferes with learning, promotes isolation and fear, and even recaptures the experience of traumatic events. All forms of dissociation, whatever the trigger or the outcome, ultimately interfere with functioning and the assessment of reality. The mechanism that helps to maintain a sense of continuity and consistency in the developmental years destroys this continuity and consistency in adulthood. Further, anyone dissociative since childhood has missed important moments in learning and experience. This adds to existing helplessness, uncertainty, and hopelessness.

Despite the negative consequences of dissociation, many clients do not view their dissociative episodes in this light. Instead, they commonly assume that dissociation is positive in that it temporarily removes them from uncomfortable feelings or situations. An important part of the group leader's role is to propose to clients that although they do get some immediate relief through dissociation, the costs are high, and the dissociative states themselves may create additional problems in their lives. One of the goals of the group is to help group members replace dissociation with more adaptive coping mechanisms for negotiating with the rest of the world.

Contextual Similarities of Dissociative Patients

There are certain common factors in the childhood contexts of dissociative clients that generate dissociative symptoms. The degree and pervasiveness of these environmental factors and the individual experiences of children living in them result in various forms of maladaptive functioning. The group leader must be alert to when this is replicated in group members' lives and in the microcosm of the group sessions. In keeping with the CT group culture of focusing on the here-and-now, these phenomena are identified and normalized in the group in terms of how likely one is to respond to familiarly perceived events in familiar ways. Reference is made to historic relevance, and an opportunity is offered for assessing the similarity between present and past. The following are some of the common childhood factors experienced by people with dissociative disorders.

1. Chaotic Events. There is usually disorder, disorganization, and unpredictability in the dissociative person's family or neighborhood. There is little or no continuity in routine, such as the scheduling of meals, health care, or bedtime. Alcoholism and other addictions, as well as financial difficulties of parents, add to the chaos and unpredictability and perpetuate this chaos intergenerationally. Group members often report similar events in their current lives and react in ways that actually contribute to the chaos. Even minor inconveniences (such as an electricity outage or the noisy refurbishing of a building next door) may be magnified or taken personally and reacted to in ways that increase stress rather than resolve it.

2. Erratic Relationships. Primary adult figures may leave or enter the developmental picture impulsively or unpredictably. Dissociative clients may have had multiple caregivers of varying ages and uneven ability to take competent charge. Carelessness, inattention, loss, abandonment, and rejection all may be experienced under these circumstances. An example of this phenomenon in the group may occur when group members become overinvolved with strangers or each other in an attempt to have relationships. Their expectations may be too high as they idealize or, conversely, devalue spouses, friends, or each other. They become too engaged or remain disengaged out of fear of being hurt. They will abandon a friend so as not to be abandoned.

3. Nonvalidation of Experience. Overwhelmed parents or caregivers may be unable or unwilling to see things from a child's point of view. Mothers afraid to be without a partner will tolerate their partner's mistreatment of themselves and their children to maintain the illusion of a family unit. Children's questions, fears, or reports of harm may be denied or discounted. Group members often question the validity of their experiences, saying they may be making it all up or calling themselves "liars" or "bad." As one member said, "If I say something, that means it's true. But that would be scary, and besides, other people might not believe me. And if anyone doesn't believe me, it's not true."

4. Pathological Attachments. Parents may be dependent on their children and use them as sounding boards, as idealized figures, or as extensions of themselves for proving excellence or strengths. The expectations generated can give too much or too little power to a child. Children may become helpless and immobilized in the face of adult demands. Deference to others, out of the conviction that other people's needs are more pressing than their own, is a common problem experienced by CT group members.

5. Violation of Personal and Role Boundaries. Role boundaries as well as physical boundaries are clouded for children in divided or stressed homes. Anger, guilt, and shame often result from the confusion that arises when a child is asked to be or do something too difficult or too uncomfortable. Group members report being unable, or they are sure they would be unable, to defend themselves (even as adults) from unwanted touch. Even when they successfully defend themselves, they feel responsible for having caused the situation. Members may inappropriately confide in or overreact negatively to what may be age-appropriate childishness in their own children.

6. Confusion in Communication. There may be mixed messages about expectations or problems understanding instructions that, for a child in certain contexts, can result in punishment or mockery. Children have difficulty explaining themselves, especially if they fear the adult's reaction. Group members prefer to remain silent rather than risk saying the wrong thing and harming or offending someone else. They often preface remarks with, "This sounds dumb, but . . ."

These are the social environments that produce trauma for children, with resulting posttraumatic stress, and the dissociation addressed in this chapter. These social contexts are perpetuated throughout the adult life of the dissociative client: The dissociative symptoms that blunt, change, or significantly alter the experience of the child who is trying to adjust to overwhelming contexts are symptoms that, combined with other factors, recreate those contexts in adulthood.

Advantages and Disadvantages of Dissociation

As mentioned earlier, clients may perceive benefits to dissociative states, and validating the temporary nature of these benefits can help them to feel understood. At the same time, the disadvantages need to be made overt, so that clients are motivated to substitute other coping mechanisms for dissociation. The following outlines the advantages and disadvantages that are often discussed in group.

1. A Familiar Reaction. A benefit of dissociation for group members, therefore, is that it is a familiar reaction to familiar circumstances. Knowing that dissociation will serve as an insulation from triggering situations can be reassuring, even comforting to a dissociative client. The down side is that this same insulation prevents access to personal resources that might otherwise be available for dealing with them. It may also increase the risk to safety because it increases a sense of helplessness.

2. A Shared Identity. Another benefit is the shared identity generated around the symptom of dissociation. A traumatic history and the symptoms that result (including dissociation) often create deep fear and suspiciousness of other people. This results in profound isolation and avoidance of social contact for most group members. They nonetheless experience a sense of belonging with each other because they do dissociate. There is a shared assumption among many dissociative clients that dissociation proves they have had the worst life experiences of anyone and that their suffering is greater. This is certainly often true. However, the particular elitism created in joining together around this belief prevents efforts to try other ways of belonging. This can create major impasses to healthy ways of building relationships. A critical part of the group treatment of dissociative clients is to address this dilemma: the conviction that dissociation makes them belong and the equally strong conviction that dissociation interferes with functioning and quality of life. This difficult personal dilemma may be seen in the CT group as patients struggled thusly: "I want not to dissociate so I can function better in the group, and yet I'm afraid that if I don't dissociate, other members (including the group leader) might think I'm not dissociative, and would not want me in the group any more —and they would be right, because everyone else is dissociative, and if I don't dissociate, I don't belong."

3. A Learned Skill. There is another aspect to dissociation that complicates things for clients and their treatment because of the advantage it offers—that dissociation can be voluntary as well as involuntary. The tension between the advantages and disadvantages of dissociating can blur the fine line that exists between control and lack of control. Some clients are more clear than others about where that line is, but the issue is a problem for everyone.

4. Shared Responsibility for Outcomes. Another benefit of dissociation is the sharing of guilt or shame for impulsive or unusual behavior. Alter-ego states may be held responsible for drinking, hostile outbursts, or childlike behavior. Being able to detach from poorly understood or poorly controlled aspects of themselves can help clients with dissociative disorders maintain a sense of steadfastness of purpose in working toward treatment goals. However, the setbacks are significant, and functioning is not improved as long as this duality continues.

Focusing on the dual nature of dissociation as an asset and a handicap is followed by challenging clients to stop dissociating in group long enough to discover other ways of processing their experiences. These include talking about a situation long enough to experience and verbalize feelings rather than to act them out; helping others to do the same by sharing one's struggle with dissociation and increasing a sense of group cohesion as a result; and sharing the benefits of greater self-confidence and higher functioning in situations in which responses other than dissociation are used.

The short-term objectives of the Level 1 group are to help dissociative inpatients 1) to remain grounded (nondissociative) for the duration of the group 2) to participate. These are appropriate short-term goals for inpatients who stay for only a few days or a couple of weeks. The long-term objectives developed in the Level 2 group (a 10-session outpatient group) as its members demonstrate an ability to maintain symptom stability on their own, are to help them learn in the here-and-now 1) to generate the beginnings of healthy relationships, 2) to engage in activities and interests outside of treatment contexts, and 3) to challenge the beliefs and assumptions that arise in this process.

Rationales Suggested for Not Dissociating

In the Level 1 group discussions on the inpatient unit, patients focus on various aspects of dissociation and their perceptions of it. In these discussions, the advantages and disadvantages of dissociating are discussed. Initially the group leader provides reasons for group members not to dissociate, but ultimately the group begins to generate these on its own. As a result, the stress and anxiety caused by the effort and a sense of risk in not dissociating is decreased. Increased connection and a sense of mastery in improved communication are experienced. The group culture absorbs the rationales and they are passed along to new members. Some of the rationales that have been developed are provided below:

Getting From and Giving to the Group

One rationale for not dissociating is that dissociating in the group can cause them to miss out on important aspects of the group's discussion and prevent them from contributing to the group according to the group's primary objectives: to maintain symptom stability and to participate. All the patient has to do to become a member is to say he or she will try to remain nondissociative. Once in the group, patients are urged to engage with the others in a way that involves offering and receiving information, support, opinions, and useful strategies.

Talking About It Is Better Than Doing It

Talking about dissociation—what it is like, when and how often it happens, and what helps to remain grounded—is more productive than demonstrating it. Dissociated group members are not in a position to discuss their, or anyone else's, dissociation. Group members who stay present and focused are more likely to learn more about dissociation in general and take better charge of their own.

Adults Relate Better to Other Adults

Group members are asked that they be nondissociative in an adult state because the group topics are adult topics, and adults need to be present to address them. If they change consciously or unconsciously into a group-incongruent state, such as becoming childlike, acting in a threatening manner, or beginning to have a flashback, they are asked if the original adult-identified person can prevail. Dissociating members are not asked who is present or what is happening, nor are they called by a different name. Instead, they are asked if they feel it would be helpful for them to leave the group and seek unit staff. It is difficult for other group members not to respond to dissociative changes in each other because these changes can be dramatic, and because elsewhere on the unit both patients and staff may reinforce dissociation by asking for more information about it. If the dissociative state resembles a childlike persona, group members might respond in soft tones and childlike voices. If the changed state appears threatening, other group members might respond by becoming belligerent or fearfully leaving the room. Similarly distressing is the onset of a dissociative state that involves a cutting, scratching, or hitting gesture. The presence of adults for the duration of the group increases the chances for more satisfactory interactions and greater confidence in what the members can expect from each other.

Limitations of One Group Leader

In inpatient groups, there may be only one group leader. No one else may be available to tend to a dissociative member while the other leader continues to lead the group. It is distracting even with two leaders. If the group leader (or leaders) has to stop the group to deal with a dissociative episode, there can be no group. The dissociative person who creates this disruption risks creating a trigger for others. It is better not to come to group at all, or to leave voluntarily if symptoms are too difficult to manage. If group members have to leave to regain control, they are asked to state why they are leaving and whether or not they will be coming back. This is so the other members are kept informed and not suffer the often-held perception that the member's departure is their fault. Decisions to leave the group, or not to enter the group at all, are acknowledged as difficult, responsible, adult decisions that other group members and the leader appreciate.

One Spokesperson Per Member

It is impossible for group members and the leader to know whether any one member is really completely focused (not dissociated) at all times. It is assumed, however, that all members do their best to stay grounded and present. Although a member might have a variety of reactions to discussions in the group, those reactions need to be represented by the one consistent adult presence who is the identified adult member. If there seems to be a significant change in that person, the member is asked about it and also if it is possible to rejoin the group as the identified member.

Interpersonal Connection Is Stronger

A frequently highlighted rationale for no dissociation is the importance of interpersonal connection. The opportunities for closeness within the boundaries of safe relationships have been limited in the developmental history of many dissociative patients. Cultivating safe interpersonal connection in their adult lives is not enhanced but is disrupted by dissociative episodes. The resulting breaks in mutual understanding and shared reality are difficult to repair. These breaks can create even more suspicion, anxiety, and fear than is commonly experienced. A powerful motivator for group members in their struggle to control their dissociative symptoms is the realization that dissociation actually causes more disconnection than connection.

A Cognitive Model for Dissociation

In the group discussions, the basic cognitive triangle is used to demonstrate simply and concretely the process of dissociation (i.e., automatic thoughts, automatic feelings, and automatic behavior). As group members talk about a common concern or difficulty, a rough sketch of the triangle is made on the dry-erase board. As members describe their problems, their perceptions of the problems, and the results of those perceptions, their experiences are mapped out on the triangle. In keeping with the major theme of the group, many of these result in dissociative episodes. Because of the clear distinction (even compartmentalization) that dissociative patients make between emotions and physiological sensations, perceptions are described as the combination of cognitions (thoughts, images, words, songs, etc.), feelings (emotions) and behaviors (described as automatic behaviors of the body such as anxiety symptoms, but also impulses and anger-related cues such as grinding teeth, etc.). The following is an example of this type of sketch. Figure 7.1 shows how this example would be mapped out.

> A group member wants to discuss her conviction that she invites threatening behavior from people. Other members are interested because they often feel the same way. She goes on to assert, "I just look like a victim." Then she describes the following situation: "I was walking past this weird person on the unit and he made a sudden gesture, like he wanted to hit me. It happens all the time. Nobody likes me. I was out of there (dissociated)! It took me an hour to come back." As she talked, the event was mapped out in the following way:

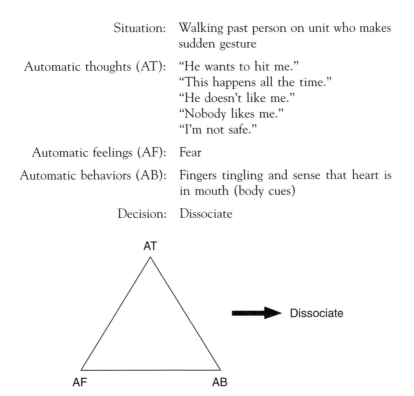

Situation: Walking past person on unit who makes sudden gesture

Automatic thoughts (AT): "He wants to hit me."
"This happens all the time."
"He doesn't like me."
"Nobody likes me."
"I'm not safe."

Automatic feelings (AF): Fear

Automatic behaviors (AB): Fingers tingling and sense that heart is in mouth (body cues)

Decision: Dissociate

Figure 7.1. A cognitive model for dissociation. Automatic thoughts (AT), automatic feelings (AF), and automatic behaviors (AB) combine and result in a dissociate state.

This version of the basic cognitive model is used to make more visual and concrete (and conceptually more manageable) the group members' descriptions of situations that cause them to dissociate (or do other regrettable activities). As a group member talks, the situation is charted on the dry-erase board. If one or more parts of the triangle diagram is left out of the description, the group mobilizes to help the person fill them in. This provides the opportunity to teach clients how to identify feelings, attend to body cues, and access the thoughts and images that accompany them. The importance of knowing all three is emphasized, because to leave out any one component is to overlook valuable and useful information.

When discussing dissociation as the outcome of these three components of perception, the group leader is introducing the controversial idea that dissocation may actually be thought of as a decision. Some group members have difficulty with this idea as it contradicts the prevailing view that dissocation is a noncontrollable "automatic" behavior. Resulting discussions can be productive in instilling hope that as automatic as dissociation may seem, determined effort, and practice, can make it a deliberate activity that one can choose to do or not.

Some group members like the idea that it is possible to have some choice about dissociating. A related idea is to consider that what seems automatic might really be acting on an assumption without waiting to gather more information about what is really happening. To suggest that dissociation is a decision rather than an automatic behavior equates it with other forms of negative problem solving such as cutting, drinking, drugging, suicide, or other self-harm, that are also actions one could make choices about.

The group leader's mapping out a patient's situation on the board, with group members helping each other articulate various perceptions of it, and all looking together at how the resulting decision is made helps remove a group member from the intensity of her experience and places her in the position of observer. It also engenders the sense of shared experience with other group members. Further, the attention of the other group members can shift from the person in question to the phenomenon being discussed. This makes it easier for them to identify with and discuss similar situations with their own thoughts, feelings, behaviors, and decisions. In the above example, group members learn how to recognize the extremes in the automatic thoughts, assess the reality of the situation with more accurate data, and tell themselves that the tendency to dissociate comes from old, bad experiences but that this may not be what is happening now. An alternative decision to the situation described above might be to regulate breathing, ground oneself, and find someone to talk to about the experience.

LEVEL 2 GROUP

Once clients are released from inpatient treatment to a partial hospitalization or outpatient program, a Level 2 group is appropriate.

Basic Differences in the Level 1 and Level 2 Groups

The Level 2 group is different from Level 1 group in the following ways:

1. Name of Group. Instead of the Dissociative Disorders Group, it is called the Cognitive Therapy Basic Skills Group. Although the group continues to be for individuals with dissociative disorders, there is a concession to a major issue that pervades Level 1 CT group. This issue is that patients ultimately feel that because they have to dissociate to join the group, they have to continue to dissociate in order to remain in the group. This is resolved in part by removing the word *dissociation* from the group name and addressing the dissociation issue in the group rules and guidelines. Dissociation is primary concern in and out of the group and it is often integral to identity among members.

2. Outpatient Versus Inpatient. It is in an outpatient setting, and as such, the risk is greater for impulsive behavior and other kinds of unpredictability. There are increased expectations for self-control. The outpatient therapist is more actively aware of the group members' goals and processes.

3. A Set of Rules. Clients are asked to sign a commitment to try to follow the rules and guidelines for the group. These are reviewed in the pregroup interview. Prospective group members are asked to review them with their therapist, and the rules are reviewed in the first group session.

4. Referral Sources. Referrals come from inpatient and outpatient mental health professionals and managed care organizations, as well as through the patient grapevine.

5. Individual Therapist on Team. Group members are in individual outpatient therapy, and they are asked that open communication be permitted between their therapist and the group leader. They are asked to sign a consent form for this.

6. Less Structure, More Stability. Group members work, are in day treatment, or attend school. These contexts provide less structure than on an inpatient basis and it is expected that group members have the ability to exercise more control over symptoms both in these contexts and in the group.

7. Number of Members. The group membership is smaller, about four to five members. This number is not intentional, it just seems to stay at the lower number.

8. Session Time. Group time is 1.5 hours, longer than the 50-minute group in the hospital. There is a 10-minute lateness rule.

9. Number of Sessions. The group is a rotating 10-session group. New group members are asked to commit to 10 sessions. At the end of this time, evidence of progress and the group's usefulness are assessed by the client with the outpatient therapist and the group leader.

In the early stages of Level 2 groups, a client who finished the first series of 10 sessions could recommit to the group and attend on an open-ended basis with a 3-session advance notice for termination. Most members who made it through the first 10 sessions wanted to stay, for time periods that varied from 4 or 5 more sessions to 2 or more years. There was too much unpredictability created by this format.

The Level 2 group consists currently of a 10-session series, with the option for renewing commitment every 10 sessions. This allows group members periodic summaries of their work in the group, gives them closure on some of their achievements, lets them set new goals, and lets them exchange feedback about the status of their relationship with other group members and the leader. The 10-session format also reduces the likelihood of unexpected departures or arrivals.

10. Goal Setting and Objectives. Level 2 group members set individual goals beyond decreasing symptom acuity and developing coping strategies that define the goals of Level 1 group members. Group members in Level 2 are expected to learn the following as a means to their goals:

- To discover the underlying beliefs and assumptions that might link dissociative episodes to each other and to other unproductive, unuseful trends and activities.
- To generate and verify hypotheses for themselves and for each other about individualized ways in which this occurs.
- To challenge these beliefs and patterns.
- To do tasks that strengthen more balanced beliefs and assumptions.

The group culture now includes the expectation of a greater level of symptom control. Group objectives change from the Level 1 focus on dissociative symptom management to the Level 2 focus on ways in which patterns of dissociation (and the perceptions that maintained them) interfer with the clients' lives. As in Level 1 groups, Level 2 groups have consisted soley of women, simply because dissociative men have not sought out the groups.

Level 2 Group Referral and Recruitment Process

The Level 2 group is advertised by word of mouth and a flyer that highlights group objectives, structure, content, and requirements for membership. Information on the flyer may vary but should include the following basic points:

- This group is for people having difficulties with symptoms related to trauma and dissociation.
- The group goal is to increase life management skills and to decrease the intrusive effects of trauma-related symptoms, including dissociative episodes.
- Group members will work individually and as a team to identify and challenge inaccurate patterns of thinking that interfere with their daily lives.
- Group members will not explore traumatic memory content.
- Each member must be in individual therapy and must allow contact between the group leader and their individual therapist.

Group members are expected to be in stable individual psychotherapy and must be referred by psychotherapists who agree with their clients' goals for the group. Group members will be asked to commit to attend all group meetings for the sake of continuity and consistency.

The group format includes agenda-setting, sharing experiences and perceptions of those experiences, suggestions for individual activities between sessions, and summary and feedback. Members work on their own goals and at their own pace while being available to each other for support, ideas, and information.

An individual pregroup evaluation session must be scheduled before the 10-group sessions begin. Each group session is 1.5 hours.

Pregroup Interview

Each candidate is required to have a pregroup interview for screening and model socialization. This session is a 50-minute session, billed at the same rate as a group session. The following points are covered in this session.

The Applicant's Understanding of the Group

There are several ways the client may know about the group—friends, the therapist, and the flyer. The pregroup interview helps to clarify what is known and what is expected. A description of Level 2 group at this interview may be stated by the group leader as follows:

> This is a group for people with trauma in their backgrounds and for whom dissociation and other trauma-related symptoms are causing problems in their lives. The group is to help sort out how certain beliefs and assumptions, developed in childhood to help you make sense of things and cope at that time, may now be working against you more than for you. Dissociation, and other symptoms and behaviors, are part of how these beliefs play themselves out. Is working on these problems in the group something you think would be of help to you?

Expectations of Members—Building Group Culture

Level 2 group members differ from Level 1 group members in the degree of control over symptoms and level of participation they are able to manage. In the pregroup interviews, each prospective member is oriented to the rules, expectations, language, and structures of Level 2. The applicant is asked what she feels she would like to get from the group and what she can give to the group. Many applicants say this is a new idea for them and have difficulty answering. When urged to think of something they feel they could offer, they say things such as "I'm a good listener," "I try to be empathic," or "I'm willing to share my experiences." Typical responses for what they want from the group are "I want to fit in somewhere" and "I want help with my thoughts."

Members are then asked what they would like to accomplish in the group. The responses are initially vague and on the order of "I keep getting in over my head in situations," "I want to have more confidence in myself," and "I'm afraid of people's anger." This is the initial brain-storming that is then brought to focus with the question, "What would you like to see change or be different?" This is the beginning of the Problem List. The new member is asked to write down her list and bring it to the first group session. The Problem List is discussed in the first group session, with the leader and other group members helping each other to set realistic goals: "What can we do here to help you get more self-confidence? How would you know you had it?" The answer might be, "I'd know I had more self-confidence if I could disagree with someone sometimes, and not agree all the time."

Prospective group members are asked about active self-mutilation, suicide attempts, addictions, and eating disorders. These problems are common among clients with dissociative disorders, and it is important to evaluate the level of individual risk and potential for interference with the group. Many dissociative clients cannot guarantee that they will stop these behaviors forever but can agree to do so for a period of time. The rationale for the request that they not engage in self-destructive behaviors while they are members of the group is that challenging rigidly-held beliefs and assumptions can be anxiety provoking, and group members must be willing to engage with each other in doing so without self-harm.

Prospective members are also told about the expectation to participate actively. They may be concerned about saying or doing the wrong thing and then not fitting in. The group leader addresses these concerns by making it clear that participation is expected of everyone, although not everyone's level of activity has to be the same. Group members are reassured that they will not be forced or put on the spot but to do the best they can.

Confidentiality is an important part of the group, and members' desire for privacy is respected. Contact must be allowed however between the group leader and the individual therapist, particularly around safety concerns. It is assumed that what is brought up in the group by any member is also known by that member's therapist. It is also assumed that group members will keep their therapists informed about progress in the group.

Group members are discouraged from having contact outside of group meetings, but if it happens, it should be reported in the group. Outside contact between members of the group becomes a part of the group process whether they want it to or not and can inadvertently cause concerns about trust and secrecy.

Prospective members are asked if they can commit to being nondissociative in the group. This requires letting the group know if they are being triggered to dissociate by another member or the leader or if outside events are increasing the likelihood of dissociation in the group. The rationale behind this request is that everyone works best together if they

know what to expect from each other. Consequently even though dissociation is discussed a lot during group sessions in both Level 1 and Level
2 groups, members are asked not to dissociate if they can help it. Prospective members are told that because of the time-limited nature of the group,
and to make the most of the time in the group sessions, they will be asked
to set up tasks for themselves between meetings. This is so they can examine their current life situations and try out small changes as they make
discoveries and grow in the group. They are assured that nonsuccess is an
opportunity for learning, that everyone should experience this a few times,
and that without it they may not be testing their limitations.

Rules and the rationale for each are reviewed with each prospective
group member in the pregroup interview. Unlike the group rules that were
constantly talked about in the Level 1 group, applicants of Level 2 groups
are expected to have an understanding of them and follow them without
frequent reminders. Each applicant is asked to sign their copy of the contract (see Exhibit 7.1).

The idea of doing tasks and experiments between sessions is introduced. These are explained as ways to try out new and balanced perceptions
that have been worked on in the group.

Finally, prospective members are urged to keep data logs, both for
jotting down ideas in the group and for observations about old and new
patterns of thinking and reacting outside of group.

Therapist Norms

In a longer term ongoing group, an organized and focused group leader
is critical to maintaining sense of safety of the members and keeping the
group on track. The following principles of group leadership help to keep
the group process productive and focused. Although these are not discussed
formally in the pregroup interview or in groups, the concepts are discussed
as they arise in group discussions.

Consistency

The therapist is responsible for making sure things go as planned.
Group members must be able to rely on a particular sequence in the group
process, and group members need to know what to expect from each other
and from the group leader. Inconsistency generates a sense of unpredictability, and unpredictability is anxiety provoking and disorganizing for clients with dissociative disorders.

Continuity

The therapist must help group members keep oriented toward their
goals and objectives. Group members need to be shown how to work in

EXHIBIT 7.1
Group Rules and Guidelines

In the group it is important that members be able to rely on each other for consistency as everyone addresses difficult issues. The following are some guidelines that help group members know what to expect from themselves and each other. Written as a formal contract, prospective members review and sign it to indicate they understand and are committed to stay within the guidelines.

- **Be no more than 10 minutes late:** Once the group has begun, it's difficult to stop for you to check-in or to fill you in on what's been said.
- **Adults only present in group:** Since the group discusses coping, symptom management, and daily life events (adult issues), it may be difficult for child or other altered ego states to understand. If a childlike or type of altered ego state does appear, it will be acknowledged and then asked to find an adult. Members are asked to choose one adult self (or ego state) to attend all groups.
- **Crises are managed with individual therapist:** It is assumed that members and their therapists have crisis plans to deal with what comes up in individual treatment. Group problems will be dealt with in the group.
- **Brief departures from group are acceptable:** If it is necessary to leave the group briefly, please come back as soon as possible to inform other members about why this was necessary. Other group members are sometimes concerned that they caused the departure, and this issue deserves clarification.
- **Respectful behavior is requested:** One of the group goals is to manage strong feelings while talking to others about people and experiences.
- **No memory work or details of abuse will be reviewed in group:** These are sensitive and personal issues that should be dealt with in individual therapy.
- **Group members may ask another member to change the subject:** It is difficult to know each other's triggers, and members need to let others know when this reaction begins to occur.
- **Reporting dissociation or asking about a dissociative episode is accepted:** Members are sometimes unaware that they have made a dissociative shift. It is important to clarify this, and group members are encouraged to check out their observations of each other.
- **The group is to be informed about out-of-group contact:** If members meet between group sessions and discuss group issues, they are asked to inform the other members at the next group meeting.
- **Adults need to drive home:** Part of the group commitment is safe, responsible travel to and from sessions.
- **Members will be billed for sessions they do not attend:** The commitment to the group is financial as well as personal. Once the group has begun, no one can take your place. (The exception is being in a hospital without approval for a pass.)

| Signed | Date | Witness | Date |

These rules are the standards for behavior within a group. Most members understand and accept that these are guidelines designed to keep the group process running smoothly and allow each member to know what to expect from the others.

Note that homework, tasks, log books, and active participation (as urged in the pregroup interview) are not part of the rules, which are for group safety and are necessary for the group to function. Homework, selected tasks, and active participation are ultimately a choice, and although they do affect the quality of the group process, the option not to do them is open to each group member.

steps and how to add up gains over time. That steps toward improvement can be made and that progress can be measured are not familiar concepts to most dissociative clients. Another important concept to infuse into the group culture is the idea that change can occur and that each member may be instrumental in the process of that change.

Communication

The therapist must model directness, interest, and patience over the course of the group sessions. Secrecy among members or between a member and the leader generates mistrust and suspicion, and yet fear of being wrong or saying too much or offending others makes members tend to be covert and secretive. Sharing information about oneself and discussing one's experiences is a skill that many dissociative clients have not had an opportunity to develop. The group context provides that opportunity with encouragement and modeling from the leader. Open communication must be valued, and each member is urged to assert her own needs and to respond to the needs of other members.

Cohesion

The group leader must work constantly for group cohesion. The internal fragmentation of dissociative clients is often replicated in a group context. The cohesion principle is based on the premise that to achieve optimal interpersonal functioning, there must be an integrated self, purpose, and history. The better dissociative clients know themselves as a unit, the better they will be able to connect to others to solidify a common group identity and purpose.

Collaboration

The group leader can foster collaboration by empowering group members to give feedback, to assert their needs, and even to disagree with the leader and with each other. Collaboration implies equal sharing of a task or an experience despite differences that arise. The idea of teamwork is an external and internal matter. Group members must work within themselves and with others in the group to move forward toward their goals.

Competence

The group leader must highlight any evidence of competence, resourcefulness, or skill manifested by group members. Treatment of dissociative clients too often tries to reduce their maladaptive ways of being in the world without giving enough emphasis to the strengths and skills they do have. Competence is increased through planning small tasks and personal experiments as clients work toward their goals. Mastery of these must be acknowledged and recorded to strengthen their sense of who they are and keep their courage at difficult times.

Level 2 Session Structure

In the first group session, the structure of all group sessions is explained as follows:

Announcements

Date changes, absences, and contact between therapists is announced, as well as any out-of-group contact between group members.

Individual Mood Check

There is a discussion of the forms that are filled out between each session: the Beck Depression Inventory (BDI), Beck Anxiety Inventory (BAI), Therapist Feedback Form. Observations are made about differences in mood, and whether their mood is consistent with ratings on the forms. There is a particular focus on the Feedback Form question: "What impressed you most in the last session?"

Review of Last Session

Members are asked to summarize the previous session and are asked if they have any further thoughts about the discussion. Any unfinished discussion is put on the current agenda.

Agenda-Setting and Homework

Each group member is asked what he or she would like to work on in the group that day. The topics should relate to the goals set in the first group, although sometimes seemingly unrelated events can result in new awareness and subsqent changes in goals. Group members are asked to refer to their problem lists, any tasks or experiments conducted since the last session, and their logbooks as they offer items for the agenda.

Agenda Discussion

The group decides how to prioritize agenda topics. Often one topic has enough relevance to all to be useful. Sometimes a group member has a quick issue or a pressing one, and all members help to order how they will be addressed.

Task-Setting

Members are asked how they will try to reinforce in the next week what is being learned in the group. Each member sets her own task, sometimes with input from the leader or other group members. This may consist of actual behaviors, observations, or practicing relaxation exercises or other symptom reduction strategies.

Individual Check-Out

Members are asked what they have found useful about the group. This is the time to give specific feedback to each other or the leader. The group leader also takes a turn, summarizing the dominant themes of the group discussion and highlighting contributions each member has made.

Take Paperwork Home

Each member takes a copy of the BDI, BAI, Therapist Feedback Form, and other handouts or worksheets such as a thought record or a feelings list.

Level 2 Group Rating Form

This is given at the end of each series of 10 sessions to allow group members to rate their progress and the group's usefulness to them.

The Dissociation Cycle

The cognitive triangle is used in the Level 2 group to help group members identify patterns and themes in thinking that suggest more entrenched beliefs and assumptions. Group members are then helped to learn ways in which these patterns become self-perpetuating cycles of dysfunction. The basic presentation of this concept is as follows:

> Dissociation seems to do one of two things: It can help to avoid or reduce the acuity of some anticipated traumatic experience (emotional, cognitive, or physical), but it also can replicate a traumatic experience. Both result in confusion, disorientation, anxiety, and even physical discomfort. This causes a person to be vigilant for cues that trauma is about to recur. The problem is that this vigilance actually lowers the threshold for dissociation, and the perception of danger is reinforced. Furthermore, because of traumatic events, and even because of the fragmentation that dissociation causes, the dissociative person often does not know how to recognize real cues of dangerous or problem situations. The effort and energy expended in looking for danger only to miss its presence until too late reinforces the uncertainty, loss of self-confidence, demoralization, and hopelessness that go along with dissociation.

Following is a look at how dissociation can fragment reality and then maintain the fragmenting condition in a way that perpetuates itself and is difficult to break out of.

1. Hypervigilance: "Something bad is going to happen to me."
2. Trigger: "I've been here before."/"This is familiar."
3. Flashback: "It's happening again." Or Escape/avoid: "Nothing is happening." "I'm not here."
4. Fragmentation/disorientation: "Things are out of control. I don't know what happened."
5. Compensatory strategy: "I must focus, get in control, feel real, quickly." (cut, drink, hit, clean)
6. Depletion/hopelessness: "Nothing works. I'm helpless. It's hopeless."

Figure 7.2 illustrates how this perpetuates itself.

In demonstrating this cycle on a dry-erase board, the group leader uses material from the agenda set by the group and asks if the cycle seems familiar or if it is relevant to what happens to the members. Group members use the cycle to try to establish their individual patterns of beliefs and assumptions that activate the steps in the cycle. The dissociative episode

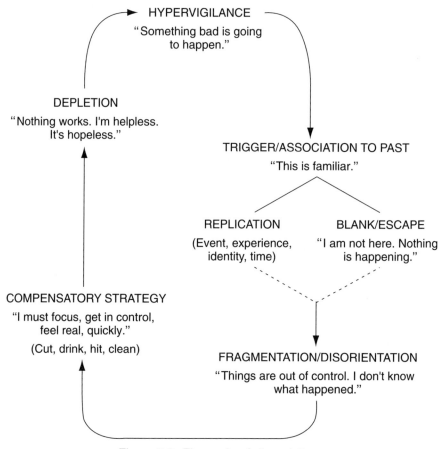

Figure 7.2. The cycle of dissociation.

and the compensatory strategies are referred to as decisions that have negative results, and group members have the opportunity to offer each other support, understanding, and coping strategies as they examine the steps in the cycle and how these steps may apply to their individual situations.

Clinical Observations

Dissociation in the here-and-now perpetuates the avoidance or reexperiencing of traumatic events and compromises the stability of group members. Years of dissociation results in skill deficits and other difficulties in functioning that can be observed in the group and reported by members about their outside lives. These skill deficits and difficulties in functioning recreate aspects of the trauma-producing environments outlined previously. In the Level 2 group, deficits caused by dissociaiton apear to cluster into four general categories: *time, events, experiences,* and *identity.* Group members have the task of not only trying to patch or rebuild what has been lost in these areas, but also to understand the inaccuracies and distortions in the beliefs and assumptions developed as a result of the fragmentation in these areas. Only by doing this skill building and by challenging related beliefs can group members deal with the effects of the past, begin to build an increasingly dependable present, and be able to expect a reasonably predictable future. The group provides the initial steps in this process.

The functional and skill deficits and related beliefs are clarified with the use of the cognitive triangle and the dissociative cycle in the discussion of the group agenda. The following sections provide a description of the fragmentation categories generated from the agenda topics.

Fragmentation of Time

The fragmentation of time interferes with a client's sense of continuity and sequence. Gaps in time, interrupted time, time juxtapositions, and confusion about developmental milestones such as age or grade level for any events (both traumatic and nontraumatic) make it difficult for clients to place themselves in time, to use time effectively, or to recreate time. This is the case for both present and past time. A client said in group, "I've been an actress, a lab technician, and have a master's degree in marketing. I've lived in a lot of different places. I don't know how I got from one thing to another or how long it took, and it scares me. I couldn't do any of those things now."

A consequence of time fragmentation is sometimes an interactive style characterized by inattention, distractibility, hypervigilance, and guardedness in the group. Efforts to normalize some memory deficits and to piece together time occur with a review of the previous session. Group members are surprised to realize they remember more than they think they can, doubly so when they remember some things better than the group leader. Dissociative people often believe that normal memory is perfect memory. A group member once said, "I wish I could remember everything that happened in my life like normal people can"—an assumption challenged by the group leader and other members, followed by a discussion about the parameters of normal time awareness and sequencing.

Fragmentation of Events

Events (traumatic or otherwise) that are not clearly remembered or not consensually remembered by family or friends cause distress in dissociative clients who don't know how to tell if they are imaginary, distorted, fabricated, or real. Internal conflict can develop from wanting to know what happened in the past even the recent past, and being unsure how to know. For example, a group member reported that one of her alters was sure she had been recently sexually molested by her outpatient therapist. The client noticed her bra was unhooked after returning home from a session with the therapist. Although she did not remember being molested by her therapist, she thought it could have happened if she was dissociated in the session. She had been raped several times as a child, and felt the same way now as then. Coincidentally, the client had also recently been mugged on the way home from work one night. She clearly remembered the mugging. She did not remember being molested by her therapist. With the group's help, she finally concluded it was unlikely that she would remember one event and not the other, and the individual therapy relationship remained intact.

Another client hesitated as she tried to remember what she had done the previous day. Her right hand came up and slapped her face. To the surprised group, she explained, "Oh, that's just a reminder not to lie." In this case, a fragment of an often-repeated event was repeated in the present.

The group addresses the issue of fragmented events by reporting incidents during the previous week in agenda-setting and challenging authomatic thoughts associated with traumatic events from the past. A group member is helped, for example, to see differences between an unpleasant quarrel with a significant other in the past week and traumatic emotional abuse by a parent in childhood.

Fragmentation of Experiences

The past experiences of group members are often too fragmented to serve as resources for addressing current problems. The fragmentation of experience results in overreaction, underreaction, naivete, or inappropriate responsiveness to situations. In this way, it prevents the growth of self-awareness and the realistic assessment of one's own strengths and deficits. Fragmented experience also calls into question the predictability of others and impairs the development of judgment in social situations. Group members may be confused about what constitutes an extreme reaction, versus a normal one. For example, a group member reported that she humiliated herself at work when she opened a drawer and found a dead mouse in it, screamed, and ran to her supervisor. The client criticized herself as a fragile trauma survivor, unable to cope. Other members discussed similar experiences, all assuming that this reaction was extreme and unusual, even though the group leader took the position that many "normal" people would have reacted similarly. Another client enrolled in a computer course and became so proficient that other students, and even the instructor, would ask her for help. The instructor drew her aside and asked her not to help the other students and mentioned they were complaining about their lack of skill. The client became depressed and anxious, and considered dropping the course. She told the group, "Why is she criticizing me? I'm not stupid! It's not my fault they're asking me for help." She associated this experience to her family, where her siblings, as well as her parents, ask her for help and information, then jeered at her, "You think you're so smart." Her reaction to this classroom situation was the result of transposing a painful experience in her family onto a current situation that highlighted her status in the class as a leader and helper.

Fragmentation of Identity

The fragmentation of identity is another consequence of dissociation. Historically, clients and therapists have assumed that an identity shift meant a new, autonomously functioning being was present, despite the fact that it is not possible to really know the degree of autonomous functioning of any altered state. Furthermore, no personality fragment (even a large one) can be reliably expected to perform a complex function or task. Even though fragmented identity is only one consequence of dissociation, it is often the most attended to in treatment. The other consequences—fragmented events, time, and experiences—may be overlooked in terms of dissociative shifts even though their relevance to treatment is as significant. It is also likely that fragments of time, events, and experiences are commonly perceived as identity fragments, again missing an opportunity to discover the more accurate nature of the fragmentation and the beliefs and assumptions that go along with it.

An example of identity fragmentation is as follows: A group member described a conflict between herself and another dissociative client in day treatment, saying, "She pushes out the kids every time I approach her. She knows I wouldn't yell at them. It's not fair." The group member assumed she could not address their adult issues because of the intentionally, generated childlike identity before her. Another member dissociated at the mention of the word *fathers*. She became childlike and began sucking her thumb. Forgetting the topic of the group, other members talked soothingly to her, as to a child. She asked one of them to be her mommy. In both instances, the dissociating members were asked to try to identify the "rule" or assumption that caused them to change focus in each situation. In the latter instance, the group member who became childlike was asked what assumption caused her to decide to become childlike.

Highlighting these four general categories of dissociative fragmentation is not to assert that they account for all problems in functioning or all perceptual distortions of dissociative clients. Identifying them does make the point that dissociation involves multiple factors, and examining it should not be limited to the assumption that dissociation is only about identity change.

Strategies That Decrease Dissociative Fragmentation

The following strategies can be used in group sessions or suggested as tasks for members to do between sessions to decrease dissociative episodes. These may be used at any time and for any group member but are particularly applicable for dissociative clients struggling with fragmentation in these four specific areas.

1. Time

   - Differentiate between past and present
   - Reconstruct the day, the past week, the last session
   - Sequence meals, bedtime preparation, a certain activity
   - Plan the next day, the next week
   - Organize time in sessions
   - Pace treatment appropriately
   - Obtain psychoeducation about memory, developmental milestones

2. Event

   - Set goals and tasks
   - Initiate small steps toward goals
   - Observe and review events, activities, contexts, and people
   - Plan in sequence
   - Predict outcomes of events and plans
   - Measure change

3. Experience

   - Report subjective reactions to people and events
   - Break experience into thoughts, feelings, and physiological responses
   - Tolerate anxiety, distress, and strong emotions longer
   - Describe progression of increase and decrease in emotions and moods

- Compare perceptions versus reality
- Establish criteria for normalcy in life and situations
- Experiment with assertiveness and new activities, behaviors

4. Identity

- Designate developmental gaps
- Practice age-appropriate activities and social skills
- Clarify social and personal roles
- Try out limit-setting and personal boundary reinforcement
- Establish concepts of internal and external teamwork and collaboration
- Assess strengths and weaknesses
- Learn major aspects of child development

These strategies and interventions are consistent with the therapist principles outlined earlier, as part of the effort to initiate change in the direction of group members' goals within the structure of the model.

Meta-Beliefs and Idiosyncratic Beliefs

A basic premise of cognitive therapy is that people's belief system influences how they perceive the realities of current life. As noted above, the belief systems held by dissociative clients are linked to dissociative fragments occurring over the course of their personal history. The chaos of group members' developmental contexts and the dissociative fragmentation that results from it causes, in addition to the specific, idiosyncratic beliefs developed by each individual, a set of beliefs generally shared by all group members. These are referred to as meta-beliefs, which because of their pervasiveness and intensity affect dissociative clients profoundly and make treatment gains difficult to achieve. Meta-beliefs question the determination of reality itself, as illustrated by the following:

1. Reality Is Uncertain. "I do not really know what I know." Nothing is certain, neither what is remembered from the past nor how accurately one perceives the present. Many current events seem to replicate past traumatic ones. There is no continuity or consistency to relationship or events. The reality of what one knows is always in question.

2. Feeling Is Intolerable. "No feeling is a good feeling." Only by being numb can one tolerate experiences without either harming someone or being harmed. Even laughter and fun result in harm or punishment. Numbness is also intolerable, however, because then one does not know what is being felt. Both emotion and the absence of emotion are considered danger signals, and as such cannot be used in the satisfactory assessment of perception.

3. Behavior Is Uncontrollable. "The body is not under my control." The body acts on its own in unpredictable ways and sometimes other people take over the actions of the body. There is therefore no choice or agency in directing behaviors. One simply does what one does. One finds oneself behaving in ways that are unusual, disturbing, and unpredictable without any clear reason why. Plans cannot be made and followed through because of the numerous contingencies that alter and control behavior.

What makes the meta-schemas so problematic is that the dissociative fragmentation that generates and maintains them also impedes the dissociative client from forming a reliable system to assess reality or even conceiving there is such a system. One objective of the cognitive group model is to help dissociative group members learn to build such a system for themselves. The beliefs and assumptions that are idiosyncratic and particular to the developmental history of each individual are more easily accessed and more readily available than the meta-beliefs to be identified, evaluated, and challenged over the course of treatment. These idiosyncratic beliefs and assumptions come up in the automatic thoughts of dissociative group members on a daily basis and are part of the agenda of the sessions. Examples of revised assumptions (called in the group New Rules to Live By) have included the following:

"I don't have to die over things."
"I can choose whether to leave or stay with things."
"A destructive action doesn't define who I am."
"I'm not responsible for other people's moods or happiness."
"It's OK to have needs and wants."
"No one will ever walk on me again."

Some of the maladaptive rules and beliefs that the group members struggle with can be guessed from the examples of positive and self-affirming new rules listed above. Group members do not suffer the illusion that the old perceptions no longer exist and will no longer pose problems; however, they do recognize these old beliefs for what they are. They are able to remind themselves of the challenges made to these old beliefs and the more balanced perceptions that have been created. This increased awareness strengthens their hope and motivation to try more new ways of interacting with the world around them.

Final Group Rating Form

At the end of each 10-session cycle, group memebers are asked to fill out a form that lists what the group has tried to provide for them. It serves as a feedback for for the leader, an assessment form for the member, and a guide for future treatment planning. Exhibit 7.2 is a sample of the form that has evolved.

Most group members report (on the basis of the BDI and BAI data

EXHIBIT 7.2
Rating Form

Listed below are some of the skills and abilities that this group has tried to make available to you. Please place *a check* by those areas in which you feel you have made progress, even if not perfectly or extensively. Keep in mind that progress is defined as a *step or two* in the right direction, NOT absolute mastery! Then *circle* those skills that personally are most important to you.

In the blank space that follows the list, please identify two or three things that you did not get enough of, or get at all in terms of your expectations and wishes. In order for the group to work better for its members, feedback about what is missing is extremely important.

1. _____ Depression decreased.
2. _____ Anxiety decreased.
3. _____ Dissociation in group decreased.
4. _____ Ability to delay impulses.
5. _____ Attach feelings to thoughts and bodily reactions.
6. _____ Identify personal cognitive errors. (Can you name one or two?)
7. _____ Recognize when thinking gets extreme/possibly distorted.
8. _____ Generate data "for" and "against" painful perceptions.
9. _____ Make a list of "pros" and "cons" in decision making.
10. _____ Break up overwhelming tasks into smaller tasks.
11. _____ Prioritize tasks.
12. _____ Manage difficult interpersonal situations.
13. _____ Recognize personal unproductive "rules" or "beliefs."
14. _____ Acknowledge successes and accomplishments in daily life.
15. _____ Identify small but significant pleasures in daily life.
16. _____ Help other members examine/challenge their perceptions.
17. _____ Brainstorm alternative ways of looking at things.
18. _____ Give feedback to other group members.
19. _____ Create tasks and experiments to test perceptions.
20. _____ Describe to others what I'm learning.
21. _____ Share my own personal difficulties with others.
22. _____ Develop new rules or beliefs and start to implement them.

Feedback regarding wishes for more, better, or different:

_____

---

collected weekly) that both depression and anxiety decreased. The therapist feedback form allows group members to acknowledge weekly what they have learned from the group and to know what options they may want to exercise for continued improvement. Discussion of their final self-ratings on the Rating Form is mutually supportive and relates back to goals set from the Problem Lists generated in the pregroup interview and the first group session.

CONCLUSION

The group context and its procedures within a cognitive therapy structure and process help to reduce the dissociative client's sense of an unpredictable and arbitrary world. As discussed in this chapter, cognitive therapy strategies help group members to identify, modulate, and tolerate a range of affects. The cognitive therapy group context also builds self-efficacy in dissociative clients and gives them the ability to make decisions and choices. It teaches group members to identify and challenge trauma-related beliefs and assumptions. Finally, it provides a means to repair skill deficits and acquire new skills.

The two models described here are the result of hundreds of hours of group therapy with dissociative disordered clients in inpatient, partial hospitalization, and outpatient contexts. Group membership has lasted from 1 day to 3 years. The observation of a minimum of acute incidents, of adherence to group structure and rules, and of the low dropout rate, as well as the self-reported benefit from clients, speaks strongly for the efficacy of groups for dissociative clients based on the cognitive model of treatment.

The cognitive therapy group models described here work well for clients with dissociative disorders in that they address those with acute, active dissociation (Level 1) and extend effectively to address the needs of those with more stability (Level 2). The principles, rules, and structure of this two-phase model allow group members to examine their perceptions and safely discover their distorted beliefs and assumptions. They do this with others with whom they can identify. Neither the cognitive model nor the individuality of the group members is compromised, because the model is consistent and predictable, and the option of choice and pacing within the model's frame is determined by the group members. The pervasiveness of distortions in their perceptions tends to limit the scope of the Level 1 group to symptom management, affiliation with other clients, and mobilization to participate. Along with the wish for improvement, however, is often the fear of change and the desire to stay "as they are" (i.e., fragmented). A major decision facing dissociative clients is whether or not to consider *not dissociating* in achieving their goals. This cognitive group model operates on the premise that it is not until after the fragmentation is at a minimum, and the basic goal of symptom stability is accomplished, that more complex goals such as assertiveness, the development of interests, satisfactory relationships, decision making, and ultimately some resolution of their traumatic past, can be sought. In the interest of these goals, the examination and revision of pathological beliefs and assumptions is critical.

REFERENCE

Beck, A. T., Rush, A. J., Shaw, B. F., & Emery, G. (1979). *Cognitive therapy of depression.* New York: Guilford Press.

8

ADULT ATTENTION DEFICIT DISORDER

WILLIAM D. MORGAN

Attention deficit disorder (ADD) is the term used in the general clinical community for the developmental syndrome marked by deficits in attention, impulse control, and activity level regulation. It is also frequently referred to as attention deficit hyperactivity disorder (ADHD) or, as in the *Diagnostic and Statistical Manual of Mental Disorders* (4th ed., *DSM–IV*; American Psychiatric Association, 1994), attention deficit/hyperactivity disorder (AD/HD). It is generally recognized that these terms represent a disorder with various subtypes, each with varying manifestations. In this chapter, ADD is used as a term to broadly include all subtypes, including attention deficit both with and without hyperactivity.

There is a growing awareness among mental health clinicians that ADD, recognized as one of the most common disorders of childhood and previously seen as a disorder of childhood only, does not always resolve in adolescence but frequently persists into adulthood. Follow-up studies show that 30% to 70% of children diagnosed with ADD continue to have either the full syndrome or significant symptoms into adulthood (G. Weiss & Hechtman, 1993).

ADD in adults is a relatively new area of study. Many mental health centers report a sizable and growing number of requests from adults for assessment and treatment of ADD and feel unprepared to provide services (Barkley, 1990). At the same time, research into its accurate assessment and effective treatment is lagging. As Kane, Mikalac, Benjamin, and Barkley (1990, p. 633) stated: "There is very little information available in scientific literature to guide the clinical management of ADHD in adults. What little exists pertains to medication treatment, and even this evidence is conflicting."

Although the assessment and treatment of ADD in adults continues to be an underinvestigated area, many clinicians have taken a special interest and have reported strategies and methods that are successful, based mostly on their clinical experience. And although published research and outcome data are scarce, there is a burgeoning interest concerning ADD's incidence, nature, recognition, and management. However undeveloped, there is now a basic understanding of the problems associated with adult ADD and effective treatments.

This chapter briefly reviews the literature concerning the treatment of ADD in adults and proposes a cognitive–behavioral therapy (CBT) time-limited group treatment protocol that is based on the literature and clinical experience.

THE NATURE OF ADD

Primary and Secondary Symptoms

ADD is commonly described as a neurobiological condition consisting of chronic difficulties in areas of inattention, impulsivity, and overactivity (American Psychiatric Association, 1994; Barkley, 1990; Quinn, 1995). Whereas in the past hyperactivity and later attention deficits received the most attention, today researchers are finding that impulsivity may be the hallmark of ADD. According to a more recent theory of ADD, the fundamental deficit is in the area of regulation of certain self-directed (executive) functions (Barkley, 1997). Poor inhibitory control results, and this lack of capacity to inhibit responses is at the core of the attentional, impulse control and activity level difficulties of ADD. In addition to these "core" or "primary" symptoms of ADD, there are other generally recognized symptoms and characteristics (American Psychiatric Association, 1994; Barkley, 1990; Ratey, Greenberg, Bemporad, & Lindem, 1992; Wender, 1995). These symptoms and characteristics, derived from a consensus of the available adult and child literature on the disorder, are summarized in Exhibit 8.1. The consensus of the literature reviewed seems to be that the symptoms and clinical features of ADD in adults are developmentally related to those in children (Wilens, Spencer, & Biederman, 1995). Adults

EXHIBIT 8.1
Common Symptoms and Characteristics of Attention Deficit Disorder in Children and Adults

Attention deficits, including easy distractibility, forgetfulness (i.e., losing or misplacing things), inability to concentrate or focus attention, lack of persistence ("stick-to-itiveness"), frequently feeling bored, short attention span.

Impulsivity, involving poor response inhibition or inability to delay response, including making decisions too quickly and without reflection, inability to delay speech or actions without experiencing discomfort, impulsive spending, changing of plans, and so on.

Overactivity, including persistent motor hyperactivity, fidgetiness, restlessness, inability to relax, being "always on the go," talking excessively.

Disorganization, interfering with the ability to complete tasks at home, school, on the job and manifesting in haphazardly shifting from one task or activity to another.

Stress intolerance, including stress sensitivity, being easily flustered or "hassled," and difficulty resolving conflicting demands.

Temper outbursts, seen as a "hot temper," frustration leading to explosive short-lived outbursts, being easily provoked, and transient loss of control.

Affective symptoms, described as emotional lability, overexcitability, and also frequent feelings of boredom. The common comorbidity of depression and anxiety is discussed elsewhere.

Memory difficulties, including semantic memory (facts, names, etc.) and prospective memory (remembering to remember) problems. Difficulty memorizing information such as names and dates.

---

may manifest these symptoms differently than children. It seems time, circumstances, and development may bring about changes in how ADD is experienced in adults (Quinn, 1995; Woods, 1986).

Associated Problems

The above-mentioned symptoms lead to difficulties in self-management functions and interpersonal relations. These problems are presumed to result from the interaction of the person's symptoms and the environment.

The symptoms of ADD are manifested in various ways that seem on the one hand to be typical but on the other hand to vary from individual to individual. Many writers have noted the common manifestations of ADD symptoms in adults (Barkley, 1990; Nadeau, 1995b; G. Weiss & Hechtman, 1993; L. Weiss, 1992; Wender, 1995). These difficulties are summarized in Exhibit 8.2.

Subtypes

Many researchers of ADD have concluded that ADD is a syndrome with distinct subtypes (Barkley, 1990; Brown, 1995; Nadeau, 1995b; Wender, 1995).

EXHIBIT 8.2
**Common Associated Problems of Attention Deficit Disorder (ADD)
in Adults**

Low self-esteem, resulting in the ADD person thinking of himself or herself as bad, stupid, inferior, or unlikable. Individuals with ADD may be especially sensitive to criticism.

Problems with planning and executing tasks, task completion, and a tendency to take on too many projects.

Generally disorganized lifestyle, typified by being frequently late, rushed, unprepared, having difficulty managing finances, a disorganized work environment, and difficulty locating necessary items.

Poor problem solving, generally characterized as poor problem-solving skills or poor means-end thinking.

Lack of persistence, which may be manifested in frequent moves or job changes, giving up on tasks that become frustrating or boring, and a pattern of taking up interests and then dropping them.

Social deficits, such as a tendency to speak without considering the consequences that the comments may elicit and to interrupt others in conversation. In addition, people with ADD may fail to attend to important social cues and lag in the development of social skills.

Chronic pattern of underachievement, commonly not performing in school commensurate with intelligence and not advancing in career as would be anticipated.

Poor peer relations, leading to frequent peer rejection, engagement in more frequent negative social behaviors, poor social performance, and difficulty maintaining long-term relationships.

Difficulty concentrating when reading, typically losing track and needing to re-read sections frequently.

Inconsistency, in the quality of work production and in performance across situations. Performance may be better or worse at certain times or in certain places. The ADD individual may be prone to slack off until the pressure is on.

The *DSM–III* (American Psychiatric Association, 1980) recognized that the ADD syndrome presents with or without hyperactivity. The *DSM–IV* (American Psychiatric Association, 1994) classified ADD as three subtypes:

1. AD/HD combined type (symptoms of inattention and hyperactivity–impulsivity).
2. AD/HD predominantly inattentive type (symptoms of inattention, fewer than six symptoms of hyperactivity–impulsivity).
3. AD/HD predominantly hyperactive–impulsive type (symptoms of hyperactivity–impulsivity, fewer than six symptoms of inattention).

Some researchers believe there may be other subtypes within the ADD syndrome (Barkley, 1990; Nadeau, 1995b). Barkley (1990) summarized research suggesting that in addition to the ADD with or without hyperactivity distinction, ADD may be subtyped on the basis of the presence of aggression (oppositional, defiant, explosive, hostile, verbally, and/ or physically aggressive behavior—correlated to later conduct disorder and antisocial behavior), the presence of internalizing symptoms (anxiety and depression), or the situational versus pervasive nature of the symptoms. Nadeau (1995b) suggested that one subtype may be prone to engage in criminal behavior whereas another subtype may be prone to substance abuse. G. Weiss and Hechtman's (1993) research suggests the presence of small subgroups of ADD correlated with antisocial behavior and substance abuse.

Perhaps the most important distinction is to recognize that a portion of ADD individuals may be significantly impaired by inattention, disorganization, forgetfulness, carelessness, and poor sustained effort, yet not display the impulsivity or hyperactivity that many clinicians look for in diagnosing ADD. Clinicians should keep in mind the clinical profile of the AD/HD predominantly inattentive type (Brown, 1995).

Comorbidities

Many writers have found that individuals presenting with ADD frequently have one or more comorbid diagnoses or associated conditions, and this may be a crucial issue in the recognition and treatment of ADD (Barkley, 1990; Biggs, 1995; Nadeau, 1995b; Wender, 1995).

Several writers have pointed out that for many adults, ADD may be camouflaged or masked by a variety of other diagnostic conditions, such as depression, anxiety disorders, substance abuse, and other problems (Nadeau, 1995b; Tzelepis, Schubiner, & Warbasse, 1995). In such cases, the ADD individual may receive treatment for the other condition, and the ADD may go undiagnosed and untreated.

Some researchers have pointed out that there is a high incidence of comorbid learning disabilities (LD) among children and adults with ADD (Barkley, 1990; Lavenstein, 1995; Mannuza, Klein, Bessler, Malloy, & LaPadula, 1993; Sandler, 1995). LD may be found in 30% to 70% of children with ADD and in 15% to 50% of adults (Gittleman, Mannuzza, Shenker, & Bonaquanna, 1985, cited in Lavenstein, 1995). Barkley (1990), using a conservative approach, stated that between 19% and 26% of ADHD children have at least one type of comorbid LD.

REVIEW OF TREATMENT

It is generally considered that adults as well as children respond best to a multimodal approach to treatment, including medication and psychological therapies (G. Weiss & Hechtman, 1993). Several controlled studies have evaluated the efficacy of various medications with adults, and clinicians indicate that 60% to 80% of adults respond favorably to medications (Hallowell & Ratey, 1994; G. Weiss & Hechtman, 1993; Wender, 1995). Although most researchers recommend a combination of drug therapy and psychological treatment, no controlled studies have evaluated the efficacy of psychological therapies for adults with ADD. However, a number of psychological therapies have been documented and are described briefly here.

Pharmacological Treatment

Stimulant medication is the mainstay of drug treatment for adults as well as children (Wender, 1995; Wilens et al., 1995). Stimulant drugs commonly prescribed for ADD adults include Ritalin (methylphenidate), Dexedrine (dextroamphetamine), and Cylert (Pemoline). Tricyclic antidepressants such as Norpramin (desipramine) and an atypical antidepressant, Wellbutrin (buproprion), have also been reported to be effective in reducing ADD symptoms and are frequently prescribed (Wender, 1995). Other medications have also been studied and are currently being explored for use in the treatment of ADD, and the reader is encouraged to consult recent literature for up-to-date information and proposed protocols. For recent summaries, see Wilens, Spencer, and Biederman (1998) and Goldstein (1997).

The effectiveness and toleration of medication vary, but numerous adults with ADD report dramatic improvement in functioning when treated with medication. The therapeutic actions of the medication reduce the core symptoms of ADD and can also improve comorbid conditions such as depression. Stimulant medication is usually the first-line choice, with antidepressants often chosen for nonresponding individuals or individuals with comorbid depression or anxiety.

Psychological Treatment

Anecdotal data indicate that pharmacological treatment may be more effective when combined with psychoeducational and psychotherapeutic interventions (Wilens et al., 1995). Pharmacological treatment is limited in the scope of symptoms for which it is effective, with core symptoms generally improved but not eliminated and many secondary symptoms and associated problems not effectively reduced by medication alone. Approximately 30% of ADD adults will not have a positive response or find they cannot tolerate available medications. Nonmedical interventions therefore have an important role in the treatment of ADD adults.

CBT is frequently cited as the treatment of choice for adults with ADD (Kane, Mikalac, Benjamin, & Barkley, 1990; Murphy, 1995). The consensus among researchers and clinicians seems to be that the best approach is one that is active, directive, supportive, and encouraging (Hallowell, 1995).

Many researchers believe that psychoeducation is one of the most important interventions for individuals with ADD (Hallowell & Ratey, 1994; Murphy, 1995; Nadeau, 1995c). An understanding of ADD will help the adult with ADD to understand himself or herself better, understand why certain things are problematic, see his or her difficulties more realistically, and suggest coping strategies. Psychoeducation often leads to some immediate relief and improvement. Psychoeducation includes information about the neurobiological nature of ADD, symptoms and characteristics, effective treatments, course through the life span, and helpful management techniques.

Various techniques and interventions have been reported useful for helping ADD adults with their attentional deficits (Goodwin & Corgiat, 1992; Nadeau, 1995c; L. W. Weiss, 1994). Attentional deficits are one of the most frequent complaints of adults with ADD, and they benefit from interventions to help with mastering distractions, increasing attention span and concentration, listening, and reading (Jackson & Farrugia, 1997; Morgan, 1996). Other core symptoms such as impulsivity and overactivity often need to be addressed in therapy. Self-instructional verbal mediation techniques such as developed by Braswell and Bloomquist (1991) may be adapted for use with ADD adults. Exercise, relaxation techniques, and other methods are useful as well (Jackson & Farrugia, 1997; Morgan, 1996).

Because most ADD adults present with significant problems in life management, including disorganization, poor task completion, difficulty planning and executing plans, and forgetfulness, methods of compensating for and accommodating their deficits are needed. Hallowell (1995; see also Hallowell & Ratey, 1994) described an effective intervention called *structuring* that has been helpful to numerous ADD adults. Structure is a set of external controls set up to compensate for the unreliable internal controls of ADD individuals. Structuring includes increased organization, patterning, developing goals, planning, and the assistance of a "coach" (someone who helps the ADD adult to plan, prepare, and organize and who provides support and encouragement).

Emotional difficulties are common with ADD adults, taking such forms as moodiness, easy frustration, temper problems, and stress intolerance. Traditional CBT interventions are successfully used for these ADD characteristics as well as comorbid emotional disorders (Morgan, 1996; Murphy, 1995). Self-esteem and relational/social functioning issues are also common among ADD adults, and interventions for these areas have been described in the literature (Jackson & Farrugia, 1997; Morgan, 1996; Murphy, 1995; Ratey, Hallowell, & Miller, 1995). Workplace functioning can be quite impaired by ADD. Nadeau (1995a) presented a number of compensatory strategies and accommodations that can be used. Finally, cognitive remediation methods have been described by Nadeau (1995c), Goodwin and Corgiat (1992), and Weinstein (1994) for those ADD adults with more significant cognitive deficits.

Group therapy is frequently used in the treatment of ADD adults and described by L. Weiss (1992), Hallowell and Ratey (1994), Jackson and Farrugia (1997), and Morgan (1996). It has the advantages of allowing interaction with people who deal with the same difficulties in life, mutual support and encouragement, a forum for psychoeducation, and the sharing of experiences, tips, and information. Many adults with ADD do not know other adults with the disorder, thus interacting with others who are struggling with similar issues decreases the sense of isolation. Many of the interventions reviewed above can be used, and the group situation can often become a laboratory where skills learned can be tried out and practiced, with feedback and mutual encouragement provided.

GENERAL CONSIDERATIONS

Targets of Treatment

On the basis of the literature reviewed above, the principal targets of treatment are the primary (core) and secondary symptoms of ADD (e.g., impulsivity, distractibility, memory problems, and restlessness) and the associated problems that result from the manifestation of these symptoms (e.g., relationship difficulties, low self-esteem, and underachievement). Comorbid conditions (e.g., substance abuse, major depression, and LD) and maladaptive characterological patterns that may have formed around the ADD are considered to be beyond the scope of this time-limited group treatment protocol.

Overall Approach

The consensus among researchers and clinicians seems to be that an active and directive approach such as CBT is more effective than traditional psychodynamic therapies in treating ADD (Hallowell, 1995; Hallowell & Ratey, 1994; Murphy, 1995; Ratey et al., 1992; Wender, 1995). The approach outlined in this chapter is distinctively a CBT approach that is active, directive, encouraging, and supportive. Most of the interventions are cognitive or behavioral in nature, requiring an active and directive stance by the therapist. In the provision of encouragement, support, and direction, the therapist is likened to a "coach." As delineated by Nadeau (1995c), the therapist fills the roles of educator, supporter, interpreter, structurer, and rehabilitation counselor.

OVERVIEW OF TREATMENT

This treatment protocol for group treatment of adult ADD is a time-limited one that typically involves ten 60–75-minute sessions held weekly. It has several components that address the variety of common ADD symptoms and associated problems:

1. Psychoeducation to impart knowledge and understanding of the impact of ADD in the individual's life.
2. A discussion of medication for ADD and referral to appropriate professionals for pharmacological and other specialized treatment.
3. Behavioral self-management skills training.
4. CBT for emotional control and coping with stress.
5. Relationship and social skills training.
6. Group interaction to provide mutual support, encouragement, reinforcement, exchange of ideas and information, and so on.

While this is designed as a time-limited group because such a group seems to have more appeal to the typical adult with ADD, it is not unusual for the participants to choose to continue the group beyond the contracted 10 sessions, allowing more depth of treatment in the targeted areas and a possible broadening of topics.

Exhibit 8.3 provides an outline of the adult ADD group treatment program. Gathering information on the needs that group members perceive can help ensure the content addresses the relevant topics for a particular group. An assessment of these needs in the first session, using a tool such as the ADD Skills Inventory (Morgan, 1997), guides the group leader in future discussions. In Sessions 2–8, selected topics that are commonly relevant to ADD adults are pursued through a combination of group interaction and psychoeducation. Topics include the etiology and neurobiology of ADD, medication, structuring, coping with core symptoms, emotional control, workplace issues, relationship issues, and self-esteem. These topics have been selected on the basis of pretreatment needs assessments and posttreatment evaluations by clients as well as the current literature.

In designing a therapy group for ADD adults, the author has incorporated several distinctive features for this population. As mentioned above, it is designed as a time-limited group because the short-term nature seems to have broader appeal to this population who seem, in general, to lose interest in things quickly. Thus, they seem more willing to make short-term commitments.

The sessions themselves are shortened to 60–75-minute sessions, taking into account the shorter attention span, restlessness, and disdain for boredom of this population of ADD adults. A "short but sweet" session

EXHIBIT 8.3
Outline of Adult Attention Deficit Disorder (ADD)
Group Treatment Program

Session 1
  Introduction/get acquainted
  Purpose and rationale for the group
  Policies
  Review/discuss basic facts about ADD
  Personal assessment of needs/ADD Skills Inventory
  Commitment to group
Session 2
  Discussion: "What does being diagnosed with ADD mean to you?" or "How
    has ADD affected you?"
  Symptoms of ADD
  Treatment options
  Medication and the underlying biology of ADD
Session 3
  Discussion
  Introduction to structuring
  Structuring methods and tools
Session 4
  Discussion
  Introduction to getting control of core ADD symptoms: inattention, impulsivity,
    and restlessness
  Discussion of inattention, impulsivity, and restlessness
  Recommended strategies for inattention, impulsivity, and restlessness
Session 5
  A continuation of topics from Session 4
Session 6
  Discussion
  Introduction to emotional control/handling feelings and impulses—orientation
    to cognitive–behavioral therapy and cognitive restructuring
  Basic concepts and methods of self-management of emotions and stress
Session 7
  Discussion
  Introduction to workplace issues
  Discussion of ADD in the workplace
  Recommended strategies for workplace functioning
Session 8
  Discussion
  Introduction to relationship issues
  Discussion of ADD in relationships
  Recommended strategies for improving relationship/social functioning
Session 9
  Discussion
  ADD and self-esteem
  Suggested methods for improving self-esteem
Session 10
  Discussion
  "Putting it all together"
  Conclusion

seems much appreciated and may help reduce attrition and keep members engaged. In addition, incorporating variety into each session is helpful. Each meeting involves a variety of segments of activity, including a sharing/discussion/feedback time, a period of psychoeducation, discussion of the presented topic, and individual work on tasks such as worksheets. Keeping the meeting moving along and lively helps keep this group engaged and coming back. Varying the sensory modalities is also helpful. Sessions can be made multisensory by incorporating the use of videos, a dry-erase board, attractive handouts, and so on.

It is especially important to provide considerable structure to the sessions for this ADD population. As may be anticipated, group members will tend to become easily sidetracked from productive discussion and will need the therapist to be active and directive, setting the direction and bringing the group back to the topic at hand. Some members, being hyperactive, will tend to talk excessively and monopolize time; the therapist will need to tactfully set limits. Communicating an agenda, being directive in moving the group along the agenda, and setting limits all help increase beneficial structure in the session. A number of therapy tools including handouts, self-help methods, and exercises are available from the author. Exhibit 8.4 lists other sources of helpful treatment material.

TREATMENT DESCRIPTION

Session 1

The goals of Session 1 are to review the basic facts regarding ADD, provide a treatment rationale and description for the group, begin to develop cohesiveness and collaboration among group members, and assess the individual needs of group members. In addition, group policies and administrative details are explained, and members are encouraged to commit themselves to the task of the group and attendance.

The beginning of the session is usually devoted to introductions and getting acquainted. Group members are called on to introduce themselves and briefly share why they are present, as well as what they hope to get out of the group. This seems to foster group cohesiveness and collaboration, which will be a foundation for future meetings. Group members often remark how immensely encouraging it was to know there were others like them. Because the struggle with ADD is often an individual one, group discussions can be a powerful tool for healing.

It is helpful to review the basic facts about ADD to begin the psychoeducational component and provide a common basis for discussion about the disorder. Flowing from this, a rationale for the group therapy

EXHIBIT 8.4
Sources of Information and Materials Useful in the Treatment of Adult Attention Deficit Disorder

Children and Adults With Attention Deficit Disorder (CH.A.D.D.)
  Newsletters, publications, symposiums, support groups
  CH.A.D.D.
  499 Northwest 70th Avenue, Suite 109
  Plantation, FL 33317
  Phone: (305)587-3700

ADD Treatment Resources
  Useful assessment and treatment tools for child and adult ADD treatment.
    Catalog available.
  ADD Treatment Resources
  P.O. Box 595
  Havertown, PA 19083

A.D.D. WareHouse
  Catalog of books, videos, assessment tools
  A.D.D. WareHouse
  300 Northwest 70th Avenue, Suite 102
  Plantation, FL 33317
  Phone: (954)792-8944

The ADHD Report
  A newsletter edited by Russell Barkley and associates providing practical and
    scholarly updates on child and adult ADHD, published bimonthly ($70.00
    per year).
  The ADHD Report
  Guilford Press
  72 Spring Street
  New York, NY 10012

program and its goals can be provided. The goals communicated are as follows:

1. To increase knowledge and understanding of ADD, its impact in one's life, and what can be done about it.
2. To improve self-management skills and address difficulties related to ADD.
3. To create an atmosphere in which adults with ADD can discuss their challenges and support each other.

A program agenda for the 10 weeks is provided.

Policies related to attendance, assignments, fees, and confidentiality need to be explained. Time is set aside for personal assessment of needs to involve participants in reflecting on their individual ADD-related difficulties. This fosters motivation and can be empowering as members gain a sense of what benefit they may get out of the group. The ADD Skills Inventory (Morgan, 1997) is used for this purpose. This information is helpful to the therapist in tailoring sessions to the needs of group members. Finally, a commitment statement is provided and members are encouraged to commit themselves to gaining better control of their ADD through the group.

Session 2

The goals of this session are to further develop group cohesion and mutual support and provide psychoeducational information regarding ADD, particularly about its symptoms, neurobiological basis, and treatment. During this session, some time is devoted to discussing medication.

To foster group discussion, the therapist presents questions such as "What does being diagnosed with ADD mean to you?" and "How has ADD affected you?" While it may seem early in the group process for such hard-hitting questions, ADD adult group members are usually very ready to open up about their hardships. A good discussion usually develops quickly, and the foundation is developed for future discussions offering mutual support to members.

When asked "What does being diagnosed with ADD mean to you?," most participants share a sense of relief and hope, typically stating, "It's a relief to know, finally, what it is that has been holding me back in my life," "It's good to know that there is a name for my problem," "All my life I feel like I've been struggling for some reason and could be doing much better. Now I know why," and "It's comforting to know that something can be done to help." Most seem encouraged and empowered by the new understanding. Some also share a sense of regret that they have the disorder, and sometimes state things such as "I wish I had known when I was young . . ." and "I wish something could have been done to help a long time ago . . ." as they reflect on all the past struggles in their life caused by the disorder. Others share a relief that their difficulties are due to a subtle neurological deficit and not to deep characterological problems or lack of intelligence.

Next on the agenda for Session 2 is a presentation of psychoeducational information about ADD and its treatment. This segment covers a detailed description of the symptoms of ADD, its neurobiological basis, and the various treatments (e.g., psychoeducation, medication, counseling, and compensatory behavioral strategies).

A significant amount of time is devoted to medications for ADD, because this is a topic that seems to be important and of great interest to group members. Handouts on each of these topics are provided. Group members often rate the discussion of medications as being highly valuable to them on posttreatment evaluations. The combination of psychoeducational information and hearing about other group members' experiences with medication is often of great impact.

Session 3

The goals of Session 3 include a furtherance of constructive and supportive sharing and encouragement among group members (a goal for each session) and to introduce structuring techniques as a way of compensating for ADD-related behavioral deficits.

As described earlier, the symptoms of ADD cause major problems in task completion, productivity, and achieving up to one's potential. Adults with ADD typically struggle to complete routine tasks such as completing paperwork, managing finances, and various work responsibilities. Disorganization, poor planning, and forgetfulness interfere with being able to juggle multiple demands effectively.

Typical examples of difficulties include remembering to pay bills on time, keeping up with routine tasks such as entering transactions in a checkbook or balancing a checkbook, following a prudent sequence of actions in the performance of job requirements, remembering to do something one has planned to do, and completing minor tasks while more important tasks are neglected.

Structuring is a set of external controls that can compensate for the unreliable internal controls common in ADD individuals (Hallowell & Ratey, 1994). Most people with ADD cannot depend on their internal controls to keep themselves organized and on task. Thus, developing a reliable system of external controls or structure is extremely beneficial to ADD adults. Such structuring includes having methods and tools for improved organization; patterning (developing routines and habits that facilitate tasks and obligations being carried out without forgetting); having clear, specific goals and reflecting on them regularly; planning—long range and short range—and laying out steps to take toward goals; and having a "coach" to help the ADD adult think things through, plan, prepare, and strategize, as well as provide encouragement and accountability.

One underemployed ADD client wanted to change from an unfulfilling career to a career in teaching (for which he had been trained but never employed). He had a general idea of what he needed to do to achieve this goal but was unsuccessful in making the necessary steps. The vagueness of his plans and his disorganized lifestyle and approach to tasks hampered him in identifying and implementing the necessary steps.

Structuring interventions were used to aid this client in accomplishing his goal. For example, he was guided in breaking down his goal into individual steps and developing a step-by-step plan, providing an increased level of structure. He was supervised in scheduling the time necessary to implement the steps of his plan on a weekly basis, using provided schedule forms. Finally, regular contacts with the therapist provided further structure.

Another client whose work involved investment transactions of many thousands of dollars had difficulty performing her work tasks without making critical mistakes. Her job involved following complex procedures with many opportunities to forget a step or make an error. She was guided in developing a visual flowchart of her task procedures, including points at which she should check her work for accuracy, thereby providing increased structure.

During Session 3, the concept and rationale for structuring are explained. Following this, the methods and techniques of structuring are described and discussed, citing many useful examples. Clients are provided handouts that outline the concepts, tools such as a weekly schedule form, and a weekly task planning sheet. Homework assignment involves the implementation of structuring methods, which will be discussed and tracked in future sessions. Some of the most valuable things that happen in ADD groups are the sharing of ideas and experiences among members related to gaining better control of their ADD difficulties.

By the conclusion of Session 3, three very important interventions for adult ADD have been introduced: psychoeducation, medication (and other treatment options), and structuring.

Sessions 4 and 5

The main goal of Sessions 4 and 5 is to describe and discuss interventions for the "core" symptoms of ADD: inattention, impulsivity, and overactivity. These sessions are designed to further help the ADD adult to gain control of their ADD difficulties.

After some discussion of the week's experiences and follow-up on structuring, the topic of the core symptoms of ADD and how they manifest is introduced. The focus then turns to practical ways of compensating for or accommodating the attention, impulse control, and activity level difficulties. Many such useful techniques are described by Morgan (1996), Hallowell and Ratey (1994), and Goodwin and Corgiat (1992). For example, breaking work into manageable portions and taking frequent breaks can aid concentration. Exercise has been found by many to improve attention/concentration and reduce restlessness and impulsivity. Self-instructional verbal mediation techniques can reduce impulsive behavior.

Many CBT techniques can be beneficially used in helping ADD adults cope with their core symptoms. For example, relaxation techniques are helpful in quieting the racing mind and physical restlessness of ADD individuals. Cognitive strategies such as covert verbal mediation (guided self-dialogue) can help ADD clients inhibit impulses and thereby stay on task, concentrate, and persist. Problem-solving techniques can help ADD adults to devise strategies to better cope with things such as environmental distractions. Behavioral techniques such as setting up rewards and punishments for task completion are almost always desirable. Through psycho-education, recommended reading, therapist suggestion, sharing of ideas among group members, and handouts, many useful strategies are provided to group members to help them gain better control of their ADD symptoms.

A group member who was an executive in a major corporation reported she tended to be impulsive when attempting to resolve problems relayed to her by subordinates or other executives she dealt with, sometimes with serious consequences because of her poor decisions when she rushed. When described a problem in a phone conversation, she would characteristically "shoot from the hip" with the first solution that seemed reasonable. As an intervention, she was taught to use covert verbal mediation to catch herself in target situations and use an inner dialogue to stop, think, and make a well-reasoned plan. Self-statements she rehearsed covertly to herself included "You don't have to answer now, buy some time to think about it first," "Think before you act," and "Slow down."

Session 6

The primary goal of this session is to introduce strategies for coping with stress and gaining better emotional control. Basic concepts and methods of self-management of emotions and stress are introduced.

Cognitive restructuring techniques are the focus of this session. The cognitive model (Beck & Emery, 1985) is introduced to the group. The group is thus oriented to the relationships among situations, emotions, and cognitions. Following this, the group is trained in cognitive strategies for coping with stress and reducing emotional distress, based on the literature (e.g., Ellis & Dryden, 1987; Meichenbaum, 1985). Skills are further developed through the application of these concepts to real-life situations and self-help assignments.

Typical affective problems of ADD adults include angry outbursts in response to ordinary frustrations and anxiety around performance situations similar to past experiences in which they performed badly, perhaps as a result of ADD symptoms. If these situations involve other people, the ADD adult's coping ability is often further challenged, sometimes leading to difficulty keeping a job or maintaining relationships. One client repeatedly lost his temper with his fiancé under routine circumstances. He was encouraged to identify self-statements, which included many "should" statements such as "She shouldn't bother me about that," "She should leave me alone," and "She shouldn't be so picky," when he incurred her criticism. Once he understood how his "demanding" views and "should" statements escalated his frustration, he was able to learn to substitute coping statements in target situations (e.g., "While I prefer that she not bother me about this, I can deal with it") to deescalate his frustration and refrain from outbursts. Practice of such cognitive restructuring methods eventually led to his being able to catch himself and slow down his reaction to such bothersome situations, thus achieving better self-control.

Although the exposure to cognitive restructuring concepts and methods is rather brief, this topic is returned to time and again in future sessions, allowing reinforcement of the concepts and practice in the implementation of the methods. Through self-help assignments and handouts, the process is further strengthened.

Session 7

The goal of Session 7 is to help group members to understand and deal with workplace problems and issues that result from their ADD deficits and tendencies, although initially time is spent reviewing cognitive restructuring principles.

It is particularly important to carry over discussion from the previous session on stress and emotional control to further develop self-management skills in this area. Application of cognitive strategies to episodes throughout the preceding week is highlighted. Following this, an introduction to the topic of this session is provided. Potential difficulties that may be presented in the workplace because of ADD are introduced and discussed. Such difficulties include task completion and follow-through, problems with details and paperwork, disorganization, poor planning and time management, relationships and communication with coworkers, and many other areas (Nadeau, 1995a). Helping group members to identify their individual work-related problems and the connection between these problems and ADD is very helpful, and discussion time is devoted to this.

Through therapist suggestion, handouts, and group collaboration, strategies for dealing with ADD-related workplace difficulties are presented. Nadeau (1995a) presented useful lists of reasonable workplace accommodations and compensatory strategies for ADD adults. For example, ADD adults who tend to "dive into" projects at work in a rather impulsive and rushed manner benefit from developing the habit of spending time at the beginning of the day in planning and setting priorities. Also, becoming better attuned to social cues can help many ADD adults to avoid interpersonal conflicts with coworkers.

Other issues that may be addressed in group are ADD and career fit, positive traits of ADD and the workplace (e.g., energy and enthusiasm, creative ideas, and good crisis intervention), whether to divulge one's ADD diagnosis, and reasonable accommodations that can be requested from employers. This session is often particularly productive in terms of group discussion, as ADD adults are often struggling in this area and feel the need to talk and find help for their difficulties. Members often appreciate the group's cohesiveness, support, and practical ideas.

Session 8

The main goal of this session is to describe and discuss interventions for relationship issues and problems as related to ADD. As with previous sessions, some time is also devoted to group sharing and discussion and review of previously presented concepts.

G. Weiss and Hechtman (1993) pointed out that, according to their research, ADD adults tend to have more frequent interpersonal problems; lack long-term close relationships; have brief and less significant hetero-sexual relationships; have frequent disputes with peers, family members, and supervisors; and may feel lonely. As with workplace issues, helping ADD adults to identify their individual relationship problems and the connection between these problems and ADD is very helpful. Many relationship problems they face are driven by ADD symptoms (Hallowell & Ratey, 1994; Murphy, 1995; Ratey et al., 1995; L. Weiss, 1992), and identifying self-defeating patterns is an essential first step. For example, ADD adults are famous for the annoying tendency of tuning out or being distracted in conversations. They also tend to interrupt and intrude on others and manifest impatience and other impulsive interpersonal behaviors. They frustrate easily, are sometimes much too open about their negativity, and may be argumentative. These are all impediments to good interpersonal relationships.

By developing greater self-awareness and particularly awareness of ADD-related self-defeating behaviors and tendencies, this session begins the process of self-enhancing change. This is furthered by the presentation of several interpersonal strategies to counter the problematic tendencies and discussion, sharing of ideas, and support among group members. Practice of strategies between sessions is encouraged. The basic intervention scheme used is to develop awareness of self-defeating patterns in communication and relationships, recognize the ADD-related barriers to intimacy (Ratey et al., 1995), and learn and improve communication and interpersonal problem-solving skills (Murphy, 1995).

Examples of specific interventions include paying attention to nonverbal cues from others, active listening techniques, bibliotherapy in the form of recommended reading on communication and relationship skills (e.g., Burns, 1985; Garner, 1980), learning to "know when to stop," and monitoring and changing stubbornness, argumentativeness, frustration, and anger. The focus is on providing compensatory strategies and increasing relationship awareness and skills. Training in these skills is facilitated by handouts on various communication skills, conflict resolution steps, and expression of negative feelings.

Session 9

The main goal of this session is to show group members how they can improve self-esteem. Low self-esteem is a common by-product of ADD owing to the accumulation of years of higher rates of negative feedback, rejection, and failure.

Reframing the past in light of ADD can be a powerful intervention with ADD adults (Murphy, 1995). Often these individuals have a sense of something being wrong but have not been able to identify what it is. They frequently attribute their problems to a pervasive characterological deficit in themselves. Helping the ADD person to see how ADD manifests in their life, now and in the past, and that their difficulties are due to a subtle neurological deficit they have little control over allows them to reframe their shortcomings and the negative messages they have received from parents, teachers, spouses, peers, and employers over the years; this helps them to rebuild their self-esteem. The empowerment that occurs through participation in the group, as members see that there are ways that, with effort, they can be more successful, also has the potential to increase self-esteem.

Another intervention for enhancing self-esteem is cognitive reappraisal (Burns, 1993). Group members are guided in identifying their personal faulty standards of self-worth and changing this to unconditional self-acceptance. Other helpful exercises include listing "what's good about me" (strengths) or "my most impressive qualities," practicing positive affirmation statements, choosing activities and vocations that fit with individual strengths, and recognizing positive traits associated with ADD.

Session 10

The goals of this session are to review the process of previous sessions, emphasize key points, empower group members, and draw the series to a fitting close. Having a time-limited group has the advantage of attracting ADD members who might shy away from a longer time commitment. However, frequently group members themselves ask if the group may continue, which is often beneficial. At this point, some if not all group members will likely choose to end their involvement, and the therapist should be prepared at some point to "put it all together" and have a wrap-up session.

I have made it a practice to distribute an outcome evaluation form that lists most of the topics and issues discussed during the course of the group and that asks for a rating of the benefit of each discussion. This can serve as a basis for discussing and reviewing concepts.

It is hoped that the last session will be empowering to the group members. This is accomplished by conveying the message that ADD does not doom one to failure and that ADD individuals can be quite successful if they persist and work at making changes (Murphy, 1995). By using the information and methods presented in group, ADD clients can make significant and sometimes dramatic improvement. This message instills hope and motivation.

CONCLUSION

ADD in adults is a common disorder that significantly impairs several aspects of the individual's functioning. ADD is a treatable disorder, and promising intervention strategies are emerging in the literature. Clinicians who treat ADD should have a clear understanding of the disorder itself and how it affects the lives of their clients. A multimodal approach to treatment appears to be the most successful. ADD adults seem to respond best to a treatment that is active, directive, supportive, and empowering. CBT is therefore a good choice and has been shown anecdotally to be effective. The group format has particular advantages. Group therapy for ADD adults should take into consideration the common and typical needs of this population as well as the individual group members and includes psychoeducation, referral for medication, compensatory behavioral strategies, emotion and stress management techniques, relationship and social skills enhancement, and group collaboration and support. CBT group therapy can also provide a sense of empowerment, hope, and motivation, and when combined with the skills discussed, such treatment can help these clients to cope with and gain better control over their ADD symptoms and related difficulties.

REFERENCES

American Psychiatric Association. (1980). *Diagnostic and statistical manual of mental disorders* (3rd ed.). Washington, DC: Author.

American Psychiatric Association. (1994). *Diagnostic and statistical manual of mental disorders* (4th ed.). Washington, DC: Author.

Barkley, R. A. (1990). *Attention deficit hyperactivity disorder: A handbook for diagnosis and treatment*. New York: Guilford Press.

Barkley, R. A. (1997). Behavioral inhibition, sustained attention, and executive functions: Constructing a unifying theory of ADHD. *Psychological Bulletin, 121*, 65–94.

Beck, A. T., & Emery, G. (1985). *Anxiety disorders and phobias*. New York: Basic Books.

Biggs, S. H. (1995). Neuropsychological and psychoeducational testing in the evaluation of the ADD adult. In K. G. Nadeau (Ed.), *A comprehensive guide to attention deficit disorder in adults* (pp. 109–129). New York: Brunner/Mazel.

Braswell, L., & Bloomquist, M. L. (1991). *Cognitive–behavioral therapy with ADHD children*. New York: Guilford Press.

Brown, T. E. (1995). Differential diagnosis of ADD versus ADHD in adults. In K.G. Nadeau (Ed.), *A comprehensive guide to attention deficit disorder in adults* (pp. 93–107). New York: Brunner/Mazel.

Burns, D. D. (1985). *Intimate connections*. New York: Penguin Books.

Burns, D. D. (1993). *Ten days to self-esteem*. New York: William Morrow.

Ellis, A., & Dryden, W. (1987). *The practice of rational–emotive therapy*. New York: Springer.

Garner, A. (1980). *Conversationally speaking: Tested new ways to increase your personal and social effectiveness*. New York: McGraw-Hill.

Goldstein, S., (1997). *Managing attention and learning disorders in late adolescence and adulthood*. New York: Wiley.

Goodwin, R. E., & Corgiat, M. D. (1992, September–October). Cognitive rehabilitation of adult attention deficit disorder: A case study. *Journal of Cognitive Rehabilitation, 10*, 28–35.

Hallowell, E. M. (1995). Psychotherapy of adult attention deficit disorder. In K. G. Nadeau (Ed.), *A comprehensive guide to attention deficit disorder in adults* (pp. 144–167). New York: Brunner/Mazel.

Hallowell, E. M., & Ratey, J. J. (1994). *Driven to distraction*. New York: Pantheon Books.

Jackson, B., & Farrugia, D. (1997). Diagnosis and treatment of adults with attention deficit hyperactivity disorder. *Journal of Counseling and Development, 75*, 312–318.

Kane, R., Mikalac, C., Benjamin, S., & Barkley, R. A. (1990). Assessment and treatment of adults with ADHD. In R. A. Barkley (Ed.), *Attention deficit hyperactivity disorder: A handbook for diagnosis and treatment* (pp. 613–654). New York: Guilford Press.

Lavenstein, B. (1995). Neurological comorbidity patterns/differential diagnosis in adult attention deficit disorder. In K. G. Nadeau (Ed.), *A comprehensive guide to attention deficit disorder in adults* (pp. 74–92). New York: Brunner/Mazel.

Mannuza, S., Klein, R. G., Bessler, A., Malloy, P., & LaPadula, M. (1993). Adult outcome of hyperactive boys: Educational achievement, occupational rank, and psychiatric status. *Archives of General Psychiatry, 50*, 565–576.

Meichenbaum, D. (1985). *Stress innoculation training*. New York: Pergamon Press.

Morgan, W. D. (1996). *Adult attention deficit disorder: A review of the literature and application to clinical practice*. Unpublished doctoral dissertation, University of Michigan, Ann Arbor.

Morgan, W. D. (1997). *ADD Skills Inventory*. Havertown, PA: Author.

Murphy, K. R. (1995). Empowering the adult with ADD. In K. G. Nadeau (Ed.), *A comprehensive guide to attention deficit disorder in adults* (pp. 135–145). New York: Brunner/Mazel.

Nadeau, K. G. (1995a). ADD in the workplace: Career consultation and counseling for the adult with ADD. In K. G. Nadeau (Ed.), *A comprehensive guide to attention deficit disorder in adults* (pp. 308–334). New York: Brunner/Mazel.

Nadeau, K. G. (Ed.). (1995b). *A comprehensive guide to attention deficit disorder in adults.* New York: Brunner/Mazel.

Nadeau, K. G. (1995c). Life management skills for the adult with ADD. In K. G. Nadeau (Ed.), *A comprehensive guide to attention deficit disorder in adults* (pp. 191–217). New York: Brunner/Mazel.

Quinn, P. O. (1995). Neurobiology of attention deficit disorder. In K. G. Nadeau (Ed.), *A comprehensive guide to attention deficit disorder in adults* (pp. 18–31). New York: Brunner/Mazel.

Ratey, J. J., Greenberg, M. S., Bemporad, J. R., & Lindem, K. J. (1992). Unrecognized attention deficit hyperactivity disorder in adults presenting for outpatient psychotherapy. *Journal of Child and Adolescent Psychophamacology, 2,* 267–275.

Ratey, J. J., Hallowell, E. M., & Miller, A. C. (1995). Relationship dilemmas for adults with ADD: The biology of intimacy. In K. G. Nadeau (Ed.), *A comprehensive guide to attention deficit disorder in adults* (pp. 218–235). New York: Brunner/Mazel.

Sandler, A. D. (1995). Attention deficits and neurodevelopmental variation in older adolescents and adults. In K. G. Nadeau (Ed.), *A comprehensive guide to attention deficit disorder in adults* (pp. 58–73). New York: Brunner/Mazel.

Tzelepis, A., Schubiner, H., & Warbasse, L. H. (1995). Differential diagnosis and psychiatric comorbidity patterns in adult attention deficit disorder. In K. G. Nadeau (Ed.), *A comprehensive guide to attention deficit disorder in adults* (pp. 35–57). New York: Brunner/Mazel.

Weinstein, C. S. (1994). Cognitive remediation strategies: An adjunct to the psychotherapy of adults with attention-deficit hyperactivity disorder. *Journal of Psychotherapy Practice and Research, 3*(1), 44–57.

Weiss, G., & Hechtman, L. T. (1993). *Hyperactive children grown up* (2nd ed.). New York: Guilford Press.

Weiss, L. (1992). *Attention deficit disorder in adults.* Dallas, TX: Taylor.

Weiss, L. W. (1994). *The attention deficit disorder in adults workbook.* Dallas, TX: Taylor.

Wender, P. H. (1995). *Attention-deficit hyperactivity disorder in adults.* New York: Oxford University Press.

Wilens, T. E., Spencer T. J., & Biederman, J. (1995). Pharmacotherapy of adult ADHD. In K. G. Nadeau (Ed.), *A comprehensive guide to attention deficit disorder in adults* (pp. 168–188). New York: Brunner/Mazel.

Wilens, T., Spencer, T. J., & Biederman, J. (1998). Pharmacotherapy of adult ADHD. In R. A. Barkley (Ed.), *Attention-deficit hyperactivity disorder: A handbook for diagnosis and treatment* (2nd ed.). New York: Guilford Press.

Woods, D. R. (1986). The diagnosis and treatment of attention deficit disorder, residual type. *Psychiatric Annals, 16,* 23–24, 26–28.

II

COGNITIVE–BEHAVIORAL GROUP THERAPY FOR SPECIFIC POPULATIONS OR SETTINGS

9

OLDER ADULTS

LARRY W. THOMPSON, DAVID V. POWERS, DAVID W. COON,
KELLIE TAKAGI, CHRISTINE McKIBBIN,
AND DOLORES GALLAGHER-THOMPSON

This chapter presents models of short-term, cognitive–behavioral therapy (CBT) for two of the most common psychological problems experienced by adults over 60 years of age: depression and the stresses of family caregiving. Group CBT is particularly suited to older adults who are often experiencing decreased social contact and who may feel less stigmatized when their problems are addressed in a group context and with an emphasis on coping (Dick, Gallagher-Thompson, Coon, Powers, & Thompson, 1996). Although our group treatment in each of these two problem areas has a somewhat different focus, each shares our emphasis on the cognitive–behavioral aspects of problem definition and solution and a similar process in terms of assessment, group socialization, goal setting, group process, and termination. We begin the chapter with a discussion of these common elements with regard to depression. Later sections of the chapter highlight areas specific to family caregiving. The model of group

This work was partially supported by Grants R01-MH37196 and T32MH19104 from the National Institute of Mental Health (NIMH) to Larry Wolford Thompson and Grants R01-MH43407 and U01-AG13289 from NIMH and the National Institute on Aging, respectively, to Dolores Gallagher-Thompson.

treatment for depression is flexible enough to be modified easily to address these and other problems, such as grief, common to older populations.

DEPRESSION IN OLDER ADULTS

Historically, depression and depressive symptomatology have been perceived as predictable responses to the common losses that occur with increasing age, such as death of one's spouse and other family members and friends; changing roles (e.g., no longer being in the labor force); decline in one's own physical health and stamina; economic reverses; and, for many, the need to take on caregiving roles (e.g., for one's spouse, adult children, and, in many cases, grandchildren as well). The prevalence of currently recognized clinical syndromes of depression in older adults is unclear, owing to methodological limitations and differences in assessment methods in various epidemiological studies. However, it is generally accepted that more older adults experience subsyndromal levels of depression than a full-blown major depressive episode; in addition, various depressive disorders tend to be more common in older adults with significant physical health problems and those who have experienced recent major losses (Blazer & Koenig 1996). Although only a minority of older adults develop severe depression, those who do actually seek help often require a range of health and mental health services. Frequently, a diagnosis of depression in older adults is often concurrent with multiple medical disorders, low socioeconomic status, and low social integration (Phifer & Murrell, 1986; Turner & Noh, 1988).

Accurate assessment and recognition of depressive symptoms and syndromes in older adults is essential because these are generally treatable conditions with a favorable prognosis. However, as indicated by the disproportionate number of successful suicides among older adults, depression continues to be unrecognized and untreated by professionals, family, and friends (Manton, Blazer, & Woodbury, 1987). Depression in older adults is often seen in combination with chronic and multiple medical disorders common in late life, such as thyroid disorder, carcinoma, or nutritional or vitamin deficiencies. Furthermore, the presence of chronic pain, somatic complaints, or dementia can complicate the diagnostic assessment. A thorough review of the complexities of diagnosing depression is beyond the scope of this chapter (for more detailed discussions, see Futterman, Thompson, Gallagher-Thompson, & Ferris, 1995; Pachana, Thompson, & Gallagher-Thompson, 1994).

Older adults who seek treatment in an outpatient setting will often present with mild to moderate levels of depression, frequently accompanied by significant anxiety (Sheikh, 1996). It is also not uncommon for older adults to present with a transient reoccurrence of depressive symptoms that do not meet the diagnostic criteria for major depressive disorder in the American Psychiatric Association's (1994) *Diagnostic and Statistical Manual of Mental Disorders* (4th ed., DSM–IV; see Blazer & Koenig, 1996). It is the clinician who must be able to determine if the older adult has a diagnosis of depression and assess the nature of the depressive syndrome so that an assessment can be made of the type of treatment that is most likely to be appropriate for that individual.

GROUP CBT FOR LATE-LIFE DEPRESSION

Group CBT is one of the most frequently used types of group therapy for older adults. Our program is derived from the original work of Beck and his colleagues (Beck, 1967, 1976; Beck, Rush, Shaw, & Emery, 1979). A major tenet of CBT renders this approach particularly well-suited for elderly individuals, who are experiencing numerous or substantive losses in their later years: The experience of loss per se does not necessarily lead to depression; rather it is how that experience is *perceived* and what its meaning is to the individual that determines whether or not depression will result. In our experience, as older adults begin to understand this concept more fully, they can more readily accept the rationale for implementing cognitive techniques and appear more amenable to adapt new ways of looking at their problems. CBT includes three key constructs for understanding the origin and maintenance of depression. These are (a) negative schemas, (b) faulty informational processing, and (c) the negative cognitive triad. In the cognitive model of depression, it is proposed that negative schemas interact with negative life events to produce depressive symptomatology. Therefore, treatment focuses primarily on modifying thoughts to change affect and behavior. Group CBT as used in our center also includes techniques based on the principles of a behavioral therapy developed by Lewinsohn (1974). As depressed older adults modify their behaviors and their thoughts, their mood is expected to improve, lifting them out of depression.

In this section, we discuss why it is helpful to use a group format with older adults, how group members are introduced to this treatment, how the CBT model is presented and cognitive techniques are introduced, how to incorporate behavioral methods, and how to get maximal gain from homework. For a more comprehensive discussion of group cognitive therapy for depression in older adults, the reader is referred to the work of Yost, Beutler, Corbishley, and Allender (1986). Detailed treatment manuals for late-life depression are also available based on individual CBT used in our programs, which can be modified for group work (Dick et al., 1996).

ASSESSING APPROPRIATENESS FOR GROUP CBT

Older adults represent a diverse group with various levels of appropriateness for cognitive–behavioral group therapy. It is therefore important for the clinician to be able to conduct a thorough assessment and then to determine the most appropriate form of treatment for each older adult who seeks treatment in an outpatient setting.

Assessment Interview

In the initial phase of the interview process, it is important to determine if the potential group participant has any hearing or speech impairments that might interfere with communication in the group. Additionally, the client's verbal, reading, and written level of comprehension needs to be evaluated, because of the emphasis on homework assignments, group discussions, and coping strategies that are taught during each group session. If the group participant is a caregiver, the clinician must also discuss with the participant about available transportation and arrangements for a family member or friend to provide respite care during the group meetings. If arrangements are not made in advance, it may become a barrier for the participant in being able to attend the group sessions on a regular basis. It is essential that the clinician explain to each participant that in group CBT, improvement requires work, practice, regular attendance, active verbal participation, and a problem-solving attitude. There are several other important areas that the clinician must address during the initial interview with each potential group participant, including the following:

1. The origins and nature of the presenting problem or problems and how this affects the participant's current functioning.
2. Complete medical history and medication history, including current illnesses and medical treatments.
3. Cognitive function to determine if the individual can process and retain new information sufficiently to benefit from CBT.
4. Information regarding cultural traditions, beliefs, and values as well as health and mental health beliefs and practices.
5. Prior health and mental health care utilization, which also includes alternative or nontraditional practices.
6. An assessment regarding suicidal risk.

Assessment Instruments

There are several self-report measures that we commonly administer to older adults prior to therapy. Level of depression is assessed with either Beck Depression Inventory (BDI; Beck, Ward, Mendelson, Mock, & Erbaugh, 1961) or the Geriatric Depression Scale (GDS; Brink et al., 1982). The BDI consists of 21 items that assess the severity of complaints, symptoms, and concerns about current depression, including somatic, cognitive, and behavioral items. This measure was originally developed and tested on young adults. Since then, psychometric studies have been conducted with older adults. Gallagher, Nies, and Thompson (1982) found that the BDI had adequate test–retest reliability and internal consistency in a sample of both community volunteers and outpatients with depression. Coefficient alpha in the community sample was .76 and in the depressed sample was .73. Gallagher, Breckenridge, Steinmetz, and Thompson (1983) examined the validity by comparing conventional cutoff scores on the BDI and selected diagnostic classifications of the Research Diagnostic Criteria using information derived from the Schedule for Affective Disorders and the Schizophrenia (Endicott & Spitzer, 1978). They found high correspondence between the two, indicating that the BDI is a sensitive index of clinical depression in older adults.

In the older adult population, a significant confound to recognizing depression is the presence of multiple somatic complaints, because these may reflect a diagnosable medical condition or chronic pain rather than depression. To reduce their impact on diagnosis, researchers developed the GDS. It contains no somatic items and is one of the few depression scales developed specifically for older adults and standardized on an older adult sample. Items in this measure are answered either yes or no, which reportedly makes it easier for older adults with low literacy or some cognitive impairment to complete the scale. Yesavage, Brink, Rose, and Adey (1983) reported an overall alpha coefficient was .94. A 15-item short form has also been developed (Sheikh & Yesavage, 1986), which is very practical for use as a screening measure in medical settings.

Assessment of suicidality is typically initiated by direct questions about suicidal thoughts and specific suicidal plans, but self-report measures such as the Hopelessness Scale (HS; Beck, Weissman, Lester, & Trexler, 1974) can also be helpful in this process. The HS is a 20-item scale that assesses a person's extent of pessimism or hopelessness about the future. Studies have shown that the presence of hopelessness can be an important risk factor for suicidal behavior, irrespective of depression level.

The Dysfunctional Attitude Scale (Weissman, 1979) was originally designed to identify a set of relatively stable attitudes (or cognitive vulnerabilities) associated with depression; the use of this scale can be helpful in identifying schemas. A number of techniques have also been developed to assist clients in changing schemas: A modification of Young's (1990) historical test of schemas is particularly suited for work with elders (Dick & Gallagher-Thompson, 1995) and can be used effectively with some clients in a group setting.

The Older Person's Pleasant Events Schedule (OPPES; Gallagher &

Thompson, 1981) provides an index of functional activities leading to pleasure attainment. This is a 66-item self-report inventory designed to assess seven domains that may bring pleasure: nature, social, thoughts and feelings, recognition from others, giving to others, competence, and leisure activities. The OPPES measures both the frequency with which activities are engaged over the previous month and the degree of pleasure derived from the event (regardless of whether the older person engaged in that event). Separate frequency and pleasantness scores are created by summing scores of items pertaining to each of the seven domains. This information is often useful in helping clients increase pleasurable activities, which are discussed in greater detail below.

PROGRESSION OF GROUP CBT FOR DEPRESSION

The type and sequencing of specific procedures in CBT with the elderly may vary substantially, depending on the capability level of the clients, personality differences of group members, whether the group is held for a fixed number of sessions or is ongoing, whether it is closed or open to new clients, whether group members are experiencing similar or diverse problems, and whether the group has a specific topical focus or more general aims. We prefer to conduct CBT groups for fixed time periods of approximately 10 to 12 sessions that are closed and tend to focus on the development of several basic skills to help clients with their depression. At the conclusion of the group, we evaluate the clinical condition of clients and at the same time obtain information on what seemed to work and what did not. Depending on their clinical status, clients could then choose to discontinue therapy, enter a new group with a different problem focus if it was available, or repeat the therapy group that focuses on basic skills. For example, after 10 sessions or so, a client may be less depressed as a result of group CBT but is still having difficulty in being assertive in certain social situations. The decision might be made that relapse or recurrence is likely unless he or she is able to resolve this problem. Rather than continuing in the same group, the client might benefit more from participation in a group with a specific focus on social skills if it was available. Regardless of what specific procedures are to be emphasized, there are a number of general features in need of attention in any CBT group designed for older adults.

Preparing Clients for Group

An initial objective is to familiarize older adults with the CBT model. Many older adults may not have previously participated in a group therapy, and even those who have may have inaccurate preconceptions about what to expect. Therefore, the general content and format of the group should be outlined during the initial contact with group members and covered in more detail in the first session. Along with a presentation of the theory, clear examples relevant to older adults are used to illustrate how thoughts and behaviors can change mood. Chapter 1 of Dick et al. (1996) gives detailed information and examples, as in the following, used by us in presenting the theory effectively to older adults.

> An example that is particularly salient for many older individuals involves an 80-year-old man named Sam who was required to take a written examination to renew his drivers license in the State of California. Sam made a few errors on the examination, but he had a sufficient number of items correct to pass the test, and his drivers license was renewed for another 5 years. Ordinarily, one might be relieved and even somewhat happy that this ominous hurdle was cleared once again. Not Sam. As Sam was driving home he began to dwell on the few errors that he made, and he became so preoccupied with his errors, he lost sight of the fact that he had passed the exam. So, rather than experiencing relief, perhaps even a little joy at having surmounted this obstacle, he became sad and remorseful at having made some foolish mistakes. Sam began to berate himself, because of his intellectual inadequacies, and he was so preoccupied that he made a wrong turn while driving home. He thought, "This just proves my mind is slipping badly. I probably am making errors in everything. I'll bet my checkbook is a mess. I've probably lost thousands of dollars. This is just more proof that my brain is deteriorating. I know my doctor is going to find that I have Alzheimer's." By the time Sam arrived home, he was visibly shaken, and he spent the remainder of the day in his study, unable to talk to anyone or convey the good news about his examination. His family thought he had failed, and they tried to plan what to do to cheer him up.

After presenting the story, we would invite clients to consider how Sam might have felt if he had not engaged in the negative filtering and also how they might have reacted in this situation.

Goal Setting

Once clients have some comprehension of the model, attention is turned to socializing the group members into treatment. This involves directly addressing the goals the group hopes to meet as well as what is expected of group members. The primary goal is to reduce and eventually eliminate group members' feelings of depression. To meet this goal, group members are expected to discuss their difficulties honestly in the group, maintain the confidentiality of the group, attend regularly, and complete homework tasks between sessions. Group members' active participation in treatment is a critical factor in treatment effectiveness. Likewise, it is important that group leaders model appropriate behavior through their active participation in the group. Another characteristic of older adult group members is that they are initially much less likely than younger group members to ask questions when they do not understand a point, thus it is the responsibility of the group leader to encourage and prompt group members to ask questions.

Group members are also asked to think about what they want to get out of therapy as a homework assignment after the first session. In the second session, each group member is asked to outline up to three target complaints they would like to address in the group. The overall goal is to reduce each group member's depression, but each group member is asked to identify specific issues to deal with. These goals serve as the focus of therapy for each group member. Categories of complaints frequently reported by elders who seek help in our programs include loneliness, problems with adult children and grandchildren returning to the nest because of insufficient finances or other adjustment difficulties, interpersonal difficulties with other community members, problems in functioning as a result of medical illness, inadequate resources, and severe emotional disturbance. Group members are then asked to develop concrete, measurable outcomes that are attainable and would reflect progress in dealing with a particular target complaint. Clients sometimes have difficulty doing this, and often this may become a source of discussion in early group sessions as group members assist one another in developing measurable outcomes. For example, Sara, a 70-year-old widow of 5 years, had a primary complaint of being lonely. After discussions in the group pertaining to life contingencies relevant to this problem, the group helped her set a goal of trying to have a pleasurable contact with a friend or relative at least three times per week. The rationale of this strategy is for clients to experience successful progress as they develop the requisite skills to address these specific outcomes. Thus, the more often they are able to reach their specific target goals, the more confident they will be in using their newfound capabilities to address other life difficulties as they arise. The assumption is that as success in dealing with problems increases, depression is likely to decrease.

Group CBT can provide several advantages over individual CBT, particularly when working with older adults. A cohesive group provides a great deal of support for older adults with depression, along with increased social contact. Group members are also able to see that they are not alone in struggling with depression, they may gain new insights into their difficulties from other group members, and they are provided firsthand evidence of how the techniques used in CBT can be effective. This seems particularly helpful for those who often are socially isolated. They are also less likely to feel stigmatized when attending a group, particularly if the emphasis is placed on learning new coping strategies (rather than dealing with psychopathology; see Dick et al., 1996).

Group Structure and Process

As mentioned earlier, the CBT approach tends to foster collaboration among group members, wherein problem solving is a primary focus during most sessions. Generally, traditional "process issues" have a low priority, unless they are directly relevant to a specific problem focus or they are interfering in some way with the group focus. Turning again to Sara, for example, she was reluctant to reach out to her friends and relatives, because she thought she would burden them and they would eventually reject her completely. This was revealed in an unhelpful thoughts record (explained below) that she completed in the group. While working on this with Sara, the group focus was to help her see the potential distortion in her thinking. As a result of group discussion, in which other members provided personal illustrations, Sara was able to see that her thoughts about her relations with others were heavily influenced by "mind reading" and "fortune telling." Not only was Sara helped by this process, but others in the group with similar tendencies also had an opportunity to see how this example might apply to their own situation.

For the most part, each session is loosely structured in the following manner. The duration of each session is approximately 90 minutes. After the first session, each group meeting generally includes initial instruction or continued elaboration in a particular cognitive–behavioral technique by the therapist, followed by group discussion pertaining to particular issues. Sessions typically begin by having clients discuss their homework assignments, highlighting any problems or issues that came up for them since the last session. The therapist also inquires whether any specific problem or issue came up that the clients would like to put on the agenda. After reviewing homework and items for the agenda, the therapist must work with group members to decide what should be the focus for additional group discussion. A general rule is that during the course of therapy each group member will have an opportunity to discuss each new technique with the group and obtain suggestions to assist them in mastering the particular technique in question. Thus, one or two clients will report on their progress per session until all clients have had an opportunity to obtain group input. Time is usually set aside near the end of each session to discuss homework assignments. If a new technique is being introduced during the session, sufficient time is set aside for demonstrations and practice to facilitate implementation and homework compliance. Each session is normally concluded with a summary of what transpired, and questions or comments are solicited from group members.

During the group discussions, group members are encouraged to provide each other with supportive suggestions for managing particular problems and to think of creative ways to use the cognitive–behavioral techniques that have been reviewed. Homework typically includes one or both of the following: (a) practicing the technique reviewed in the most recent session and (b) specific assignments tailored through group discussion to fit each group member's own goals. Homework assignments in the initial sessions are more likely to be similar for all group members as they are learning the CBT techniques. As the group continues, however, group members will mix and match the techniques to fit their own needs, resulting in very different homework tasks for different group members. Our experience is that older adults generate very creative and effective homework assignments in group as they become more experienced with the techniques.

Successive approximation is also emphasized when goals are addressed. An experienced CBT therapist does not require or even expect that group members will go home and immediately use each technique to perfection, thus attaining their goals immediately. Rather, homework assignments are seen as skill-building opportunities. Difficulties with assignments are seen as opportunities for the individual and the group to learn more and to custom fit the techniques to the life situation and characteristics of the older adult who is using them.

If the group is "closed" such that membership of the group does not change over time, the group leader will be less involved over time in technique instruction and more involved in providing support for the group and facilitating constructive interaction among group members. If the group is "open" and membership changes across the life of the group, the therapist must continue to play a more active role to be certain that techniques are clearly understood by the newer members.

COGNITIVE–BEHAVIORAL TECHNIQUES

Specific techniques introduced will depend in part on the focus of the group. However, a few techniques are fundamental to the effective implementation of CBT for older adults and should be presented irrespective of any other specialized procedures that might be presented. These include mood monitoring, increasing pleasurable activities, and learning how to monitor dysfunctional thoughts using a Daily Record of Unhelpful Thoughts. Each of these is discussed in more detail in this section. Additional techniques, such as relaxation training, are described in a later section on family caregiver groups. As mentioned earlier, homework assignments are provided in each of these areas and provide the material for the group discussion each week. The amount of time spent explaining CBT strategies to the group tends to decrease gradually after the first several sessions, and more time is spent on addressing particular problems individual group members are experiencing, with all group members participating in designing and implementing the techniques that have been discussed.

The order of presentation of the techniques should be decided on the basis of the needs and characteristics of the members in each group, but we recommend mood monitoring and increasing pleasant events, as described by Lewinsohn, Munoz, Youngren, and Zeiss (1986), as the initial techniques to be covered in group CBT with depressed older adults. Mood monitoring helps group members recognize when they are not doing well, when they are feeling better, and what events are associated with mood changes. This skill is critical in the group members' ability to recognize what techniques are working for them and what situations are particularly difficult for them. One self-monitoring mood assessment commonly used is the Daily Mood Rating Form, which asks the older adult to rate his or her mood for each day (i.e., "how good or bad you felt") using a 9-point scale. The specific increments on the 9-point scale are as follows: 1 = *very depressed*, 5 = *so-so*, and 9 = *very happy*. On each day of the week, the older adult fills out each of the three columns on the form, which includes (a) date, (b) mood score, and (c) "Why I think I felt this way?" At the next cognitive–behavioral group therapy session, the older adult brings the form to be discussed with other group members.

Mood Monitoring

This technique typically provides group members with firsthand direct experience of the relationship between mood changes and pleasurable activities. The essential ideas for group members to understand with this exercise is that "Events can affect our mood in a positive or negative direction. To a greater or lesser degree, we can increase the frequency of pleasant events in our lives. Therefore, we have the capability to control our mood." Of course, this is not exactly a revelation to most people, but when individuals are experiencing noticeable depression or anxiety it is often easy to lose sight of such basic contingencies. The concrete realization of this simple relationship by monitoring mood on a daily basis can often provide the rationale and incentive for attempting to increase pleasurable activities.

Rita, a 69-year-old housewife, had retired from a management-level position in marketing approximately 3 years before coming to the clinic. Her target complaints were (a) boredom with household activities, (b) increasing problems with her husband who also retired about 3 years ago, and (c) insufficient energy to get anything accomplished. Rita began monitoring her mood on a daily basis, and within 2 weeks she noted that her mood and energy level were higher on days when she was engaged in some activity that involved other people. She was surprised by this finding, because she had always minimized the importance of social contacts in her life. At the third group session, she announced that she had had an "amazing" insight. For years she said she had been having lunch with her cousin every couple of months and always thought she did this out of family obligation. However, now that she was monitoring her mood, she realized that when she did this, her mood was much higher, and from now on she was going to go out to lunch with her more often.

Increasing Pleasurable Activities

The next technique serves two key purposes: (a) Often, this quickly results in improved mood for a group member who has successfully increased the number of pleasant events occurring each day. (b) This, in turn, can serve as a model for other group members who are having difficulty accepting the principle as a useful tool for decreasing the intensity of negative emotions. Sharing with other group members the success of implementing this technique provides them with evidence that they, too, can exert effective control over how they feel, rather than assuming they are helpless in being able to change their depression. A key to the success of this technique is to have an appropriate set of pleasant activities to monitor and attempt to increase at any given point in time. Most older persons are comfortable with monitoring 10 or so pleasant activities while attempting to increase their frequency of occurrence on a daily basis. We have found that this number of events works well for clients participating in group therapy.

Selecting a list of activities can be a challenge for both the therapist and the client. Activities selected should be pleasurable for the individual and should be ones that can be carried out with minimal difficulty but typically are not being done on a regular basis. The OPPES can be helpful in developing a useful list of activities. Frequency and Pleasantness scores are each plotted for the seven domains (i.e., nature, social, thoughts and feelings, recognition from others, giving to others, competence, and leisure activities) on the same scale on a simple graph that provides a quick and easy visual display of how frequent activities were engaged in, for comparison with their degree of pleasantness. The goal is to pinpoint activities to increase or decrease, in accordance with the degree of pleasure each event creates for the individual. Thus, highly pleasurable events should be increased if their frequency falls far below the degree of pleasure derived. Similarly, if events that bring little pleasure are done more frequently, perhaps they may be decreased and time allotted to do a more pleasurable activity. (Note that copies of the measure, along with scoring instructions and graphs, can be obtained from the first author on request.)

Figure 9.1 shows a graph of the data from the OPPES for George, a 71-year-old married man who developed a moderately severe depression after retiring from his position as a civil engineer. Notice that, compared with the normative sample, George has a disproportionately high frequency of activities in categories pertaining to nature, reflections, and leisure time

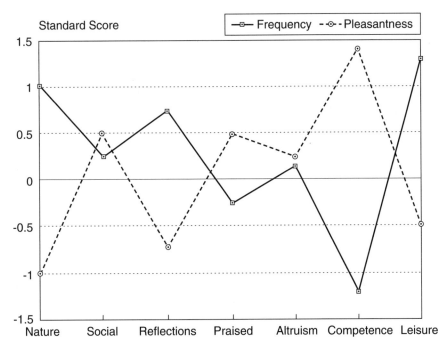

Figure 9.1. Frequency and level of pleasure ratings on the Older Person's Pleasant Events Scale for George, a 71-year-old retired engineer. Events are grouped into seven categories: experiencing nature; being in social situations that are pleasant; spending time alone reflecting and meditating; being praised by others for some activity; giving to others; being involved in activities in which competence is demonstrated; and traditional leisure time activities.

(e.g., reading, listening to music, and going to museums) and a disproportionately low frequency of activities in the category that demonstrates his competence or effectiveness. Yet his degree of pleasure obtained from these activities is in distinct contrast. He derives very little pleasure from activities pertaining to nature, being alone and thinking about things, or engaging in many other leisure time activities and an immense amount of pleasure from accomplishing things and being recognized for his accomplishments. After reviewing this graph, it was relatively easy for George, the therapist, and the group, working collaboratively, to come up with a brief list of activities for George to try to increase. Among them was the activity of doing volunteer work at a local hospital. George's skill and efforts at the hospital were greatly appreciated, and he found it sufficiently rewarding that he decided to commit three half-days per week to this activity. Soon after starting this routine, his depression began to decrease in intensity and his participation in other pleasant activities also increased. Within a few months, he was able to regulate the type and frequency of pleasurable activities, such that his attitude about being retired completely changed.

Similarly, Mabel, a 75-year-old married caregiver noted in her graph that she rarely engaged in activities that created a sense of "competence," one of the domains assessed by the OPPES. However, she rated feeling competent as highly pleasurable. Together with the group, she brainstormed about different activities that engendered a sense of competence. Earlier in her life she had taken painting classes at her community arts center, and she recalled that many individuals had been very appreciative of her work. She was even able to sell some of her work at local art shows. She added that creating her work gave her a feeling of pride and accomplishment. With reassurance from the group, she decided to resume art classes two evenings per week. Mabel also observed that she tended to engage in "giving to others," another domain assessed by the OPPES, considerably more than the normative group. Furthermore, she also observed that she found this activity far less pleasant than her age-peer group. Mabel reported that seeing the information about her activities and pleasantness before her eyes encouraged her to decrease her helping behaviors for others and to increase the time she spent incorporating more pleasant activities into her life.

Daily Record of Unhelpful Thoughts

A basic cognitive technique that is generally well received by older group members is a modification of the Dysfunctional Thought Record (Beck et al., 1979), which we refer to as the Daily Record of Unhelpful Thoughts (DRUT). This tool is based on the premise that negative emotions result from the negative thoughts about a particular situation, and that people who are likely to become depressed characteristically have distorted negative thoughts about particular situations, about themselves, and about the future. These distortions tend to occur automatically and in the case of persons who experience depression or other serious negative emotions, they often are accepted as veridical with little further scrutiny. The DRUT helps the client understand the relationship between thoughts and feelings and provides a useful aid in learning how to identify the automatic distortions and develop rational constructions to replace them. The six most common ways of distorting information about situations seen in older clients in our work are the following:

1. Thinking in "all-or-nothing" terms, which is the tendency to perceive situations, events, or things as either all good or all bad.
2. "Mental filtering," which can be described as overgeneralizing, exaggerating, or reducing the significance of an event or filtering out all the positive and only thinking about the negative aspects of a situation or event.

3. "Jumping to conclusions" occurs when the older adult uses "mind reading" or attempts to predict the future instead of obtaining all the facts about the situation or event.
4. Thinking "I should" or "what if" or "I shouldn't have," which involves becoming one's own critic.
5. "Labeling" is an extreme form of generalization and often involves labeling oneself as a "bad person" or "no good."
6. "Personalization" occurs when the older adult assumes responsibility for events or others' behavior when this is uncalled for.

We use both a three-column and five-column DRUT. We start with the simpler three-column to help clients first understand the relationship between thoughts and feelings and to give them practice in monitoring their thoughts about situations that provoke emotional reactions. We then move to the five-column DRUT to help clients develop challenges to their distortions and then evaluate the impact of this intervention on the intensity of the emotions. Table 9.1 shows a five-column DRUT for Sara, mentioned earlier. Note that the automatic thoughts about the fact that her son and his family had decided to go to the in-laws for the holidays rather than to come and visit her precipitated fairly intense negative emotions. However, after writing the thoughts down and reviewing them carefully, Sara was able to develop constructive challenges that lessened the emotions substantially. Working on Unhelpful Thought Records in the group setting is extremely productive, both for the individual who is presenting the material and for the other group members who participate in developing appropriate challenges for the automatic unhelpful thoughts. Frequent repetition of this exercise soon begins to facilitate the client's ability to detect and challenge automatic thoughts before they have an opportunity to result in the development of serious negative emotions.

In addition to these basic tools, there are a variety of other cognitive and behavioral techniques that are frequently used as an integral part of CBT for depression. More detailed explanation of these techniques are provided in several sources (Beck et al., 1979; Dick et al., 1996; Gallagher & Thompson, 1981; Lewinsohn et al., 1986). Along with mood monitoring and increasing pleasant events, relaxation exercises and learning problem-solving skills to facilitate behavioral changes are good behavioral techniques for improving mood. Identification and challenging of unhelpful thought patterns, using such techniques as examining the evidence, becoming a scientist (i.e., doing experiments to confirm or refute hypotheses about oneself), listing advantages and disadvantages of retaining an unhelpful belief about oneself, imagery exercises, scheduling of "worry time," and problem-solving strategies are some of the key cognitive techniques that can be helpful for older adults with depression (see Dick et al., 1996,

TABLE 9.1
Sara: 69-Year-Old Widow in Excellent Health

Situation	Automatic Unhelpful Thoughts	Feelings	Challenges	Results
Describe the event that led to your unpleasant emotions	What are your negative thoughts? Identify your unhelpful thought patterns. How strongly do you believe in these thoughts? (from 0% to 100%)	What are your feelings? (sad, angry, anxious, etc.) How strong are these? (from 0% to 100%)	Replace the negative thoughts with more helpful ones. How strongly do you believe in these thoughts?	What are your feelings now? Rate (from 0% to 100%)
John called to say they were going to Barb's parents for Christmas. He said my gift would be coming in the mail, and that I didn't have to send gifts.	How can they do this? My only chance to see my grandchildren: 90% John thinks more of them than he does of me: 80% They have more money and a better home. The kids will like them better. They won't even miss me. I can't compete with them: 80% I'm not important: 90% What's the use. I'm a failure: 50%	Angry: 70% Sad: 100% Disappointed: 100% Bereft: 80% Heartbroken: 40% Unimportant: 80% Forgotten: 95%	It's a long way to come. John may not get time off. They came last year. Barb writes a lot. She cares. Money isn't the only thing. When the kids are here we do things they really like. The Lees want me to come. This will give me a chance to do some things with them.	Angry: 0% Sad: 25% Disappointed: 30% Bereft: 0% Heartbroken: 0% Unimportant: 15% Forgotten: 0%

Five-column Daily Record of Unhelpful Thoughts completed by Sara, a 69-year-old widow, for a specific event that precipitated negative emotions. Ratings for intensity: 0% = *not at all*; 100% = *completely*.

for descriptions of these techniques in language appropriate for older adult group participants).

Homework Assignments

Homework remains an essential part of group CBT with older adults regardless of the length or composition of the group. Any difficulties with completing homework must be addressed in order for the group to be as beneficial as possible for the members, and the difficulties should always be addressed in a manner that helps group members become interested in figuring out how the homework can help them. For example, older adults may be embarrassed to ask questions when they do not understand an assignment, particularly in the first few sessions. They may also feel so hopeless that they believe the homework will not help, and therefore do not want to try when failure is "certain." The homework task may have been too ambitious in scope, particularly if the guideline of successive approximation was not considered. If homework is assigned rather than the result of a collaborative effort in which the client had an active role in making the decision, the client may become resentful and lose motivation. Problems with homework will likely increase if they are addressed in a manner that frames an incomplete or missed homework as an error that is either explicitly or implicitly held against the group members.

Termination

Termination is a final issue to deal with in group CBT. The strategy for termination as outlined in Thompson, Gallagher-Thompson, and Dick (1996) can be readily modified to work in a group setting. Clients are encouraged to work collaboratively with the group leader and other group members to develop maintenance or "survival" guides. This is a specific document, which consolidates the group members' experience in therapy. The skills learned in therapy are reviewed. Danger signals for possible relapse or recurrence are highlighted. Finally, procedures are developed and rehearsed, detailing what the group member should do in the event that danger signals are experienced. Information about procedures to be followed in the event of a relapse (e.g., who to contact and where to go) is also included as part of the maintenance guide.

GROUPS FOR STRESSES INVOLVED IN FAMILY CAREGIVING

Older adults can often find themselves providing considerable care to failing family members or friends, and over time these caregiving responsibilities may ultimately wear down the psychological and physical resources of these informal helpers. This stress process frequently leads to a considerable amount of psychological distress across the course of caregiving, including feelings of depression, frustration, anger, anxiety, fear about the future, loneliness, and guilt (Gallagher, Wrabetz, Lovett, DelMaestro, & Rose, 1989; Mittelman et al., 1995; Schulz, O'Brien, Bookwala, & Fleissner, 1995; Wright, Clipp, & George, 1993).

Because the precipitant for psychological distress in caregivers is usually due in large part to the excessive burdens they experience, we have found that it is more beneficial to work with them in groups designed specifically to assist them in learning to cope with the stresses of prolonged caregiving. The groups incorporate many of the features in group CBT in terms of process and early sessions, but they clearly differ in terms of structure and emphasis. In fact, we described them as psychoeducational group interventions that incorporate cognitive and behavioral change strategies, tailored to address the personal needs of stressed and distressed caregivers. In particular, a major focus is placed on strengthening the caregiver's self-management skills. We have found outreach to older adults for these types of interventions is noticeably easier than traditional psychotherapy groups given their classroom-based structure in which considerably less stigma is attached to their participation. In psychoeducational interventions, caregivers are not only offered new information, but they are also taught ways to develop new skills to enhance their coping abilities. Interventions focused at caregiver self-management can include strategies such as relaxation training, problem solving, or teaching caregivers to increase pleasant activities in their lives (Greene & Monahan, 1987, 1989; Haley, 1989; Lovett & Gallagher, 1988; Whitlatch, Zarit, & von Eye, 1991).

Generally, these interventions share characteristics found in traditional CBT groups, including small numbers of participants (generally six to eight), structuring the time at each meeting so that group members can share thoughts and feelings, and providing the opportunity for class leaders to give individualized attention by focusing the discussion on problems and processes of particular members. Yet, psychoeducational interventions do differ from "traditional" forms of CBT by using a great deal of active participation in the learning process through role plays and skill demonstrations in session, along with significant homework opportunities designed to encourage the practice of new skills outside the group (Gallagher-Thompson, 1994; Gallagher-Thompson, Coon, Rivera, Powers, & Zeiss, 1998; Thompson & Gallagher-Thompson, 1996). In addition, these psychoeducational programs are always time limited and can vary in length, based on their target audience of older adults and the goals of the class. For example, a program to improve communication skills with other family members might last 4 to 6 weeks, whereas a program designed to teach assertiveness skills, relaxation training, and cognitive restructuring would last longer—often 8 to 10 weeks.

Finally, psychoeducational groups also differ from traditional psychotherapy groups by following a very detailed agenda at each meeting that delineates the specific goals to be achieved in that class, and the steps to get there, that are applied across all the members. A typical session lasts for approximately 2 hours, with a 20-minute break for refreshments and social activity. Each session starts with a review of homework, followed by a brief presentation of a new skill or topic to be considered for the next week. Then a break occurs, at which time a group leader or leaders can assist any group member who seems to be having difficulty understanding the material. Following the break, the group practices the techniques to be used in the coming week, using role play and discussing material in breakout groups or whatever might be appropriate to assist group members in learning the material in question. This is followed by a brief review that emphasizes any problems arising in the practice. Questions are addressed before the conclusion of the session.

Empirical data have shown that psychoeducational groups are effective in reducing caregiver stress, anxiety, and depression (Gallagher-Thompson et al., 2000). Interventions that focus on specific skills such as anger management versus a broad array of skills such as problem solving appear more effective at reducing caregiver distress. Generally, caregivers have reported high levels of satisfaction with these interventions, indicating that they have increased feelings of self-efficacy and are better equipped to deal with caregiver problems after their group experience (Haley, Levine, Brown, & Bartolucci, 1987; Steffen, Gallagher-Thompson, Zeiss, & Willis-Shore, 1994; Toseland, Rossiter, & Labrecque, 1989).

We have developed two different psychoeducational classes with accompanying leader and participant manuals that were either adapted or designed specifically for family caregivers. These include a "Coping With the Blues" class for increasing life satisfaction and a "Coping With Frustration" anger-management class. Both classes have eight weekly sessions followed by two monthly booster sessions. Table 9.2 shows the content covered in both of these classes. We find both of these classes to be practical in format length, reasonably inexpensive to implement, and acceptable to older adult caregivers.

There are several similarities between both types of classes as well as some significant differences. To begin with, the Coping With Frustration class targets feelings of anger and frustration, whereas the Coping With the Blues class focuses primarily on depression. In both classes, a CBT rationale for the particular target is presented. Also, a relaxation exercise is used at each session, which is based on standard techniques of visualization and deep breathing. Individuals keep a relaxation log in which they rate their tension on a 5-point scale (ranging from 1 = *not at all tense* to 5 = *terribly tense*) before and after the relaxation exercise, both in session and as part of their ongoing homework. The final sessions of both classes

TABLE 9.2
General Content Outlines for "Coping With Frustration" and "Coping
With the Blues" Classes

Sessions	"Coping With Frustration" Class	"Coping With the Blues" Class
1 through 3	Present the cognitive–behavioral model and treatment rationale. Discuss sources of depression, frustration, and anger in caregiving situation and typical ways people respond. Introduce relaxation and start relaxation logs for monitoring.	
4 through 6	Introduce cognitive techniques, self-talk, and active listening to deal with daily stressors. Develop self-statements.	Introduce mood monitoring. Identify potential pleasant events. Obtain baseline data.
7 and 8	Learn assertion techniques. Practice technique "broken record" and learn to express feeling appropriately. For example, when you say X and feel Y, and that results in Z. X: "I can't help you this weekend." Y: "I feel frustrated." Z: "I feel unsupported by my family in my caregiving role." Review practice and identify barriers to implementation.	Develop self-change plan for increasing daily pleasant events. Problem-solve ways to overcome barriers.
9 and 10 Booster Sessions	Review successes and problems in applying techniques. Highlight reasons for successes and determine source of problems, if any. Encourage anticipation of future problems and rehearse application of new skills in coping.	

are devoted to review of skills emphasized and discussion of their application to troublesome situations likely to occur as caregiving progresses. From Session 4 onward, the two groups have separate foci.

In the Coping With Frustration class, standard cognitive techniques for eliciting and examining negative thoughts are used (Beck et al., 1979; Dick & Gallagher-Thompson, 1996), with an emphasis on thoughts that foster feelings of frustration. For example, when Harold (a 70-year-old man with dementia living at home with his wife) repeatedly asks "When is lunch?" within 30 minutes after having had lunch, his wife Maude expresses her thoughts: "There he goes again! He's just trying to get my goat. He could stop that if he wanted to." In class Maude would be taught to challenge these thoughts by examining empirical evidence that significant impairment in short-term memory is a classic feature of dementia, and that by thinking more adaptively (e.g., "He really can't help it. This is part of the disease."), her negative emotions will decrease, thus enabling her to cope more effectively with this recurring situation. In this class, participants are next taught common techniques of assertion. The "broken-record" technique, for example, could be helpful to Maude in dealing with Harold's repeated requests. (For a more detailed description, this class manual can be requested from the first author.)

In the Coping With the Blues class that focuses on depression management, typical behavioral techniques for identifying and increasing pleasurable activities are used (Lewinsohn et al., 1986). They include (a) daily mood monitoring using a simple 9-point scale in which mood is rated from best to worst the client has ever experienced, (b) development of individual lists of potential daily pleasant activities, and (c) discussion of barriers to having them included in everyday life. For example, most caregivers initially say that they cannot add anything more into their crowded schedules, but when specific activities are generated (such as talking on the phone with a friend, going for a brisk walk in the neighborhood, or planning to watch a favorite TV show), they are more hopeful about being able to actually gain more control over events in their lives. Once individualized lists have been developed for each participant, the class focuses discussion on ways to overcome practical barriers that arise, such as finding a responsible person to sit with their relative with dementia so that they can participate in a pleasurable activity without concern about the care recipient.

Although the majority of caregivers are women, a substantial number of men also assume this role (Stone, Cafferata, & Stangl, 1987), and they too can report feelings of frustration or sadness (Gallagher-Thompson et al., 1998; Schulz & Williamson, 1991). Some authors have suggested that male caregivers might also benefit from psychoeducational classes based on cognitive–behavioral principles that are specifically designed to address their needs (Moseley, Davies, & Priddy, 1988). In particular, groups for male caregivers should remain small, should be closed rather than open-ended, and should present a balance of specific information about caregiving and emphasize group support and techniques for coping (Moseley et al., 1988). However, little empirical data are available regarding the effectiveness any kind of group treatment with older male caregivers.

Closely related to the group treatment of family caregivers lies the issue of treatment for cognitively impaired older adults themselves. Individualized behavioral treatments in particular have proved effective in ameliorating depressive symptoms and managing care-recipient problem behaviors, often working with the caregivers teaching them how to monitor and change these behaviors by shaping, cuing, and reinforcement (Pinkston & Linsk, 1984; Pinkston, Linsk, & Young, 1988; Teri & Logsdon, 1991; Teri & Uomoto, 1991). These techniques are thought to benefit both the care recipient and the caregiver by reducing depressive symptoms in both and by reducing problem behaviors in the care recipient that upset the caregiver (Teri & Gallagher, 1991). However, we are aware that some practitioners and local chapters of the Alzheimer's Association have begun to explore group intervention efforts for early-stage dementia victims. Although it is too early to discuss the potential demand for such interventions or the effect these interventions will have on the cognitively impaired and their caregivers, the step toward group interventions for these older adults is a potentially promising one. And, given the positive effects of individualized behavioral interventions for this population, groups that introduce and reinforce these behaviors with older adults and their caregivers could prove fruitful.

WHERE DO WE GO FROM HERE?

Opportunities exist to extend CBT approaches into group treatment for a good number of other late-life problems, particularly problems in which individual CBT has proved effective in reducing elders' distress. There are several important reasons to consider expanding the types of CBT groups targeted to elders, including some we have already mentioned before:

1. CBT groups, and psychoeducational groups based on cognitive–behavioral principles in particular, provide an interactive, learning-focused approach that reduces older adults' concerns regarding the stigma associated with more traditional forms of psychotherapy.
2. Older adults can often feel out of place with much younger group participants whom they may perceive as unfamiliar not only with their chief problems and complaints but also with their societal views and life experiences.
3. CBT offers older adults the opportunity to collaborate with group leaders in developing individualized strategies to meet their diverse needs in light of their complex situations and comorbid conditions.
4. The time-limited nature of CBT groups can be beneficial for elders on fixed incomes with limited financial resources.

We believe this model could be applied to other problems, such as coping with chronic physical illness in older adults. For example, older adults with chronic physical illness, chronic pain, or those recovering from acute illness episodes might benefit from CBT groups that combine behavioral strategies, including relaxation, guided imagery, and pleasant physical activities, with various cognitive interventions that identify unhelpful thinking patterns that further discourage them in their current situations. CBT-based groups or psychoeducational classes that identify problem behaviors and beliefs that undermine medical protocol adherence and compliance have the potential to significantly impact physical health functioning.

Individuals undergoing grief may also benefit from group CBT, either in a traditional therapy format or presented in a psychoeducational framework. Many of these individuals are experiencing depression, anxiety, sleep disorders, and significant role changes because of the loss of their loved one (Gallagher & Thompson, 1996). By learning appropriate cognitive–behavioral skills (e.g., challenging the belief that they can no longer function adequately without their loved one, and then learning needed behavioral skills for acquiring new acquaintances), some distress associated with bereavement may be mitigated over time.

Group therapy for older adults with substance abuse problems that teaches more helpful behavioral strategies and uses cognitive interventions to address problems underlying the abuse (e.g., multiple loss, chronic pain, depression, or anxiety) could assist these older individuals who are frequently ignored in society. Many elders who lack effective communication skills could benefit from CBT group interventions that teach and role play assertiveness skills, identify and substitute more adaptive cognitions for negative thoughts that impede assertiveness, and in turn, practice these *in vivo* to better manage problems, ranging from the anxiety experienced in new social situations after retirement relocation to stress and conflict with adult children over opposing role expectations or personal values.

Finally, the door is wide open to investigate the effectiveness of CBT-based groups within the traditions and norms of various ethnic and racial groups in the multicultural society of the United States (Yeo & Gallagher-Thompson, 1996). It is clear that a diverse array of beliefs and customs exists within any cultural group, and how strongly a person identifies with those beliefs is a complex interaction of the individual and the sociocultural context. However, creative interventionists are needed to help us learn how to identify and incorporate successful strategies that may be used within and across groups along the acculturation continuum while remaining sensitive to cultural differences and developing their cultural competence.

REFERENCES

American Psychiatric Association. (1994). *Diagnostic and statistical manual of mental disorders* (4th ed.). Washington, DC: Author.

Beck, A. T. (1967). *Depression: Causes and treatment*. Philadelphia: University of Pennsylvania Press.

Beck, A. T. (1976). *Cognitive therapy and the emotional disorders*. New York: International Universities Press.

Beck, A. T., Rush, A. J., Shaw, B. F., & Emery, G. (1979). *Cognitive therapy of depression*. New York: Guilford Press.

Beck, A. T., Ward, C. H., Mendelson, M., Mock, J., & Erbaugh, J. (1961). An inventory for measuring depression. *Archives of General Psychiatry, 4,* 561–571.

Beck, A. T., Weissman, A., Lester, D., & Trexler, L. (1974). The measurement of pessimism: The Hopelessness Scale. *Journal of Consulting and Clinical Psychology, 42,* 861–865.

Blazer, D., & Koenig, H. (1996). Mood disorders. In E. W. Busse & D. G. Blazer (Eds.), *Textbook of geriatric psychiatry* (2nd ed., pp. 235–263). Washington, DC: American Psychiatric Press.

Brink, T. L., Yesavage, J. A., Lum, O., Heersema, P. H., Adey, M., & Rose, T. L. (1982). Screening tests for geriatric depression. *Clinical Gerontologist, 1,* 37–43.

Dick, L., & Gallagher-Thompson, D. (1995). Cognitive therapy with the core beliefs of a distressed, lonely caregiver. *Journal of Cognitive Psychotherapy: An International Quarterly, 9,* 215–227.

Dick, L., & Gallagher-Thompson, D. (1996). Assessment and treatment of late-life depression. In M. Hersen & V. B. Van Hasselt (Eds.), *Psychological treatment of older adults: An introductory textbook* (pp. 181–208). New York: Plenum.

Dick, L. P., Gallagher-Thompson, D., Coon, D. W., Powers, D. V., & Thompson, L. W. (1996). *Cognitive–behavioral therapy for late-life depression: A client manual*. Palo Alto, CA: Veterans Affairs Palo Alto Health Care System.

Endicott, J., & Spitzer, R. L. (1978). A diagnostic interview: The Schedule for Affective Disorders and Schizophrenia. *Archives of General Psychiatry, 35,* 837–844.

Futterman, A., Thompson, L. W., Gallagher-Thompson, D., & Ferris, R. (1995). Depression in later life. In E. Beckham & R. Leber (Eds.), *Handbook of depression: Treatment, assessment and research* (2nd ed., pp. 494–525). New York: Guilford Press.

Gallagher, D., Breckenridge, J., Steinmetz, J., & Thompson, L. (1983). The Beck Depression Inventory and Research Diagnostic Criteria: Congruence in an older population. *Journal of Consulting and Clinical Psychology, 51,* 945–946.

Gallagher, D., Nies, G., & Thompson, L. W. (1982). Reliability of the Beck Depression Inventory with older adults. *Journal of Consulting and Clinical Psychology, 50,* 152–153.

Gallagher, D., & Thompson, L. W. (1981). *Depression in the elderly: A behavioral treatment manual*. Los Angeles: University of Southern California Press.

Gallagher, D., & Thompson, L. (1996). Bereavement and adjustment disorders. In

E. Busse & D. Blazer (Eds.), *Textbook of geriatric psychiatry* (2nd ed., pp. 313–328). Washington, DC: American Psychiatric Association Press.

Gallagher, D., Wrabetz, A., Lovett, S., DelMaestro, S., & Rose, J. (1989). Depression and other negative affects in family caregivers. In E. Light & B. Liebowitz (Eds.), *Alzheimer's disease treatment and family stress: Directions for research* (pp. 218–244). Washington, DC: National Institute of Mental Health.

Gallagher-Thompson, D. (1994). Direct services and interventions for caregivers: A review of extant programs and a look to the future. In M. H. Cantor (Ed.), *Family caregiving: Agenda for the future* (pp. 102–122). San Francisco: American Society on Aging.

Gallagher-Thompson, D., Coon, D. W., Rivera, P., Powers, D., & Zeiss, A. M. (1998). Family caregiving: Stress, coping and intervention. In M. Hersen & V. B. Van Hasselt (Eds.), *Handbook of clinical geropsychology* (pp. 469–493). New York: Plenum Press.

Gallagher-Thompson, D., Lovett, S., Rose, J., McKibbin, C., Coon, D., Futterman, A., & Thompson, L. W. (2000). Impact of psychoeducational interventions on distressed family caregivers. *Journal of Clinical Geropsychology, 6,* 91–110.

Greene, V. L., & Monahan, D. J. (1987). The effect of professionally guided caregiver support and education groups on institutionalized care receivers. *The Gerontologist, 27,* 716–721.

Greene, V. L., & Monahan, D. J. (1989). The effect of a support and education program on stress and burden among family caregivers to frail elderly persons. *The Gerontologist, 29,* 472–480.

Haley, W. E. (1989). Group intervention for dementia family caregivers: A longitudinal perspective. *The Gerontologist, 29,* 481–483.

Haley, W. E., Levine, E. G., Brown, S. L., & Bartolucci, A. A. (1987). Stress, appraisal, coping and social support as predictors of adaptational outcome among dementia caregivers. *Psychology and Aging, 2,* 323–330.

Lewinsohn, P. M. (1974). A behavioral approach to depression. In R. Friedman and M. Katz (Eds.), *The psychology of depression* (pp. 157–176). New York: Wiley.

Lewinsohn, P., Munoz, R., Youngren, M., & Zeiss, A. (1986). *Control your depression* (2nd ed.). New York: Prentice Hall.

Lovett, S., & Gallagher, D. (1988). Psychoeducational interventions for family caregivers: Preliminary efficacy data. *Behavior Therapy, 19,* 321–330.

Manton, K. G., Blazer, D. G., & Woodbury, M. A. (1987). Suicide in middle age and later life: Sex and race specific life table and cohort analyses. *Journal of Gerontology, 42,* 219–227.

Mittelman, M., Ferris, S., Shulman, E., Steinberg, M., Ambinder, A., Mackell, J., & Cohen, J. (1995). A comprehensive support program: Effect on depression in spouse-caregivers of AD patients. *The Gerontologist, 35,* 792–802.

Moseley, P. W., Davies, H. D., & Priddy, J. M. (1988). Support groups for male caregivers of Alzheimer's patients: A followup. *Clinical Gerontologist, 7*, 127–136.

Pachana, N., Thompson, L. W., & Gallagher-Thompson, D. (1994). Measurement of depression. In M. P. Lawton & J. Teresi (Eds.), *Annual review of gerontology and geriatrics* (Vol. 14, pp. 234–256). New York: Springer Press.

Phifer, J. F., & Murrell, S. A. (1986). Etiologic factors in the onset of depressive symptoms in older adults. *Journal of Abnormal Psychology, 95*, 282–291.

Pinkston, E. M., & Linsk, N. L. (1984). Behavioral family intervention with the impaired elderly. *The Gerontologist, 24*, 576–583.

Pinkston, E. M., Linsk, N. L., & Young, R. N. (1988). Home based behavioral family treatment of the impaired elderly. *Behavior Therapy, 19*, 331–344.

Schulz, R., O'Brien, A. T., Bookwala, J., & Fleissner, K. (1995). Psychiatric and physical morbidity effects of dementia caregiving: Prevalence, correlates, and causes. *The Gerontologist, 35*, 771–791.

Schulz, R., & Williamson, G. M. (1991). A 2-year longitudinal study of depression among Alzheimer's caregivers. *Psychology and Aging, 6*, 569–578.

Sheikh, J. (1996). Anxiety and panic disorders. In E. W. Busse & D. G. Blazer (Eds.), *Textbook of geriatric psychiatry* (2nd ed., pp. 279–289). Washington, DC: American Psychiatric Press.

Sheikh, J., & Yesavage, J. (1986). Geriatric Depression Scale (GDS): Recent evidence and development of a shorter version. In T. Brink (Ed.), *Clinical gerontology: A guide to assessment and intervention* (pp. 165–172). New York: Haworth Press.

Steffen, A. M., Gallagher-Thompson, D., Zeiss, A. M., & Willis-Shore, J. (1994, August). *Self-efficacy for caregiving: Psychoeducational interventions with dementia family caregivers.* Paper presented at the 102nd Annual Convention of the American Psychological Association, Los Angeles.

Stone, R., Cafferata, G. L., & Stangl, J. (1987). Caregivers of the frail elderly: A national profile. *The Gerontologist, 27*, 616–626.

Teri, L., & Gallagher, D. G. (1991). Cognitive–behavioral interventions for treatment of depression in Alzheimer's patients. *The Gerontologist, 31*, 413–416.

Teri, L., & Logsdon, R. (1991). Identifying pleasant activities for individuals with Alzheimer's disease: The Pleasant Events Schedule—AD. *The Gerontologist, 31*, 124–127.

Teri, L., & Uomoto, J. (1991). Reducing excess disability in dementia patients: Training caregivers to manage patient depression. *Clinical Gerontologist, 10*, 49–63.

Thompson, L., & Gallagher-Thompson, D. (1996). Practical issues related to maintenance of mental health and positive well being in family caregivers. In L. Carstensen, B. Edlstein, & L. Dornbrand (Eds.), *The practical handbook of clinical gerontology* (pp. 129–150). Thousand Oaks, CA: Sage.

Thompson, L. W., Gallagher-Thompson, D., & Dick, L. (1996). *Cognitive–behavioral therapy for late-life depression: A therapist manual.* Palo Alto, CA: Veterans Affairs Palo Alto Health Care System.

Toseland, R. W., Rossiter, C. M., & Labrecque, M. D. (1989). The effectiveness of peer-led and professionally led groups to support family caregivers. *The Gerontologist, 29,* 465–471.

Turner, R. J., & Noh, S. (1988). Physical disability and depression: A longitudinal analysis. *Journal of Health and Social Behavior, 29,* 23–37.

Weissman, A. N. (1979). The Dysfunctional Attitude Scale: A validation study. (Doctoral dissertation, University of Pennsylvania, 1979). *Dissertation Abstracts International, 40,* 1389–1390B.

Whitlatch, C. J., Zarit, S. H., & von Eye, A. (1991). Efficacy of interventions with caregivers: A reanalysis. *The Gerontologist, 31,* 9–14.

Wright, L., Clipp, E., & George, L. (1993). Health consequences of caregiver stress. *Medicine, Exercise, Nutrition, and Health, 2,* 181–195.

Yeo, G., & Gallagher-Thompson, D. (Eds.). (1996). *Ethnicity and the dementias.* Washington, DC: Taylor & Francis.

Yesavage, J. A., Brink, T. L., Rose, T., & Adey, M. (1983). Development and validation of a geriatric depression screening scale: A preliminary report. *Journal of Psychiatric Research, 39,* 37–49.

Yost, E., Beutler, L., Corbishley, M. A., & Allender, J. R. (1986). *A treatment approach for depressed older adults.* New York: Pergamon.

Young, J. (1990). *Cognitive therapy for personality disorders: A schema-focused approach.* Sarasota, FL: Professional Resource Exchange.

10

MEDICAL PATIENTS

PAUL G. RITVO, M. JANE IRVINE, JOEL KATZ, AND BRIAN F. SHAW

Medical patients face increased risks of morbidity and mortality in addition to the immediate experiences of pain and distress caused by their medical condition. Adapting to the reality of these risks and physical and emotional distress requires significant cognitive adaptation. The Risk Adaptation Model was developed to clarify the process of adaptation to illness (Katz, Ritvo, Irvine, & Jackson, 1996; Ritvo, 1994). This model, reviewed in the next section, is used to structure our cognitive–behavioral group therapy program for these patients, which we describe in detail in this chapter.

THE RISK ADAPTATION MODEL

We have attempted to explain why individuals, when confronted with illness, undertake health-oriented behaviors. Our model is based on viewing healing as an active, decision-driven process. Whereas physical changes may occur without a person specifically changing their actions or attitudes, personally adaptive changes are actively initiated and maintained. As such, one's choice of taking or not taking a health-oriented approach is continuously confronted in each situation. Even deciding to be behaviorally passive is an active cognitive choice and, in the right circumstance, a healthy alternative.

While continually confronted with decisions, our medical patients are often distressed about risks and limitations, and inabilities to overcome them. To the degree a collaborative–empirical mapping of healthy pathways can occur, intelligently adaptive decision making can follow. Ideally, the Risk Adaptation Model (RAM) functions as an orienting vehicle, illuminating the optimal pathways for patients amidst conceivable choices.

The RAM thus supports the patient's pragmatic confrontation with risk and with pain. The relevant risks invariably summate to mortality risks, to the risks of experiencing worsening disease and distress, and to the risks of experiencing limitations that may not escalate but, nonetheless, reduce quality of life. Similarly, illness-associated pain can be subdivided into physical and psychic components, with the former and latter sometimes merging, sometimes remaining distinct.

According to the RAM, medical patients first encounter the question of how *modifiable* their situations are. Given the difficulty of estimating modifiability without engaging in trial and error, questions follow about the consequences of trying to change as opposed to remaining passive. These questions become clearer as attention is directed and regulated toward addressing them. Patients may progressively explore these issues, seeking useful information about them, or they may disengage from or deny them altogether, consequently becoming distracted and fragmented.

The processes of estimating *modifiability/consequentiality* and *regulating attention* estimates are affected by individual factors, the most salient being expectancy style. Predispositions toward positive (optimism) and negative (pessimism) expectancies are particularly relevant. Optimists have been observed to engage in more active coping strategies when recovering from coronary artery bypass surgery (Scheier et al., 1989) and when adapting to breast cancer (Carver et al., 1993). This tendency toward active coping perhaps explains why optimists appear to recover faster and have better outcomes following coronary artery bypass surgery (Scheier et al., 1989). In heart transplant patients, optimism is associated with a greater adherence to health care recommendations and with better health outcomes (Leedham, Meyerowitz, Muirhead, & Frist, 1995). Optimism has also been associated with better adherence to health protective practices in men who tested positive for HIV (Taylor et al., 1992). This research suggests that in adapting to illness, a person with an optimistic expectancy style has a greater tendency toward active engagement in health-oriented behavior and in better health outcomes. It is, therefore, reasonable to propose that general expectancy style, in this case optimistic versus pessimistic style, shapes specific appraisals regarding risk modifiability and thus gives rise to greater motivation to engage in healing behaviors.

Taken together, the RAM proposes that when sufficient attention is directed toward estimating the probability that a behavior will result in positive versus negative change and to the consequences of attempting versus not attempting it, insightful decisions follow about whether to attempt change. In the course of decision making, a patient's attention is directed toward finding the best tools to make the change (*response efficacy*) and the know-how for using these tools effectively (*self-efficacy*; see Bandura, 1986). Modifiability and consequentiality estimates are naturally in constant evolution, as is the regulation of attention.

From this view of risk adaptation, what indications can be derived for approaching cognitive group therapy with medical patients?

RAM-BASED INTERVENTIONS

Attention Regulation

The increasing recognition that cognitive adaptation begins with *attention regulation* has led to interest in attentional states observed in people recovering from trauma and illness (Bremner et al., 1993; Horowitz, Wilner, & Alvarez, 1979). A curvilinear relationship has been identified (Horowitz et al., 1979), with the extremes of dysfunctional attention characterized by distractibility-avoidance on one side and instrusiveness on the other. Under extreme stress, individuals often avoid focusing on distressing events, frequently finding, however, an unwelcome, chaotic intrusion of distressing thoughts. As indicated by the RAM, insufficient attention directed toward adaptation results in poor decision making. Thus, stimulating and supporting attention regulation is necessary to improving the patient's immediate status and longitudinal adaptation. This process often focuses on helping the patient to move from avoidant to nonavoidant positions in relation to salient issues and problems to down-regulate the hyperarousal associated with poor judgment and the feeling of being overwhelmed.

Cognitive group therapy can support attention regulation in medical patients in several ways. First, the patient is introduced to relaxation-oriented techniques that reduce the frequency and intensity of stress—anxiety (hyperarousal) states hindering regulation. These techniques assist the patient in intentionally focusing attention, amidst competing stimuli (stressors). Although this characteristic is common to many relaxation approaches, it is most clearly represented in mindfulness practices (Kabat-Zinn, 1982, 1990; Kabat-Zinn, Lipworth, & Burney, 1985; Kabat-Zinn, Lipworth, Burney, & Sellers, 1986; Kutz, Borysenko, & Benson, 1985; Segal, Williams, Teasdale, & Gemar, 1996; Teasdale, Segal, &

Williams, 1995). *Mindfulness* refers to states of optimal regulation attained through deliberately mobilizing attentional capacities toward intended targets. All mindfulness techniques promote these states, often guiding individuals toward healthy releases of tension while attention is observed and regulated.

In mindfulness practices, the trial and error of attentional deployment occurs in contexts where the goal is attaining a relaxed, peaceful state. In such circumstances, attentional patterns, and particularly the thoughts dominating attention, are readily identified. In accord with mindfulness principles, however, thoughts are simply noted or monitored, with attention directed back to breathing sensations. As can be seen in Figure 10.1, activity is purposely limited to two aspects of cognitive change: *identification* and *detachment*. The other two aspects, namely *judgment* and *substitution*, are deemphasized. In other words, attentional efforts are restricted to observing rather than implementing change.

Thus, in the application of mindfulness techniques, there are no identifiable failures or successes in personal change. The willful suspensions of such judgments support unbiased observations of cognition. Freed of feeling compelled to judge or to change, the individual explores cognitive realities without typical prohibitions, transcending fixed routines to more in-depth perspectives that influence the way situations are viewed, including the potential for meaningful change.

In the context of such unbiased observations, the cognitions associated with strong emotions are readily identified. At the same time, mindfulness practice is restricted to observation and detachment, regardless of how "hot" a cognition may be. To the degree an individual remains relaxed and detached in the face of emotion-provoking cognitions, he or she gains perspective about previous reactions and becomes less prone to automatically react.

Mindfulness or thought-monitoring techniques also help medical pa-

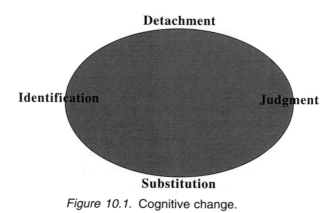

Figure 10.1. Cognitive change.

tients prioritize change needs while strategizing change efforts more effectively. Although the patient may conceive of many health-oriented changes, only a few can be effectively made at any point in time. With adequate attention regulation, the patient is able to marshal resources decisively toward the most important, timely changes.

Along these lines, Prochaska and DiClemente's framework of *stages of change* (Prochaska & DiClemente, 1983, 1992) provides a helpful structure, differentiating levels of readiness with respect to specific changes. Whether a patient is precontemplative (not systematically thinking of change) or contemplative (thinking systematically), in preparation (actively preparing for change) or in action (actively changing), stage has proved a significant predictor of successful change (Prochaska et al., 1994). The stages-of-change model thus supports the perspective that specific goals are associated with different motivational levels (i.e., stages) which, in turn, affect outcome (Prochaska, Velicer, DiClemente, & Fava, 1988; Velicer et al., 1993). Improved attention regulation helps the patient identify which stage he or she is in with respect to specific change attempts such that expectations for success become more realistic and preparations for change more effective.

Perhaps because of its Asian-meditative origins, the idea of mindfulness assisting attention regulation and prioritization may seem initially strange to many North American-trained therapists. But most of the features of mindfulness practice have been integrated into the standard repertoire of psychotherapeutic skills for decades. Many therapists allow patients to "ventilate" distressing cognitions and emotions, while timing their introduction of new, reorganizing structures so that patients are optimally "ready" to receive them. During such periods of ventilation, therapist listens nonjudgmentally, placing little or no emphasis on change. Of course, the therapist is simultaneously role modeling for the patient a nonjudgmental, yet consciously self-monitoring position. Along a different vector, desensitization procedures have assisted patients in down-regulating dysfunctional arousal and reducing excess reactivity. Mindfulness is innovative in bringing these therapeutic components together in a single, autonomous practice.

Perhaps a description of the response of one of our patients to mindfulness may illustrate some advantages of such autonomous application. Having survived a serious heart attack in his mid-30s, Bob was intent on applying stress management techniques with the same hyperactivity that characterized his lifestyle. When first instructed in mindfulness, he reacted by expressing a lack of confidence in being able to do it "right." He felt "something more definitive" should be happening experientially and was surprised at thoughts "crowding in" while he was trying to "clear" his mind. He also expressed doubt that a technique so simple could help him relax. We responded by instructing him to neutrally observe the flood of thoughts besieging him whenever he undertook practice. We pointed out this "flood" represented an overflow of concerns and anxieties that prevented him from being able to relax without tranquilizing medications. Mindfulness, if practiced consistently, would help him detach from unrealistic expectations of exerting exacting control over such large domains of personal activity. If he could simply monitor and detach from the thoughts that flooded him, his less crucial concerns would fade away while the concerns most important to him would clarify.

Bob's responses over the next few weeks illustrated progress in coming to terms with realistic perspectives regarding control. He experienced relaxed mental states during which he calmly related to whatever "came up." At the same time, he placed more value on the quieter, more meaningful events in his life, particularly time spent with his children. Being able to review his life without having to make decisions all the time helped him more calmly "review it all," permitting a prioritization he could trust in terms of where to direct attention and where to detach, so as to reduce tensions in his daily existence. Over time, he stated that what he had found in the group was quite different from what he expected. Rather than just a way of calming down, he had found a new way of viewing his life, including a new perspective on what was important, as well as a new way of connecting his thoughts, feelings, and values.

Although the application of mindfulness techniques assists attention regulation in our groups, it is not a group therapy approach, per se, until it is strategically integrated with the dynamics of guided social support. Although the benefits of social support are documented, the mechanisms by which support enhances adaptation remain unclear (Lyons, Sullivan, & Ritvo, 1995). Social support can affect attention regulation positively when peer interest and emotional stimulation help patients to functionally focus on specific aspects of their situation. Peer support, guided therapeutically, affects the inquiring, specifying, and clarifying functions of regulated attention. The patient is motivated to examine more closely, when peers express interest and concern. Peers also directly assist in inquiring, specifying, and reality testing in dialogues focused on achieving the optimal outcome through strategic change.

In marshalling supportive group resources, however, the therapist faces a complex task. While he or she wishes to motivate patients, there is the responsibility of *not* overmotivating them. Discharging this responsibility means guiding them *away* from the unrealistic prospects of change likely to prove self-defeating. In this respect, the therapist carefully monitors group expectancies, ensuring an *optimistic* focus (positive adaptation is possible) and a *realistic* focus (within a range of achievable outcomes). In our group therapy with medical patients, we present *realistic optimism* as a distinct process that aids attention regulation.

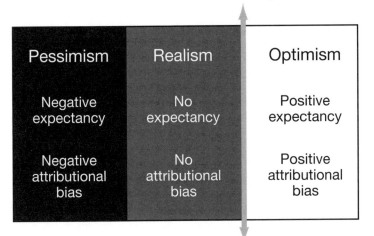

Realistic–Optimistic
Boundary

Pessimism	Realism	Optimism
Negative expectancy	No expectancy	Positive expectancy
Negative attributional bias	No attributional bias	Positive attributional bias

Figure 10.2. Expectancies as tools of change.

Optimizing Expectancies in the Service of Healing

Seligman, Scheier, Carver, and others (Abramson, Seligman, & Teasdale, 1978; Kamen & Seligman, 1987; Lin & Peterson, 1990; Peterson, 1988; Peterson, Maier, & Seligman, 1993; Peterson & Seligman, 1987; Scheier et al., 1989; Scheier & Carver, 1985; Scheier & Carver, 1987; Scheier & Carver, 1992; Scheier, Weintraub, & Carver, 1986; Self & Rogers, 1990; Taylor et al., 1992; Vaillant, 1978) have demonstrated that optimistic expectancies promote positive adaptation. Debate still continues, however, about the degree to which expectancies are inherent *traits* versus attitudinal *states*. While considerable time may elapse before these parameters are finally defined, the practical question, therapeutically, is how the expectancies of patients can be guided beneficially. Expectancy guidance can have immediate effects on mood and anxiety and can influence which adaptive changes are attempted and the degree of effort invested in them.

We take a collaborative–empirical approach to guidance, presenting patients with a spectrum of possible expectancies, ranging from *pessimistic* through *realistic* through *optimistic* (see Figure 10.2). Because expectancies are presented as tools of change in their dual function of informing and energizing change efforts, no implicit value is placed on optimism over pessimism. Both states are important pieces in the puzzle of successful change. Pessimism can preventively curtail futile efforts wasting precious resources. When sufficiently realistic, optimism can contribute information and energy to the change attempt. In contrast, unrealistic optimism may lead to a squandering of resources or to dangerously lax reactions to high-risk situations.

While optimism is best tempered by realism, how can this be conveyed to patients untrained in the complexities of expectancy? In our experience, it is important to emphasize the experiential boundary between optimism and realism: The *optimistic–realistic boundary* is the interface where these processes of deriving expectancies meet (see Figure 10.2).

As can be seen in Figure 10.3, when optimism, realism, and pessimism are contrasted in terms of expectancy and attribution, one finds an interesting result. Whereas pessimism and optimism are linked to negative and positive expectancies and external versus internal attribution, realism is defined by the absence of defined expectancies and attributional biases. In other words, the relativity of these terms lays bare the fact that realism, for the most part, is defined negatively—as an absence of expectancy and attributional bias. Accordingly, we assert the impossibility of completely escaping either pessimistic or optimistic biases when being realistic and, furthermore, the preferability of being optimistically realistic rather than pessimistically realistic. In the most practical terms, it is preferable to conceive a best *possible* scenario when attempting change, with the most productive thinking likely to occur along the optimistic–realistic boundary, where optimism is informed by realism and realism is energized by optimism.

This process, of course, has further relevance to prioritizing personal change goals. One cannot simply manufacture realistic optimism about a goal. One must find goals that one *can be* realistically optimistic about achieving. These, in turn, are likely to be the goals most likely achieved.

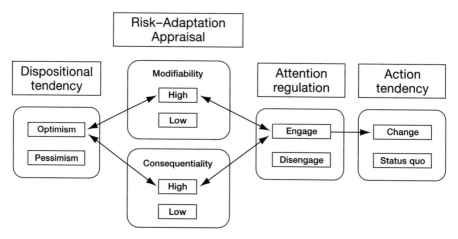

Figure 10.3. Risk–adaptation model.

The ability to derive a realistic–optimistic perspective is then another measure for determining which behavior changes should be attempted.

Perceptions of Modifiability

The process of estimating the modifiability of behaviors and achieving modifications is complex. As reviewed above, expectancies exert powerful influences that work for or against successful change. What we believe modifiable often is, whereas what we believe not to be modifiable often is not, because of our beliefs. Thus, perceptions of modifiability affect whether attempts are made, as well as the degree of vigor and determination invested. The reciprocal relationship between perceptions of modifiability and the ability to modify must be acknowledged. In contemporary theory, this relationship is often explained in terms of self-efficacy theory (Bandura, 1977, 1986).

Self-efficacy focuses on outcome expectancies relevant to specific behavior changes (Bandura, 1977, 1986). Like generic expectancies, specific expectancies inform a person about how likely change is to be successful (if attempted) while supporting positive momentum for change. The RAM suggests that both functions should be maximized in cognitive group therapy through therapeutic guidance. In other words, patients are guided in caretaking their decision-making process (concerning which changes to attempt) and their change skills (in increasing their skills and avoiding discouraging, no-win situations). The pragmatic phrase consolidating this guidance is that confidence (i.e., self-efficacy) is cultivated like a garden. The metaphor is apt because, like a garden, confidence is cultivated during dynamic goal seeking and emerges within a dynamic process of change.

Just as the medical patient is confronted with taking or not taking a health-oriented approach in each situation, he or she confronts situations in ways that either increase or decrease confidence. We point out to patients that easily performed tasks (e.g., ones that do not challenge limitations) boost confidence when well done. Conversely, the same tasks, done poorly, undermine confidence. Such insights are relevant to medical patients adapting to new handicaps. It is predictably difficult to adapt to simpler, less challenging tasks when they are all one can do, because of reduced endurance and capability. Nevertheless, patients remain acutely aware of the ups and downs of their confidence. The key linkage then is to associate confidence building with doing simpler tasks well, particularly in preparing for incrementally more challenging tasks, where performance signals progress. Our therapeutic goal then is an awareness of self-efficacy theory sufficient to guide an autonomous "pacing" of tasks, which amplifies confidence.

Perceptions of Consequentiality

In some circumstances, assisting medical patients to address the consequences of *not* adopting a healthy behavior makes the difference between life and death. When patients fail to adhere to medication regimens or to undertake rehabilitative efforts, a downward spiral of avoidance-denial-discouragement-depression evolves. In such cases, it is difficult to promote change by emphasizing modifiability, attention regulation, or realistic optimism. Often the transformative interactions boil down to confronting them about averting potentially dire consequences.

Ultimately, the importance of different sets of consequences, widely varying in time and magnitude, must be integrated by the patient in a rational, decision-making process. The potentially negative consequences of *not* changing (e.g., mortality or increasingly severe illness) must be weighed with the potentially positive consequences of changing (e.g., decreased risk and symptomatology). The more immediate consequences (positive and negative) related to the pros and cons of simply attempting change must also be weighed.

When a medical patient becomes apathetic about health management, however, he or she also usually becomes apathetic about decision making. Anxiety about risk and loss is often the alarm awakening new motivation, with confrontation frequently the medium for sounding the alarm, be it carried out by peers or a therapist. A basic message that penetrates the "shell" of apathetic and ambiguous "automatic" thinking is that although things may be unsatisfactory, they can become worse if change does *not* occur. It is important to note that findings are quite variable about the effects of fear-arousing interventions on health-oriented outcomes. Although effects seem potentially positive when the aroused fear is at a moderate level, they are frequently negative when too much fear is provoked (Leventhal, Singer, & Jones, 1965; Leventhal & Watts, 1966; Meyerowitz & Chaiken, 1987). Thus, the therapist's skill is tested in the initiating and managing of confrontations related to consequences, with the goal being a conscientiously critical weighing of the pros and cons of change. The ultimate endpoints of meaningful adaptations, however, are often mediated by highly charged emotions. This is because apathetic responses and an underlying strata of ambiguous–automatic thinking are frequently defenses against the deeper feelings of despair, anger, frustration, and grief. In terms of emotions, anxiety is usually the key that, when acknowledged and confronted, unlocks other forms of distress. The path to adaptive, critical thinking is sometimes discovered through a ventilation of intense negative emotion where the skill of the therapist is appropriately directed toward mobilizing and guiding the patient through emotionally dominated thinking to more rational thinking.

BASIC STRUCTURE AND MANAGEMENT OF
OUR GROUP PROGRAM

Given this exploration of applied theory, it is natural for questions to emerge about practical program aspects. Our therapy groups with medical patients are linked with the outpatient services of a large teaching hospital. Patient referrals originate from different medical services, the most prevalent referrals being patients contending with cardiovascular and cancer-related illness. A phone-based interview precedes group participation but deliberately avoids extensive psychological evaluation. We have found it more useful to describe the group carefully, accenting the personal commitment to engage in focused self-reflection and daily practice of mindfulness-based relaxation techniques for the 10-week duration. We have found that patients who are discouraged by this intensity are simply inappropriate for this type of group. We have also found that participation is infrequently followed-through by patients with serious comorbid psychiatric conditions. Nonetheless, several patients, at entry, have qualified for diagnoses ranging from mild to moderate depression to various types of adjustment disorder. Again, our experience has been that the patient's motivation for this type of group is more important than their diagnosis with respect to positive participation. There are typically 6 to 10 patients in each of our groups.

The group is led by two leaders and uses a structure that combines psychoeducation with opportunities for patients to challenge and discuss content, while undertaking personal disclosure and integration work. Stress reduction in the form of mindfulness and thought-monitoring techniques is practiced at the start of each session. Our approach uses a sitting position, with patients encouraged to adopt a relaxed, erect posture, either using a regular chair or a "zabuton"-type seat cushion. Patients sit for 20 minutes while receiving quietly verbalized instructions encouraging focus on breathing sensations and emphasizing full exhalations, in which the "letting go" of breath promotes a simultaneous release of tension. They are further instructed to relate to each thought arising in awareness, noting it, and deliberately detaching attention from it, a process underlined by silently verbalizing the word *thinking*. These instructions, while specific, are not presented in a demanding manner, and patients are encouraged to find their own adaptation (within a reasonable range) of the technique described.

As participants become accustomed to mindfulness practice, they have many questions about the technique, such as why it is presumed to be healthy and what changes they should expect to see. We respond to these questions by emphasizing the contrast between their experience sitting meditatively and their experience during psychological distress. We emphasize that the experience of breathing accurately reflects personal levels of stress. One focal metaphor we frequently use is *catching your breath*, that is, finding a well-regulated form of breathing that reflects a relative degree of relaxation. We readily point out that, when in such a state, one's thinking tends to be clearer and less biased by emotional reactivity. Consequently, it follows that judgments, under these conditions, are more rational and less emotionally driven.

Emphasizing careful reflection on improving one's health, we introduce the functions of *mapping* (discerning where one is and is headed), *protecting* (identifying risks and needs to reduce them), *optimizing* (making one's current situation work in the best possible way), and *changing* (deciding what to change and then doing it decisively). These functions are introduced as naturally evolving processes; the group context simply catalyzes and supports their progression. The progression serves to re-regulate the patient's living experience, understandably disordered by illness.

The psychoeducational component of the group is deliberately intended to challenge patients to consider a more active, health-oriented lifestyle. First, eight booklets are distributed to each group member. Each details step-by-step approaches to improving health along distinct lines of development. They include the following titles: *Raising Confidence; Moving Toward Freedom; Exercising for Health and Energy; Better Sleep, Rest and Relaxation; Increasing Vital Energy; Managing Stress and Anxiety; Finding the Support You Need;* and *Eating Right and Liking It.* The supply of step-by-step approaches are intend to eliminate, as much as possible, the problem of insufficient information about alternative directions for change. Within our group sessions, and in supplemental phone counseling sessions, we then focus on personal resistances to change, applying the RAM, as described. These resistances are discussed as normative for all individuals and as common in individuals coping with illness. Patients are invited to disclose their personal resistances and, in our experience, have engaged in quite meaningful levels of disclosure and discussion, without extensive probing and direction. We have found that the group mindfulness practice provides momentum in terms of meaningful disclosure. The group leaders simply guide disclosure, emphasizing linkages between the experiences of different members and reflections of the underlying truths of behaviour change. Sometimes the group agenda includes another 20-minute mindfulness practice session, but most often group discussion is so vigorous that patients prefer continuing with mutual exchanges.

While we emphasize group support, we most often emphasize the support of autonomous decision making in the service of evolving new lifestyles. Once decisions are arrived at, support is directed to actualizing particular changes, both as a way of testing the validity of decisions made and as proof of the capacity to change.

INTEGRATING ATTENTION REGULATION, OPTIMISTIC EXPECTANCIES, MODIFIABILITY, AND CONSEQUENTIALITY

The test of guiding models is their identification of therapeutic factors that, linked together, provide cohesive explanations of behavior. The RAM is most helpful when its four components are understood dynamically, with effects in one component influencing others. For example, in a positive sequence, the more attentive a patient is in estimating the consequences of change (vs. no change), the more likely these estimates are to become accurate. The more accurate the patient's estimates of consequences, the more likely he or she is to regulate attention toward estimating the modifiability of key behaviors related to consequences. The more accurate these estimates, the more likely he or she is to develop a realistic–optimistic perspective about making changes and to approach change tasks with higher levels of focal attention. These conditions, in turn, are conducive to specific positive outcome expectancies and to the development of response and self-efficacy (see Figure 10.3).

The model, however, is not linear, although most conveniently described this way. Changes in attention regulation do not necessarily precede changes in perceptions of consequences or modifiability, or in generic or specific expectancies. Obviously, a single change in either modifiability or consequentiality can influence a change in attention regulation. Or a change in the perceptions of consequences can affect a change in the perceptions of modifiability and vice versa. Rather than a linear chain of events, the RAM represents a series of feedback loops identifiably evolving in either positive or negative directions. In any given situation, either pattern may be adaptive, as the patient rouses himself or herself to adapt in relevant ways while rejecting activities judged as being of little value.

ELICITING THE INTEGRATIVE FIELD

As therapists, we often strive to create a healing environment within which specific transactions occur. In our work, we use the terms *integrative field* to describe such an environment. The term *field*, borrowed from physics, refers to a fluidly interactive context. The term *integrative* refers to attempts by people to synthesize and harmonize perspectives, both interactively and individually. Ideally, in cognitive group therapy, participants productively compare and contrast views, helping one another in problem solving efforts and in deriving functional cognitive adaptations.

How can the RAM guide and facilitate the development of an integrative, healing environment? There are a number of ways the RAM organizes this effort.

1. Empathic Identification. To empathically identify with each other, group members need structures that facilitate comparisons of their similarities and differences. Particularly within time-limited groups, structures catalyzing this process enable groups to accelerate progress. The RAM provides group members with a structured method of co-reviewing their lives, the decisions confronting them, and their decision-making processes.

2. Deriving a Realistic–Optimistic Orientation. Group support is largely based on transactions that bolster positive expectancies among members, based on either faith in a specific belief system (e.g., religious groups) or more eclectic views. While therapy groups are inherently evidence based, research on optimism and on response/self-efficacy has progressed to the point where positive expectancies are rightfully used as tools for self-change. The RAM provides a structure of decision making that guides group members in discovering a reasonable (realistic) set of positive expectancies about their current situation and about changing it. Explicit reference to the realistic-optimistic boundary challenges patients to integrate, socially and individually, cognitions classified as optimistic/realistic/pessimistic and to explore emotions and cognitions that propel them toward positivism or negativism, realism or illusion.

3. Normalizing Anxiety, Its Resolution, and In-Depth Personal Exploration. Anxiety is often the gateway experience to in-depth emotional and cognitive exploration. Its normalization in the context of risk adaptation facilitates group norms that support members in exploring and transcending anxieties and in thoroughly reviewing associated emotions (e.g., grief, sorrow, hope, relief) relevant to adaptation.

4. Reframing Adversity as a Stimulus for Learning and Empowerment. The normalization of risk adaptation (i.e., adapting to potential and immediate adversity) is the initial step toward reframing. It provides a foundation for patients to view the management of adversity as a regular life function, yielding valuable lessons about one's self and capacity for growth and maturation.

5. Demystifying Mental Health and Personal Integration. Medical patients entering group therapy differ, decidedly, from patients entering therapy because of psychiatric problems. The medical patients typically have not undergone the role inductions associated with seeking help. They see themselves as primarily having adjustment problems and psychological problems reactive to physical disease. Especially in time-limited groups, it is important to overcome the erroneous beliefs these patients have about what constitutes mental health and personal strength. For example, instead of embracing a static stoicism, the RAM provides these patients a practical structure for adopting a dynamic perspective using all forms of information (cognitive and emotional) in sound decision making. This provides a stepping stone for helping medical patients adopt more realistic views of mental health and personal integration altogether.

SUMMARY AND CONCLUSIONS

This chapter describes the RAM, an orienting model in cognitive–behavioral group therapy that provides medical patients a collaborative–empirical method of mapping health pathways defined by individual and group values. By providing patients a foundation in mindfulness practice, a healing environment, and an integrative field in which group exchanges yield new insights and changes in behavior, the model enables individual members and the group, as a whole, to function in a more integrated manner. Lastly, the RAM provides the medical patients of our group a structure for managing personal and group expectancies as important tools in deriving sound decision making and successful personal change.

In our work, we are further studying the RAM to explore its empirical applicability to a variety of medical patient populations, as well as its refinement in guiding group cognitive therapy.

REFERENCES

Abramson, L. Y., Seligman, M. E. P., & Teasdale, J. D. (1978). Learned helplessness in humans: Critique and reformulation. *Journal of Abnormal Psychology, 87,* 49–74.

Bandura, A. (1977). Self-efficacy: Toward a unifying theory of behavioral change. *Psychological Review, 84,* 191–215.

Bandura, A. (1986). The explanatory and predictive scope of self-efficacy. *Journal of Social and Clinical Psychology, 4,* 359–373.

Bremner, J. D., Scott, T. M., Delaney, R. C., Southwick, S. M., Mason, J. W., Johnson, D. R., Innis, R. B., McCarthy, G., & Charney, D. S. (1993). Deficits in short-term memory in posttraumatic stress disorder. *American Journal of Psychiatry, 150,* 1015–1019.

Carver, C. S., Pozo, C., Harris, S. D., Noriega, V., Scheier, M. F., Robinson, D. S., Ketcham, A. S., Moffat, F. L., & Clark, K. C. (1993). How coping mediates the effects of optimism on distress: A study of women with early stage breast cancer. *Journal of Personality and Social Psychology, 65,* 375–390.

Horowitz, M., Wilner, N., & Alvarez, W. (1979). Impact of Event Scale: A measure of subjective stress. *Psychosomatic Medicine, 41,* 209–218.

Kabat-Zinn, J. (1982). An outpatient program in behavioral medicine for chronic pain patients based on the practice of mindfulness meditation: Theoretical considerations and preliminary results. *General Hospital Psychiatry, 4,* 33–47.

Kabat-Zinn, J. (1990). *Full catastrophe living: Using the wisdom of your body and mind to face stress, pain and illness.* New York: Bantam Doubleday Dell.

Kabat-Zinn, J., Lipworth, L., & Burney, R. (1985). The clinical use of mindfulness meditation for the self regulation of chronic pain. *Journal of Behavioral Medicine, 8,* 163–190.

Kabat-Zinn, J., Lipworth, L., Burney, R., & Sellers, W. (1986). Four year follow-up of a meditation-based program for self regulation of chronic pain: Treatment outcomes and compliance. *Clinical Journal of Pain, 2,* 159–173.

Kamen, L. P., & Seligman, M. E. P. (1987). Explanatory style and health. *Current Psychological Research and Reviews, 6,* 207–218.

Katz, J., Ritvo, P. G, Irvine, M. J., & Jackson, M. (1996). Coping with chronic pain. In M. Zeidner & N. S. Endler (Eds.), *Handbook of coping* (pp. 252–279). New York: Wiley.

Kutz, I., Borysenko, J. Z., & Benson, H. (1985). Meditation and psychotherapy: A rationale for the integration of dynamic psychotherapy, the relaxation response, and mindfulness meditation. *American Journal of Psychiatry, 142,* 1–8.

Leedham, B., Meyerowitz, B. E., Muirhead, J., & Frist, W. H. (1995). Positive expectations predict health after heart transplantation. *Health Psychology, 14,* 74–79.

Leventhal, H., Singer, R., & Jones, S. (1965). Effects of fear and specificity of recommendation upon attitudes and behavior. *Journal of Personality and Social Psychology, 2,* 20–29.

Leventhal, H., & Watts, J. C. (1966). Sources of resistance to fear-arousing communications on smoking and lung cancer. *Journal of Personality, 34,* 155–175.

Lin, E. H., & Peterson, C. (1990). Pessimistic explanatory style and response to illness. *Behavior Research and Therapy, 28,* 243–248.

Lyons, R., Sullivan, M. J., & Ritvo, P. G. (1995). *Relationships, illness and disability.* Newbury Park, CA: Sage.

Meyerowitz, B. E., & Chaiken, S. (1987). The effect of message framing on breast self-examination attitudes, intentions, and behavior. *Journal of Personality and Social Psychology, 52,* 500–510.

Peterson, C. (1988). Explanatory style as a risk factor for illness. *Cognitive Therapy and Research, 12,* 119–132.

Peterson, C., Maier, S. F., & Seligman, M. E. P. (Eds.). (1993). *Learned helplessness: A theory for the age of personal control.* Oxford, England: Oxford University Press.

Peterson, C., & Seligman, M. E. (1987). Explanatory style and illness. *Journal of Personality, 55,* 237–265.

Prochaska, J. O., & DiClemente, C. C. (1983). Stages and processes of self-change of smoking: Toward an integrative model of change. *Journal of Consulting and Clinical Psychology, 51,* 390–395.

Prochaska J. O., & DiClemente C. C. (1992). Stages of change in the modification of problem behaviors. In M. Hersen, R. M. Eisler, & P. M. Miller (Eds.), *Progress in behavior modification* (pp. 184–214). Sycamore, IL: Sycamore Press.

Prochaska, J. O., Velicer, W. F., DiClemente, C. C., & Fava, J. (1988). Measuring processes of change: Applications to the cessation of smoking. *Journal of Consulting and Clinical Psychology, 56,* 520–528.

Prochaska, J. O., Velicer, W. F., Rossi, J. S., Goldstein, M. G., Marcus, B. H., Rakowski, W., Fiore, C., Harlow, L. L., Redding, C. A., Rosenbloom, D., & Rossi, S. R. (1994). Stages of change and decisional balance for 12 problem behaviors. *Health Psychology, 13,* 39–46.

Ritvo, P. G. (1994). Quality of life and prostate cancer treatment: Decision-making and rehabilitative support. *Canadian Journal of Oncology,* IV(Suppl. 1), S43–S46.

Scheier, M. F., & Carver, C. S. (1985). Optimism, coping, and health: Assessment and implications of generalized outcome expectancies. *Health Psychology, 4,* 219–247.

Scheier, M. F., & Carver, C. S. (1987). Dispositional optimism and physical well-being: The influence of generalized outcome expectancies on health. *Journal of Personality, 55,* 169–210.

Scheier, M. F., & Carver, C. S. (1992). Effects of optimism on psychological and physical well-being: Theoretical overview and empirical update. *Cognitive Therapy and Research, 16,* 201–228.

Scheier, M. F., Magovern, G. J., Sr., Abbott, R. A., Matthews, K. A., Owens, J. F., Lefebvre, R. C., & Carver, C. S. (1989). Dispositional optimism and recovery from coronary artery bypass surgery: The beneficial effects on physical and psychological well-being. *Journal of Personality and Social Psychology, 57,* 1024–1040.

Scheier, M. F., Weintraub, J. K., & Carver, C. S. (1986). Coping with stress: Divergent strategies of optimists and pessimists. *Journal of Personality and Social Psychology, 51,* 1257–1264.

Segal, Z. V., Williams, J. M., Teasdale, J. D., & Gemar, M. (1996). A cognitive science perspective on kindling and episode sensitization in recurrent affective disorder. *Psychological Medicine, 26,* 371–380.

Self, C. A., & Rogers, R. W. (1990). Coping with threats to health: Effects of persuasive appeals on depressed, normal, and antisocial personalities. *Journal of Behavioral Medicine, 13,* 343–357.

Taylor, S. E., Kemeny, M. E., Aspinwal, L. G., Schneider, S. G., Podriguez, R., & Herbert, M. (1992). Optimism, coping, psychological distress, and high-risk sexual behavior among men at risk for acquired immunodeficiency syndrome (AIDS). *Journal of Personality and Social Psychology, 63,* 460–473.

Teasdale, J. D., Segal, Z. V., & Williams, J. M. (1995). How does cognitive therapy prevent depressive relapse and why should attentional control (mindfulness training) help? *Behaviour Research and Therapy, 33,* 25–39.

Vaillant, G. E. (1978). Natural history of male psychological health: IV. What kinds of men do not get psychosomatic illness. *Psychosomatic Medicine, 40*, 420–431.

Velicer, W. F., Prochaska, J. O., Bellis, J. M., DiClemente, C. C., Rossi, J. S., Fava, J. L., & Steiger J. H. (1993). An expert system intervention for smoking cessation. *Addictive Behaviors, 18*, 269–290.

11

LATINOS

KURT C. ORGANISTA

There is consensus in the psychotherapy literature that group treatment is an especially viable modality for Latino clients (Acosta, 1982; Arredondo, 1991; Delgado, 1983; Delgado & Humm-Delgado, 1984; Franklin & Kaufman, 1982; Herrera & Sanchez, 1976; Hynes & Warbin, 1977; McKinley, 1987). These reports discuss how group therapy is particularly well suited to Latino clients struggling with migration and acculturation-related stress and isolation, the breakdown of the extended family, the difficulty of not speaking English, and the experience of discrimination.

Hays (1995) argued that cognitive–behavioral therapy (CBT) is well suited for people of color for many reasons, including the emphasis on tailoring treatment to the client's particular circumstances, empowering clients through self-change skills, and its attention to conscious process and specific behaviors. On the same topic, Casas (1988) noted that CBT emphasizes action and not just verbal expression, that it can be used to change environmental factors causing psychological distress, and that explanations of problems are more plausible and less abstract than in other therapies.

With regard to Latinos, CBT is consistent with the expectations of traditional clients, which include immediate symptom relief, guidance and advice, and a problem-centered approach (M. R. Miranda, 1976). Short-term, directive, problem-solving therapies are also more consistent with the expectations of low-income groups whose pressing life circumstances frequently demand immediate attention and interfere with long-term treatment (Goldstein, 1971; Torres-Matrullo, 1982).

In this chapter, a culturally sensitive, time-limited CBT outpatient group for depression is described that has been tailored to meet the needs of the Latino population in San Francisco's predominantly Latino Mission District. Members are typically drawn from groups in which poverty, low acculturation, and medical problems are common. This population has been served by this CBT clinic through the auspices of the San Francisco General Hospital (SFGH), University of California, San Francisco.

SFGH is located in the Mission District, where Latinos of Mexican descent are most numerous but where there are almost as many Central American refugees. For example, in 1990, there were 38,326 Latinos of Mexican descent and 34,119 Central Americans in San Francisco (U.S. Department of Commerce, 1993). Latinos make up 14% of the city's total population, and those who use medical and other services at SFGH are typically low income, without health insurance, and occasionally undocumented residents.

Nationally, there are approximately 27 million Latinos, or 10% of the U.S. population (U.S. Bureau of the Census, 1994). Most Latinos are of Mexican descent (64.3%), followed by Puerto Ricans (10.6%), Cubans (4.7%), Central and South Americans (13.4%), and "other" Latinos (7% not self-identified with these groups). In terms of socioeconomic status (SES), the annual median family income is $20,654 for Puerto Ricans, $23,018 for Mexican Americans, and $30,095 for Cuban Americans as compared with $39,239 for non-Latino Whites. Only about 10% of non-Latino Whites live below the poverty level as compared with 39% of Puerto Ricans, 30% of Mexican Americans, and 18% of Cuban Americans (Healey, 1995).

With regard to education, the percentage of Latinos over 25 years of age who have completed high school is 62% for Cuban Americans, 61% for Puerto Ricans, and 45% for Mexican Americans as compared with 83% for non-Latino Whites. These figures are important when one considers the very stable inverse relation between SES and psychopathology (Bruce, Takeuchi, & Leaf, 1991; Kessler et al., 1994).

Common elements across the diverse Latino groups in the United States include family roots in Latin American countries, the Spanish language, and the blended cultural traditions of the Spanish colonists and the indigenous peoples of the Americas. Latinos may also belong to various racial groups, including those with roots in Europe, Africa, Asia, and the Middle East. The more clinicians knows about particular Latino groups in different areas of the country (e.g., Mexican Americans in East Los Angeles or Central Americans in San Francisco), the better they can respond to the mental health needs of that group.

The remainder of this chapter is organized according to a framework of culturally responsive mental health services for Latinos conceptualized at Fordam University's Hispanic Research Center (Rogler, Malgady, Costantino, & Blumenthal, 1987). This framework describes effective mental health services for Latinos as consisting of three broad levels:

1. The first foundational level refers to increasing the utilization of mental health services on the part of Latinos by decreasing obstacles to treatment.
2. The second level refers to selecting treatment approaches that are compatible with Latino culture and experience.
3. The final and most complex level of the framework refers to modifying mainstream treatment approaches in ways that are compatible with Latino culture or in ways that sensitively deviate from Latino culture in the interest of the client's well-being. This final level involves incorporating elements of Latino culture into mainstream treatment approaches and/or expanding the adaptive capacities of Latino clients adjusting to their ethnic minority, bicultural experience in the United States.

These three levels are used to frame the remainder of this chapter.

LEVEL I: INCREASING LATINO UTILIZATION OF MENTAL HEALTH SERVICES

Latino Service Utilization and Mental Health

Over 30 years ago, Karno and Edgerton (1969) coined the term *epidemiological paradox* to refer to the underutilization of mental health services on the part of Mexican Americans despite their suspected high risk for mental disorders given their significant rates of urban poverty, migration and acculturation-related stress, and experience of prejudice and discrimination. Since this report, numerous studies have documented the underutilization of mental health services on the part of Latinos in proportion to their population size (Acosta, 1979; Barrera, 1978; Padilla & Ruiz, 1973; Sue, 1977; Sue, Fujino, Hu, Takeuchi, & Zane, 1991). For example, in a chart review of patients in the Los Angeles County mental health system during a 5-year period, Sue et al. (1991) found that although Latinos comprised 33.7% of the county, they comprised only 25.5% of county mental health patients. In contrast, non-Hispanic Whites comprised 44.2% of Los

Angeles County and the nearly identical rate of 43% of county mental health patients.

While not definitive, current research indicates that Latinos may be at higher risk for problems such as depression, anxiety, and somatization disorders as compared with the general population. For example, results from the National Comorbidity Survey (NCS; Kessler et al., 1994), which are based on a national probability sample (N = 8,098), showed that as compared with non-Latino Whites and African Americans, Latinos had significantly higher prevalence of currently diagnosable affective disorders as well as active comorbidity, meaning three or more concurrent mental disorders.

Prior to the NCS, reports from the Epidemiologic Catchment Areas (ECA) study showed that Island Puerto Ricans were higher than U.S.-born and Mexico-born Mexican Americans and non-Latino Whites in somatization disorder (Shrout et al., 1992). Escobar et al. (1987) used the Los Angeles ECA data to compare somatization disorder in Mexican Americans (N = 1,242) and non-Hispanic Whites (N = 1,309) and found that Mexican American women over 40 years of age were higher in somatization than their non-Latino White counterparts. Somatization in Mexican American women was also found to be positively correlated with age and negatively correlated with level of acculturation. And, looking just at women who met criteria for depression or dysthymia, Escobar et al. found that about 50% of Mexican women also met criteria for somatization disorder as compared with 20% of non-Latino White women. The comorbidity of depression and somatization has been found in other large surveys of Latinos (Angel & Guarnaccia, 1989; Kolody, Vega, Meinhardt, & Bensussen, 1986).

Although no epidemiological data currently exist for the estimated 1 million plus Central Americans in the United States, studies of community samples show higher symptoms of depression, anxiety, somatization, and interpersonal sensitivity as compared with the general U.S. norms (Plante, Manuel, Menendez, & Marcotte, 1995), as well as higher depression and migration-related stress (Salgado de Snyder, Cervantes, & Padilla, 1990), and posttraumatic stress disorder (PTSD; Cervantes, Salgado de Snyder, & Padilla, 1989), as compared with Mexican immigrants.

The above reports suggest a prototypical Latino client remarkably consistent with my own caseload and with descriptions of typical Latino clients in the psychotherapy literature (Acosta, 1982; McKinley, 1987): middle-aged, female, low in acculturation and SES, Spanish-speaking, with complaints of depression, anxiety, and bodily aches and pains either with no organic basis or in excess of what would be expected from existing medical problems. The comorbidity of depression and PTSD for Central American clients would also not be unusual. Few male clients are seen in the clinic because depression is twice as high in women and because Latino gender roles influence men to seek professional help for emotional problems less than women.

With regard to Latino underutilization of mental health services, it is currently the consensus of minority mental health experts that this is a function of numerous institutional barriers to mental health services (Snowden, 1982). Nearly 20 years ago, the President's Commission on Mental Health under Jimmy Carter conducted a national study of ethnic minority underutilization of mental health services. In this massive report, the commission summarized the following four major reasons for ethnic minority underutilization: (a) availability (i.e., too few existing services for minorities); (b) accessibility (existing services too distant and unaffordable); (c) acceptability (too few culturally acceptable services that are consistent with the cultural needs and expectations of minority clients); and (d) accountability (lack of consultation with minority groups regarding services desired; Parron, 1982).

Decreasing the above barriers is the first major step toward increasing mental health service utilization on the part of Latinos and other ethnic minority groups. For example, Sue et al. (1991) tested the "ethnic match" hypothesis by examining 12,000 Los Angeles county mental health charts, 3,000 per each of four ethnic groups: Latinos, Asians, Blacks, and Whites. This hypothesis holds that by matching ethnic minority clients with bilingual, bicultural therapists of similar background, utilization and treatment outcome will improve because such mental health services are more culturally acceptable to clients. Results showed that ethnic and/or linguistic matching was indeed related to lower dropout and better treatment outcome for Latino and Asian clients low in acculturation.

Whereas Latinos underutilize mental health services, it is also well known that they overutilize medical doctors for emotional and psychological problems (Karno, Ross, & Caper, 1969; Padilla, Carlos, & Keefe, 1976). For example, Muñoz and Ying (1993) found rates of current major depression to be as high as 25% in Spanish-speaking primary care patients, which is about four times the rate in the general population (Kessler et al., 1994). Thus, medical staff also need to be actively involved in mental health outreach to Latinos in hospital settings (Muñoz, 1995).

Increasing Latino Utilization of Group CBT for Depression

The SFGH Cognitive–Behavioral Depression Clinic minimizes barriers to mental health services by providing free (affordable), hospital-based (available and accessible) mental health services with linguistically and ethnically matched therapists (acceptability). In terms of outreach, primary care physicians and medical staff have been trained to recognize and refer clients presenting with depressed affect, multiple somatic complaints, or both.

Referral forms containing a checklist of the *Diagnostic and Statistical Manual of Mental Disorders* (4th ed.; American Psychiatric Association, 1994) criteria for major depression are used by primary care staff to screen clients for a referral to the clinic. Referrals sent to the clinic are distributed to therapists who call or write clients and offer them an evaluation for depression on the basis of their physician's recommendation, which facilitates the acceptance of mental health services. The clinic receives about 300 referrals a year, and about half of these are Spanish-speaking Latino primary care clients, predominantly first-generation immigrants from Mexico and Central American refugees.

Outpatient group CBT is offered to clients who meet criteria for unipolar major depression without psychotic features. Persons with active substance abuse, cognitive disorders, or other Axis I psychiatric diagnoses are referred out for appropriate services. However, clients with concomitant anxiety disorders (e.g., generalized anxiety, panic disorder, PTSD) or somatization disorder are not excluded. Also, persons currently in treatment for their substance abuse problems are allowed to enter group CBT.

LEVEL II: SELECTING TREATMENTS THAT FIT LATINO CULTURE AND EXPERIENCE

Group Therapy as a Viable Treatment Modality for Latinos

In Delgado's (1983) review of the literature on group therapy with Latinos, he categorized factors that facilitate culturally competent group work with this population. Under organizational issues, Delgado included (a) locating groups near or within generic and natural support settings where Latinos are likely to go for help (e.g., medical or family agency settings vs. mental health settings); (b) concerted outreach efforts; (c) responding to the culture-based preference for relating to individuals versus institutions; and (d) cultural sensitivity training for staff. Regarding group process factors, he included (a) pretreatment preparation for group through education about the structure and process of group psychotherapy; (b) bilingual services that facilitate the full range of verbal and emotional expression in Latino clients; and (c) targeting common Latino problem themes such as interpersonal or family conflicts and low SES-related stressors.

With regard to acculturation levels of group members, Delgado included (a) attending to female gender-related issues given the predominance of Latina women in group therapy; he noted how (b) varying levels of acculturation among group members is advantageous to group process. Finally, regarding group leader factors, Delgado emphasized the need for a therapist who is an active, expert, authority figure who gives answers and advice, targets concrete problems, informs clients about community resources, and engages in enough self-disclosure as to establish a personalized professional relationship. As discussed below, all of the above factors can be incorporated into CBT with Latinos.

The Group CBT Protocol for Latinos With Depression

Task Focus

The clients in our clinic are offered 16 weeks of standardized, manual-driven, group CBT provided by bilingual, bicultural Latino therapists. Groups meet once a week for 2 hours, and the treatment protocol consists of three four-session cognitive–behavioral modules (Muñoz, Aguilar-Gaxiola, & Guzman, 1986; Muñoz & Miranda, 1986) adapted from the self-help book, *Control Your Depression* (Lewinsohn, Muñoz, Youngren, & Zeiss, 1986). The three therapy modules focus on the following:

1. Activity schedules designed to break the vicious cycle of depression leading to low activities and vice versa.
2. Assertiveness training to increase interpersonal effectiveness.
3. Cognitive restructuring designed to identify and change depression-related thinking and core beliefs.

The didactic style of CBT quickly orients the clients to treatment by educating them about mental disorders and how CBT is used to conceptualize and treat their problems. The use of therapy manuals, homework assignments, and chalkboard-aided teaching resulted in our clients referring to therapy as *la clase de depresión*, which we believe helps to alleviate any stigma attached to therapy.

Each participant is given a copy of the treatment manual, which includes outlines of each of the 12 sessions as well as weekly homework assignments consisting primarily of daily mood monitoring in relation to activities, interpersonal contacts, and thoughts–beliefs. Homework is reviewed at each session to teach clients the relations among thoughts, behaviors, and mood.

New clients enter the ongoing groups at the beginning of each module so that there are usually clients who are just beginning therapy, others who are midway, as well as some close to termination. This strategy allows us to meet our clinic's demand for services but also populates each group with clients at different stages of treatment, which can be advantageous, as when new and overwhelmed clients are assured by those closer to termination that they felt similarly when they started but are now feeling better. Note that although there are only 12 sessions in the manual, each client repeats his or her first module to make 16 sessions.

Group Cohesion

Constant care is taken to achieve a delicate balance between teaching CBT techniques and attending to specific client problems and group process. This balance is partly achieved by using the first hour of therapy to review CBT agenda in a lecture/discussion format, followed by reviewing homework and applying CBT techniques to actual problems during the second hour. This way of ordering the agenda increases the likelihood of completing the didactic component of CBT, which the reverse order does not.

Historically, the CBT literature has emphasized theory and technique at the expense of therapeutic process (Hollon & Shaw, 1979; Rose, Tolman, & Tallant, 1985). This is especially true for CBT groups in which interventions are targeted at the individual level and fail to consider the powerful advantages of therapeutic group process (Satterfield, 1994). As such, conscious attention is paid to process and other general therapy factors to promote group cohesion.

Satterfield (1994) advocated for cognitive–behavioral "hybrid groups" that systematically use group dynamics so that CBT can be conducted through a group experience rather than simply in a group setting. For example, I consistently instigate and reinforce intermember behaviors such as sharing and feedback to build cohesion within the group. When reviewing homework on the chalkboard, I routinely list one client's mood graph and related thoughts and behaviors, but then ask other group members to discuss the board work. Furthermore, several group-as-a-whole exercises are included in the treatment manual (e.g., making a list of pleasant activities in San Francisco that cost little money; sharing behavioral contracts to do reinforcing activities between sessions, and setting and sharing short- and long-term goals).

In addition to group cohesion building, I have also found that generous amounts of empathy are essential to the successful application of CBT techniques to sensitive client problems. While this might seem obvious, Burns and Nolen-Hoeksema (1992) have noted that the role of empathy in CBT is somewhat controversial in the literature, with some experts downplaying its importance in relation to technique. In their study of therapeutic empathy and recovery from depression in CBT, Burns and Nolen-Hoeksema found that the clients of therapists who were rated as warmest and most empathic improved significantly more than the clients of therapists with lower empathy ratings, even when controlling for factors such as initial depression severity and homework compliance. These researchers concluded that even in a highly technical form of therapy, the quality of the therapeutic relationship has a moderate to large causal effect on clinical recovery separate from therapist skill. Exactly how our CBT techniques are modified for Latinos is described in detail below.

LEVEL III: MODIFYING GROUP CBT TO FIT LATINO CULTURE AND EXPERIENCE

According to Hays (1995, p. 313), "the key to multicultural applications of CBT lies in the need for explicit attention to cultural influences and minority populations that have traditionally been ignored." She also noted that such applications require considerable creativity and flexibility in the absence of informative research. For example, she recommended CBT that promotes bicultural competency versus just mainstream skills, that defines problems in relation to cultural norms, and that is used to foster social change (e.g., teaching skills to challenge oppressive social situations). These suggestions as well as other considerations are described below.

Engagement Strategies

Given the high dropout of Latinos from psychotherapy compared with their non-Latino White counterparts (Sue, 1977), the first few client contacts are crucial for engaging Latinos in treatment. At the Cognitive–Behavioral Depression Clinic, clients are invited to a pretreatment orientation session in which they meet bilingual, bicultural Latino staff and therapists and learn about the structure and process of group therapy over coffee and cookies. This type of "role preparation" is highly recommended for decreasing dropout in low-income (Orlinsky & Howard, 1986), ethnic minority (Acosta, Yamamoto, & Evans, 1982), and Latino clients (Delgado, 1983).

Engagement is further enhanced during the first session of group therapy by incorporating the salient Latino value of *personalismo* into a culturally sensitive relationship protocol. Personalismo refers to a valuing of and responsiveness to the personal dimension of relationships, including task-oriented professional relationships such as psychotherapy. As such, the mainstream practice of immediately focusing on the presenting problem in therapy can be perceived as impersonal by Latino clients, especially if it is at the expense of the social lubrication needed to build *confianza*, or trust (Roll, Millen, & Martinez, 1980).

It is important not to confuse personalism with informality. That is, it would be a mistake to come across too casually or overly friendly. As described by Roll et al. (1980), the task of the culturally sensitive psychotherapist is to find the balance between task-oriented formality and personalized attention to the client. To achieve such a balance, it is necessary for the therapist to engage in sufficient small talk, or *plática*, that includes judicious self-disclosure.

Hence, during the first session, time is allotted for *presentaciones* in which therapists and clients share personal background information about where they are from, their families, work that they have done, personal interests, and so on. The importance of everybody getting to know each other a little before dealing with problems is stressed in this session. The similarities among clients in terms of countries of origin, types or work, interests, and so on naturally elicit questions and small talk. Following presentations, therapists educate clients about the diagnosis of depression and the CBT model. Finally, clients are asked to share their experience of depression, with special emphasis on how it affects their activities, interpersonal relationships, and thinking.

As a preliminary assessment of depressed thinking, clients are asked to speculate about the causes of their depression. For example, a middle-aged Central American woman attributed her extreme depression to the death of her son, who had been killed 12 years earlier in Nicaragua where young men were frequently the targets of either government or guerilla forces during the country's civil war. The woman recalled with tears the trauma of having to identify her son's bullet-riddled body in the morgue. It is interesting that when we asked her what about her son's death made her so depressed, she claimed that his death was her fault because the two of them had argued on the morning of his death and in his anger he had stormed out of the house to meet his unfortunate fate. This case is noteworthy for illustrating the difference between normal bereavement and guilt-ridden self-blame that exacerbates bereavement and can result in major depression. It also illustrates the kinds of hardships that Central American refugees sometimes bring into therapy.

In the above case, it was imperative to eventually challenge the woman's belief that she was responsible for forces beyond her control. The woman eventually learned to think, "Yes it's true that my son and I argued, and that he left the house in anger on the day of his death, but that doesn't mean that his death was my fault." We also reminded the woman that her son's life included much more than his tragic death and asked her to recall some pleasant memories of him. She eventually shared that her son had been quite a joker and recalled a few of his pranks that made her laugh for the first time in years.

Addressing Common Problem Themes in Latino Clients

Fortunately, most problem themes that emerge in therapy with Latino clients are not as dramatic as the above example. In Delgado and Humm-Delgado's (1984) review of 28 published reports on group therapy with Latinos, they reported that the most common problem themes that emerged revolved around interpersonal conflicts in marriage and family. Comas-Díaz (1985) conducted a content analysis of problem themes in her CBT group work with depressed Puerto Rican women and found that therapy time centered on problems in interpersonal relationships, children, spouse/lovers, culture shock, and symptoms of psychological distress. Acosta (1982) categorized problems in his group work with Latinos into family breakdown, acculturation stress, and discrimination.

Although it is not known whether Latinos present to therapy with more interpersonal and family problems than their non-Latino White counterparts, many Latino mental health experts (e.g., Szapocznik, Santisteban, Kurtines, Perez-Vidal, & Hervis, 1986) speculate that the stress of immigration and acculturation exacerbates normal family problems for Latinos. For example, generation gap problems between parents and children can become exacerbated by acculturation gap problems in which parents become critical of their children for being too Americanized, whereas children become critical of their parents for being too "old fashioned." Similarly, couple problems may become exacerbated by the stress of changes in traditional gender roles in which women need to work outside of the home for economic survival.

Because Latino clients are predominantly women, therapists need to be cognizant of traditional gender roles prescribing that Latinas be submissive, self-sacrificing, and enduring of suffering inflicted by men (Comas-Díaz, 1985). As Comas-Díaz (1985) and Torres-Matrullo (1982) noted in their work with Puerto Rican women with depression, depressed thinking appeared related to unrealistic sex role expectations faced by these women with respect to prohibiting the expression of anger, remaining married despite the quality of the marriage, and the expectation to give help but not to request it. The above problem themes and gender issues provide therapists with consistent intervention targets when working with Latinos.

Activity Schedules

Activity schedules and behavioral contracts to increase reinforcing activities are used to break the vicious cycle of depression and anhedonia that leads to low activity levels, which in turn maintain depression. I have also found activity schedules to be helpful in countering agoraphobia related to panic disorder in my clients (Organista, 1995).

When applying cognitive–behavioral techniques, therapists must be aware of underlying mainstream American cultural assumption. Hays (1995) noted that CBT is based on several dominant group values assumed to be universal but that are not always universal priorities (e.g., change, assertiveness, verbal ability, and personal independence). For example, an implicit assumption underlying activity schedules emphasizes the need to "take time out for one's self," based on the value that one must take care of one's self before others. Although such an assumption is undoubtedly adaptive in the individually oriented U.S. society, it can run counter to the emphasis in Latino culture, especially for women, to put the needs of family members ahead of one's own. This cultural contradiction is further complicated by the fact that although traditional Latino female gender role expectations may be more realistic within intact extended family and community systems (with their many compensating resources), such expectations become unrealistic in the United States, where Latino families have become more nuclear with fewer traditional resources.

Consider, for example, the excessiveness of one female client who had the bulk of homemaker and parenting responsibilities in her family, in addition to working full time outside of the home. To make matters worse, this woman also had few family members or friends living close by. For this client, it was important to balance her many responsibilities with some time for pleasant relaxation. But how? It was also important to teach this client how to set limits with her husband and other family members regarding housework and child care.

Latino clients can be persuaded to do pleasant activities with family members. The woman in the above example began increasing pleasant activities by taking her children to the park after work and by visiting a coworker who also had children. The two women talked about work over coffee while their children played together.

Our clients have also taught us over the years that they are willing to increase pleasurable activities in order to *distraerse*, or distract, themselves from worry, conflict, and problems. This common perception of pleasant activities as a way of temporarily escaping problems provides practitioners with an opening for encouraging this effective intervention strategy. The woman in the above example considered visiting with her coworker friend a pleasant distraction from her daily chores and stress.

In addition, because Latino clients are disproportionately poor, care needs to be taken to generate discussions and lists of local activities that cost little or no money (e.g., free admission to museums and zoo on the first Wednesday of the month, crocheting, or preparing a favorite meals). Group members enthusiastically participate in the exercise of generating such lists, and one client can be asked to write out the list, which can be copied and distributed to members upon completion. Next, obstacles to doing such activities are addressed (e.g., *falta de ganas*, or loss of desire to do activities because of depression). Because Latino clients are fond of sayings, we discuss sayings such as, "You can lead a horse to water but you can't make him drink" as a way of increasing motivation.

Finally, teaching clients to assertively set limits on excessive demands from family members is another helpful way of decreasing obstacles to doing activities. For instance, the woman in the above example practiced how to ask her husband to spend more time with the children after school while she shopped for the family. However, getting a traditionally oriented Latina to make such assertive requests requires a culturally sensitive approach to assertiveness training.

Assertiveness Training

In traditional Latino culture, communication and behavior are strongly governed by traditional institutions such as the extended family, community, and the church, as well as by values such as deference to those of higher status based on age, gender, and social position. As such, assertive communication can run contrary to the culture's emphasis on communication that is polite, nonconfrontational, deferential, and even purposefully indirect (e.g., asking one relative to speak to another on one's behalf). Such communication is especially true for women who are taught to defer to and obey men and to subordinate their needs to those of the family (Comas-Díaz, 1985). Unfortunately, such a traditional system of communication is subject to breakdown in modern society, in which the mediating functions of traditional institutions are rapidly deteriorating. As such, the need for members of U.S. society to assertively convey their needs and desires is imperative for optimal adaptation.

Despite the sociocultural dilemma of teaching a modern, Western, and particularly American style of communication to traditionally oriented individuals (Rakos, 1991), the argument to do so with Latino clients is compelling. For example, Soto and Shaver (1982) studied a sample of 287 Puerto Rican women and found that women highest in gender role traditionalism were the least assertive and the most psychologically distressed. Thus, the question that remains is how to conduct assertiveness training in a culturally sensitive manner. Encouraging descriptions of assertiveness training with Latinos have been reported (Acosta, 1982; Boulette, 1976; Herrera & Sanchez, 1976; Torres-Matrullo, 1982), as well as culturally sensitive guidelines for conducting assertiveness training with ethnic minorities in general (Wood & Mallinckrodt, 1990) and with Latinas in particular (Comas-Díaz & Duncan, 1985).

The cognitive–behavioral models of assertiveness training (e.g., Lange & Jakubowski, 1977) emphasize the concept of "personal rights" as a way of motivating assertiveness; however, such a concept can be foreign to the nondemocratic, nonegalitarian family and friendship systems of Latino clients. Thus, in our clinic, we sensitively deviate from traditional Latino culture by encouraging clients to expand their bicultural capabilities by adding assertive communication skills to their traditional communication style. That is, we "biculturate" clients by describing assertiveness as an effective communication skill in mainstream American society in areas such as work, school, agency settings, and interpersonal relationships. The emphasis on biculturation is based on an "additive" model of therapy, in which the task is to add mainstream communication skills to the client's current repertoire without devaluing traditional communication styles.

Care is taken to stress culturally compatible aspects of assertiveness, such as the emphasis on communication that is not only direct but also honest, respectful, a way of cultivating family relationships, and a good way of teaching one's children how to be interpersonally effectively in mainstream society.

On the basis of Comas-Díaz and Duncan's (1985) guidelines, Latino cultural factors that mitigate against developing assertiveness are discussed in group, as well as strategies for dealing with predictable negative reactions from spouses and other higher status individuals. For example, Comas-Díaz and Duncan taught Puerto Rican women to preface assertive expressions with phrases such as *con todo respeto* (with all due respect) and *me permite expresar mis sentimientos?* (would you permit me to express my feelings?). In addition, clients are taught to respond to negative reactions to their assertiveness with explanations such as, "Expressing my feelings makes me less upset and better able to handle things."

For example, one seemingly passive woman in our group learned how to respond more assertively toward her overly critical and domineering mother. On one particular occasion, the client was very hurt because when she had shared with her mother the possibility of getting a job she had applied for, her mother responded by saying, "And just how do you expect to work a job when you can't even speak English?" When we asked the client why she did not express her hurt feelings to her mother, she replied that she did not want to be disrespectful. This latter point is noteworthy because although Latinos are as likely as anybody else to be passive, the client's reason for enduring her mother's insensitivity stemmed from her culture-based practice of respectful behavior toward one's parents and not passivity per se.

With the help of modeling by therapists and role play, the woman was finally able to say to her mother, "With all due respect, *mamá*, could you please be more supportive in my efforts to get a job? It hurts my feelings when you are so critical and discouraging." Both surprised and angered, the client's mother criticized her daughter for "talking back" and called her a *mal criada*, which refers to a poorly raised child without manners. But role playing and group discussion had prepared this client for this assertion mitigating response, to which she replied, "Would you permit me to say something about that?," to which the mother could hardly say no, and the client continued, "If you don't let me express my feelings to you, I'm going to feel bad and resentful toward you, which I really don't want to do." In this case, group discussion was extremely helpful in differentiating an honest and respectful assertive communication from the rude, disrespectful, and aggressive expressions of a *mal criada*.

Another excellent way of motivating Latino clients to consider assertiveness is to ask them what happens when they hold their negative feelings inside. Almost without exception, clients describe the exacerbation of existing physical illness such as high blood pressure, diabetes, heart disease, gastrointestinal, and other somatic symptoms. For example, one woman who had survived a heart attack became very motivated to become assertive as a way of decreasing the probability of a second attack by not holding in anger and resentment toward her husband, who drank excessively and became insulting and neglectful when intoxicated.

The above approach is important because Latino clients commonly report a tendency to *guardar*, or hold in anger, rather than express it to spouses, family members, and others with whom they are upset. The tendency to *guardar* can be viewed as part of a larger culture-based style known as *controlarse*, which refers to the disciplined self-control of negative thoughts and feelings leading to either resignation or efforts to overcome hardship (Cohen, 1985).

Cognitive Restructuring

In Orlinsky and Howard's (1986) landmark review of the literature on psychotherapeutic process and outcome, they concluded that therapist factors such as problem exploration, interpretation, and active confrontation were more effective than support, advice giving, and therapist self-disclosure. Cognitive restructuring necessitates confronting clients about their unhealthy thinking and core beliefs. As mentioned earlier, empathy is key to this intervention in combination with modifying traditional methods of cognitive restructuring.

For years, therapists in our clinic have tried to use Albert Ellis's seemingly simple A-B-C-D method as a way of teaching clients how to identify and change problem thinking (Ellis & Grieger, 1977). However, not only does the acronym A-B-C-D not translate well into Spanish, but rarely do our clients master mapping out the Activating event, Beliefs about the activating event, the emotional Consequences of beliefs, and how to Dispute irrational beliefs related to negative emotional consequences.

In view of this problem, I teach Latino clients the difference between "helpful" thoughts that help to reduce symptoms and initiate adaptive behaviors and "unhelpful" thoughts that do the opposite. In addition, I streamline cognitive restructuring by teaching what I refer to as the "Yes, but . . ." technique, in which clients are taught that much of problematic thinking amounts to "half-truths" about problems that need to be made into "whole-truths." Rather than provoking defensiveness by labeling client beliefs as irrational or distorted, therapists make clients feel understood when they communicate that client thoughts are understandable in view of their circumstances.

For example, we treated a bright, middle-aged Central American woman who survived 12 years of serious spouse abuse and whose depression stemmed from the core belief that "If only I hadn't remained in that marriage so long, my children would not have been emotionally harmed." The depression-related self-blame in this belief, as well as the omission of the client's significant accomplishments, was addressed by asking the client to complete the following half-truth: "Yes, it is sad that I remained in an abusive marriage so long and that my children were exposed to this situation, but . . ." to which the client eventually replied, "But I did finally leave him and I raised two good children here in the United States all by myself!" The client was also asked to describe her children, now adults, to group members, who were asked by the therapist if these sounded like emotionally damaged individuals.

Another common problem is that many of our middle-aged clients must often stop working and limit their responsibilities because of chronic medical problems, disabilities, and depression. For example, in a sample of 176 of our clinic patients with depression, 52% had chronic medical conditions (Organista, Muñoz, & González, 1994). Sadly, a common conclusion that both male and female Latino clients make is No sirvo para nada [I'm good for nothing], because their sense of self-worth is overly invested in providing tangible forms of support to their family. Again, we teach cognitive restructuring by asking clients to complete statements such as, "Yes, my health problems do limit what I can do, but . . .," to which clients respond with something like, "but, that doesn't mean I'm worthless" or "there are still some things I can do for my family."

Because the majority of our clients are practicing Catholics, we regard religion as a cognitive–behavioral domain in which therapists need to work with traditional, religious Latino clients. We reinforce church going and prayer as behavioral and cognitive activities, respectively, that help clients deal with stress and negative mood states. However, we have also learned to explore and challenge forms of prayer that seem to lessen the probability of active problem solving. For example, when clients report that they "just prayed" as a way of coping with their problems, we ask them to share their prayers in group. They often reply that they simply asked God to alleviate their suffering or to solve their personal problems. In such cases, we help clients to shift prayers in a more active direction with techniques such as discussing the saying, Ayúdate, que Dios te ayudará, which is the Spanish equivalent of "God helps those who help themselves." Following this, we model for clients, and ask them to recite prayers in which they ask God for support in trying out new behaviors (e.g., God, please give me the strength to increase my daily activities, learn how to be more assertive, and so on).

On a more serious note, we have encountered clients who were noncompliant with diets and medications for medical problems because they chose to put their fate in the hands of God. For example, an elderly Latino man from Mexico, who chose not to follow his diet and medication for diabetes, claimed that if it was God's will that he die, then he would do so. We quickly informed the man that he was "testing" God's will and asked the group, "Who are we to do so?" I told the man that this would be like me putting a bullet into the chamber of a gun, spinning the chamber, holding the barrel to my head, and saying, "Let's see if it's God's will that I live or die." Furthermore, I tell such clients that if they really want to know God's will, they need to use all of the resources that God has provided them and then see what happens.

On a humorous note, I frequently tell clients the story of the middle-aged woman whose town is flooding but who refuses to get into a rescue car because she claims to have faith that God will save her. With the water level continuing to rise, the woman later refuses to board a rescue boat and later refuses a rescue helicopter, sitting on the roof of her home insisting that God will save her because she has always been a strong, practicing Catholic. We end the story by informing clients that the poor woman drowns, goes to heaven, and demands to know why God did not save her, a woman of such great faith. God replies that he tried several times to save her; first by sending a rescue car, next by sending a rescue boat, and finally by sending a rescue helicopter!

SUMMARY

Unfortunately, extremely little outcome research on the efficacy of CBT with Latinos and other ethnic minorities has been conducted (Casas, 1988). For example, in my review of the CBT outcome literature on depression, I found only one randomized, controlled outcome study on Latinos. In this study, Comas-Díaz (1981) investigated the efficacy of group cognitive therapy and behavior therapy in a small sample of 26 depressed, Spanish-speaking, unmarried Puerto Rican mothers from low SES backgrounds. Results showed significant and comparable reductions in depression for both cognitive and behavioral treatments compared with a waiting-list control group.

In a preliminary outcome study of group CBT with 175 of our SFGH clients, nearly half of whom were Spanish-speaking Latinos, we found significant pre- to posttreatment reductions in depression (Organista et al., 1994). However, these reductions in depression were from severe to moderate symptomatology, whereas CBT outcome studies typically report reductions from moderate to mild symptoms (Nietzel, Russell, Hemmings, & Gretter, 1987). This difference is not surprising, considering that research participants in the CBT outcome literature are highly motivated for treatment and are almost exclusive non-Hispanic White, middle-class participants screened for the kinds of problems that characterize our clients (e.g., medical conditions, substance abuse, and concomitant anxiety disorders).

Our clinical research team has just completed an auspicious report on a radomized trial comparing group CBT with and without clinical case management (CCM; J. Miranda, Azocar, Organista, Dwyer, & Arean,

2000). Clinical case management services were examined as a way of enhancing group CBT and addressing the multiple needs of our low income and ethnic minority clients. In addition to providing traditional social work case management services, case managers also function as co-therapists in group CBT and could therefore reinforce clinical work during individual case management sessions (for a full description of CCM, see Organista & Valdes Dwyer, 1996). Participants were 199 clients (77 Spanish-speaking Latino, and 122 English-speaking predominately non-Latino White and African American clients). Results revealed less drop-out from the group CBT plus CCM condition versus group CBT alone. Group CBT plus CCM was also more effective in decreasing depression and improving functioning but only for Spanish-speaking Latino clients. This latter finding is consistent with past research by Sue et al. (1991) demonstrating that ethnic and linguistic matching in therapy improved retention and outcome for Latino and Asian clients low in acculturation, but not for Anglo or African American clients. Miranda et al. (2000) concluded that Latino clients were most responsive to group CBT plus CCM because of their special linguistic and other acculturation related needs.

Given the paucity of research to inform us about the efficacy of culturally sensitive applications of CBT, we are dependent on the experience, creativity, and flexibility of clinicians who conduct CBT with Latinos and other diverse groups to share what they believe is effective. As such, descriptive reports in the literature on this topic are consistent in discussing the good fit between group therapy in general and CBT in particular with Latino culture and experience in the United States. In addition to incorporating salient Latino values into CBT to increase its appeal, therapists can also teach Latino clients mainstream American skills in the spirit of making them more biculturally effective. Group therapy is an ideal modality for conducting CBT with Latinos given the strikingly similar problem themes of traditionally oriented Latino clients.

In addition to basic CBT outcome research with Latinos, future directions in this area also need to include theorizing about the interaction between traditional Latino values and role prescriptions, characteristic social circumstances (e.g., poverty), and mental health problems. For example, the drawbacks of traditional gender role for Latinas with depression could be explicated and reviewed with these clients in ways analogous to Young's (1994, p. 13) schema-focused approach in which he delineated early maladaptive schemas that drive interpersonal problems (e.g., "Subjugation/Lack of individuation—The voluntary or involuntary sacrificing of one's own needs to satisfy others' needs, often with an accompanying failure to recognize one's own needs"). Deference to authority is another example (i.e., "It is disrespectful to disagree with or to express anger towards authorities such as elders, professionals, bosses, etc."). Although these cultural values may be more functional in traditional settings, they could be excessive and limiting in the United States where the Latino experience is more modern and bicultural.

Furthermore, acculturative stress needs to be studied for its role in triggering unhelpful, culturally based attributions in the areas of personal or interpersonal problems. For example, in Szapocznik's work with Cuban families, he found that parents frequently blame family problems on their children's over-Americanization, whereas the children, in turn, blame their parents for being too old fashioned. In his Bicultural Effectiveness Training, Szapocznik et al. (1986) taught all family members to "blame" the acculturation process and challenged them to assist each other's adaptation to American society (e.g., how can parents help their children adapt to American society while still being respectful and responsible to the family?).

REFERENCES

Acosta, F. X. (1979). Barriers between mental health services and Mexican Americans: An examination of a paradox. *American Journal of Community Psychology, 7,* 503–520.

Acosta, F. X. (1982). Group psychotherapy with Spanish-speaking patients. In R. M. Becerra, M. Karno, & J. I. Escobar (Eds.), *Mental illness and hispanic Americans: Clinical perspectives* (pp. 183–197). New York: Grune & Stratton.

Acosta, F. X., Yamamoto, J., & Evans, L. A. (1982). *Effective psychotherapy for low-income and minority patients.* New York: Plenum Press.

American Psychiatric Association. (1994). *Diagnostic and statistical manual of mental disorders* (4th ed.). Washington, DC: Author.

Angel, R., & Guarnaccia, P. J. (1989). Mind, body, and culture: Somatization among Hispanics. *Social Science Medicine, 28,* 1229–1238.

Arredondo, P. (1991). Counseling Latinas. In C. C. Lee & B. L. Richardson (Eds.), *Multicultural issues in counseling: New approaches to diversity* (pp. 143–156). Alexandria, VA: American Association for Counseling and Development.

Barrera, M., Jr. (1978). Mexican-American mental health service utilization: A critical examination of some proposed variables. *Community Mental Health Journal, 14,* 35–45.

Boulette, T. R. (1976). Assertion training with low income Mexican American women. In M. R. Miranda (Ed.), *Psychotherapy with the Spanish-speaking: Issues in research and service delivery* (Monograph No. 3, pp. 16–71). Los Angeles: University of California, Los Angeles, Spanish-Speaking Mental Health Research Center.

Bruce, M. L., Takeuchi, D. T., & Leaf, P. J. (1991). Poverty and psychiatric status: Longitudinal evidence from the New Haven Epidemiologic Catchment Area Study. *Archives of General Psychiatry, 48,* 470–474.

Burns, D. D., & Nolen-Hoeksema, S. (1992). Therapeutic empathy and recovery from depression in cognitive–behavioral therapy: A structural equation model. *Journal of Consulting and Clinical Psychology, 60,* 441–449.

Casas, J. M. (1988). Cognitive–behavioral approaches: A minority perspective. *The Counseling Psychologist, 16,* 106–110.

Cervantes, R. C., Salgado de Snyder, V. N., & Padilla, A. M. (1989). Post traumatic stress disorder among immigrants from Central America and Mexico. *Hospital and Community Psychiatry, 40,* 615–619.

Cohen, L. M. (1985). *Controlarse* and the problems of life among Latino immigrants. In W. A. Vega & M. R. Miranda (Eds.), *Stress and Hispanic mental health: Relating research to service delivery* (DHHS Pub. No. ADM 85-1410, pp. 202–218). Rockville, MD: U.S. Department of Health and Human Services.

Comas-Díaz, L. (1981). Effects of cognitive and behavioral group treatment on the depressive symptomatology of Puerto Rican women. *Journal of Consulting and Clinical Psychology, 49,* 627–632.

Comas-Díaz, L. (1985). Cognitive and behavioral group therapy with Puerto Rican women: A comparison of content themes. *Hispanic Journal of Behavioral Sciences, 7,* 273–283.

Comas-Díaz, L., & Duncan, J. W. (1985). The cultural context: A factor in assertiveness training with mainland Puerto Rican women. *Psychology of Women Quarterly, 9,* 463–476.

Delgado, M. (1983). Hispanics and psychotherapeutic groups. *International Journal of Group Psychotherapy, 33,* 507–520.

Delgado, M., & Humm-Delgado, D. (1984). Hispanics and group work: A review of the literature. *Ethnicity in Group Work Practice, 7*(3), 85–96.

Ellis, A., & Grieger, R. (1977). *Handbook of rational emotive therapy.* New York: Holt, Rinehart & Winston.

Escobar, J. I., Golding, J. M., Hough, R. L., Karno, M., Burnam, M. A., & Wells, K. B. (1987). Somatization in the community: Relationship to disability and use of services. *American Journal of Public Health, 77,* 837–840.

Franklin, G. S., & Kaufman, K. S. (1982). Group psychotherapy for elderly female Hispanic outpatients. *Hospital & Community Psychiatry, 33*(5), 385–387.

Goldstein, A. P. (1971). *Psychotherapeutic attraction.* New York: Pergamon.

Hays, P. A. (1995). Multicultural applications of cognitive–behavior therapy. *Professional Psychology: Research and Practice, 26,* 309–315.

Healey, J. F. (1995). Hispanic Americans: Colonization, immigration, and ethnic enclaves. In J. F. Healey (Ed.), *Race, ethnicity, gender, and class: The sociology of group conflict and change* (pp. 341–401). Thousand Oaks, CA: Pine Forge Press.

Herrera, A. E., & Sanchez, V. C. (1976). Behaviorally oriented group therapy: A successful application in the treatment of low income Spanish-speaking clients. In M. R. Miranda (Ed.), *Psychotherapy with the Spanish-speaking: Issues in research and service delivery* (Monograph No. 3, pp. 73–84). Los Angeles: University of California, Spanish-Speaking Mental Health Research Center.

Hollon, S., & Shaw, B. (1979). Group cognitive therapy for depressed patients. In A. Beck, A. Rush, B. Shaw, & G. Emery (Eds.), *Cognitive therapy of depression* (pp. 328–353). New York: Guilford Press.

Hynes, K., & Warbin, J. (1977). Group psychotherapy for Spanish-speaking women. *Psychiatric Annals, 7*, 52–63.

Karno, M., & Edgerton, R. B. (1969). Perceptions of mental illness in a Mexican-American community. *Archives of General Psychiatry, 20*, 233–238.

Karno, M., Ross, R. N., & Caper, R. A. (1969). Mental health roles of physicians in a Mexican American community. *Community Mental Health Journal, 5*, 62–69.

Kessler, R. C., McGonagle, K. A., Zhao, S., Nelson, C. B., Hughes, M., Eshleman, S., Wittchen, H., & Kendler, K. S. (1994). Lifetime and 12-month prevalence of *DSM–III–R* psychiatric disorders in the United States. *Archives of General Psychiatry, 51*, 8–19.

Kolody, B., Vega, W., Meinhardt, K., & Bensussen, G. (1986). The correspondence of health complaints and depressive symptoms among Anglos and Mexican-Americans. *Journal of Nervous and Mental Disease, 174*, 221–228.

Lange, A. J., & Jakubowski, P. (1977). *Responsible assertive behavior: Cognitive/behavioral procedures for trainers.* Champaign, IL: Research Press.

Lewinsohn, P. M., Muñoz, R. F., Youngren, M. A., & Zeiss, A. M. (1986). *Control your depression* (Rev. ed.). New York: Prentice Hall.

McKinley, V. (1987). Group therapy as a treatment modality of special value for Hispanic patients. *International Journal of Group Psychotherapy, 37*, 255–268.

Miranda, M. R. (Ed.). (1976). *Psychotherapy with the Spanish-speaking: Issues in research and service delivery* (Monograph No. 3). Los Angeles: University of California, Los Angeles, Spanish-Speaking Mental Health Research Center.

Miranda, J., Azocar, F., Organista, K. C., Dwyer, E., & Arean, P. (2000). *Treatment of depression in disadvantaged medical patients.* Unpublished manuscript, Georgetown University Medical Center, Washington, DC.

Muñoz, R. F. (1995). Toward combined prevention and treatment services for major depression. In C. Telles & M. Karno (Ed.), *Latino mental health: Current research and policy perspectives* (pp. 183–200). Los Angeles: University of California, Los Angeles, Neuropsychiatric Institute.

Muñoz, R. F., Aguilar-Gaxiola, S., & Guzman, J. (1986). *Manual de terapia de grupo para el tratamiento cognitivo–conductual de depresion* [Group therapy manual for cognitive–behavioral treatment of depression]. Unpublished manual, San Francisco General Hospital, Depression Clinic, San Francisco.

Muñoz, R. F., & Miranda, J. (1986). *Group therapy manual for cognitive–behavioral treatment of depression.* Unpublished manual, San Francisco General Hospital, Depression Clinic, San Francisco.

Muñoz, R. F., & Ying, Y. W. (1993). *The prevention of depression: Research and practice.* Baltimore: John Hopkins University Press.

Nietzel, M. T., Russell, R. L., Hemmings, K. A., & Gretter, M. L. (1987). Clinical significance of psychotherapy for unipolar depression: A meta-analytic approach to social comparison. *Journal of Consulting and Clinical Psychology, 55,* 156–161.

Organista, K. C. (1995). Cognitive–behavioral treatment of depression and panic disorder in a Latina patient: Culturally sensitive case formulation. *In Session: Psychotherapy in Practice, 1,* 53–64.

Organista, K. C., Muñoz, R. F., & González, G. (1994). Cognitive–behavioral therapy for depression in low-income and minority medical outpatients: Description of a program and exploratory analyses. *Cognitive Therapy and Research, 18,* 241–259.

Organista, K. C. & Valdes Dwyer, E. (1996). Clinical case management and cognitive–behavorial therapy: Integrated psychosocial services for depressed Latino primary care patients. In P. Manoleas (Ed.), *The cross-cultural practice of clinical case management in mental health* (pp. 119–143). New York: The Halworth Press.

Orlinsky, D. E., & Howard, K. I. (1986). Process and outcome in psychotherapy. In S. L. Garfield & A. E. Bergin (Eds.), *Handbook of psychotherapy and behavior change* (3rd ed., pp. 311–381). New York: Wiley.

Padilla, A. M., Carlos, M. L., & Keefe, S. E. (1976). Mental health service utilization by Mexican Americans. In M. R. Miranda (Ed.), *Psychotherapy with the Spanish-speaking: Issues in research and service delivery* (Monograph No. 3). Los Angeles: University of California, Los Angeles, Spanish-Speaking Mental Health Research Center.

Padilla, A. M., & Ruiz, R. A. (1973). *Latino mental health: A review of the literature.* Washington, DC: U.S. Government Printing Office.

Parron, D. L. (1982). An overview of minority group mental health needs and issues as presented to the President's Commission on Mental Health. In F. V. Muñoz & R. Endo (Eds.), *Perspectives on minority group mental health* (pp. 3–22). Washington, DC: University Press of America.

Plante, T. G., Manuel, G. M., Menendez, A. V., & Marcotte, D. (1995). Coping with stress among Salvadoran immigrants. *Hispanic Journal of Behavioral Sciences, 17,* 471–479.

Rakos, R. F. (1991). *Assertive behavior: Theory, research, and training.* New York: Routledge.

Rogler, L. H., Malgady, R. G., Costantino, G., & Blumenthal, R. (1987). What do culturally sensitive mental health services mean? *American Psychologist, 42,* 565–570.

Roll, S., Millen, L., & Martinez, R. (1980). Common errors in psychotherapy with Chicanos: Extrapolations from research and clinical experience. *Psychotherapy: Theory, Research and Practice, 17,* 158–168.

Rose, S., Tolman, R. M., & Tallant, S. (1985). Group process in cognitive–behavioral therapy. *Behavior Therapist, 8,* 71–83.

Salgado de Snyder, V. N., Cervantes, R. C., & Padilla, A. M. (1990). Gender and ethnic differences in psychosocial stress and generalized distress among Hispanics. *Sex Roles, 22,* 441–453.

Satterfield, J. M. (1994). Integrating group dynamics and cognitive–behavioral groups: A hybrid model. *Clinical Psychology: Science and Practice, 1,* 185–195.

Shrout, P. E., Canino, G. J., Bird, H. R., Rubio-Stipec, M., Bravos, M., & Burnam, M. A. (1992). Mental health status among Puerto Ricans, Mexican Americans, and non-Hispanic whites. *American Journal of Community Psychology, 20,* 729–752.

Snowden, L. R. (Ed.). (1982). *Reaching the underserved: Mental health needs of neglected populations.* Beverly Hills, CA: Sage.

Soto, E., & Shaver, P. (1982). Sex-role traditionalism, assertiveness, and symptoms of Puerto Rican women living in the United States. *Hispanic Journal of Behavioral Sciences, 4,* 1–19.

Sue, S. (1977). Community mental health services to minority groups: Some optimism, some pessimism. *American Psychologist, 32,* 616–624.

Sue, S., Fujino, D. C., Hu, L., Takeuchi, D. T., & Zane, N. W. S. (1991). Community mental health services for ethnic minority groups: A test of the cultural responsiveness hypothesis. *Journal of Consulting and Clinical Psychology, 59,* 533–540.

Szapocznik, J., Santisteban, D., Kurtines, W., Perez-Vidal, A., & Hervis, O. (1986). Bicultural effectiveness training: A treatment intervention for enhancing intercultural adjustment in Cuban American families. *Hispanic Journal of Behavioral Sciences, 6,* 317–344.

Torres-Matrullo, C. (1982). Cognitive therapy of depressive disorders in the Puerto Rican female. In R. M. Becerra, M. Karno, & J. I. Escobar (Eds.), *Mental health and Hispanic Americans* (pp. 101–113). New York: Grune & Stratton.

U.S. Bureau of the Census. (1994, March). Hispanic Population the United States, 1993. *Current Population Reports* (Series P20-475). Washington, DC: U.S. Government Printing Office.

U.S. Department of Commerce. (1993). *1990 Census of Population: Social and Economic Characteristics of California* (1990 CP-2-6). Washington, DC: U.S. Government Printing Office.

Wood, P. S., & Mallinckrodt, B. (1990). Culturally sensitive assertiveness training for ethnic minority clients. *Professional Psychology: Research and Practice, 21,* 5–11.

Young, J. (1994). *Cognitive therapy for personality disorders: A schema-focused approach* (2nd ed.). Sarasota, FL: Professional Resource Press.

12

WOMEN'S SEXUALITY

SUSAN WALEN AND JANET L. WOLFE

Time-limited all-women's sexual enhancement and preorgasmic groups have provided powerful demonstrations of how effectively and efficiently sex therapy can be done when the appropriate learning conditions are provided. In some of the early studies (e.g., Barbach, 1974; Heinrich, 1976), the majority of group participants learned how to have an orgasm in masturbation and, over time, a majority were able to generalize their sexual skills to partner situations. Other frequently reported results included reduction of sexual anxiety, reduction of sexual inhibitions, increased self-acceptance, enhanced body acceptance, increased confidence in the ability to feel pleasurable and sexual feelings, and increased desire for sex (Barbach, 1980; Walen & Wolfe, 1983).

A major therapeutic element that has been identified in group therapy is the relief from self-blame and anxiety that comes from the discovery of the group members' shared suffering and the acceptance by others despite one's flaws (Yalom, 1985). Groups are less costly than individual therapy or conjoint therapy, which also requires a cooperative partner. Most importantly, women's groups seem to provide a context ideally suited to providing women with powerful corrective emotional experiences and a highly facilitative learning environment. A major ingredient is the increased communicational freedom that the same-sexed group seems to provide. Meador,

Solomon, and Bowen (1972, p. 338) found that "women together talk differently from the way they do in the presence of men. The cultural conditioning which most women have assimilated rises to the fore if only one man is present."

An important influence in women's difficulties in sexual enjoyment has been their sex role scripting that has taught them to be passive and dependent, to value themselves and their bodies largely on the basis of their ability to lure and secure a man, and to rely on a man to come along and light their orgasmic fire. The all-women's sexuality group provides a place where a woman can come and, shutting out the psychosocial influences of her past, enter a supportive and protective place where she can discuss, learn, and practice an entirely different set of attitudes about herself and her sexuality. In the climate of warmth, support, playfulness, and caring that rapidly occurs, a woman can experience her own power as a person, develop a more positive relationship with herself and her body, and take responsibility for her own sexual pleasure and her own orgasms.

Between sessions, when she is doing her homework on masturbation, the group member is comforted at the thought that there are at least six other women in her community who are also masturbating. Back in the group, she is provided with a set of reinforcement contingencies that are often the reverse of those in the "outside world." In contrast to the impatience or blame she may have gotten from her spouse or lover, she receives hugs and cheers from other group members for the first tingle she elicits in her clitoris, or for her first stumbling attempts at asserting herself. A plain-looking unpartnered woman in her 50s—often not seen as a sexual person on the outside (by others and by herself)—experiences herself for the first time as an envied "sexpot" and is complimented on her new "glow" when she reports to the group her sexual experimentation with water massagers and new masturbation positions. Group members are reinforced and supported in a new belief system that is the basis of their sexual self-determination: that they have a right to get satisfaction for their own wants (sexual and nonsexual) rather than merely taking care of others, and they are in charge of their lives and their sexuality. And finally, in a group whose members all have the same kinds of genitals and essentially the same long-time freeze on sexual discussion, they receive much-needed practice in sharing sexual feelings and communicating about sex that will become the bridge to their more comfortably communicating these feelings to their partners.

A COGNITIVE–BEHAVIORAL GROUP MODEL

It is our purpose in this chapter to describe in some detail how we conducted our own women's groups and to outline procedures for dealing with typical kinds of problems. Because an important ingredient in the groups is dealing with problems in a flexible, individualized manner, it is recommended that the chapter be used not as a rigid blueprint for how one *must* run the group, but rather as a set of suggestions on procedures and issues emerging from the groups we have conducted. Although research has not yet been done dismantling the effective components of the treatment, we believe that a major difference between our groups and those run by other professionals is our heavy focus not merely on behavior change or skill acquisition through the use of sex therapy techniques, but on teaching a more expanded set of skills for restructuring the attitudes and cognitions that are seen as underlying sexual dysfunctioning and attendant emotional distress. It is this teaching of a general disturbance-combating cognitive self-help approach that accounts for what appears to be a typically rapid elimination of many target problems (e.g., over 90% of the women in our groups learn to orgasm in only six 2-hour sessions) and for the broader generalization to other areas of the women's lives (Wolfe, 1976).

The goals of the group encompass a broad range of cognitive and behavioral changes:

1. Becoming more comfortable talking about sexuality with others.
2. Unveiling and debunking erroneous sexual myths and sex role programming that interfere with autonomy and self-determination in sexual and nonsexual areas.
3. Increasing knowledge of anatomy and physiology of female sexuality and sexual health.
4. Learning more about and becoming more comfortable with one's own body through self-exploration and directed masturbation.
5. Permission-giving to increase sexual pleasure and playfulness; information-giving to expand the sexual repertoire.
6. Overcoming emotional blocks to sexual freedom (guilt, anxiety, self-downing, and anger) by challenging dysfunctional cognitions.
7. Improving ability to assert oneself and to communicate sexual preferences to one's partner.
8. Developing plans for continuing sexual enhancement when the group concludes.

GROUP COMPOSITION AND SELECTION

We generally have found the optimal group size to be between six and nine women. Although having female cotherapists tends to facilitate the group (and especially the construction and troubleshooting of home-work assignments), it is possible for one therapist who is highly experienced in sex therapy and in conducting groups to lead a sexuality group. Because the existence of a mastery model with perceived similarity to group members appears to be a powerful factor in the group's success (Yalom, 1985), a female rather than a male therapist is seen as mandatory. The all-female membership also reinforces the important idea that women are the best authorities on their own sexuality.

In the settings in which we work (private practice or outpatient clinic), group members have generally been self-referred or referred by colleagues. Although prescreening might appear to be an absolute requirement of such groups, the fact is that in several years of running the groups we have not encountered anyone who was not able to effectively participate in them. Those who have never participated in therapy groups, women who previously have had difficulty in relating in mixed-gender groups, and even borderline clients have, in the unusually supportive atmosphere of the theme-centered all-women's group, been able to open up fairly readily and to participate actively, abetted considerably by a "go around" format that allows each woman to speak up at least two or three times during each session.

Although our groups are generally either preorgasmic groups or general sexual enhancement groups, group composition is not rigidly restricted to women with the same problem. Typically, there will be two or three women in the preorgasmic group who define themselves as anorgasmic either because they are having orgasms but not labeling them as such or because they are having orgasms in masturbation but not in intercourse. There also will be two or three anorgasmic women in the sexual enhancement group. Not only have we not encountered any real difficulties in running mixed-problem groups, but rather, we have experienced the mixing as beneficial in that the members often derive encouragement from the presence of coping models. Not uncommonly, for example, a preorgasmic group member will encourage another by saying, "I used to be where you are, and now I can do it. Here's something that worked for me that maybe you might want to try." The already orgasmic member in a preorgasmic group also illustrates the important lesson that orgasmic ability is not a panacea—that having the ability to reach orgasm is no guarantee of a problem-free sex life.

Ages of the group members generally range from early 20s through the 60s. Although it is not mandatory to have each age group represented, it is generally helpful, where possible, to have an approximate matching to avoid a feeling of being "the odd woman." Thus, having two women in the 50-to-70 age group, or two women with orthodox religious backgrounds, can enhance feelings of belonging and support and provide better opportunities for vicarious learning. In our experience, having at least two of any age group or background comes about naturally, without any need for additional recruitment. Ultimately, however, the increasing awareness that there are more commonalties than differences among group members despite disparate ages and backgrounds wins out over alienation.

PORTRAIT OF A TYPICAL GROUP

Looking at a woman in her 60s who has been married for 40 years, another in her 30s who recently "came out" as a lesbian, another a young woman who lives alone and has few friends, and a fourth a bubbly active person with two lovers, one might at first wonder what they have in common and how they are going to identify with each other. Common elements quickly become apparent as they introduce themselves and discuss what they think they "should" be doing sexually. The following is a sample of the presenting problems taken from some of our most recent sexual enhancement groups:

- My husband's and my sex life has gotten dull and routine; I know I should be enjoying sex with him and giving more to him.
- I should be able to have sex without fantasy.
- I almost never feel turned on. I could take sex or leave it.
- I only have orgasms with a vibrator. If I were really healthy, I'd be able to come in "sex."
- The only way I can come is when I'm lying on my stomach.
- My boyfriend says I should have orgasms during intercourse, and I'm denying him the pleasure of giving me an orgasm.
- I'm not sure if I have orgasms. I've heard that if you don't know for sure, you haven't had one.
- I know I should be able to express my needs, but I'm uncomfortable. It feels unfeminine. And besides, if I tell him now —after 7 years of faking it—he'll really be hurt.
- I always have to initiate sex if I want it. If I didn't, my husband would just lie in bed and channel-surf.
- I am always afraid my partner will be turned off by my stretch marks. I can't even stand to look at myself in a full-length mirror.

Most readily apparent—even in the most highly educated members —is a great deal of sexual ignorance and inappropriate expectations. The typical group member has feelings of shame and disgust toward her genitals and basically dislikes her body. She may be looking for the earth to move, for "coming" during intercourse or without having to inform her partner as to what she needs. She does not trust her own experience and does not think she is a "real" woman. She has labeled herself as frigid, as has her partner and (occasionally) her doctor if she is not having orgasms in intercourse. She may think she is incapable of a good sex-love relationship. As a result, she has become more uptight, finding it harder than ever to let go and thus anticipating sex with dread and experiencing arousal in terms of fright. She may dissociate or distance herself from the sexual experience. There is at least one sexual practice (fantasizing, using a vibrator, wanting oral stimulation) that she has set up as the *sine qua non* of sexual health and for which she condemns herself—for doing it, for not doing it, or for both.

Almost invariably, we watch the members' facial expressions change from anxious amusement to being moved and relieved as they listen to each woman in turn provide a description of a set of problems overlapping remarkably with hers. She expresses genuine surprise as she becomes aware that all of her well-put-together-looking, "normal" appearing group mates are not the perfect, emotionally integrated creatures she has imagined them to be in other settings—but in fact are very much like her. She thus experiences tremendous relief within the first hour of the group at discovering she is not the terribly inadequate sexual "freak" she always imagined herself to be. She has received and given to herself few positive messages about her sexuality and has had few good models. The group provides her with corrective information, helps her redefine her problems without the cognitive castigation she usually imposes on herself, and helps her replace her negative attitudes and feelings with more positive ones—all in a climate of support and permission-giving.

TREATMENT FORMAT AND ROLE OF LEADER OR LEADERS

Both the sexual enhancement groups and preorgasmic groups are conducted on a time-limited, topic-centered basis. (An additional format we sometimes use is to devote four sessions of a general ongoing women's group to the topic of sexual enhancement.) The range of time for such groups as revealed in the literature is 6 to 12 weeks, with the group meeting one or two times each week for 1.5 to 2 hours. Although our own groups are conducted for 6 weeks, meeting once a week for a 2-hour session, we strongly recommend that therapists who are not highly experienced in working with groups or in the area of female sexuality schedule a longer (8 to 12 weeks) group. With increasing experience, the therapist can conduct the workshop more efficiently. We have found that with a six-session format, the pressure of the limited time encourages clients to accomplish the work of therapy more efficiently and directly. The greater efficiency of therapy when clients know it is to be time limited has been reported by

Muench (1964) and Paul (1966). In our groups, the bibliotherapy and behavioral homework assignments, as well as encouragement to keep sharing histories and discoveries with other women friends outside the group, help to extend the amount of therapy time the group members are getting beyond the 12 hours spent in group.

The initial sessions of the groups are more highly structured than later sessions. Especially in the first two meetings, the therapists contribute the majority of the agenda items in order to (a) define each client's problems and socialize the client to the group and to the cognitive focus of therapy; (b) provide experiences that will encourage group members to evaluate specific attitudes; and (c) teach clients accurate information about sexuality. Throughout each session, however—more so from the third session on (after the didactic groundwork has been laid)—members are encouraged to present and work on their own individual sexual problems.

During the course of the group, the therapists use a number of styles of presentation, including brief lectures, experiential exercises, group discussion, individual problem focus, handouts, audiovisual aids, and assignment and review of homework. (Examples of these techniques are described later.) Varying the format in this way maintains the interest of group members at a very high level and thus maximizes learning and retention.

The role of the therapist is a difficult but challenging one. It is up to her to create a climate of support and encouragement while still confronting resistance. She will be giving permission to push on and try new things, or not to try so hard—to slow down and relax. She serves as a participant model, yet she also needs to keep the group moving, pick up on group process issues, and tie together themes and group members with similar problems. If the therapist is well-trained clinically, she will be able to identify underlying issues and work with such problems as clinical depression, low self-esteem, relationship distress, and couple's communication. To maximize her value as an educator, she needs to be informed and up-to-date about female sexuality, birth control, and other sexual health issues.

One of the leader's first tasks is to state clearly the theme that will be reiterated again and again in the course of the group: that sex is a natural function that has been inhibited in the women by psychological blocks and that their goal in the group will be to help each other erase their old inaccurate information and destructive attitudes and feelings to reclaim and take control of their sexuality. This is facilitated from the start by helping the group members to accurately label their problems. "Bad communication," for example, may mean many different things, among which may be a woman's fear of being assertive, her lack of skill or vocabulary for assertiveness, or not even knowing what she wants, amatively or sexually. The therapist needs to clarify and correct the woman's self-diagnosis.

GENERAL THEMES

We outline a number of general themes that recur across sessions to give the reader a sense of the flavor of the workshop series.

1. Use of a "Flooding" Model. From the first moments of the first session, the therapists actively and directively move to encourage frank and open discussions of sexuality. Through modeling by the therapists, a flooding rather than a cautious desensitization model is used. The cognitive message transmitted by this model is that sex is neither taboo nor frightening and that the group members are not fragile children who must approach a "dangerous" topic obliquely. Further desensitization is encouraged by having the women discuss a list of topics back and forth with at least one outside woman friend and by reading as much material on the sexuality reading list as possible.

2. Use of Informal and "Lusty" Language. An examination of the language of sexuality proves very revealing. In English, there is a relative paucity of terms for many aspects of female sexual functioning. For example, there are no direct synonyms for *clitoris*, the female sex organ. This fact suggests the cultural devaluation of the woman's sexuality and may, in part, account for the difficulty many women experience in talking about sex. Similarly, the majority of colloquialisms used for *masturbation* are descriptive only of male masturbation (e.g., "play pocket pool"). An additional problem of our language of female sexuality is that terms are used loosely and with inaccurate referents. As Hite (1976) reported, even when women are describing an activity about which they have positive feelings (e.g., cunnilingus), they tend to describe it in "spare, tight, unenthusiastic and secretive language."

It is pointed out to group members that if a hallmark of good partner sex is good communication—the ability to express sexual preferences clearly, directly, and comfortably—then developing and practicing a new sexual vocabulary is very important. When people think about their own genitalia and the sex acts in which they engage, they do not think in technical or medical terminology. We believe strongly that therapists should better be prepared to accept this fact and freely model such behavior. When therapists comfortably use the informal and lusty language of sex, they may meaningfully illustrate a different attitude toward sexuality —the playful, demystified attitude we wish to project. In addition, because many women have only passive sexual vocabularies, therapist modeling may help clients move these terms from a passive to an active vocabulary and find and share comfortable ways of expressing themselves.

3. Focus on Sex Role Socialization Messages. An important theme in our workshops is consciousness raising about the unequal position of women in U.S. society. We stress that it is unlikely that women will obtain sexual equality if they are not working toward human equality. For example, many women grow up with the cultural notion that most of their worth as people depends on their "feminine allure." They are encouraged to use their sexuality *indirectly* to get what they want from men but are not supposed to actually initiate sex or be too active or lusty.

We also provide some of the disturbing figures on sexual abuse of women as a means of highlighting a pervasive societal tendency toward derogating women and viewing them chiefly as means to serve men's sexual and other needs.

Whenever it is relevant, we point out the importance of socialization messages that may be continuing to interfere with the women's sexual enjoyment and general self-actualization, and encourage group members (especially those with no previous exposure to feminist writings) to read some of the recommended "consciousness-raising" literature on the effects of traditional female sex role socialization. (See some of the items with asterisks in the References.)

4. Focus on Self-Acceptance. Whether or not group members want to change their attitudes or learn new skills, we believe that an important first step is *acceptance of the now*. By this we mean acceptance of oneself, acceptance of one's partner, and acceptance of reality. Very commonly, group members may be heavily blaming themselves or blaming their partners for not doing what they want them to do. The resultant emotions— anger, anxiety, or depression—are incompatible with good sexual functioning. We therefore encourage the women to focus first on feeling better about the sex they are doing, rather than merely on doing better sex. Once this nondemanding philosophy is accepted, they can move forward far more efficiently.

5. Focus on Changing Cognitions. Group members are consistently aided in identifying and challenging the dysfunctional thoughts that result in emotional blocks to good sexual functioning and enjoyment. They are helped to examine their perceptions and evaluations of their own sexual functioning, their partner's behavior, and environmental events. The cognitive focus is taught by minilectures on the techniques of cognitive and rational–emotive behavioral therapy (REBT), and these techniques are demonstrated on individual problems as they are brought up by the group members. A reading list of general cognitive therapy and REBT self-help material is useful.

6. Focus on Changing Behavior. One way to feel better, to change attitudes, or to reinforce attitude change is to *behave* differently. This message is presented repeatedly at all sessions. Group members are encouraged to practice new behaviors and challenge themselves with new behavioral risks both within the group sessions (e.g., asking for clarification or help with a problem) and in their homework assignments. These new behaviors may be sexual or nonsexual in nature.

7. Focus on Hedonism. Many of the cognitive and behavioral assignments used in the group are designed to encourage and strengthen a general hedonic philosophy. Assignments are not merely sexual, therefore, but rather are more broadly self-pleasuring. They are designed to dispute the sex role socialization message that "it's selfish to pursue my own pleasure." Until a woman fully accepts her right to nurture and pleasure herself, she often will have great difficulty allowing herself pleasure in sexuality.

The difficulty in attending to one's own needs is particularly strong in women with strict religious upbringing or those who are deeply embedded in their roles as wives and mothers. By defining their role as that of taking care of other people, these women have almost totally neglected the habit of doing nice things for themselves. Homework assignments such as taking a leisurely bubble bath or buying flowers for oneself may serve to combat guilt or thoughts of "selfishness" and may encourage a more general acceptance of hedonic self-pleasuring.

8. Use of Humor. Humor is another way in which the hedonic philosophy is asserted. We attempt, when appropriate, to keep a light, playful attitude, replete with puns and witticisms. Humor is another way of teaching women that it is appropriate and healthy to have fun, and that humor is a helpful anxiety desensitizer. Not only is it all right to have fun, but it is also all right to make fun of things. Obviously, the group members are never the butt of a joke, although their cognitive distortions may be. It is our experience that an efficient way to explode myths and attack taboos is to help clients realize the absurdity of some of these notions.

9. Focus on Women's Health. Because of the large amount of ignorance regarding their bodies and what happens to them, time is always required in the groups to inform women about sexual health issues, such as the relative risks of different birth control methods, how to detect some of the common "female problems" (such as vaginal infections), and proper ways to go about treating them. Information is provided on the role of good nutrition and other health practices in helping the body and mind function at optimal levels. Information is given on medications that may block sexual desire or functioning, as well as ones that may enhance it (such as antidepressants). Frequently this material evokes some further demystification of the role of "doctors as sex experts" as the women become aware of the inadequate treatment almost all of them have received at one time or another and learn how to deal more assertively with physicians in the future so as to receive better care. *The New Our Bodies, Ourselves* (Boston Women's Health Collective, 1992) is highly recommended as a handbook for the healthy functioning of their bodies. The companion volume, *Ourselves, Growing Older* (Doress, Siegal, & the Midlife and Older Women Book Project, 1987) is also strongly recommended.

10. Leaders as Participants. The cotherapists in our groups function very much as participant models rather than as distant or aloof experts. As leaders, we are very self-disclosing about our own sexuality as well as ways we have learned to handle "performance anxiety" and develop self-acceptance. In nearly every exercise in which group members are asked to self-disclose intimately (e.g., sharing details of how we masturbate), the group leaders participate and demonstrate free disclosure and a coping (or successfully "coped") model. As Yalom (1985) pointed out, a therapist who is self-disclosing; who models open, direct, and uninhibited communication; and who has had similar problems but overcome them greatly increases the therapeutic power of the group.

11. Participants as Leaders. One of the most significant themes of the group is that other women are often the best sources of information about female sexuality—not male psychologists, doctors, or other "sex experts." An important cognitive message given to the group is that there is no "right way" to have sex; rather, it is up to each woman to define her sexuality and sexual preferences for herself. Both within and outside the group, members are encouraged to find out how other women think and feel about sexuality and how they go about it. They learn to acquire the capacity to abstract personally relevant information and helpful hints even when the spotlight of attention is not directly focused on them. They give each other substantial support and permission to be sexual. They share with each other by providing in-group practice in taking risks, communicating feelings, and sharing their own specific sexual practices. This in-session sharing helps enormously in building better facility in talking to and dealing with their partners outside the group. Although *The Hite Report* (Hite, 1976) was compiled over 20 years ago, it is still recommended reading because, as a pooling of questionnaire responses of over 3,000 women, it serves to amplify the theme of women as experts. By reading about other women's experiences, group members feel less like "patients" and more like individuals striving to increase their knowledge of sexual options, their ease in discussing sexual matters, and their sexual self-determination.

SESSION-BY-SESSION FORMAT: A SAMPLE MODEL

The following format is used in both our preorgasmic and sexual enhancement groups. The main difference between the two types is that the amount of time spent on troubleshooting masturbation homework assignments is understandably shortened in the enhancement groups.

Session 1

Once the group is convened, the therapist opens the first meeting by congratulating the women for attending and for challenging their first sexual stereotype: that sex should be naturally perfect. We ask the members to give their first names and set forth the group rule of absolute confidentiality, explaining its importance in allowing the women to be as free as possible to express themselves. Each participant is then asked to tell the group something about herself, incorporating the following information into her responses: What are you worried or concerned about sexually? Are you orgasmic? Are you currently in a relationship or not, and what are your feelings about this? How does your partner feel about your being here? Each woman typically speaks for 5 to 10 minutes. If the target questions are not answered or if the client digresses or speaks for a prolonged time, the therapists guide her back to task.

Let us introduce three women from one of our groups, describing how they presented their complaints.

> Margaret was a 53-year-old homemaker in her second marriage whose complaint was that she could only orgasm occasionally and only when she used her vibrator. She chided herself for her "slow progress despite all the reading" she had done. She also expressed anger at her husband for showing little interest in her sexually and said that her life was "boring."

> Laura was a 25-year-old secretary, the daughter of two alcoholic parents. She was in a troubling sex/love relationship with a woman. She often felt inadequate and alternated between being overly deferential or breaking off the relationship.

> Patricia was a 31-year-old teacher whose parents had told her she was so ugly that she would never find anyone who could be attracted to her. Shy and unconfident, she described herself as "asexual." She had never orgasmed during masturbation, but thought that she might have come once with a partner. She had little dating experience and no sexual contact in the previous 2 years.

The next phase of the meeting is devoted to illustrating some of the detrimental sexual stereotypes that women encounter. An exercise that we have found especially useful is to ask the women to call out words or phrases that come to mind for each of the following categories: (a) women who are sexually active; (b) women who prefer not to be sexually active; (c) men who are sexually active; (d) men who prefer not to be sexually active; (e) women who are assertive; and (f) men who are assertive. The responses are written in columns on a blackboard or tag board, and the women are asked what trends they notice in the responses. What clearly emerges from this "nasty names" exercise is that men who are sexually active are prized (e.g., called *macho* or *studs*), whereas women who are sexually active are condemned (e.g., referred to as *whores, promiscuous,* or *loose*). Women who are inactive are castigated (e.g., *frigid* or *dyke*), whereas men who are inactive are derogated by associating them with females (e.g., *momma's boy, fairy*). Finally, women who are assertive are seen as pushy or aggressive and destructive of male sexual prowess (e.g., *ball buster* or *castrating woman*), whereas there are few if any derogatory names for assertive men. This exercise—a powerful consciousness-raiser—is followed by a discussion of the lack of adequate models for healthy sexuality in women, including a review of some statistics on the sexual oppression of women.

The goal in this section of the workshop is to provide women with valid understanding of their problems in dealing with their sexuality. The message is that *they* are not deficient but have been raised in a culture in which different standards exist for men and for women. Some brief facts are presented on violence against women and social and economic oppression, with active contributions from the group members, at least 50% of whom generally have been raped or sexually molested at some time; who have worked as hard and long as men but for less money; or who have been treated like sex objects or patronized ("don't bother your pretty little head" about financial and mechanical things). Slowly, the women come to see that although they certainly may at times have collaborated in perpetuating their helplessness and dependency, the facts of reduced power and respect in a male-dominated society unfortunately requires them to work long and hard at countering both internal and external forces if they wish to claim their fullness, strength, and autonomy.

During the second hour of the first session, basic education about the anatomy and physiology of sex is provided through handouts and discussion. During the anatomy lesson, the therapists continue to stress the role of the clitoris by referring to it as "the clitoris, *your sex organ*." The message passed down in the culture and often reinforced by the male partner is that the vagina is "where it's at." The term "having sex" is used by a vast majority of men and women as synonymous with intercourse. In sex education classes, girls still for the most part are taught that they have two ovaries, a uterus, and a vagina. Group members frequently report that they never even masturbated or heard of the clitoris until they were in their 20s, 30s, or even later. Boys, on the other hand, are generally taught about their sex organs and about masturbation in their sex education classes.

An image that many group members report as powerful and corrective is viewing intercourse as male masturbation (i.e., rubbing of his sex organ against the walls of her reproductive organ), thus making it a small wonder that the woman often finds this stimulation insufficient to induce orgasm. It is stressed over and over again that orgasm is a learned response and that failure to experience it is not a sign of neurosis but of faulty or inadequate early learning, and that in a culture in which millions of men and women barely recognize women or their orgasms, it is no surprise that women have not learned how to reach orgasm. In the end, failure to achieve that shining, male-established goal of female orgasm-in-intercourse is, as Hite (1976) pointed out, not a deficiency but a *normal response to insufficient stimulation*, since only one third of women report having regular orgasms through intercourse.

Next we review the physiology of the sexual response cycle. In this segment, we particularly stress the fact that vaginal lubrication is a very early sign of sexual arousal and does not mean that the woman is near her orgasmic threshold. This bit of information may be corrective for her partner who, in many cases, tests her readiness for intercourse by inserting his finger into her vagina to see if it is wet. In this, as in all phases of the group, we avoid the use of technical language. Thus, rather than use clinical language, we simply describe the genital arousal and plateau stages in terms such as "blood flows to the vagina and swells the tissues, much in the same way as blood flows to a man's penis and causes it to swell."

Finally, we explore the group members' attitudes and feelings about their bodies, following the "go-around" format that allows all the women to talk at least two or three times, from the first session on. They may be asked to imagine themselves looking at themselves nude in the mirror. They then share with the group whether their feelings were positive or negative; to what extent their feelings about their bodies influence how they feel about themselves as a sexual person; and to what extent they feel they are valued (or devalued) by others for their bodies. They are encouraged to work on accepting themselves and on giving themselves the right to be sexual persons, whether or not they have perfect bodies. We conclude the first session by encouraging the women "to ask any dumb questions you've ever had about sex and were afraid to ask," adding, "you can even ask an intelligent question!" We are thereby accomplishing several tasks at once: (a) picking up on loose ends, (b) allowing the group members to take responsibility for their own sex education, and thus their own sexuality, (c) providing practice in verbally communicating about their sexual wants, and (d) reinforcing the message that it is all right to sound "dumb," to make mistakes, and to show they are imperfect. At the end of the question-and-answer period, we hand out the first homework assignment.

Homework for Session 1[1]

The homework for this first session is a rich and complex set of assignments, largely drawn from the work of Lonnie Barbach (1975, pp. 38–115). The participants are asked to stretch and push vigorously forward in their work on exploring sexual *attitudes*, for example, by choosing a female friend outside the group with whom to share a set of discussion questions. The questions move from easier ("What were your parents' attitudes toward sex?") to harder ("Do you remember any sexual traumas such as child-adult sexual contact, rape, or other frightening sexual experiences?"). The next

---

[1]From *For Yourself: The Fulfillment of Female Sexuality*, by Lonnie G. Barbach, 1975, New York: Doubleday.

part of the assignment sheet reviews *anatomy* and provides a guide to exploration of her genital anatomy, encouraging the woman to repeat the exercise daily until it feels comfortable. The third homework segment consists of a handout titled "Why Masturbate?," which stresses the message that masturbation is a metaphor for taking charge of one's own sexuality, and a handout of instructions for beginning masturbation.

Even at the first session, homework assignments can be somewhat tailored to address the concerns of individual group members. For example:

> Margaret, who was angry at herself as well as her husband, was encouraged to give herself the message that "being frustrated is highly inconvenient, but not awful; just because I'm not enjoying sex much now doesn't mean I never will."

> Laura, who had been browbeaten by her parents and was perhaps overly sensitive to her partner, Hilary, was encouraged to practice accepting love from Hilary without feeling undeserving or guilty. Her homework was to dispute the irrational belief that she was "damaged goods."

> Patricia, the shy teacher, was asked to challenge the belief that "because my parents think I'm a washout, it must be true." She was also encouraged to rehearse the message, "I have a right to, and capacity for, sexual pleasure."

Sessions 2–3

We begin the session by asking the group members for their reactions to the first session. If they experienced any distress, we help them to identify and challenge their dysfunctional automatic thoughts. We then review their homework assignments, thereby learning more about each participant and helping anyone who had difficulty in doing the homework to identify her emotional blocks and other resistances. Not uncommonly, several members will plead that they were "too busy" or "too tired" to do the exercises, or that their kids were underfoot. Low frustration tolerance (avoiding the anxiety accompanying difficult and uncomfortable situations) and lack of belief in their right to take time and space for themselves are pinpointed by the leaders as being contributory to these resistances, and appropriate cognitive and behavioral homework assignments are suggested, along with practical advice (such as borrowing a friend's empty apartment).

Patricia told us that when she was discussing sexual histories with two friends, she learned that *they* did not know some common sexual facts. She felt greatly relieved at discovering that she was not as "backward" as she had thought. In addition, after completing three sessions of self-exploration, she reported feeling "freer to spend more time touching my body than ever before." However, she was still doubtful about her orgasmic potential.

The focus of this session is on masturbation and on the women increasing comfort with their bodies. Group members are asked for their feelings about touching their bodies and about being their own sex partners. A great deal of the ensuing discussion entails cognitive challenges to feelings of guilt, anxiety, or revulsion. The claim made by members that sex is "so much better with a partner" than alone is met with the explanation that 95% of women who masturbate have orgasms most of the time —a far higher percentage than occurs in partner sex and thus a more reliable way to reach orgasm. Other advantages given are the freedom from being observed and its attendant anxieties; the fact that one does not need to have an available partner to have sexual pleasure; and that women tend to have difficulty in seeing themselves as having sexual feelings and desires other than those resulting from male initiation. Finally, it is explained that if they can learn comfortably and reliably to reach orgasm with themselves, they are likely to enjoy sex all the more with a cooperating partner.

During the final segment of this session in the sexual enhancement groups, each woman describes in detail the various ways she masturbates. All group members are encouraged to ask each other as many direct questions as they wish. For most women, this exercise may be the first time they have ever spoken to anyone about masturbation and it is almost always the first time they have explicitly verbalized their masturbation procedures. Participants often decide to give themselves the assignment of trying out someone else's method, just for fun, thereby providing the originator with perhaps her first exhilarating experience in being a *teacher* in sexuality.

This exercise also allows us to identify any potentially troublesome styles of masturbation. For example, one woman had trained herself since early childhood to reach orgasm only while curled in a fetal position, one that clearly would make good partner sex quite difficult. Additionally, we can provide cognitive corrections about masturbation (e.g., "I'm probably the only person who masturbates—or *doesn't* masturbate" or "I'm sure I'm doing it the wrong way"). Finally, we can help the group members to identify and correct their cognitive blocks to orgasm.

The women are asked to share with the group a description of "the sexiest experience you ever had *with yourself*." As in all such disclosure exercises, the leaders share one of their own experiences. The women then are asked, "What prevents you from doing more of that for yourself?" Again, guilt reduction is the typical therapeutic focus. Because many of the women's sexiest experiences tend to be their more unusual ones (e.g., masturbating on a secluded beach or with a cucumber), the group members (talking for perhaps the first time about their "dark secrets") receive practice in seeing that the "freaky" things they have done sexually were in fact not so abnormal or shameful after all. This tends to pave the way for increasing levels of self-disclosure. At the next session, for example, a woman may share the information that she is having an affair and is almost sick with anxiety and guilt about it.

We also initiate a discussion of sexual fantasies, stressing the positive value of fantasies, discriminating between fantasy and reality (e.g., one may enjoy a particular fantasy—such as having sex with the entire church choir —without having to worry about acting it out). We encourage the women to develop and expand their fantasy life, recommending books that women tend to find erotic, such as Friday's (1975) *My Secret Garden*.

The focus of the latter part of this session is on clarifying the role of REBT techniques in overcoming emotional blocks to sexuality. The theory of REBT is described. It is then applied to problems brought up by group members, so that participants learn both directly and vicariously how to apply these methods to their problems of anger, anxiety, guilt, depression, and especially, low frustration tolerance. One way we have found particularly effective in helping group members identify their main dysfunctional cognitions is to give them several handouts and do a sample "A-B-C" exercise on the board to illustrate the REBT model. Each woman is asked to identify two of the irrational beliefs she plans to work on over the next week by disputing them on a self-help form. She is encouraged by the leaders to reinforce her new rational countermessages "every hour on the hour" if possible.

The session concludes with individualized assignments to the members. These include *behavioral* assignments, such as self-nurturance or the taking of some new risks. For example, one woman assigned herself the task of telling her partner that she wanted him to "go down" on her. Another gave herself the homework assignment of installing a lock on her bedroom door and informing her children that she wanted them to knock if they wanted to enter. A woman currently not in a relationship gave herself the homework of treating herself to a massage and speaking up to a difficult coworker. The members also give themselves a *cognitive* assignment as well: for example, one woman agreed to work on her guilt by disputing the idea that it would be awful if it required 15 minutes of clitoral stimulation by her partner for her to come.

> Margaret, by the end of Sessions 2–3, had completed three masturbation sessions at home and reported that she was close to orgasm twice, but was "afraid to let go . . . lose control." Her homework assignments were *cognitive* (Challenge the belief that "something awful will happen if I orgasm") and *behavioral* (Role play a cataclysmic orgasm, making crazy noises and thrashing about; do this shame-attacking assignment several times to desensitize yourself to your fear of appearing crazy or out of control).

> Laura had been working on showing her partner, Hilary, the specific ways she liked to be stimulated by guiding her with her own hand. At the same time, she had been working against her irrational belief that

"I *must* have an orgasm every time we have sex—even if I'm not in the mood." She practiced *not* going for an orgasm while not feeling angry or defective. Nonetheless, she remained anxious about the possibility of being rejected by her lover, which she recognized was contributing to her distractibility during sex. Laura's homework was to dispute her belief that "if my lover rejects me, it proves I'm defective and will never have a successful sex/love relationship." In addition, she committed to calling at least two close friends each week so that all her "relationship eggs" wouldn't be in one basket!

Patricia had been working at proceeding at her "own sexual pace" and was experimenting with reading *My Secret Garden* (Friday, 1975) to help her maintain her erotic focus. Nevertheless, she continued to report that "I think I'm the only one in the group who's not going to make it." Further discussion revealed that when she was getting close to orgasm, Patricia became scared that she would "lose control . . . or lose consciousness . . . maybe even die." Another group member volunteered the suggestion that before beginning each masturbation session, Pat call her and request that she phone 1½ hours later to check in to see if she (Pat) was okay.

Session 4

We begin this session by asking for "reports from the field." This open-ended structure allows more opportunity for group members to use this session to bring up their individual problems for therapeutic intervention. The majority of this session is spent doing individual problem solving, with group members serving as "adjunct therapists" in helping other group members, which in turn helps their own proficiency in using REBT with themselves.

A main agenda item we introduce in the latter part of the second hour is how to carry over what the women are learning about their own sexuality to their relationships with their partner or partners, now or in the future. An important point that is emphasized is that while women's accepting themselves as active sexual creatures is certainly a positive change, many men may feel threatened by their new assertiveness. We define assertive behavior and discuss the factors responsible for women's especially heavy problems in this area, focusing on sex role socialization messages (e.g., "Be sweet," "Don't rock the boat," "Take care of others," "Don't express anger—it's unfeminine"). Part of taking charge of one's sexuality, it is pointed out, involves challenging the old notion that it is up to a man to satisfy a woman; that he will do so if he really loves her without any coaching; and that if she lets him know what she wants, she will "hurt" him or be " a castrating female." Particular attention is paid to handling sexual initiations and refusals and "asking your partner for what you want."

Related topics that are often raised by the women include dealing with a partner's resistance to engaging in the kind of stimulation she wants or to having a vibrator join them in bed; expressing negative feelings about her partner's behavior in nonsexual areas; asking for more snuggling and cuddling; and expressing positive feelings. A belief system that supports assertive behavior is developed with the group members and typically includes the following concepts: (a) I have a good deal of choice in how I feel about my partner; (b) I am able to make appropriate choices about how I relate to my partner; and (c) I am a strong and centered person, with the right to be treated with respect, to have my desires considered, and to have my time taken seriously. Role playing and feedback are used to help members get practice in communicating their thoughts and feelings in more helpful ways, along with modeling by the therapist or other group members, where appropriate.

During this session, the therapists elaborate the evolving list of common myths about sex, along with corrective information (Wolfe, 1993). Beliefs such as "sex should happen spontaneously—not be scheduled" or "normal couples have sex several times a week" are disputed with corrective information. Some time is spent as well discussing society's preoccupation with sex, and the resulting escalation of performance standards and feelings of inadequacy when they fail to achieve them. An excerpt from Ehrenreich and English (1978) is often read:

> the human need for sex is made to bear the burden of all our bodily starvation for contact and sensation, all our creative starvation, all our need for social contact, and even our need to find a meaning in our lives. (p. 319)

In line with this theme, a discussion of ways women who do not have a sexual partner can get their "skin hunger" needs met is held. It is pointed out that there are many ways to have physical contact—with pets, kids, and platonic friends. It is also pointed out that women these days are finding new ways to "rewrite" the traditional relationship script. These expanded options may include a woman's choosing not to be in a sex/love relationship, to be in a love relationship with herself, to love one other woman or one other man or a series of other women and/or men, or to single-parent if she strongly wants children but has not found a partner.

By this session, homework assignments are usually given by the women to themselves, with the help of other group members and with the leader picking up any loose ends or making additional suggestions. This process underscores the group members' ability to create their own solutions and fades out some more of their reliance on "authority figures." As an additional assignment, each member is asked to think about the following questions: What do you want done to you? What, if anything, do you want to do to your partner? Members are asked especially to think of things that they have never tried before and then to try at least one of them during the week, thus incorporating risk-taking and assertiveness assignments into one.

Let us check in with the three women we have been following:

Margaret had experienced her first orgasm in manual masturbation. Unfortunately, she told her husband somewhat aggressively that it was clearly *he* who had a sexual problem and he had better shape up; he then withdrew further. The group pointed out that anger is a sexual turn-off and made several suggestions for new things the couple might try. She agreed to challenge the idea that "my husband must be perfectly sexually cooperative right away, and it's awful if he's not." Margaret also decided on a behavioral assignment of making a "sensual exchange contract" with her husband, in which each could offer to give the other nongenital "treats," thus not making orgasm the goal.

Laura and Hilary had an unresolved argument; Laura felt so anxious about it for 3 days that she messed up an important work assignment. She was convinced that everything was her fault, that she was a "total screw-up" and incapable of having a good relationship. In discussion, Laura realized that some of her core beliefs came from living with her alcoholic parents. She decided to dispute three of these beliefs: "It must be my fault and I have to fix it," "I am responsible for my lover's happiness and should put my own desires aside," and "Sometimes my partner will be angry at me and that means either I'm a bad person or she is a total jerk." Laura also decided to buy a relaxation tape to help reduce her anxiety and the tension in her head and neck, and to practice with it for three 20-minute sessions.

Patricia felt much more relaxed during masturbation, so she did not feel the need to call her group colleague but reported being "very reassured to know I had someone who could help if I was in trouble." She felt very close to orgasm, got scared, pushed herself for another minute or two, and then gave herself permission to stop. The group offered several suggestions to help Pat distract herself from "spectatoring" (e.g., incorporating erotic imagery and focusing on her erotic sensations). She decided to try two new masturbation techniques, either from the group's suggestions or from the *Hite Report* (Hite, 1976).

Session 5

This session begins with the usual follow-up on homework. Members are positively reinforced for their efforts, and any dysfunctional feelings and cognitions are identified and worked on. Most of the remainder of this session is basically nonstructured, thereby allowing participants maximum opportunity to bring up their own agenda items. Two topics generally emerge: (a) dealing with anger at their partner for inconsiderate sexual or nonsexual behavior and (b) handling difficulties in dealing with their partner's focus on goal-directed sex (orgasm) rather than on intimacy, kissing, cuddling, sensuous stroking, and the other activities they love. (Almost invariably, the group sighs in unison when asked to get in touch with their feelings about snuggling through an experiential exercise often introduced at this point.) The problem of encouraging their partners to get off an intercourse focus is dealt with by introducing "informational massages" and other sensate-focus procedures. A handout with instructions for several such exercises (Wolfe, 1993) is given to group members with a caution not to go ahead with them if there is a significant relationship problem or a partner who flatly refuses to participate in nonorgasmic sex. In these situations, couples counseling is strongly recommended.

Members are encouraged to bring up situations involving anger at their partner (or other people close to them), and a review is made of how to dispute anger cognitions. This is followed by role playing and group feedback.

> Margaret's husband had agreed to do their sensual exchange but then did not initiate it on the agreed-upon night. Margaret withdrew and sulked and depressed herself over the possibility of never having good sex with him. The group pointed out her demandingness that he change right away and reminded her that anger on her part tends to elicit further withdrawal from him. Margaret practiced challenging her anger cognition: "When I assert myself, he *must* respond positively each and every time." She decided to reinitiate the sensual exchange contract and follow through even if her husband did not do the initiating. In addition, she would try in general to express her feelings to her husband without attacking.

> Laura was feeling considerably less anxious about her relationship with Hilary, but was self-downing because she had let it distract her for several weeks from working on her writing. She said she was afraid that she was deluding herself about having any writing talent. Laura's cognitive assignment was to remind herself that "what I write does not have to be brilliant and does not reflect my worth as a human being." She was also to work on accepting herself even when she did not do all the tasks she had set out for herself. She gave herself a behavioral assignment to spend three 45-minute periods a week writing and to reward herself "no matter how lousy the writing is."

> Patricia reported that she felt her legs tensing, followed by a relaxed, mellow feeling, but was not sure it was an orgasm. The group applauded, and group members assured her that it almost certainly was, and would probably get more and more clearly punctuated the more she practiced. She was going to continue to masturbate and try using her vibrator in a "teasing" fashion while continuing to use her favorite fantasies. Pat also brought up the topic of her fears of meeting men and being rejected by them. She agreed to dispute the idea that it was "awful to be rejected" or to be uncomfortable in social situations. The

group suggested several ways she might meet men, and Pat agreed to go to one social event and approach and converse with two new men.

Toward the end of the session, the therapists begin to discuss how the women can continue their work after the group ends. Each member is asked to respond to the following questions: How will you try to make sure that you don't backslide? What will you plan to do for yourself in the next month? What are your future goals for yourself in nonsexual areas? In the area of sexuality and sensuality? Additional risk-taking exercises and other supplementary assignments also may be suggested by the other group members and the leaders. The sixth (and final) session is then scheduled in approximately 3–4 weeks.

Session 6

This follow-up session is conducted in a very relaxed atmosphere, frequently with refreshments provided by the leaders and group members. The first agenda item is a review of each woman's progress, checking for backsliding or new problems. Not uncommonly, significant changes have occurred in the women's lives (e.g., loss of a partner, change of job), and the impact of these changes on sexuality is assessed. As a result, the follow-up meeting frequently revolves around general life-change stresses and developing coping strategies for handling them. In such cases, sex may be the tip of the iceberg. If there are emotional problems relating to such issues as health, finances, or relationship crises, it generally is best to deal with these first, and further individual therapy may be recommended.

> Margaret reported that her husband cooperated beautifully in the sensual exchange. She initiated sex another time; both enjoyed it and though she did not come, she felt confident that she would with time. She described improved marital communication, with less attacking by her and more active participation by him. Margaret's long-range cognitive task was to continue to "antiawfulize" about not always getting her desired sexual and nonsexual response from her husband. She was to work on accepting the fact that she may always be the main initiator and even prefer sex more than her husband, without concluding that she has a miserable marriage or is unattractive. She was also to work on positively reinforcing her husband for assertive behaviors and sexual initiations, and to join an assertiveness group to improve her personal and vocational communication skills.

> Laura had completed only two writing sessions but was pleased that she had gotten back into it and was not putting herself down for not having done more. She'd also treated herself to a massage and realized that she could enjoy purely sensual time with Hilary without any genital stimulation. She pledged to continue to dispute two core beliefs: "Because I come from a dysfunctional family, I'm doomed to a life of

insecurity and unhappiness" and "When there is a criticism or difference of opinion, I am wrong and the other person is right." She also wanted to continue to develop her skill and pleasure in writing, as well as to take some time each week to "smell the flowers" and nurture her other friendships.

Patricia was having more clearly articulated orgasms. She felt ready to approach partner sex, saying that through the group work she had "gone from being asexual to actually being horny—I think about sex at work and can't wait to get home and try it!" To prepare herself for both nonsexual and sexual risk taking, she was encouraged to read *The Assertive Woman* (Phelps & Austin, 1997) and to broadly increase her assertive behaviors: giving and receiving compliments, asking for favors, and making spontaneous comments at work and in social situations.

Another common focus of the sixth session is to provide what amounts to an advanced course in sexuality. Since the group's inception, many of the women will have taken new risks, tried new sexual experiences, and read a great deal on the topic of sexuality—all of which may open new areas for questions. Therefore, we ask group members at some point in the meeting to pick some item, hopefully one that always has been particularly difficult or embarrassing for them to discuss, and to throw it out to the other group members for their response. For example, in a recent follow-up group, questions such as the following were raised: "Do you swallow your partner's cum when you go down on him?" "How do you protect yourself against VD or AIDS if you think your lover may be sleeping with other women?" and "Is anal sex bad for you?"

During this final meeting it is common for the members—by now closely involved in each other's lives—to express sadness that the group is ending. The therapists may suggest that group members exchange names and phone numbers, and that if they wish they may arrange for periodic reunions, with or without the leaders. This suggestion typically leads to the group electing an informal secretary to take charge of arranging such reunions and clearing them with the leaders' schedules.

CONCLUSION

All-women's sexuality groups can be a powerful way of helping women redefine their own sexuality and determine the form of their own sexual expression. In an important paper on women's sexuality (Childs, Sachnoff, & Stocker, 1975), the characteristics of the sexually self-affirmed woman were summarized. The self-affirmed woman

is a woman who: (1) can enjoy her own body apart from others ("I have a primary sexual relationship with myself"); (2) can have sexual experiences for her own reasons; (3) can experiment and experience; (4) has her own standards and uses herself as the measure of her own experience. The self-affirmed woman understands the interpersonal issues found frequently in relationships that are sexual. She knows ways to negotiate, to fight, to settle, and to forgive. She knows when to leave relationships that are too costly. (Childs et al., 1975, p. 3)

Although these goals are rarely perfectly accomplished, it is our observation that cognitive–behaviorally oriented sexual enhancement groups, such as those we have described in this chapter, provide corrective emotional experiences and accomplish an impressive range of results in a relatively short period of time. Sexual reeducation, a climate of openness and support, and skills teaching (especially assertiveness training) are important ingredients in this process. It is the cognitive focus, however—the teaching of general anxiety-, anger-, and depression-combating philosophies—that is seen as being particularly responsible for helping the women develop an expanded set of skills for more clearly defining and pursuing their sexual and nonsexual goals.

REFERENCES

Readings marked with an asterisk are on the reading list for group members.

Barbach, L. G. (1974). Group treatment of preorgasmic women. *Journal of Sex and Marital Therapy, 1,* 139–145.

*Barbach, L. G. (1975). *For yourself: The fulfillment of female sexuality.* New York: Doubleday.

Barbach, L. G. (1980). *Women discover orgasm: A therapist's guide to a new treatment approach.* New York: Free Press/Macmillan.

*Barbach, L., & Levine, L. (1981). *Shared intimacies: Women's sexual experiences.* New York: Bantam Books.

*Borcherdt, B. (1996). *Head over heart in love.* Sarasota, FL: Professional Resource Press.

*Boston Women's Health Collective. (1992). *The new our bodies, ourselves.* New York: Simon & Schuster.

*Cash, T. (1995). *What do you see when you look in the mirror? Helping yourself to a positive body image.* New York: Bantam Books.

Childs, E., Sachnoff, E., & Stocker, E., with a Committee of the Whole of Association for Women in Psychology. (1975, March–April). Women's sexuality: A feminist view. *AWP Newsletter,* 1–4.

*Dodson, B. (1992). *Sex for one: The joys of selfloving.* New York: Crown.

*Doress, P. B., Siegal, D. L., & the Midlife and Older Women Book Project. (1987). *Ourselves, growing older.* New York: Simon & Schuster.

*Ehrenreich, B., & English, D. (1978). *For her own good: 150 years of the experts' advice to women.* New York: Anchor/Doubleday.

*Ellis, A., & Harper, R. (1997). *A guide to rational living.* North Hollywood, CA: Wilshire Books.

*Ellis, A., & Tafrate, R. C. (1997). *How to control your anger before it controls you.* Secaucus, NJ: Carol Publishing Group.

*Friday, N. (1975). *My secret garden.* New York: Pocket Books.

*Gottman, J., Notarius, C., Gonso, J., & Markman, H. (1976). *A couples' guide to communication.* Champaign, IL: Research Press.

Heinrich, A. (1976). *The effect of group and self-directed behavior-education treatment on primary orgasmic dysfunction in females treated without their partners.* Unpublished doctoral dissertation, University of Minnesota.

*Hite, S. (1976). *The Hite report.* New York: Macmillan.

Meador, B., Solomon, E., & Bowen, M. (1972). Encounter groups for women only. In N. Solomon & B. Beerzon (Eds.), *New perspectives on encounter groups* (pp. 335–348). San Francisco: Jossey-Bass.

Muench, G. (1964, April). *The comparative effectiveness of long-term, short-term, and interrupted psychotherapy.* Paper presented at Western Psychological Association, Portland, OR.

Paul, G. (1966). *Insight vs. desensitization in psychotherapy.* Stanford, CA: Stanford University Press.

*Phelps, S., & Austin, N. (1997). *The assertive woman.* San Luis Obispo, CA: Impact.

*Reynolds, M. (Ed.). (1990). *Erotica: Women's writing from Sappho to Margaret Atwood.* New York: Fawcett Books.

*Russianoff, P. (1985). *Why do I think I am nothing without a man?* New York: Bantam Books.

Walen, S. R., & Wolfe, J. L. (1983). Sexual enhancement groups in women. In A. Freeman (Ed.), *Cognitive therapy with couples and groups.* New York: Plenum.

*Wolfe, J. (1976). *How to be sexually assertive* [Pamphlet]. New York: Institute for Rational Living.

*Wolfe, J. (1993). *What to do when he has a headache: Renewing desire and intimacy in your relationship.* New York: Penguin Books.

Yalom, I. (1985). *The theory and practice of group psychotherapy* (3rd. ed.). New York: Basic Books.

13

PARENT TRAINING

JONATHAN STERN

This chapter describes a parent-training group that differs from traditional cognitive–behavioral parent-training groups in that the focus is not primarily on teaching specific parenting skills, such as time-outs and positive and negative reinforcement. Although such skills are modeled during the course of the group, the primary focus of the group described here is on enhancing the motivation of the parents to change by helping them relinquish certain negative parenting behaviors that are strongly linked to their self-image and to how they were parented. This involves concentrated attention to the long-standing effects of shame, rage, and self-pity that may be hampering parents in their efforts to improve their parenting.

Before describing this 12-session parent-training group in detail, I first present the theoretical rationale for the group and review the characteristics of more traditional parent-training approaches. Then I describe cog-

I would like to thank Richard Wessler, Sheenah Hankin Wessler, and Mildred Borras for their inspiration, mentorship, and input on the development of the cognitive appraisal therapy parenting group. I would also like to thank Anne Hamel for her invaluable help, collaboration, and substantial input in the organization and inauguration of these groups, as well as Beverly Grunfeld, Ronnie Gambardella, and Jeremy Robinson for the opportunity to run these groups with different populations and thereby improve the groups' effectiveness (as well as my own).

nitive appraisal therapy (Wessler, 1987; Wessler & Hankin Wessler, 1986, 1997), a form of therapy from which my parent-training group was adapted.

WHY SOME PARENTS DO NOT CHANGE IN PARENTING GROUPS

As therapists, we all have had clients say they want to change but then do everything possible to maintain the status quo. Many of us have had clients remark that they *know* that what they are thinking is illogical or incorrect but they still *feel* it to be true (e.g., "I know I'm not stupid—I even have concrete evidence that I'm smart—but I still feel like an idiot"). These two situations in and of themselves mitigate against working with clients from a solely cognitive–behavioral perspective.

Likewise, in doing parent training, I have found that parents fall into two basic groups: those who say they want to use behavioral tools and do so effectively, and those who say they want to use these tools and then instead use a variety of strategies to undermine the effectiveness of these tools (J. Stern, 1996). The second group seem as earnest as the first in professing that they want to improve their children's lot in life, as well as their own as parents. They often appear to be amenable, sometimes enthusiastically, to trying out the various behavioral strategies I suggest to them. However, week after week, after many modifications and trouble-shooting sessions, these parents are still unable to follow through with their prescribed assignments. Instead, they prefer to tell me of yet more horrendous terrorist tactics used by their 5-year-old son; to regale me that I just do not understand how headstrong and downright frightening their child can be; to come up with many creative reasons why they were unable to implement the behavioral strategies we discussed; or to complain bitterly that all their lives they have been the overly responsible caretaker while everyone around them (including me) makes unrealistic and uncaring demands of them. Nevertheless, many of these same parents keep on returning to therapy. (I remember that, as a naive and overzealous psychology intern running behavioral parenting groups, I used to think, "I've given you all you need to know to change your kid's behavior. Damn it, why aren't you using it?")

From these experiences, I came to see that behavioral interventions can be effective in treating both the child's and parent's behavioral *symptoms*, but they do not address underlying *personality* characteristics in the parents that can often sabotage their willingness to comply with behavioral assignments. I have also found that challenging illogical thoughts, as a rational–emotive therapist might do, is not enough to help some parents change, because their long-standing feelings dominate their logic. By dint of how they grew up and how they saw themselves in relation to the world around them, some parents (those whom Yalom, 1985, called help-rejecting complainers) seem more invested in maintaining their roles as downtrodden, victimized, unappreciated, and ineffective parents than in changing these roles. Others prefer to maintain their roles as the rescuers of their "incompetent" children, as they covertly encourage their offspring not to change. Still others opt to be taken care of by their children rather than addressing the children's resulting problematic behaviors (e.g., school phobia, resistance to sleeping apart from the parent, and psychosomatic symptoms).

Rather than questioning the genuineness of clients' motivation to change, I have found it more useful to consider their motivation in another way, which has been articulated by Wessler and Hankin Wessler (1997). Following Bowlby's (1969) work on attachment, Wessler and Hankin Wessler stressed that people are motivated and predisposed to seek out familiar affect and avoid novel (and therefore uncomfortable) feeling states. This is compatible with Daniel Stern's (1985) finding that the infant's sense of who he or she is and what the world is grows out of preverbal feelings that are elicited by and define the parent–child relationship. Thoughts and behaviors spring up around these feelings, but it is the core attachment-based feelings themselves that are least mutable. Therefore, in adulthood, if a person's behavior or belief does not evoke familiar affect in a person, then the person must change what he or she does and thinks to rekindle this affect. If a client has predominantly felt angry and ashamed, for example, then he or she will not be motivated to act or think in ways that relinquish these feelings (which are linked psychologically to one's parents and, initially, to one's survival).

Understanding parents from this perspective helped me see that my cognitive–behavioral interventions could be highly threatening to parents because they required the relinquishing of some affectively charged aspects of their self-image—aspects that these parents may have believed to be immutable. This attachment-based self-image requires parents to reexperience certain emotions (e.g., rage, shame, and self-pity) while parenting to be on familiar ground and thus feel secure. Without addressing these affects in parent training groups, parents will be unable to make use of cognitive–behavioral interventions, as the following example illustrates:

> Joe, a 46-year-old father of three adolescent girls, felt victimized and helpless in his family. According to Joe, his wife would undermine any decisions he would make, harshly criticize him in front of his children, and then the daughters would align themselves with the mother (who pampered them) and would criticize and ignore Joe. Joe came to see how this paralleled his relationship with his highly critical mother, who often would set him up to fail and would then berate him. Joe passive–aggressively rebelled against his mother and, later, his wife, by drinking and having affairs, which would in turn pull for more criticism and

disapproval, as well as self-hatred. In the parenting group, Joe came to see this recurrent pattern and how he presently set himself up to be a victim. The group then generated some helpful ways that he could devictimize himself, all of which Joe then ignored. The group then got angry and frustrated with Joe, true to the interpersonal pattern of the help-rejecting complainer (Yalom, 1985), and he thus felt victimized once more. Only when Joe began to focus on and understand the affect (rage, shame, and self-pity) inherent in his victim stance and how he uses others to rev up these feelings, and only when he learned how to diminish these feelings using cognitive and experiential strategies, did he begin to behave differently and see himself and others in a different light.

In this chapter, I describe an approach to working with such parents in parent-training groups that is an adaptation of Wessler and Hankin Wessler's (1986) cognitive appraisal therapy (CAT). First, I briefly review some traditional approaches to parent training and then describe how a parenting group based on CAT can address some of the limitations of these groups. Following this, I describe a protocol for a 12-session parent-training program based on CAT principles.

TRADITIONAL PARENTING-GROUP APPROACHES: STRENGTHS AND WEAKNESSES

Schaefer and Briesmeister (1989) pointed out that approaches to parent training can be categorized into those that focus on teaching parents new skills and those that work to improve the parent–child relationship. The former mostly adheres to a protocol that outlines behavioral and developmental principles and then helps parents to implement these principles as they parent (e.g., Anastopoulos & Barkley, 1989; Douglas, 1989). The latter often observes the parent–child interaction and then gives parents suggestions, either by having a therapist model a recommended interaction with the child or by having the parent try out a new way of interacting with the child in the therapeutic setting (e.g., Jernberg, 1989; Trad, 1992). Both approaches are essentially behavioral in that they focus on a parent's doing something different and cognitive in that they try to alter the parent's knowledge base and perception of what the child's behavior means and communicates.

Parent-training groups have been found to be a cost-effective format to help clients change their parenting styles and diminish problematic behaviors in their children for as long as 4.5 years after treatment (Christiansen, Johnson, Phillips, & Glasgow, 1980; McMahon & Forehand, 1984). However, some research exists that indicates that parental issues can block the use of behavioral tools. Griest and Forehand (1982) reviewed studies that conclude that family variables (e.g., marital distress and maternal depression) can impede productive use of parent training. Horne and Patterson (1980) noted that 50% of the participants in their parent-training program were not able to implement the requisite skills and needed up to a year of subsequent treatment to work through interfering conflicts and improve their negotiation skills.

The role that parents' emotions play in their noncompliance with parent training is still speculative; however, some studies suggest that parenting can be improved by helping parents soothe interfering negative feelings. Joyce (1995) found that children's behavior problems were significantly reduced and associated with changes in their parents' irrational beliefs about their self-worth and ability to reduce stress 10 months after their parents participated in a rational–emotive parent education group. Nixon and Singer (1993) found a significant improvement in the parenting of children with severe disabilities by teaching parents to decrease their guilt, self-blame, internal negative attributions, and depression using cognitive–behavioral techniques in a group format.

The Rekindling of Shame in the Parenting Group: There's No Place Like Home

I have found that parents who participate in but do not make use of a behavioral or cognitive–behavioral parenting program are often riddled with shame, the feeling that "I am a defective, flawed, unlovable person/ parent" (Nathanson, 1992; Tangney, 1991; Wessler & Hankin Wessler, 1997). Therefore, a parent-training group will be a countertherapeutic experience for these parents if their shameful feelings are enhanced. Moreover, if parents are primed by years of shame-seeking thoughts and behaviors to reinvoke shameful feelings, they often use therapy to do so. Thus, inherent in a behavioral or cognitive–behavioral "protocol" is the possibility that failure to comply or succeed with such a program indicates that one is not good enough, is incapable, is stupid, and so on. It is my belief that shame-seeking parents may participate in such programs in order (totally nonconsciously) to fail. They can then get angry at themselves, fellow group members, or the therapist, feel sorry for themselves, and ultimately feel like a failure, thus replaying old familiar feelings and interpersonal patterns.

Offering Sympathy Rather Than Empathy in the Parenting Group: The Inner Child Outshouts the Inner Adult

Some parenting groups that are more humanistic in nature tend to offer "support" to parents. Naturally, validation and support can be important elements of a group therapy (Yalom, 1985); however, they can often be confused with sympathy (feeling sorry for another) rather than associated only with empathy (understanding how another feels). While it is important to acknowledge how difficult parenting can be and how hard it can be to effectively change a child's behavior, a group therapist must not focus on this to the exclusion of having parents assume responsibility for changing their parenting style.

Parents who are prone to feeling ashamed of themselves and pulling sympathy from others will attempt to do so in the parenting group. If such a group tends toward the Rogerian, members may be encouraged to feel sorry for such parents frequently, and whining will become the group norm. If the group norm is particularly "supportive," then other members' anger may surface passive–aggressively or, ultimately, in a resentful, fed-up confrontation. Self-pity and rage (the voice of one's "inner child") may reign supreme. Instead, empathy (an adult behavior) should be given to these parents rather than sympathy, and self-pity should be discouraged or ignored.

COGNITIVE APPRAISAL THERAPY

Cognitive appraisal therapy, or CAT, was created by Richard Wessler and Sheenah Hankin Wessler (Wessler, 1987; Wessler & Hankin Wessler, 1986, 1997) to work with difficult, often personality disordered, clients. In brief, CAT posits that people nonconsciously recreate long-standing feelings that are derived from early attachments to feel the security of familiarity. People are motivated therefore not to seek out pleasure or avoid pain, but to rekindle familiar feelings and avoid novel ones (Wessler, 1993a; Wessler & Hankin Wessler, 1997). Long-standing, attachment-based feelings, which CAT terms *personotypic affect*, can be either positive or negative depending on the dominant feelings in a person's relationships with his or her parents.

Wessler and Hankin Wessler (1997) found that shame, self-pity, and rage are the three personotypic affects that their clients seek to rekindle nonconsciously, either by acting in ways that result in these feelings (called *security-seeking maneuvers*) or by holding beliefs that explain or reinforce these feelings (called *justifying cognitions*). Thus, the noncompliant client is really not being "resistant" but is instead using therapy to recreate his or her familiar interpersonal dynamic and personotypic affect.

In doing CAT, I came to understand that parents who do not comply with behavioral or cognitive–behavioral protocols are doing so to rev up personotypic affect. "My child is too difficult to respond to behavioral interventions" reinforces one's victim feelings of self-pity and perhaps rage. "I'm not capable of using these behavioral strategies" reinforces the parent's long-standing shame. And "You, Mr. or Ms. Therapist, are not being sympathetic to how difficult my situation is with my child by giving me all these behavioral things to do" rekindles rage and self-pity. Unless a non-compliant parent's personotypic affect is highlighted in a nonshaming way and the parent's noncompliance is reframed as part of a lifelong security-seeking pattern, behavioral and cognitive–behavioral interventions with this parent will not be successful.

PREPARING FOR THE CAT PARENT-TRAINING GROUP

The CAT parenting group is a 12-session therapy that helps parents to understand and diminish the power of long-standing negative feelings that prevent them from making use of behavioral tools and knowledge of child development. As such, the group integrates didactic information concerning behavioral parenting strategies and child development with experiential interventions to access personotypic affect and justifying cognitions and with cognitive strategies to help parents soothe affect and access logical, helpful thoughts instead. It should be noted that, although I describe the behavioral and developmental information that I present to parents, this part of the group can be left up to the therapist's personal preference. It is the group's integrative nature, philosophy, and affect-oriented interventions that are most unique to CAT and that can be integrated with the therapist's own behavioral and developmental approach.

Structuring and Screening

The optimal CAT parenting group consists of 12 weekly 90-minute sessions, with 6 to 10 members. I prefer to mix parents of different-age children in my CAT groups so that parents of older children can help preview (Trad, 1993) for parents of younger children what they might expect from them in the future. Parents of older children sometimes have their confidence boosted by such an experience. For example, many parents of younger children react to what is termed the "terrible twos" with feelings of anger and rejection. Their sweet, loving, relatively compliant infant is now a toddler who pushes them away sometimes and just will not take no for an answer. This shift can often reinforce parents' shame-based personotypic affect, and parents instead must learn to understand that the independence gained during this stage is vital to the child's developing self-confidence, competence, and autonomy (Trad, 1993). Thoughts of "My child hates me. What did I do wrong?" or "My child is turning into a little monster" can give way to "How can I foster my child's independence while setting limits and maintaining a positive relationship with him/her?"

I have not found it essential to ensure that there be at least two parents of similar-age children in the group, although it is certainly a bonus when this occurs. It is the empathic, nonjudgmental tone of the group, coupled with the discussion of developmental stages that includes all parents, which makes the parent of a child who is different in age from those of the other parents still feel welcomed in the group.

Potential participants should be screened for the 12-session group. It should be explained to parents that they are expected to attend all 12 sessions and arrive on time, no excuses accepted, if they are to benefit from the group. The screening interview contains many questions that I would ask as part of any intake interview, but some extra questions are added to give me an initial assessment of the parent's personotypic affect, justifying cognitions, and security-seeking maneuvers, as well as a sense of the parent's own upbringing that created them. (See Exhibit 13.1 for a list of these questions.) Questions such as "During a particular conflict (have parent think of recent typical parent–child conflict), how did you feel right after it happened?" when paired with "How did the parent's parents typically make him/her feel?" begin to elicit personotypic affect. Questions such as "What changes need to take place in your family in order to solve the

EXHIBIT 13.1
Screening Interview Questions Used to Assess Personotypic Affect, Justifying Cognitions, and Security-Seeking Maneuvers

---

Parenting Style: Affect
1. During a particular conflict (have parent think of recent typical parent–child conflict), how did you feel as it was happening? Right after it happened?
2. What thoughts did you have along with these feelings?
3. What do you think your child was feeling and thinking during his/her misbehavior? After he/she was disciplined by you?

Parenting Style: Behavior/Discipline
1. What have you tried so far to discipline your child? How has it worked? What happens? (If parent acknowledges that it has not succeeded, how does parent explain this? Where is the difficulty located?)
2. Where did you learn your discipline strategies? Is this how your mother/ father would have responded to a similar situation? Why or why not?
3. Repeat these questions for partner. Also: Where do you and your partner agree and disagree in terms of discipline? How do you negotiate disagreements?

Parents' Parents
1. How do your parents respond to your child? To your form of discipline? What kind of relationship did you have with them? How is it different now?
2. How do your parents typically make you feel?
3. Ask same questions for partner's parents.

Parental Motivation
1. What do you want out of being in this group?
2. What changes need to take place in your family in order to solve the problem? Who needs to change in your family in order to make things better? How do they need to change? How will this happen? How might the group help this to happen?

---

problem?" give an estimation of how much responsibility the parent takes for the problem. Asking the parent about what the child might be feeling during the conflict not only elicits the degree of empathy and perspective taking a parent currently has (Newberger 1985) but also yields some of the parent's justifying cognitions (e.g., "My child is thinking 'this will really stick it to Dad'" or "My child is only thinking about herself; she's always cared only about her feelings"). Finally, once a parent's problems are outlined, the therapist can give an indication of how the CAT group might help to resolve them as a way of forming an alliance with a parent.

Because the CAT parenting group was formed to work with parents who are difficult to change and difficult to work with, not too many parents are rejected for the group on the basis of the screening interview. More often, it is the parents themselves who self-select on the basis of the initial screening. Presumably, those who do not want to attend all 12 sessions, those who do not want to show up on time, and those who do not want to do all of the work that is described to them during the screening choose not to participate in the group when contacted subsequently. I make certain that all parents know that the group requires a high degree of dedication and commitment so as to screen out any parents who at least initially are not up to the task.

Parents who have been court-ordered to participate in a parenting group are accepted for the CAT group. However, I am quite clear with them that if they are merely punching in a time-clock to fulfill their required obligations and if they do not participate to the fullest, I will contact the referring agency and express my opinion that they are not yet fit to assume parental responsibilities.

Occasionally, I have an initial screening with a parent who discloses currently abusing substances or physically abusing a child. I reject these parents, as they need to ameliorate these problems before being able to make use of the CAT group, and I notify the referring clinician or agency of these problems, as well as the department of social services in the case of child abuse.

Finally, the screening interview indicates the level of insight and responsibility that a parent is willing or able to take at present. As such, if I am able to run more than one CAT group at a time owing to volume of referrals, I try to run one group for parents with a greater degree of insight, cognitive sophistication, and proneness to taking responsibility for their actions, and another for those who are lower on these dimensions. I have found that, in a mixed group, parents with a higher degree of insight and cognitive sophistication tend to feel slowed down and ultimately angry at the parents who are struggling to master some of the more basic concepts of the group, and the latter parents can feel intimidated and ultimately embarrassed in front of the former group. Dividing parents in this way also allows me to modify my presentation and expectations for the group accordingly, rather than having to shuttle between making more and less sophisticated interventions.

Creating a Shame-Free Therapeutic Environment

Because CAT holds that those parents who are nonconsciously motivated to remain the same are often driven by long-standing shame-based feelings, the group therapist must do all that he or she can to make participation in the group a shame-free experience. This engenders what Safran and Segal (1990) called an experiential disconfirmation of one's typical cognitive–interpersonal pattern, as the client interacts with others without shame for perhaps the first time in his or her life.

Wessler (1993b) reviewed four ways in which shame is often dealt with by group therapy members: (a) avoiding and withdrawing; (b) denying shame by being active in focusing on others' feelings; (c) using humor to avoid disclosing riskier feelings or being humorously self-effacing to preempt possible criticism by others; and (d) "shame-defended rage," or turning underlying shameful feelings into threatening anger to keep others at a safe distance. Although the CAT parenting-group therapist may during the course of the group point out these shame-related defenses as they play out in the group dynamic as well as in the parent's life, the group should be structured to preempt the surfacing of shame as much as possible. As such, group members are told during the first session to be empathic, to share similar experiences, and to imagine how they might feel in another parent's shoes, but they must not give advice, criticize, or tell another member what he or she is thinking or feeling. The therapist stops group members from doing the latter and uses this opportunity to model more appropriate responses (Wessler, 1993b). The group's highly structured format and the presentation of much information also serve to diminish the playing out of shame-based behaviors.

Shame can also be reduced with therapist self-disclosure (Wessler, 1993b; Wessler & Hankin Wessler, 1986). The therapist can take the lead in the group by disclosing problematic experiences and feelings in his or her own parenting or, if the therapist is not a parent, with a partner, a parent, a coworker, and so on. Every therapist has experienced shame, rage, and self-pity and has thought himself or herself to be incompetent, unloved, or ineffectual. Sharing these similar feelings, thoughts, and behaviors turns the therapist into a well-informed colleague rather than placing parents in the shame-inducing position of disclosing embarrassing shortcomings to a distant "expert."

I often share with group members a problem I have had in raising my son, who is currently a little under 2 years old, and I try to do so with humor to give the message, "It's not a big deal here to share personal shortcomings." Also, by linking my parenting problems to how I was raised, I set the stage for parents doing this later.

> My mother, while well-intentioned, panics easily when she believes something is unsafe, either for herself, for me, or, now, for my son— and she believes that many objects, behaviors, and situations are unsafe. She herself was the youngest of three children in a poor family with a single mother who worked 20 hours a day during the Depression. She describes herself as a somewhat lonely, fearful, "latchkey kid," so it is not difficult to imagine how she might have grown up feeling lonely, afraid of the world, and longing to have her fears soothed by another. Nevertheless, while growing up, I used to resent her many fears, her sometimes leaning on me to take care of them, and her valuing safety and security above all else. I swore that I would never be excessive in my worries like her, and that I would not impose them on others. Well, when my son was 9 months old, he took my glasses off of my head, which he occasionally did to amuse himself. This time, however, he appeared to poke himself in the eye with one of the side pieces. I screamed out, froze, and did absolutely nothing that was helpful—much as my mother, paralyzed by her fearful helplessness, might have done. I handed my son to my wife, who I assumed would be better equipped to handle the situation. After seeing that my son had in fact not poked himself (although he was crying, surely in reaction to my scream), my wife looked at me with her and-you-call-yourself-a-child-psychologist look. I realized at that moment that I had internalized not only my mother's fearful beliefs (her justifying cognitions) but, more centrally, her underlying shame-eliciting belief that I as an incompetent parent am incapable of preventing danger from befalling my son (and only my highly more competent wife, whom I must depend on, is worthy to care for him). Well, that was the last time I reacted that way, although it was not the first. I still feel embarrassed and exposed sharing this story, and I still feel uncertain (though not incompetent) when faced with an injury to my son, although I try to do the appropriate thing.

Finally, nonblame can arise from exploring how the parents' *parents* influenced their current parenting style. Feelings and thoughts in reaction to the child can be likened to those either elicited in the parent by his or her parents or modeled by them. Personotypic affect and justifying cognitions can then be attributed *not* to the parent but to the way the parent was raised. Once parents begin to see that their shame-eliciting parenting style was learned in childhood—when a child has no other choice but to accept and thrive on the type of attachment offered by the parent—then the parent's self-blame and rage at the child can begin to abate. Moreover, group members tend to be extremely empathic toward current struggles when they hear what difficult childhoods many of their comembers had. Anger at a group member who screams at and physically threatens his children turns into empathy (but hopefully not forgiveness) when other members hear how he was repeatedly beaten and humiliated as a child, for example.

THE CAT PARENTING GROUP

I consider a group to be successful (a) if parents are able to focus on what they are feeling before, during, and after a problematic interaction with their child; (b) if they can link at least some of these feelings to personotypic affect and take responsibility for these feelings ("My child doesn't *make* me feel this way. *I* do."); and (c) if parents learn how to manage their affect while they parent, enabling them to use behavioral tools appropriately and to depersonalize their child's misbehaviors using basic knowledge of child development.

Sessions 1 and 2: Goals, Feelings, and Cohesiveness

Plutchik (1981, p. 142) maintains that the sharing of emotion is essential to group cohesiveness, more so than didactic lessons taught by the therapist: "That the crucial element is the sharing of emotions and not the exchange of information is evident from the fact that people who simply attend a lecture do not thereby become cohesive." Parenting groups that rely solely on didactic instruction and parenting skills training may have less need to focus on building cohesion. The CAT parenting program, with its additional focus on managing affect, requires that the therapist pay stronger attention to facilitating group cohesiveness and eliciting empathic comments from members.

Toward this end, the first two sessions overtly focus on the members' (a) sharing their stories of why they are attending the group and (b) formulating goals for changing their children's behaviors or their relationships with their child. Implicitly, the therapist uses these early sessions to have group members acknowledge the difficulty of each other's situations and to begin to make a list of what they are feeling while they are parenting.

Group members are asked to describe why they are attending the group, and the therapist makes sure that each member gets equal time to tell his or her story. Noncritical reactions (e.g., discussing similar difficulties, voicing empathic remarks) are welcomed from group members. As clients tell their stories, the therapist asks for their feelings while they are parenting and lists these on the blackboard. Typical feelings are anger, helplessness, frustration, anxiety, guilt, and powerlessness. The therapist also uses this opportunity to help parents become more specific in describing their feelings. The parent who responds "I felt bad" or "I felt that I wanted to run away," for example, is asked to substitute a more specific feeling for this description. If the parent is unable to do so, group members are asked to "fill in the blank" from their similar experiences. The therapist is also encouraged to share a problem he or she has had with a child and the related feelings as a way of modeling self-disclosure and linking thoughts and behaviors to feelings. At this point, nothing more is done with this list of parents' feelings. This exercises is done simply to make it a group norm to discuss feelings in a noncritical environment.

Next, parents' goals for themselves in the group are listed on the board. Typical goals that parents set include "I want to communicate better with my child," "I want my child to obey me more without such a hassle every time," "I want to feel better about myself as a parent," "I want to understand better why my child does what she does," and "I'm afraid of hitting my son when he doesn't listen to me. I need more alternatives as a parent."

Many parents begin the CAT group believing that it is not they but their children who have to change. In these cases the therapist can still encourage these parents to formulate goals that focus on their feeling differently about themselves and their child. For example, a parent might set the goal "I want to feel like parenting is less of a hassle" or "I want to be more respected as a parent." It is hoped these parents will come to realize that, even if they do not want to change their parenting style, they can attain their goals by changing their perception of their child and themselves; this realization usually accrues slowly over sessions.

Parents then list their hopes and fears for the group. This is done again mostly to encourage the open sharing of feelings to facilitate cohesiveness and self-disclosure. The therapist begins by sharing his or her greatest hope and fear for the group. At times, I have said that my greatest hope is that parents will find that the group is of value to them and that it has helped them to achieve the changes that they wish for themselves and their family. My greatest fear is often that parents will think that group is a waste of time and that "I'm a moron." (I make the last statement not to be self-effacing but to open up the possibility of such self-disclosures from parents.)

Typical hopes from parents are "that I will see that other parents have similar struggles and problems," "that I'll learn more parenting information and skills," and "that other parents will see that I'm smart and that I have something to offer." Typical fears include "of talking in front of others," "that the other parents will think I'm a bad parent," and "of coming across as dumb to others."

Toward the end of the first session, the therapist outlines what the general goal of the entire CAT parenting group is: emotional self-care. The therapist spends some time discussing with parents how feelings can get in the way of doing the "right thing" for their children, feeling positively about themselves as parents, and "tuning in" to what their children are experiencing. The therapist then emphasizes that, by the end of the CAT group, parents will be able to put aside unhelpful, painful feelings that they experience while parenting to enable them to parent more effectively.

During the second session, the therapist writes a more detailed, feeling-focused version of the A-B-C child behavior model (Baker, Brightman, Heifetz, & Murphy, 1976) on the board (see Table 13.1). The ensuing discussion, which often continues into Session 3, focuses on how the parent feels step-by-step during a typical altercation with the child and how these feelings may influence a parent's behavioral response. For example, one mother said that she feels enraged when her daughter does not listen to her and thinks, "She treats me like garbage" (B). Believing that the only way to earn respect will be to hit her daughter, as the mother's parents did to her, and feeling helpless to change her daughter (C), the mother chooses to retreat into her room, avoid the situation, and feel sorry for herself and "depressed."

Parents are also asked to imagine what the child is feeling during this interaction. Most often, at the beginning of the CAT group, many parents have either not considered this before or project thoughts and feelings onto the child that justify their own reactions. A mother of a 5-year-old girl who cries when she is told to clean up her elaborate Lego creations in the living room of a two-room apartment said she believes her daughter cries "just to start with me and aggravate me. She has to have her own way" (E). She would then typically yell at her daughter in a very critical way. Parents as well as other group members are asked to put themselves in the child's place and imagine what they might feel if they had this done to them. The therapist can ask group members to close their eyes if they want to and visualize the situation to access their feelings. The mother of the 5-year-old was told to imagine that she had created a masterpiece of which she was extremely proud (D) and was then told it must be destroyed. The mother reported that she would feel "angry, frustrated, and disrespected" (F). She then concluded that maybe she should respond more "gently" and try to move the Lego creation, with her daughter's help, to another area of the apartment.

It is important to diffuse any shameful feelings parents may have during this session by normalizing their situations: On a daily basis, parents have their own routines and agendas that they must complete and they

TABLE 13.1
Chart of Feelings During a Typical Parent–Child Interaction

Feelings	Situation Before Behavior	Child's Behavior	Your Response
Your feelings	A	B	C
Child's feelings	D	E	F

cannot always take into account their children's needs and experiences. Rather than beating themselves up subsequently, it is more useful to self-correct and continue trying in the future without self-recrimination.

Sessions 3 and 4: Behavioral Tools

Parents naturally come into the CAT group with varying degrees of knowledge about child development and behavioral parenting strategies. I first try to get all parents on a par with each other in these domains. Moreover, Dubey, O'Leary, and Kaufman (1983) have found that parents participating in groups to address their children's behavior difficulties are more likely to attend sessions and find them more relevant if the initial emphasis is on behavior management.

As such, these sessions present the basic behavioral interventions that every parent should know and be able to use, followed by applying them to problematic child behaviors. The therapist can teach whatever behavioral program he or she prefers, as long as this program includes such concepts as natural consequences, logical consequences, when to reward and when to punish, time-outs, how to modify behavioral programs to suit the child's age, and mistakes parents can make in implementing behavioral strategies (e.g., rewarding negative behaviors, ignoring positive changes). I teach the basic behavioral interventions from Clark's (1985) SOS! Help for Parents because this book applies to a wide range of behavior problems and is written in a clear, parent-friendly style. I do not assign this book to parents, but I do recommend it to them.

About the first third to half of Sessions 3 and 4 are didactic in nature, followed by group discussion. I begin by making the basic points that many problematic behaviors can be avoided (a) by praising positive behaviors, achievements, and compliant behaviors, even if small; and (b) by establishing specific negative consequences ahead of time and sticking to them consistently. I stress that taking away a privilege is my preferred consequence for most negative behaviors, as basic positive behaviors (doing chores, working hard in school, and following rules) are what is expected of all of us and therefore should not be rewarded.

This is followed by a discussion of hitting as punishment. I discuss studies that have shown that parents who hit have children who are physically aggressive more frequently, as the children learn from their parents' modeling that hitting is the way to express feelings and problem-solve. These children also learn to value power and strength in relationships instead of verbal expression and sharing. I have worked with many parents who punish their children for hitting another person by hitting them, without seeing the connection. I tell parents that, if they hit their child and then the child hits others, they should be flattered, as the child is effectively using the parents as role models.

I then give handouts from Clark (1985), the first of which lists natural consequences (e.g., mishandling a cat and getting scratched; not combing one's hair and being teased by other children) and the second listing logical consequences (e.g., taking away a child's bike for a week if he or she rides it in the street; taking away phone privileges for 2 days if the child breaks phone use rules). A list of methods of punishment (scolding and disapproval, behavior penalties, and logical consequences) is then reviewed, with special attention to using time-outs when a child is behaving aggressively or throwing tantrums. Ignoring nonviolent tantrums and anger-provoking behaviors in the child is also discussed.

This presentation almost always leads to a lively discussion by parents of behavioral interventions they have already tried, their successes and failures with them, and how they might alter these strategies in the future. During this discussion, I write three columns on the blackboard: behaviors you are trying to change in your child, what you have already tried, and what you can try in the future. Each parent is asked to generate new ways of handling the situation behaviorally. If a parent is having difficulty generating new solutions, I ask him or her if other parents might help him or her apply the behavioral tools we have discussed. Usually, parents do not feel ashamed if others offer suggestions here, as this exercise takes on a more problem-solving rather than confessional tone.

Finally, we practice how to implement behavioral strategies with each parent's child (or children) by role playing difficult situations. The parent assumes the role of his or her child, both because the parent knows the child best and to avoid the parent's repeating not being able to react appropriately to the child and then feeling embarrassed and ashamed. In a playful atmosphere, other parents form a "tag team" and step into the parenting role as they try out new behavioral interventions on the "child." The therapist coaches them on how to set up rules with the child and then implement them clearly, simply, and effectively. Finally, the parent might step into the parenting role and use some of the strategies that the other parents already tried out.

At this point in the group, parents are *not* encouraged to implement new behavioral strategies at home. Instead, the gauntlet is thrown down by the therapist, who guarantees that these behavioral interventions will not be successful unless parents get better at managing interfering feelings. Some parents choose to use this challenge as a paradoxical intervention (Haley, 1976), although it is not so intended, and they independently implement a behavioral program at home.

Session 5: A Developmental Reframe

This session is devoted to reviewing developmental stages, again focusing on how parents may typically feel when faced with a child's misbehaviors at each stage. The therapist's additional objective is to help parents reframe some of their children's misbehaviors as developmentally appropriate, thus diminishing the parents' taking such misbehaviors overly personally and using them to support their personotypic affect and justifying cognitions. If many (but certainly not all) misbehaviors are seen as part of normal development, parents can then view their responses as opportunities to help their children negotiate the developmental task at hand. This is not to imply that parents should pardon or overlook developmentally appropriate misbehaviors; they still might need to set negative consequences and boundaries for them that will be helpful to the child. Nor, of course, should parents rule out that some misbehaviors are reactions to environmental stressors or the parents' own behaviors.

The developmental chart presented during this session appears in Table 13.2. It has been adapted from the work of various parent-training manuals (Forehand & McMahon, 1981; Patterson, 1976) and has been altered to suit CAT's purposes. After reviewing this chart, each parent is encouraged to select an example of his or her child's misbehavior, describe it, and then reframe it in terms of the child's developmental stage. Parents are then asked if, having done this reframe, they would feel differently about their child's behavior and might react differently. (Some parents might choose to feel and react in the same way which, in some cases, might be perfectly appropriate.)

A brief discussion of temperament is often inserted here, as parents can also use a child's temperamental predisposition to feed personotypic affect and justifying cognitions. I use Kagan's (1989) model of the inhibited (shy and easily overstimulated) and uninhibited (easily engaged, curious, and not easily overstimulated) child, as this distinction is relatively easy for parents to grasp. One mother, for instance, was concerned that her 12-year-old son has never discussed much with her. She said it made her feel "rejected" by him and she would occasionally yell at him in frustration. After ruling out that he was reacting to anything she was doing in particular and discovering that he has always been this way with everybody, I could help her reframe her son as temperamentally inhibited and in need of acceptance and gentle, patient, playful encouragement to come out of his shell (Greenspan, 1992). This mother then realized that she could not take her son's silence so personally and she needed to soothe her own anger and frustration instead.

Sessions 6 and 7: Identifying How Shame, Rage, and Self-Pity Can Drive Parenting

Traditional cognitive–behavioral groups teach parents to identify automatic and unhelpful thoughts while parenting (Beck, Rush, Shaw, & Emery, 1979; Evans & McAdam, 1988). The CAT program goes a step

TABLE 13.2
Stages of Child Development (Chart Used in the CAT Group)

Facets of Development	Age (in Years)			
	0–1	2–4	5–12	13–18
What kids are learning	Attachment Belonging Trust	Autonomy ("No! I'm myself! I'll do it my way!")	Role modeling ("What are the rules about how to behave?")	Independence Autonomy ("I'm not like you. I want my own identity.")
How kids misbehave	Attention-seeking ("I belong only when I'm noticed")	Tantrums and moods Breaking rules Challenging you ("No! I'm the boss!")	Break social rules Copying parent	Asserting independence ("I'm the boss!") Moods!
How parents often feel	Annoyed Confused Overwhelmed Scared Needed	Angry ("I have lost my power and authority") Hopeless Rejected	Hurt/mocked Angry Hopeless Flattered	Enraged ("My authority's challenged.") Rejected
What to do to help child learn	Encourage Ignore misbehavior	Set choices and consequences ahead Follow through with plans Withdraw from power struggle with choices	Avoid taking it personally Stop criticism Be good model	Set consequences Choices Withdraw from conflict

Note. CAT = cognitive appraisal therapy. Adapted from Forehand, R. L. and McMahon, R. J. (1981).

further by eliciting the feelings that accompany automatic thoughts and reframing and grouping these feelings into three categories: rage, shame, and self-pity.

In doing individual work with parents, I will often use the emotional language of the client. For instance, a client might feel ashamed but tell me "I feel inadequate," "I feel worthless," "I feel unloved," or "I feel like a wimp." Because these words are emotionally salient for that individual, I will use them instead of the word *shame*, which might have little valence for the client. However, because the CAT group is didactic, is short term, and involves members speaking a common language, I group parents' feelings under the headings *shame, anger,* and *self-pity* at this point. I have found that this is easy to do without having to force feelings into artificial categories. Feelings such as embarrassment, hopelessness, and powerlessness are facets of or synonyms for shame (Tangney, Wagner, Fletcher, & Gramzow, 1992). If the therapist probes other feelings, such as guilt, fear, or worry, shame issues almost always emerge. For example, a mother who said she feels guilty while thinking "What did I do wrong?" was then asked "What would it mean to have done something wrong while parenting?" She responded, "That I am a bad parent," thus exposing a shame-related justifying cognition. A mother who said she feels afraid that "Something is very wrong with my kid" as she parents him then revealed that this would mean she is a failure as a parent, again indicating that her fear is ultimately about feeling ashamed of herself. Finally, a mother who feels powerless, thinking "I can't change anything," said that she feels incompetent to change anything in her life, again suggesting shame with the use of the word *incompetent*.

The same can be done with anger and self-pity. Resentful, annoyed, and even sometimes anxious can be grouped under anger. With regard to anger, Wessler and Hankin Wessler (1997) have found that if the feelings coinciding with reported anxiety are probed, anger is often predominant. A typical CAT discussion of this might be as follows:

Client: I was feeling anxious.

Therapist: What were you feeling anxious about?

Client: That I wasn't going to get my way.

Therapist: And how would you feel if you didn't get your way?

Client: Well, anxious.

Therapist: Would you feel anything else in addition to anxious?

Client: Well, upset that I didn't get what I wanted.

Therapist: What thought might you have as you felt upset?

Client: "Damn it, give me what I want for once in my life!"

Therapist: What tone of voice were you using there?

Client: Anger. It was an angry tone. I guess I'd be feeling angry as I thought that.

Feelings such as pain, protectiveness, and resentfulness may lead to a discussion of self-pity. A father recently said he felt "protective" while disciplining his daughter, as he thought, "The world is hard enough on her as it is." He then revealed that he (falsely) assumed this because he believes that the world has treated him unfairly. A parent who said she felt "resentful" and thought "Ay, another problem to deal with" revealed the additional thought (a justifying cognition): "I always have to deal with everybody's crap. Why don't they solve their own problems and leave me alone." While there is certainly some anger in this statement (which almost always goes hand-in-hand with self-pity), exploration of this belief led to a "poor me" feeling in the parent.

Once feelings are grouped, the therapist can explain that these emotions are quite normal in parents sometimes and are nothing to be ashamed of or embarrassed about; however, they are *unhelpful* to their children as well as to themselves. Moreover, the therapist can discuss CAT's motivational theory here—second departure from other cognitive–behavioral parenting groups: All parents are nonconsciously driven to repeat familiar, long-standing feelings in spite of consciously wanting to do the "right thing" for their children. Parents are then asked to look at their thoughts and feelings while parenting and think of other situations in their lives during which they have had similar thoughts and feelings. Almost always, group members begin to make connections: They feel this way at work or with a spouse or with their parents. The idea of security-seeking maneuvers is then introduced (without using the term itself) as the therapist suggests that all individuals have lifelong behavior patterns that we unconsciously create to stir up familiar but unhelpful old feelings.

Finally, the therapist links long-standing feelings to how the parents were parented: "As innocent kids, we all followed our parents' lead concerning how we felt about ourselves and others. This was all we knew, and it came to define who we were and are."

Once group members understand how their parenting is influenced by their own parents' parenting, the therapist introduces the idea of parenting styles. A handout of parenting styles that Richard Wessler (personal communication, August 5, 1996) derived from his clinical experience is distributed (see Table 13.3). Each parenting style is discussed in the context of parents identifying their own parents' dominant parenting styles and how they affected the parents both as individuals and as parents. This is usually one of the liveliest parts of the group. Members noncritically help each other to make the connections between how they were raised and how they are raising their own children. Moreover, how they were raised

TABLE 13.3
Wessler's (1996) Grid of Parenting Styles and Their Impact
on Children

Parenting Style	Children's Feelings	Children's Responses	Kids Become as Adults
Yelling and abuse	Intimidation, resentment	Obey because of fear	Passive, dependent, unassertive
Whining and complaining	Pity for parents	Obey because of guilt	Whiny, complaining people-pleasers
Defer to kids	Entitled	Nothing to obey —kids have the power	Selfish, antisocial, prone to addiction
Kind but domineering	Incompetent	Obey without question	Dependent, immature, fearful
Respectful, encouraging	Secure	Cooperative	Autonomous, yet loyal to family

Note. From R. Wessler, August 5, 1996, personal communication. Reprinted with permission.

is linked to what parents often feel (personotypic affect) while disciplining their children. The parenting style of each parents' parents is written on the blackboard (titled "How Your Parents Raised You"), followed by the parents' personotypic affect ("What You Usually Feel As You Parent") and justifying cognitions ("What You Think While Parenting").

Sessions 8 Through 11: Learning to Manage Feelings While Parenting Logically

The next session begins with a review of the parenting flowchart presented here as Exhibit 13.2. This integrates all of the components that have been presented up to this point. Step 1 of the flowchart incorporates some of the behavioral strategies discussed and practiced in Sessions 3 and 4: that parents must anticipate behavioral problems and establish clear and appropriate behavioral consequences before such problems occur, and that they must communicate these consequences clearly to the child. Step 2 involves what the group discussed in Sessions 6 and 7: understanding and identifying personotypic affect and related justifying cognitions during parenting. Step 2 also stresses that these are signals to the parent that these feelings must be dealt with therapeutically if the parent is then to respond to the child effectively.

Step 4 incorporates the developmental reframes that parents learned in Session 5. This helps parents to avoid misinterpreting the child's misbehaviors in order to feed and rekindle personotypic affect. Instead, parents can see their child's difficult behaviors as a normal part of growing up or as a normal extension of their particular temperament. Step 5 is the end

EXHIBIT 13.2
Parenting Flowchart

Step	Parent's Task
1	Even before any misbehavior happens, establish rules and reasonable logical consequences for misbehaviors in your child. Let your child know ahead of time what will happen when he/she misbehaves.
2	When the misbehavior happens, be aware of what you are feeling. Old familiar feelings are red flags: WARNING—WORK AHEAD!
3	Put the feelings in your back pocket for the time being.
4	What is the (positive) message of your child's misbehavior? For example, is he/she trying to tell you "I need to feel independent" or "I need to feel strong" or "I need to know the limits of your rules?"
5	How will you respond? What is the predetermined consequence for this misbehavior (see Step 1)? What is the best message for you to give your child so that he/she learns best and with the least conflict (and least hassle for you)?

result of calming down personotypic affect and reframing the child's misbehaviors more empathically: How can the parent respond to the child's behavior effectively, with the least parent–child conflict, and in a way that will help the child to learn what is most developmentally helpful?

The emphasis of the following sessions, parents are told, will be on Step 3: putting their feelings in their "back pockets" while interacting with and disciplining their children. Wessler and Hankin Wessler (1997) defined emotional self-care as consisting of "soothing one's feelings, reducing their intensity, and reassuring oneself" (p. 183). In the CAT parenting group, this consists of (a) breaking one's emotional ties to one's parents, (b) learning to calm down one's personotypic affect, and (c) strengthening the influence of logical thoughts over personotypic affect and justifying cognitions.

Breaking Emotional Ties to One's Parents

Group members practice identifying feelings and thoughts familiar to them from childhood that arise while parenting. They then each generate statements they can say to themselves to combat these thoughts and feelings. Role playing (Greenberg, Rice, & Elliott, 1993) often facilitates the discovery of powerful, useful statements that rebuff personotypic affect. I might have a parent role play his or her parent saying something that generates personotypic affect. Then, I ask the parent to respond to this statement in a mature, logical way. The client may have to shuttle between role playing his or her parent and himself or herself until a series of helpful statements are generated. Clients may respond to the role-played parent, for example, with "Leave me alone," "You are not helpful to me," or "I am tired of your criticism." They then shape these responses with statements they can make to themselves, and they rehearse them.

Soothing Personotypic Affect

Clients are then asked to think of statements that will calm down shame, anger, and self-pity while parenting. They are asked to close their eyes (only if they want to) and think of someone in their life who has been successful at calming them down while they were experiencing those feelings—to imagine what they said and how they said it. Sometimes, parents say they have never been soothed by another person, so I ask them to imagine what they *would have* liked someone to say to them and then to stay with this fantasy for a while. I then ask parents to have their imagined person generate other soothing statements and practice saying these. Parents then share these images and statements with one another.

> Bob, a 28-year-old father, said that his mother was too self-involved and his father too dependent on him to ever take note of or calm down his feelings. Bob realized that he did not want to imagine either parent soothing his feelings, as he still felt too angry at them, but instead wanted to conjure up a "personal trainer" who could serve as a mentor, coach, and cheerleader for him. Once this trainer could be imagined by Bob, he could easily generate a series of statements and ideas that he could say to himself to manage his angry, fearful feelings.

It should be noted that this process is different from other cognitive–behavioral parenting groups that stress "rational and coping thoughts" to debate automatic thoughts that emanate from feelings. For example, Evans and McAdam (1988, p. 230) had parents respond to the automatic thought "Why can't I control my child?" with the self-statement, "I can control him/her a lot of the time." However, in my experience, a parent will not be able to do this when his or her feelings are flowing at full power. Feelings must first be addressed before thoughts can be debated logically. For this reason, Taffel (1991) acknowledged that angry parents may need to remove themselves from a heated conflict with their child, calm themselves down, and return to the situation later (essentially giving themselves a time-out) if they cannot successfully calm down their feelings in the moment.

Locking the "Inner Child" in the Closet

Parents then practice generating logical, adult responses to the justifying cognitions that are intertwined with their personotypic affect, much as various cognitive–behavioral approaches to dealing with negative feelings do (e.g., Evans & McAdam, 1988; Joyce, 1995; Nixon & Singer, 1993). Parents are asked to split themselves into what I call the *feeling part* (personotypic affect and justifying cognitions) and the *logical part*. After having both parts describe themselves, the logical part then responds to the feeling part with mature statements that set limits on and debate the childlike (and childish) statements of the feeling part. This process often resembles experiential techniques such as splits and the two-chair dialogue described by Greenberg et al. (1993) and Greenberg and Safran (1987), but rather than using these techniques to enhance affect, here affect is softened as cognition is strengthened. A typical dialogue between the logical and feeling parts might go something like this:

Feeling Part (FP): I'm so tired of trying to discipline my kid without results.

Logical Part (LP): Don't sacrifice your child's development to your own feelings.

FP: I don't care!

LP: You're acting like a spoiled child. You know that if you keep trying, you'll have some success. You just can't expect immediate results, like a little kid would. Be patient!

FP: I don't think I'll make it.

LP: You're just assuming that to feel sorry for yourself. You don't know if you'll make it or not. Just hang in there—it's worked for you in the past. Now—get to work!

FP: But I don't want to!

LP: Then don't expect anything to change. And then don't complain about it.

There is no "cookbook" method by which parents can calm down personotypic affect and replace it with logical thoughts. Just as young children are different in how they can be soothed effectively, so too are parents different in what stops the expression of their personotypic affect. Some parents find it helpful in calming down their personotypic affect to access the voice of someone else who can or could calm them down when upset (a friend, relative, teacher, or coach). Other parents need to yell at themselves ("Just cut it out already!") to diminish personotypic affect. Others access a helpful image, such as a picture of themselves as a wimpy, tantruming child, which embarrasses them out of feeling personotypic affect. Still others use humor to joke themselves out of the melodramatic feelings of rage, shame, and self-pity, whereas others make themselves feel guilty for indulging in having such unhelpful, self-involved feelings. Finally, others sometimes find it helpful to say to themselves: "I sound just like my father/mother. That's the last thing I want!" to use cognitive dissonance to shock themselves out of experiencing personotypic affect.

Once parents have amassed and practiced various strategies for calming down personotypic affect and accessing logical thoughts, they then revisit the parenting flowchart (see Exhibit 13.2) and apply it to various problematic situations with their children. Parents are asked to describe a typical difficult parent–child interaction, to review how they handled the situation in the past, and then to apply the flowchart and, if applicable, new behavioral strategies they have learned.

Loida described how, when her 14-year-old daughter yells at her and refuses to do what she asks (a chore, homework, etc.), Loida's first impulse is to hit her, as Loida's parents used to do to her when she was a child. Instead, Loida goes to her bedroom, shuts the door, and becomes "depressed" until her husband comes home from work and addresses the situation. Loida said that she wants to be able to handle these situations herself—to learn other parenting alternatives and also to teach her daughter that she cannot always have her way with others.

During Session 9, and using the flowchart and what she learned during previous group meetings, Loida set these logical consequences for her daughter: If her daughter does not do one chore and at least 1 hour of homework each weeknight, she will not watch any television or make any telephone calls to friends that evening. If her daughter "raises a stink" about this when reminded of these consequences, she will be grounded that Friday evening (Step 1).

In group, Loida then imagined how she would feel as her daughter does not accept these consequences and begins to have an adolescent-style tantrum. Loida said she would feel enraged ("How dare you disobey me") but also scared of her own anger, and hopeless ("I want to hit her, but I can't. I'll do nothing."). Loida then practiced saying to herself, "Wait a minute. This means I have to slow down and work on my feelings here. Don't go into the bedroom and do nothing!" (Step 2).

Loida then decided that she would in fact go into her bedroom, but only for a few minutes in order to calm herself down. Loida then practiced emotional self-care (Step 3). She practiced saying to herself (her logical voice), "You do not have to hit your child like your parents did to you. You are not your mother; you are not your father." Loida then decided that she would access the soothing voice of her grandmother, the only adult who nurtured her as a child. Her grandmother's voice would say to her, "You can do it! You don't have to hide in your room. I have faith in you, Loida. You can be strong; you can. Go out there and be a good mother. I know you can do it." With the therapist's prompting, Loida then accessed her feeling part and responded, "But I may mess up, Grandma. It's safer in the bedroom." The Grandmother voice then replied, "But you will not help your daughter this way. Be there for her the way I was for you. If you mess up, you can always try again. You've never hit her even once, so you won't start now. Go, go." Loida practiced variations of this conversation four or five times in the group.

Loida also reminded herself that her daughter's oppositionalism is a normal developmental breaking away from parental control in order to begin to establish her own identity and autonomy during adolescence (Step 4). Loida acknowledged that she and her daughter were extremely close, and this made this developmental process more painful for her. A group member then pointed out that her daughter's dramatic pushing away was a testimony to how much she loved Loida: "If she didn't care so much for you, she wouldn't need to push you away so hard." Loida said that she would remind herself of this when feeling rejected by her daughter.

Finally, Loida practiced reminding her daughter of the preestablished consequences for her misbehaviors, and saying this in a firm but not enraged or hurt tone of voice (Step 5). She also practiced telling her daughter, "I know you're a teenager and need your space and want to do things your way. I love that about you, but you still are a part of this household too and you go to school, and you need to do your responsibilities. Be you and also be responsible."

By the end of this exercise, Loida had gone through the entire parenting flowchart three or four times as she practiced her new parenting strategies. The group members praised Loida during and after the exercise.

After verbally running through an application of the flowchart, each parent then coaches another group member on how to role play his or her child (group members often know each other's children by this time), and they then role play themselves applying the flowchart to the situation. If needed, parents repeat this role play several times to consolidate it.

In addition, parents are encouraged to try out what they have role played between sessions and to report back to the group. Parents will most probably not succeed the first time they apply what they have learned, because it is hard to break old habits, especially in the actual situation with the child. When parents report that they were not successful, the group then collaborates in (nonjudgmental) problem solving, and the parent then tries again.

Session 12: The Past and the Future

The last session is an opportunity for parents to review not only what they have learned but also to assess whether their personal goals for the group were met. Members are then encouraged to formulate goals for themselves as parents that they will work on in the future, and they attempt to formulate how they will go about achieving these goals. The therapist often offers to continue working individually with parents on an as-needed basis as they begin to implement what they have practiced in the group.

The therapist also asks for feedback concerning the strengths and weaknesses of the group—what was most helpful and least helpful to them. Many of the best innovations of the group, such as the parenting flowchart, have come from parents' suggestions.

SUMMARY

This chapter has reviewed how cognitive appraisal therapy, or CAT (Wessler, 1987; Wessler & Hankin Wessler, 1986, 1997), can be used in a group format to help parents who are normally "resistant" to changing their parenting styles (but who nevertheless often join such groups, ostensibly to change). Traditional cognitive–behavioral parenting groups often run the risk of enhancing these parents' shame, rage, and self-pity by presenting them with an opportunity to fail to follow the group's protocols. Humanistic "parent support" groups often enhance these parents' self-pitying complaining by providing them with infantilizing sympathy rather than with empathy and firmness.

An exploration of these parents' feelings in the group often yields the information that they nonconsciously use the parent–child relationship to mirror other relationships in their lives and to rekindle long-standing negative affect (in particular, shame, rage, and self-pity) associated with these relationships. CAT can serve as a model that integrates a focus on long-standing affect and emotional self-care with more traditional cognitive and behavioral approaches to parenting. It was argued in this chapter that, for some parents, unless they learn how to identify and manage long-standing negative affect that gets stirred up in the parent–child interaction (and to see how they unconsciously maneuver this interaction to rev up such feelings), they will not be able to make use of new parenting strategies.

A 12-session parenting group was outlined that uses the general CAT principles of creating a shame-free therapeutic environment while focusing on shame, rage, and self-pity in the parent. Approximately the first half of the group provides a model by which parents can learn to identify their negative feelings while implementing more traditional behavioral and developmental parenting principles, which are also presented to group members. The second half of the CAT group uses role playing as well as experiential and cognitive interventions to help parents practice emotional self-care, which consists of breaking emotional ties to one's parents, soothing long-standing negative feelings, reducing their intensity, and reassuring and encouraging oneself. All facets of the group are ultimately integrated, as parents practice emotional self-care and reframing their children's misbehaviors within a developmental framework while implementing appropriate behavioral strategies.

REFERENCES

Anastopoulos, A. D., & Barkley, R. A. (1989). A training program for parents of children with attention deficit-hyperactivity disorder. In C. E. Schaefer & J. M. Briesmseister (Eds.), *Handbook of parent training: Parents as co-therapists for children's behavior problems* (pp. 83–104). New York: Wiley.

Baker, B. L., Brightman, A. J., Heifetz, L. J., & Murphy, D. M. (1976). *Behavior problems*. Champaign, IL: Research Press.

Beck, A. T., Rush, A. J., Shaw, B. F., & Emery, G. (1979). *Cognitive therapy of depression*. New York: Guilford Press.

Bowlby, J. (1969). *Attachment*. New York: Basic Books.

Christiansen, A., Johnson, S. M., Phillips, S., & Glasgow, R. E. (1980). Cost efficiency in family behavior therapy. *Behavior Therapy, 11*, 208–226.

Clark, L. (1985). *SOS! Help for parents*. Bowling Green, KY: Parents Press.

Douglas, J. (1989). Training parents to manage their child's sleep problem. In C. E. Schaefer & J. M. Briesmseister (Eds.), *Handbook of parent training: Parents as co-therapists for children's behavior problems* (pp. 13–37). New York: Wiley.

Dubey, D. R., O'Leary, S. G., & Kaufman, K. F. (1983). Training parents of hyperactive children in child management: A comparative outcome study. *Journal of Abnormal Child Psychology, 11*, 229–246.

Evans, E. H., & McAdam, E. (1988). Training parents to be effective. In W. Dryden & P. Trower (Eds.), *Developments in cognitive psychotherapy* (pp. 218–238). London: Sage.

Forehand, R. L., & McMahon, R. J. (1981). *Helping the noncompliant child*. New York: Guilford Press.

Greenberg, L. S., Rice, L. N., & Elliott, R. (1993). *Facilitating emotional change: The moment-by-moment process*. New York: Guilford Press.

Greenberg, L. S., & Safran, J. D. (1987). *Emotion in psychotherapy: Affect, cognition, and the process of change*. New York: Guilford Press.

Greenspan, S. I. (1992). *Infancy and early childhood: The practice of clinical assessment and intervention with emotional and developmental challenges*. Madison, CT: International Universities Press.

Griest, D. L., & Forehand, R. (1982). How can I get any parent training done with all these other problems going on?: The role of family variables in child behavior therapy. *Child and Family Behavior Therapy, 41*, 73–80.

Haley, J. (1976). *Problem-solving therapy*. San Francisco: Jossey-Bass.

Horne, A. M., & Patterson, G. R. (1980). Working with parents of aggressive children. In R. R. Abidin (Ed.), *Parent education and intervention handbook* (pp. 159–184). Springfield, IL: Charles C Thomas.

Jernberg, A. M. (1989). Training parents of failure-to-attach children. In C. E. Schaefer & J. M. Briesmseister (Eds.), *Handbook of parent training: Parents as co-therapists for children's behavior problems* (pp. 392–413). New York: Wiley.

Joyce, M. R. (1995). Emotional relief for parents: Is rational–emotive parent education effective? *Journal of Rational–Emotive and Cognitive Behavior Therapy, 13,* 55–75.

Kagan, J. (1989). *Unstable ideas.* Cambridge, MA: Harvard University Press.

McMahon, R. J., & Forehand, R. (1984). Parent training for the noncompliant child: Treatment outcome, generalization, and adjunctive therapy procedures. In R. F. Dangel & R. A. Polster (Eds.), *Parent training: Foundations of research and practice* (pp. 298–328). New York: Guilford Press.

Nathanson, D. L. (1992). *Shame and pride: Affect, sex, and the birth of the self.* New York: Norton.

Newberger, C. M. (1985). Parents and practitioners as developmental theorists. In E. H. Newberger & R. Bourne (Eds.), *Unhappy families* (pp. 131–144). Littleton, MA: PSG Publishing.

Nixon, C. D., & Singer, G. H. (1993). Group cognitive–behavioural treatment for excessive parental self-blame and guilt. *American Journal of Mental Retardation, 97,* 665–672.

Patterson, G. R. (1976). *Living with children: New methods for parents and teachers.* Champaign, IL: Research Press.

Plutchik, R. (1981). Group cohesion in psychoevolutionary context. In H. Kellerman (Ed.), *Group cohesion.* Baltimore: Grunne and Stratton.

Safran, J. D., & Segal, Z. V. (1990). *Interpersonal process in cognitive therapy.* New York: Basic Books.

Schaefer, C. E., & Briesmseister, J. M. (1989). *Handbook of parent training: Parents as co-therapists for children's behavior problems.* New York: Wiley.

Stern, D. N. (1985). *The interpersonal world of the infant.* New York: Basic Books.

Stern, J. (1996). A cognitive appraisal approach to parent training with affect-driven parents. *Psychotherapy, 33,* 77–84.

Taffel, R. (1991). *Parenting by heart.* Reading, MA: Addison-Wesley.

Tangney, J. P. (1991). Moral affect: The good, the bad, and the ugly. *Journal of Personality and Social Psychology, 61,* 598–607.

Tangney, J. P., Wagner, P., Fletcher, C., & Gramzow, R. (1992). Shamed into anger? The relation of shame and guilt to anger and self-reported aggression. *Journal of Personality and Social Psychology, 62,* 669–675.

Trad, P. V. (1992). *Interventions with infants and parents: The theory and practice of previewing.* New York: Wiley.

Trad, P. V. (1993). *Short-term parent–infant psychotherapy.* New York: Basic Books.

Wessler, R. L. (1987). Listening to oneself: Cognitive appraisal therapy. In W. Dryden (Ed.), *Key cases in psychotherapy* (pp. 176–212). London: Croom-Holm.

Wessler, R. L. (1993a). Cognitive appraisal therapy and disorders of personality. In K. T. Kuehlwein & H. Rosen (Eds.), *Cognitive therapies in action: Evolving innovative practice* (pp. 240–267). San Francisco: Jossey-Bass.

Wessler, R. L. (1993b). Groups. In G. Stricker & J. R. Gold (Eds.), *Comprehensive handbook of psychotherapy integration* (pp. 453–464). New York: Plenum.

Wessler, R. L., & Hankin Wessler, S. W. R. (1986). Cognitive appraisal therapy (CAT). In W. Dryden & W. L. Golden (Eds.), *Cognitive–behavioural approaches to psychotherapy*. London: Harper & Row.

Wessler, R. L., & Hankin Wessler, S. (1997). Counseling and society. In J. S. Palmer & V. Varma (Eds.), *The future of counselling and psychotherapy* (pp. 167–190). London: Sage.

Yalom, I. D. (1985). *The theory and practice of group psychotherapy*. New York: Basic.

14

CLIENTS IN PARTIAL HOSPITALIZATION SETTINGS

AMY S. WITT-BROWDER

This chapter originally began when I (a therapist working in a traditional partial hospital program who is thoroughly convinced of the superior benefits of cognitive–behavioral therapy) was asked to research the use of cognitive therapy in a group setting and to provide a model for its use in a partial hospital program. The results of the research pointed to the efficacy of a comprehensive cognitive milieu in partial hospitalization. I was then requested to develop a protocol for such a comprehensive program. This chapter is based on that proposal and is not an example of a program that has been fully implemented. The clinical examples of cognitive techniques and client exchanges are based on actual interactions within a partial hospital program that uses cognitive therapy but does not represent a strict, comprehensive cognitive milieu.

In this chapter, I discuss the rationale for the development of a comprehensive cognitive milieu within a partial hospital setting. The chapter briefly looks at the benefits of the comprehensive milieu as compared with an add-on model. The steps necessary for the development and implementation of such a program, including staff requirements and training, patient screening and orientation, and treatment planning and programming, are discussed. An example of a schedule for a typical partial hospital day and examples of the use of cognitive therapy in programming are provided.

USE OF COGNITIVE GROUP THERAPY IN PARTIAL HOSPITALIZATION

Most research and writing regarding cognitive group therapy have dealt with the practice of therapy in outpatient groups. However, cognitive group therapy has also been used in inpatient treatment programs (Freeman, Schrodt, Gilson, & Ludgate, 1993) and in psychiatric partial hospital programs (Loring & Fraboni, 1990). A partial hospital program is an intensive, time-limited, outpatient treatment program that offers therapeutically intensive, coordinated, and structured clinical services within a stable therapeutic milieu. Partial hospital programs provide a minimum of 20 hours of programming per week in which clients participate in a variety of interconnected therapeutic activities, most of which take place in a group setting. The partial hospital program provides clients with the security and structure of an inpatient program during the day while allowing them to return home in the evening. The goal of partial hospitalization is to stabilize patients with the intention of averting or shortening a hospital stay (Block & Lefkovitz, 1994; Dibella, Weitz, Poynter-Berg, & Yurmark, 1982).

Clients admitted to partial hospital programs experience psychiatric symptoms severe enough to cause significant impairment in daily social, vocational, educational, or personal care activities. Such clients have usually already proved themselves unable to make sufficient clinical gains in an outpatient setting, or the severity of their presenting symptoms raises doubt about the appropriateness or success of traditional outpatient therapy. A referral to a partial hospital program, rather than inpatient hospitalization, is usually made when the following criteria are met: (a) The client can exhibit adequate behavioral control such that he or she is not considered a danger to self or others; (b) the client is able to physically attend and actively participate in daily programming; and (c) he or she has a living situation that assists in maintaining minimum functioning within the least restrictive environment (Block & Lefkovitz, 1994).

There are two basic models for partial hospital programs. Some programs offer more extended clinical services for high-risk or seriously impaired clients with persistent emotional and behavioral problems (i.e., severe psychotic disorders, multiple diagnoses, and extreme cases of personality disorder). In such cases, the partial hospital program may serve as an alternative to long-term institutionalization. Other programs focus on an acute-care model that stresses crisis stabilization to avert hospitalization or to help clients transition from hospitalization into community life. The acute focus of this model tends to create an environment in which clients have a wide range of diagnoses and may vary tremendously in terms of their level of functioning (Block & Lefkovitz, 1994; Dibella et al., 1982). To accommodate this diversity, some partial hospital programs may offer separate programming tracts such as special groups for geriatric clients, clients with substance abuse and dual diagnosis issues, or clients who are higher and lower functioning in terms of their verbal skills, concentration, and intellectual abilities. At times clients from different tracts may come together in larger groups for specific activities. Despite the many differences among partial hospital clients, Loring and Fraboni (1990) noted that most clients in their partial hospital program shared common symptoms of depression, poor self-esteem, anxiety, interpersonal problems, and difficulty dealing with stressors.

The time-limited, symptom-oriented, economical nature of cognitive therapy makes it a logical choice for practice within the acute-care partial hospital setting. Wright, Thase, Ludgate, and Beck (1993) identified models for the practice of cognitive group therapy in inpatient settings, which could be applied in the partial hospital setting. The first is an "add-on" model in which the cognitive therapy group is used to supplement treatment in an existing milieu (Wright et al., 1993). For example, the partial hospital client could spend 1 or 2 hours of the program day in a cognitive therapy group and spend the rest of the time in more psychodynamic group therapy, art therapy, movement therapy, or recreational therapy. Loring and Fraboni (1990) discussed the application of such groups in a partial hospital setting. They initially used a cognitive group therapy format in an open-ended, heterogeneous stress management group and later in a group of higher functioning schizophrenics focusing on interaction skills. In both instances, higher functioning clients tended to understand concepts, complete homework assignments, and benefit from cognitive therapy, while many lower functioning clients found the concepts of cognitive therapy incomprehensible. Loring and Fraboni (1990) later obtained more effective therapeutic results with smaller closed groups (five clients per group) that met for a predetermined period of twelve 2-hour sessions. The clients in such groups were selected on the basis of (a) requesting cognitive therapy and (b) willingness to do regular homework. These results indicate that cognitive therapy may not be appropriate for lower functioning or more severely impaired partial hospital clients but may be empowering to higher functioning clients.

Loring and Fraboni (1990) also reported that in using an add-on model, attendance of other noncognitive groups tended to blur the emphasis on the cognitive concepts and homework. Similar problems in the use of add-on groups exist in inpatient settings. Wright et al. (1993) noted that if other therapists or staff members do not agree with the cognitive model, clients may become confused, and cognitive therapists may be required to spend excessive therapeutic time defending the model. They maintain that the add-on model limits the potential success of cognitive therapy and that a comprehensive cognitive milieu therapy is more beneficial. Such a comprehensive cognitive model has been implemented in numerous inpatient facilities (Wright et al., 1993). However, utilization of comprehensive cognitive milieu therapy in a partial hospital program has not yet been reported. Nonetheless, such a model does appear adaptable to the partial hospital format.

DEVELOPING A COMPREHENSIVE COGNITIVE PARTIAL HOSPITAL PROGRAM

The steps necessary for developing a comprehensive cognitive partial hospital program are almost identical to those listed by Wright et al. (1993) for the development of a comprehensive cognitive therapy inpatient unit. The first step is to describe the rationale for establishment of such a program, and the second step is to establish goals for the program. When reviewing the fundamental goals of acute partial hospitalization and the fundamental goals of cognitive therapy, the rationale for a combination of the two seems obvious. By definition, partial hospital programs strive to provide intensive, active, and structured clinical services within a limited time frame. Cognitive therapy has been designed to be intensive, active, structured, and time limited and has been proven effective. The cognitive model also provides an excellent framework for the presentation of educational information and can be used to impose structure within the group setting (Yost, Beutler, Corbishley, & Allender, 1986). The establishment of a structured environment and presentation of educational information are considered fundamental aspects of partial hospitalization (Dibella et al., 1982). The comprehensive cognitive therapy model also focuses on case conceptualization and formulation of a comprehensive treatment plan. Likewise, acute partial hospital programs place much emphasis on the development of, and adherence to a comprehensive treatment plan (Block & Lefkovitz, 1994). Furthermore, therapists in partial hospital programs, like cognitive therapists, attempt to establish a collaborative relationship with clients and to actively involve clients in the formulation of their treatment plans as well other aspects of treatment.

Establishment of a comprehensive cognitive milieu does not mean that a purist version of cognitive therapy is practiced throughout all aspects of the treatment program. However, in the cognitive milieu, all staff members share a common philosophy of treatment. Psychotherapists focus on cognitive theory and techniques as the basis of treatment, whereas adjunct staff (recreational therapists, occupational therapists, art therapists, nurses, etc.) provide therapeutic activities that reinforce the learning of cognitive principles (Wright et al., 1993).

Staff Requirements and Training

The development of a comprehensive cognitive milieu necessitates extensive training and development of all staff, including psychiatrists, psychologists and psychological associates, social workers, nurses, and other adjunct staff, such as occupational therapists, art therapists, and activities therapists. All staff must be well versed in the principles and goals of cognitive therapy and cognitive–behavioral techniques and be specifically adept in the application of cognitive–behavioral therapy within a group setting. Partial hospital programs are often primarily staffed by professionals with master's and bachelor's degrees who may have had little or no training in the principles of cognitive therapy. This may necessitate more extensive staff training but can be considered beneficial in that staff do not enter into the training process with erroneous or poorly conceived notions regarding cognitive technique. In her discussion of the development of a comprehensive cognitive inpatient milieu, Padesky (1993) noted that training in cognitive therapy can be provided by cognitive therapists already affiliated with a program or institution, by outside cognitive therapy consultants, or by sending staff members to training sessions conducted by professionals at other facilities. Training experiences generally include participation in workshops or continuing education classes, reading, watching and discussing videotapes, and on-site supervision. Padesky (1993) stressed that ongoing education and supervision are essential to maintaining quality services, especially in the first year of a program. The extensive training required of all staff prior to implementation of the program and the ongoing training of any newly hired staff can be very time consuming and expensive. Therefore, the creation of such a comprehensive partial hospital program may be difficult unless it is affiliated with an already existing inpatient cognitive therapy unit or possibly an outpatient clinic specializing in cognitive therapy.

Staff continuity is an important aspect of any partial hospital program, but it becomes an even greater issue when attempting to establish a comprehensive cognitive milieu. Ideally, all staff members work in the partial hospital setting on a full-time basis, but often this may not be financially feasible. Partial hospital programs are often forced to contract certain services on a part-time basis or to share staff with outpatient or inpatient programs within the same facility. However, it is essential that at least some core staff members are present full time within the partial hospital setting to provide day-to-day consistency and continuity. Full-time staff members become familiar with clients' specific issues and schemas as well as their most frequently occurring automatic thoughts and cognitive distortions. This allows the staff to set up behavioral experiments and graded task assignment and follow through with the results. Full-time staff members can provide this information to part-time staff to coordinate treatment goals. Part-time staff members may find themselves entering the cognitive milieu after spending several hours involved in programming with a more psychodynamic, strict behavioral, or interpersonal focus. This can result in difficulty transitioning to the cognitive milieu. However, daily treatment planning and group supervision meetings can help to promote a team approach to treatment in which staff feel comfortable asking for and receiving assistance and feedback from others.

Patient Screening and Orientation

Hollon and Shaw (1979) stressed the importance of the intake evaluation in screening clients who are appropriate for cognitive group therapy. Clients who are judged inappropriate for a cognitive therapy group because of severe psychosis or organic impairment should be referred to alternative behavioral or activities-based programs. Hollon and Shaw also discussed the necessity of using the intake evaluation to orient clients to the principles and goals of cognitive therapy. This becomes especially important in an acute partial hospital setting in which clients typically start and exit treatment at varying times, forcing groups to adhere to an open-ended format. Providing information about cognitive therapy to clients prior to their entering group can help prevent excessive review or duplication of information within the ongoing group. Clients should be given orientation information on cognitive therapy and told about the basic procedures of the program in simple terms. The following is an example of a therapist's explanation used effectively with clients of diverse levels of functioning:

> The goal of this program is to help people meet their goals for feeling and functioning better. We know that thoughts, emotions, behaviors, and biological processes affect each other. (This concept is often best explained through a chart or by drawing on the chalkboard.) For example, let's say that you are depressed. Usually, when you are depressed you emotionally feel sad, you have negative thoughts that everything is terrible and it's never going to get better. You also feel physically bad, tired all the time, have sleep problems and appetite problems, and you often can't do your regular activities. Does that sound right? Okay, let's say something happens to upset you. You burn dinner and you start to have negative thoughts about it. Those thoughts cause you to feel worse emotionally, which can cause you to feel worse physically and even cause chemical changes in your body. Then because of your thoughts, emotions, and biology, you have a harder time performing necessary behaviors. This causes you to have more negative thoughts and feel sadder until you end up in a downward spiral and everything seems hopeless. The same type of downward spiral can occur with other emotions such as anxiety. This downward spiral presents a chicken-and-egg puzzle. That is, thoughts, emotions, biology, and behavior affect each other but often no one knows where the process starts or

what problems come first. The process may actually start in different places for different people. However, the important issue is that we need to intervene and stop the process somewhere. Your psychiatrist prescribes medication with the purpose of changing the biological part of this process. In therapy, we try to stop this process by changing thoughts and behaviors. While you are here, we are going to be talking a lot about your thought processes and doing activities that focus on changing thoughts and behaviors. We want you to learn ways that you can change this process yourself outside of therapy.

Treatment Planning

Treatment planning is an essential part of the partial hospital program. In the treatment planning process, staff members cooperate to translate clinical assessment and case conceptualization into a specific set of goals and methods for bringing about behavioral change. The *Standards and Guidelines of Partial Hospitalization: Adult Programs* (Block & Lefkovitz, 1994) specify that a treatment plan should be formalized and documented within 5 treatment days of the client's beginning a partial hospital program. Clients gain a sense of control and involvement in their treatment through participation in the formulation of their treatment plan. One way of involving clients is by having them make a list or complete a worksheet providing their own ideas about their current problems and goals for treatment. Although a variety of clients with diverse diagnoses may be entering the same partial hospital program, many include on their lists problems such as depression, poor self-esteem, relationship difficulties, and anxiety. This list can be used to help formulate an official treatment plan. Once staff members complete the treatment plan, it is reviewed individually with the client, and all aspects are explained in terms that the client can understand. The client can then ask questions and give input regarding any changes or additions that should be made to the treatment plan; these alterations can be negotiated. An example of a possible treatment plan is presented in Exhibit 14.1.

There are many acceptable formats for development of client treatment plans, but the selected format should include certain elements. The treatment plan must list the problems to be addressed. Because of the limited time frame of the acute partial hospital model, it is usually helpful to limit the treatment plan to no more than four target problems. This allows staff and clients to focus treatment, set reasonable goals, and identify issues to be addressed in follow-up care. Target problems must be defined in specific behavioral terms that make it possible to identify (a) clear outcome goals in terms of behavioral change; (b) short-term behavioral, cognitive, and affective objectives that form the steps toward meeting the overall outcome goal; and (c) the cognitive–behavioral strategies and tech-

EXHIBIT 14.1
Sample Treatment Plan

Name: Pat S. Date: 06/12/96 Global Assessment of Functioning (GAF): 45

Problem 1: Major depression evidenced by depressed mood, loss of interest, poor concentration, fatigue, insomnia, suicidal ideation, and problems attending to personal hygiene. Symptoms present for past 2 months.

Treatment Objectives:
1. Pat will contract for suicide
2. Pat will discuss in group personal and environmental issues related to depression
3. Pat will complete homework assignments
4. Pat will practice identifying dysfunctional thought patterns
5. Pat will work to develop healthier thought patterns and coping strategies

Interventions:
1. Appointments with psychiatrist for medication monitoring
2. Therapeutic recreation to increase social interaction and physical activity
3. Psychological education regarding depression to focus on symptoms of depression, automatic thoughts, and cognitive distortions
4. Group therapy to examine specific issues related to depression
5. Homework: Activities scheduling, Daily Record of Dysfunctional Thoughts

Outcome Goals:
1. Reduce depressive symptoms (evidenced by reduction in Beck Depression Inventory score)
2. Increase ability to monitor and change dysfunctional thought patterns (evidenced by homework, observation of group participation, and self-report)

Problem 2: Pattern of repeated involvement in physically and emotionally abusive relationships.

Treatment Objectives:
1. Pat will learn to identify behavior that leads to abuse
2. Pat will develop a list of appropriate coping skills to avoid abuse
3. Pat will practice setting appropriate limits with others in group

Interventions:
1. Psychological education regarding self-esteem
2. Psychological education regarding assertiveness training
3. Group therapy to examine
   (a) client's attraction to abusive partners
   (b) cognitions related to abuse
   (c) factors that cause client to choose to stay in relationship
4. Homework: Make list of escalating behaviors that occur prior to abuse, list alternative strategies for dealing with abuse, complete self-esteem worksheets

Outcome Goals:
1. Learn to identify escalating patterns of behavior that lead to abuse and develop strategies for preventing abuse
2. Make changes in patterns that lead to repeated involvement in abusive relationships

niques that will be implemented to assist clients in meeting their goals. The treatment plan format should allow therapists to tailor goals to the specific needs and problems of the client whether these are specific psychiatric issues or more interpersonal difficulties. The treatment plan must also be written in terms that the client can understand. Treatment plans should be reviewed daily by staff in order to coordinate care. Treatment goals and progress should also be reviewed with the client on a regular basis. In the example provided in Exhibit 14.1, the Treatment Objectives section provides a list of what is expected of the client, whereas the Interventions section provides a format for staff to provide treatment. It is helpful for staff to list intervention strategies for all aspects of programming, including recreational therapy, art therapy, and psychological education.

The Daily Schedule

As stated earlier, partial hospital programs are required to provide at least 20 programming hours per week, although some may provide as much as 30 hours or more. Some programs offer different treatment tracts that meet for longer or shorter periods and place clients according to their needs and level of functioning. Other programs provide a full day of treatment 5 days per week but allow some clients to attend on a part-time basis. In trying to establish a comprehensive milieu, therapists will find that it does not seem beneficial to mix groups of full-time and part-time clients. Keeping clients together on an ongoing basis provides a sense of continuity in treatment and promotes affiliation. A possible schedule for the partial hospital day based on a 6-hour programming day is presented in Table 14.1.

The day for partial hospital staff begins with an 8:00 a.m. staff meeting before the clients arrive. The staff reviews each individual's progress in the program, looks at individual treatment plans and goals for the day, and coordinates specific programming to ensure that current individual and group needs are being met. For acute partial hospital programs in which client composition changes frequently, it is particularly important to review programming agendas to ensure that daily activities are meeting current population needs. The daily staff meeting can also serve as a time for orientation of part-time staff and a forum for staff to ask for assistance with anticipated problems.

Community Meeting

The day starts for clients at 9:00 a.m. with a community meeting in which group members take care of any "business for the day." Community meeting generally involves tasks such as assignment of client chores (i.e., making coffee, straightening the group area), ordering lunches, and discussing upcoming absences. It is also a time to review ground rules and

TABLE 14.1
Possible Schedule for Partial Hospital Programming

Time	Monday	Tuesday	Wednesday	Thursday	Friday
9:00–9:30	Community meeting	Community meeting	Community meeting	Community meeting	Community meeting
9:30–10:00	Psychological education	Psychological education	Psychological education	Psychological education	Psychological education
10:00–12:00	Group time	Group time	Group time	Group time	Group time
12:00–1:00	Lunch	Lunch	Lunch	Lunch	Lunch
1:00–2:00	Therapeutic recreation	Therapeutic recreation	Therapeutic recreation	Therapeutic recreation	Therapeutic recreation
2:00–3:00	Journaling	Medication education	Journaling	Medication education	Journaling
2:45–3:00	Wrap-up	Wrap-up	Wrap-up	Wrap-up	Wrap-up

daily schedules. Community meeting may also provide the opportunity for clients to complete daily cognitive therapy self-report forms used for treatment, research, and quality-control purposes. Tools such as the Beck Depression Inventory and the Beck Anxiety Inventory can monitor client progress and demonstrate positive changes, thus reinforcing client participation in therapeutic activities. Clients can also be asked to predict how much they will enjoy the day's scheduled activities. This information can be compared with reported outcomes at the end of the day.

Psychological Education

Psychological education is essential in the development of a comprehensive cognitive milieu. Through psychological education, clients obtain information that forms the basis for understanding experiences and interventions that occur during the partial hospital day. This information enables clients to provide appropriate and effective feedback to peers, often adding to the potency of the feedback and the cohesiveness of the milieu. The psychological education component of the partial hospital day is similar to the educational cognitive therapy group discussed by Free, Oei, and Sanders (1991). However, because the partial hospital schedule often allows clients to spend more time involved in therapy than outpatient treatment, or even an inpatient stay, several differences may arise. For example, more topics may be covered, schema work may receive greater focus, and written and behavioral exercises may be completed within the group to augment educational lectures.

The list of potential psychological education topics is almost inexhaustible, and virtually any issue that can be addressed from a cognitive–behavioral perspective is a possibility. Because the nature of the acute partial hospital setting leads to periodic variation in the type of population treated, it is helpful to create a number of basic educational modules that can be incorporated into the partial hospital curriculum according to the needs of the group. Regardless of the varied diagnoses of clients within the group, most clients can relate to and learn from educational modules focusing on topics such as depression, anxiety, control issues, and self-esteem. Although some clients may find that one topic is more applicable to their situation than another, all can benefit from seeing how thoughts affect behavior and how cognitive–behavioral techniques can be used to affect feelings and actions. One useful strategy is to have weekly educational themes. Clients seem to retain more information when it is reviewed each day of the week; however, they sometimes lose interest if a particular topic is the focus for a long period of time. Educational modules usually consist of brief lectures that provide information on cognitive–behavioral theory or techniques or both. These lectures are followed by structured activities that provide opportunities for further learning, discussion, and personal application. Such activities may involve written worksheets, role play, art projects, and behavioral exercises among others. The use of such techniques and the reliance on group input in discussions may cause educational groups within the partial hospital setting to appear less structured or less purely cognitive than traditional cognitive–behavioral educational groups.

The following excerpts from a psychological education module focusing on self-esteem are good examples of techniques that can be used in programming. In the initial step, the therapist gives a brief interactive lecture to the group using a large chalk board for illustration. The therapist poses the questions to the group, "What is self-esteem? What do we mean when we talk about self-esteem? Can anyone give me a definition?" This usually generates a long list of answers. The therapist guides clients to the appropriate answers and writes them on the board. The list generally includes "how you feel about yourself," "ideas about your value as a person," and "how you view yourself compared with others." The therapist then explains that individuals with positive or high self-esteem have the ability to feel that they are worthwhile regardless of situations, whereas people with negative or low self-esteem often feel inferior in spite of external successes. The therapist then asks the group, "What are the characteristics of people with high self-esteem?" This should generate a list of descriptors such as, "They can feel secure about themselves despite criticism," "They have their own opinions and values," "They can admit and accept failures without feeling like a failure," "They aren't afraid to try new things," and "They don't compare themselves with others and aren't overly competitive." The therapist then leads the group into a discussion on the question, "Does self-esteem depend more on actual qualities or on one's attitude?" Such a question usually results in an involved group discussion with the therapist striving to make the point that self-esteem depends on one's attitude. The group can also be given a handout on "successful failures," listing examples such as Abraham Lincoln and Harry Truman, to facilitate the discussion.

During the next session, the focus of the lecture moves to current barriers to self-esteem, specifically cognitive distortions that affect self-esteem. Each client receives a list of common cognitive distortions explaining how these relate to one's sense of self-esteem (see Exhibit 14.2). The list of cognitive distortions is based on McKay, Davis, and Fanning's (1987) work on cognitive stress intervention. Clients take turns reading the definitions to the group, and each cognitive distortion is discussed to assure that the definition and process are understood. Clients are then given a self-esteem worksheet (see Exhibit 14.3). The group is told that there may be several correct answers to each problem and that problems will be discussed as a group. After clients have successfully completed the worksheet and are familiar with the principles discussed, the therapist asks them to

EXHIBIT 14.2
Cognitive Distortions That Affect Self-Esteem

1. **Personalization:** Thinking that everything that someone does is a reaction to you. Also involves comparing oneself with others to determine who is smarter, better looking, and so on. People with low self-esteem constantly compare themselves with others.
2. **Polarized Thinking:** Things are either black and white, all good or all bad. If you are not perfect, then you are a failure.
3. **Overgeneralization:** Coming to a general conclusion about yourself based on a single incident. If you make one mistake, you expect it to happen over and over again.
4. **Mind Reading:** Without their saying so, you know what people are thinking of you and how they feel about you. You worry about what they will think if you behave in a certain way.
5. **Catastrophizing:** You expect disaster and worry about the worst possible consequences. "What if I fail?"
6. **Control Fallacies:** People who are externally controlled see themselves as helpless victims of fate. Internally controlled individuals can sometimes take too much responsibility and assume that they should be able to control everyone and everything.
7. **Emotional Reasoning:** You believe that what you feel must be true. If you feel stupid and boring, then you must be stupid and boring. If you feel like a failure, then you must be a failure.
8. **Shoulds:** You have a list of ironclad rules about how you (and others) should act. You should look like this. You should be this. You should accomplish this. You feel guilty and worthless when you don't live up to these standards.
9. **Being Right:** You are continually on trial to prove that you are right. Being wrong is unthinkable and you will go to any length to demonstrate your rightness.
10. **Heaven's Reward Fallacy:** You expect that your sacrifice and self-denial will pay off as if someone were keeping score. You feel bitter when the reward doesn't come and assume that you are unworthy of the reward or that others don't care about you.

create their own example of statements that include cognitive distortions. These are collected and mixed. Each client draws and tries to identify the cognitive distortions exemplified. Answers are discussed within the group.

The principles learned in the early discussions and lectures should be reviewed at the beginning of later psychological education sessions. Handouts of the information discussed can be very helpful to clients and can be added to a psychological education notebook that clients take with them at the end of treatment. A discussion later in the module might focus on the question, "What would I do differently if I had more self-esteem, and what gets in the way of my behaving in that manner?" This is often a good way to generate role-play topics for the group or graded task assignments. Another session could address the issue of "Setting yourself up to fail." In this educational session, the therapist helps clients generate a list of ways in which they self-sabotage. This list includes problems such as setting unrealistic goals, being perfectionist, refusing to ask for help, taking a pas-

EXHIBIT 14.3
Self-Esteem Worksheet

The following statements are examples of distorted thinking. Read each statement and identify the cognitive distortions that are being used.

1. I said "Hi" to my boss this morning and he walked past me without looking up or saying anything. I know he is mad at me and dissatisfied with my work. He is probably getting ready to fire me.
Cognitive distortion: _____

2. My mom thinks that I am a failure because I didn't get the kind of job she thinks that I should have. She has never actually told me she is disappointed in me, but I know that she is. She probably tells her friend how disappointed she is in me.
Cognitive distortion: _____

3. I can't believe that I misplaced my keys again. I always do this! I lose everything. I am always so stupid.
Cognitive distortion: _____

4. The other day I said to my husband, "it would be nice to go on a picnic sometime." He said, "Yeah, we'll see about it." I know that we will never go. He doesn't like to spend time with me anymore. I won't bother to ask again, because it will probably just make him mad.
Cognitive distortion: _____

5. Last week when I was playing in a softball game, I made the final out and our team lost. I was so ashamed. I used to be a good player, but I'm just no good anymore. I think I might as well quit the team.
Cognitive distortion: _____

6. I can't stand to watch TV anymore because I hate looking at all those gorgeous models with hourglass figures. It makes me feel so ugly. Nobody could ever find me attractive. If I looked like Cindy Crawford, then I'd feel good about myself.
Cognitive distortion: _____

7. I can't stand up to my husband. If I disagree with him, he yells at me and I feel stupid. It's his fault that I have all these problems. He puts me down all the time and makes me feel like I'm worthless. I can't do anything about it.
Cognitive distortion: _____

8. My kids don't respect me. I work hard to provide for them, but they don't appreciate it. If they cared about me, they would do their chores without me having to gripe at them all the time. I must have failed as a mother if I raised such ungrateful kids.
Cognitive distortion: _____

9. My girlfriend and I were watching a cowboy movie and we got into an argument about American history. I told her that there was no way that she was right. Later I looked the question up in the encyclopedia and found out that she was right. I can't let her know that I was wrong because I'll feel so ashamed. She always thinks that she is smarter than I am and this will just add fuel to the fire.
Cognitive distortion: _____

10. My friends want me to go water skiing with them, but there is no way I'm going. I can't water ski! What if I fall on my face and make a fool of myself? I won't be able to do it and they will all laugh at me.
Cognitive distortion: _____

sive stance, assuming the martyr role, and being masochistic. The thought processes and schemas behind the self-sabotage can then be examined.

Other activities throughout the week are designed to elicit automatic thought patterns and to generate discussion of cognitive distortions. For example, clients can be asked to make two lists: "How I view myself" and "How my best friend views me." Differences between the lists are discussed, and cognitive distortions are pointed out and challenged. The "pass the plate" exercise is often extremely effective when the group is supportive and people in the group know each other fairly well. Clients are given a paper plate and asked to write three qualities that they feel describe them on the back of the plate. Plates are then passed around so that each peer and therapist have an opportunity to write a quality to describe the person named on the plate. The results and differences are compared, and each client gets a chance to ask others to explain what they meant by their comments. The collective feedback of the group (which is usually positive) placed in writing can be a powerful tool in disputing negative cognitions. This exercise usually leads to a discussion of what it is like for people to accept compliments (or in some cases receive criticism). Clients are encouraged to save the plate and review it frequently. Creative and expressive activities not traditionally used in cognitive therapy may also help to involve clients in the group process and reinforce the principles of cognitive therapy. For example, clients often enjoy and benefit from using one of the last psychological education sessions in a module to create a drawing or collage illustrating things that help them feel good about themselves and ways they can improve their self-esteem. These are discussed and processed within the group and then can be taken home to serve as a visual reminder of the principles and strategies learned in psychological education sessions.

Group Therapy

A major part of the partial hospital day is devoted to more traditional cognitive–behavioral group therapy. This "group time" is generally the longest period of the partial hospital day because it is here that clients have the greatest opportunity to discuss their individual issues. Group time builds on principles learned in psychological education sessions and can be used to discuss issues that arise in other segments of the partial hospital day. While the psychological education component of the day is a time in which the therapist performs a teaching role and structures clients in the completion of specific activities, group time is less structured and allows clients to bring up any personal issues that they wish to discuss. During group time, the therapist acts more as a facilitator and encourages greater peer input and group discussion of issues.

Group time starts with agenda setting. The therapist makes sure that adequate time is allotted to clients who have issues to discuss and that individual homework assignments are reviewed. The therapist may place time on the agenda to speak to a client who consistently remains reticent and address the process behind the reluctance to participate in the group. The therapist must also try to ensure that one person does not consistently monopolize the discussion. Although group time frequently focuses on issues in clients' lives outside the program, thoughts and feelings regarding the group process and interactions within the milieu are seen as valid topics for discussion. The following is an example of a group time discussion:

Therapist: Okay. Today Ron wants to talk about his weekend, Susan wants to talk about her phone call from her mom, and Bill want to discuss returning to work. We also need to make sure that we allow time to go over Nancy's homework. Who wants to go first?

Ron: I'll go first and get it over with if that's okay.

Therapist: Is that okay with the group? Go ahead, Ron.

Ron: Well, this weekend was my son's 9th birthday. My ex-wife gave him a party on Saturday, and I went over to take him a card. I couldn't afford to get him a present since I haven't been able to work for the last 6 months and I don't know where my disability application stands. Anyway, his grandparents and aunt on his mom's side were there when I walked in. I said "Hi" and they smiled and my ex-father-in-law asked me how I was doing. I said I was fine, but I just tried to get away from them as quickly as I could.

Susan: Why did you feel that you had to run away?

Therapist: What thoughts were going through your mind at that time?

Ron: I was starting to feel suicidal just being there.

Therapist: Ron, how were you feeling before you got to your ex-wife's house?

Ron: Fine. Well, I was a little nervous about going and kind of sad about not having a present for him, but I was really looking forward to seeing him.

Therapist: So you went from feeling pretty much okay to being suicidal within a matter of an hour or so. That's pretty serious. Have you thought about how you got from one point to the other?

Ron: I felt that they were all looking at me and thinking what a loser I am because they know that I was in the hospital again and that I haven't been working. Plus my son had gotten all these gifts and I felt so rotten walking in without one. I'm sure that they were thinking, "What kind of a father are you?" And my son came and grabbed me and started in, "Daddy, Daddy, look what Mom got me and look what this one and that one got me." I know he's just a kid and I tried to act happy when he was showing me his stuff, but I just had to get out of there. I left as soon as he got distracted. On the way home I started feeling suicidal, and all of those thoughts started coming back. I had to walk home another way because I was afraid that if I walked over the bridge, I would jump off.

Terry: He's mind reading again.

Therapist: Terry, can you say that directly to him.

Terry: Ron, you're mind reading again, just like you do with us in group. You're assuming that you know what your in-laws and everybody else is thinking of you. You said yourself that they were being polite to you. Maybe they were thinking that, and maybe they weren't—you don't know.

Susan: Terry's right. Besides, why do you care what they think? I mean, these are your ex-in-laws, right? How often do you see them, and why does what they think of you matter?

Ron: I guess it really doesn't. I mean most of the time I don't care what they think of me, but I care what people think about me as a father.

Therapist: Ron, it sounds like not having a present for your son stirred up a lot of feelings about your worth and ability as a father. You seem to be taking your own thoughts and feelings and projecting them onto your in-laws.

Ron: Yeah. I guess so.

Therapist: Do you know what thoughts and beliefs were going through your mind when you walked in without a present?

Bill: I know I always felt like I had to provide for my kids to be a good father. My folks taught me that is a father's role. I know how he feels. There were some hard times when I was out of work and my kids had to go without a lot of things. I felt like a failure.

Ron: Yeah. I feel that if I don't provide for my kid I'm falling down on the job, like I'm a dead-beat dad. I shouldn't be depressed. I should be working. My son deserves a dad who can be normal and provide for him. Sometimes I just think that he'd be better off without me.

> Denise: But that isn't the only part or the most important part of being a dad. Ron, you've told us about how much you love your son and how you spend time with him. How do you think your son would feel if you killed yourself?
>
> Susan: You're using a lot of shoulds again.
>
> Therapist: You do seem to be going to extremes by assuming that because you feel bad for not being able to afford a gift you are a failure as a father. Is that your only role as a father?

As the group discussion continues, the therapist encourages Ron to challenge his negative thoughts by examining the positive aspects of his relationship with his son. The example illustrates the important role the group can play in providing peers with a sense of universality, helping them recognize dysfunctional cognitive patterns, and providing evidence to help dispute negative automatic thoughts. In addition, group members often report that they learn how unreasonable their own cognitive distortions are when they hear peers reporting the same thoughts about situations.

While the previous discussion provides an example of interactions between nonpsychotic clients, high-functioning psychotic clients are often able to participate effectively and greatly benefit from cognitive group therapy within the partial hospital setting, as evidenced by the work of Loring and Fabroni (1990). Although some of these individuals may have more difficulty grasping the basics of cognitive therapy, the reinforcement of principles throughout all aspects of a comprehensive milieu contributes to their learning, understanding, and being able to implement cognitive principles. Individuals experiencing paranoia who are stable enough to accept that their delusional beliefs are the result of mental illness often find the examination of their paranoid delusions in terms of cognitive distortions (personalization, mind reading, etc.) to be very helpful. They are then often able to practice using cognitive techniques to assist in reality testing. Even some people with schizophrenia who experience persistent "background" auditory hallucinations (which never fully resolve despite the best efforts of pharmacotherapy) are often able to practice using cognitive techniques to dispute some of the disturbing messages that they hear from these voices. They may learn to use cognitive techniques to improve their ability to keep these voices in the "background" and focus on external reality. The following is an example of the use of cognitive techniques with a high-functioning paranoid schizophrenic client who had been stabilized on medication:

> Therapist: Todd, I believe that you asked for some group time.
>
> Todd: Yes. I want to talk about what happened just before I went into the hospital. It's hard for me to talk about.
>
> Therapist: Just try to start and we will help you by asking questions if you feel stuck.

Todd: I have trouble being around people. It always seems that wherever I go people don't like me. They talk about me and look at me. When I get really depressed, it seems like I can hear them talking about me behind my back. That's why I avoid people and stay at home. It's been hard for me to come to this group, but it's starting to get easier. I like talking to a lot of the people here.

Therapist: Todd, what do you think that people in group are thinking of you right now?

Todd: I don't know.

Therapist: Do you have any ideas?

Todd: Earlier, when we were on break, Karen and Kim were saying something and laughing. I thought that they must be laughing at me.

Therapist: Why don't you ask them and check it out.

Todd: (very hesitantly) Were you guys laughing at me?

Kim: No Todd. We weren't laughing at you. I was telling Karen about a funny show that I saw on TV. It didn't have anything to do with you. I feel that we've gotten to be friends in group and I would tell you the truth if we were talking about you.

Karen: That's right, Todd, she was talking about a show. Other people from group were there too, and they can tell you that we weren't talking about you at all.

Therapist: What do you think of what Karen and Kim have told you. Do you believe them?

Todd: Yes, but I'm embarrassed that I said anything. I shouldn't have said anything.

Therapist: It may seem embarrassing, but what would you feel like if you hadn't said anything?

Todd: I guess that I'd still be thinking that they were talking about me.

Therapist: Would that be better than feeling embarrassed? What would that be like for you?

Todd: No, because then I would feel hurt and I wouldn't want to be around them anymore. I guess saying something was better.

Kim: Isn't what he's doing one of those cognitive distortions that we've been learning about?

Therapist:	Yes. Todd, do you know which cognitive distortion you just gave us an example of?
Todd:	(After briefly referring to a handout received earlier in treatment) I think it's personalization. I do that all the time. When we went over this stuff (worksheet), that really made sense to me. My parents always tell me that I take things to personally, but I just didn't think they understood. It helps me to see that there is a name for it and that other people do it too.

The previous example testifies to the importance of group cohesiveness and the establishment of the sense of belongingness discussed by Yalom (1985). It was only after participating in the program long enough to establish trust that Todd was able to take the risk necessary to reality-test his thoughts with the group and accept feedback. Participating in a group comprising nonpsychotic clients also often contributes to the quality of feedback received by psychotic clients.

Recreational Therapy

Many new clients are hesitant to participate in recreational therapy, stating that they do not feel like it or that they did not come to therapy to play games. In such cases, therapists explain to clients that when people are experiencing mental illness or emotional difficulties, especially depression, they often tend to avoid physical exercise, social interaction, and pleasurable activities. An important aspect of recovery can be to change behavior and participate in activities even when one does not want to do so. Making such behavioral changes can eventually lead to cognitive, emotional, and biological changes. Complaints must be viewed as negative automatic thoughts that can be processed with the client through Socratic questioning. Questions regarding why the person is hesitant, what he or she is thinking and feeling, and what might happen if he or she participated in the activity are used to uncover dysfunctional attitudes. Participating in recreational therapy can be the equivalent to completing behavioral homework tasks and can be one of the first steps in a graded task assignment intervention. Recreational therapy allows clients to practice new behavior in a safe environment before going on to try social or recreational activities outside of the group.

Numerous recreational activities can be used within the cognitive milieu. All activities should, however, be structured so that every client, including the elderly or physically disabled, can participate. If this is not possible, as in the case of severely disabled individuals, alternative programming must be provided. Recreational activities may be competitive or noncompetitive and individually or team oriented, but in either case they should be designed to promote success experiences. Therapists provide encouragement for participation and positive reinforcement for display of effort. Recreational activities often serve a diagnostic function by allowing therapists to observe clients' coordination, energy level, motivation, mirth response, and ability to engage in cooperative activities. Games requiring individuals to take turns being "it" or perform while others watch can be used to assess and discuss what it is like to be the focus of attention. Team games can be used to assess and discuss assumptions clients make about how others are evaluating their performance and what people think of them if they make a mistake and "let the team down." Some activities clients respond well to include volleyball (using a soft, oversized ball), sit-down volleyball (which involves sitting on tumbling mats and hitting a plastic ball across a low net), group jungle (which involves passing a number of balls between clients in a specific pattern), obstacle courses, parachute games, shuffleboard, and bowling, just to name a few.

It is important to allow time for processing at the end of recreational therapy. This is a time to ask those individuals who had negative expectations going into the game to compare their expectations with their actual experience and to look at the differences, or at how expectations may have affected outcome. Clients are encouraged to examine their perceptions of what others may have been thinking about them and receive feedback from the group. They usually learn that their own criticism is much more negative than that of the group. Through therapeutic recreation, some clients may begin to change long-standing negative schema regarding their physical or social abilities. Many clients remark that they quit playing sports or active games long ago because they were always chosen last or teased when they made mistakes. Through therapeutic recreation, they learn that they can enjoy games even when they are not perfect.

Journal Group and Wrap-Up

Clients often find it helpful to keep a journal detailing their experiences within the partial hospital program. Although some clients report that they cannot "get into" journaling, everyone is encouraged to keep some type of record of their time in the program. Journal time can be used for clients to reflect on and synthesize the events of the partial hospital day or events at home. They can also make notes of information that they learned in the program or record thoughts, feelings, or self-revelations. Clients can be encouraged to incorporate the "three-column technique" in their journal to describe an event by breaking it down into distinct descriptions of their thoughts/cognitions, emotions, and behavior. Individuals have the option of sharing their journal entries with the group and asking for comments and feedback. One important role of the journal is to provide a record of cognitive and emotional changes that take place during the course of treatment. Clients are often surprised to see the differences in their journal entries across time. These differences can also attest to the efficacy of cognitive techniques. After the completion of treatment, clients often benefit from reviewing their journals as a reminder of what they accomplished and learned in the group. The journal can also be used to access the supportive presence of the group.

Medication Education

Medication education group is generally facilitated by a trained medical staff member, such as a psychiatrist, nurse, or psychiatric resident. This time may consist of a brief lecture on a topic such as the use of antidepressants or other psychiatric medications, the importance of taking medications as directed, or the danger of mixing medications with alcohol or drugs. The time may also be used as a question-and-answer session. Clients often have many questions about their medication, especially regarding side effects, and may be more likely to comply with their medication regime when they have proper information. By discussing medication issues with the group, staff members can more closely monitor compliance as well as the effectiveness of particular medication regimens.

Other Potential Components of a Comprehensive Cognitive Milieu

The partial hospital program schedule discussed here represents one possibility in a vast array of potential therapeutic formats. Other adjunctive therapies, such as art therapy, movement therapy, occupational therapy, and music therapy, can also play important roles in the comprehensive cognitive milieu. Occupational therapy in particular can provide excellent opportunities for graded task assignments and in vivo rehearsal experiences that assist in increasing coping skills and developing self-esteem (Wright et al., 1993). Clients who fear being able to function effectively upon returning to work or resuming household responsibilities can be asked to perform similar tasks within an occupational therapy setting and process negative, self-defeating thoughts, which may hinder task performance, as they occur. Art therapy assignments can be used to help clients become aware of underlying negative attitudes about their creative abilities or difficulty taking risks in self-expression for fear of being criticized or judged harshly. Movement therapy assignments can be used to look at similar thoughts and feelings and also to examine negative or distorted cognitions regarding one's body.

SUMMARY

Most literature regarding cognitive group therapy focuses on outpatient groups; however, cognitive group therapy is also practiced in inpatient settings and in partial hospital settings. Cognitive group therapy is well suited for implementation in an acute partial hospital setting because it is time limited, symptom oriented, and economical. Cognitive therapy can be implemented in the partial hospital setting as a discreet segment of the programming day that is added on to more traditional psychodynamic and activities programming. Research on the use of such an "add-on" model in inpatient settings suggests that this model may not be as effective as establishment of a comprehensive cognitive milieu. The development of a comprehensive cognitive milieu within a partial hospital setting requires extensive training and development of all staff members as well as proper screening and orientation of potential clients. Such a program would apply cognitive–behavioral principles and techniques not only to the traditional group therapy and educational group settings but also to adjunctive therapies. A possible protocol for a comprehensive cognitive milieu within a partial hospital program is presented and treatment issues are discussed in the chapter.

REFERENCES

Block, M. A., & Lefkovitz, P. M. (1994). *Standards and guidelines for partial hospitalization: Adult programs* (2nd ed.). Alexandria, VA: American Association for Partial Hospitalization.

Dibella, G. A. W., Weitz, G. W., Poynter-Berg, D., & Yurmark, J. L. (1982). *Handbook of partial hospitalization*. New York: Brunner/Mazel.

Free, M. L., Oei, T. P. S., & Sanders, M. R. (1991). Treatment outcome of a group cognitive therapy program for depression. *International Journal of Group Psychotherapy, 41*, 533–547.

Freeman, A., Schrodt, G. R., Gilson, M., & Ludgate, J. W. (1993). Group cognitive therapy with inpatients. In J. H. Wright, M. E. Thase, A. T. Beck, & J. W. Ludgate (Eds.), *Cognitive therapy with inpatients* (pp. 121–153). New York: Guilford Press.

Hollon, S. D., & Shaw, B. F. (1979). Cognitive group therapy for depressed patients. In A. T. Beck, A. J. Rush, B. F. Shaw, & G. Emery (1979). *Cognitive therapy depression* (pp. 328–353). New York: Plenum.

Loring, M. J., & Fraboni, E. (1990). The use of cognitive therapy in groups. *International Journal of Partial Hospitalization, 6*, 173–179.

McKay, M., Davis, M., & Fanning, P. (1987). *Thoughts and feelings: The art of cognitive stress intervention*. Oakland, CA: New Harbinger.

Padesky, C. A. (1993). Staff and patient education. In J. H. Wright, M. E. Thase, A. T. Beck, & J. W. Ludgate (Eds.), *Cognitive therapy with inpatients* (pp. 393–413). New York: Guilford Press.

Wright, J. H., Thase, M. E., Ludgate, J. W., & Beck, A. T. (1993). The cognitive milieu: Structure and process. In J. H. Wright, M. E. Thase, A. T. Beck, &

J. W. Ludgate (Eds.), *Cognitive therapy with inpatients* (pp. 61–87). New York: Guilford Press.

Yalom, I. D. (1985). *The theory and practice of group psychotherapy* (3rd ed.). New York: Basic Books.

Yost, E. B., Beutler, L. E., Corbishley, M. A., & Allender, J. R. (1986). *Cognitive group therapy: A treatment approach for depressed older adults*. New York: Pergamon Press.

AUTHOR INDEX

Numbers in italics refer to listings in the reference section.

Garfinkel, P. E., 128, 129, 130, 131, 133, 134, *146*, *147*
Garner, A., 228, *231*
Garner, D. M., 100, *123*, 128, 129, 130, 131, 133, 134, *146*
Garrow, J. S., 100, *123*
Gauthier, J. G., 63, *91*, *92*, *94*
Gelder, M., *92*
Gelernter, C. S., 89, *93*
Gemar, M., 265, *279*
George, L., 252, *261*
Gilson, M., 30, 60, 362, *383*
Glasgow, R. E., 334, *358*
Glover, D., *92*
Gobel, M., 63, *94*
Godbout, C., *91*
Goff, G., *147*
Goisman, R. M., 64, *93*
Goldfried, M. R., 15, *24*
Golding, J. M., *300*
Goldsmith, R. J., 150, 153, *172*
Goldstein, A. P., 282, *300*
Goldstein, M. G., *279*
Goldstein, S., 216, *231*
Gollan, J. K., *93*
Gonso, J., *329*
González, G., 296, *302*
Goodsitt, A., 128, *146*
Goodwin, F., *172*
Goodwin, R. E., 217, 218, 225, *231*
Gottman, J., *329*
Gould, R. A., 63, *93*, *94*
Gramzow, R., 349, *359*
Gray, J. A., 73, *94*
Greaves, C., *123*
Greenberg, L. S., 352, 354, *358*
Greenberg, M. S., 212, *232*
Greenberg, R., 17, *23*
Greenberger, D., 9, *24*
Greene, V. L., 252, *259*
Greenspan, S. I., 347, *358*
Gretter, M. L., 297, *301*
Grieger, R., 295, *300*
Griest, D. L., 334, *358*
Griez, E., 66, *96*
Guarnaccia, P. J., 284, *299*
Gursky, D., 65, *96*
Guzman, J., 287, *301*

Hackmann, A., *92*
Haley, J., 346, *358*

Haley, W. E., 252, 253, *259*
Hall, A., 127, *146*
Hallfrisch, J., *124*
Hallowell, E. M., 216, 217, 218, 224, 225, 228, *231*, *232*
Hamra, B. J., *95*
Hanis, C., *125*
Hankin Wessler, S., 144, *147*, 156, *173*, 332, 333, 334, 335, 336, 340, 349, 352, 357, *360*
Hanna, H. H., *96*
Hanson, C. F., 100, *124*
Harlow, L. L., *279*
Harper, R., *329*
Harper-Guiffre, H., 128, *146*
Harris, E. L., *95*
Harris, S. D., *277*
Hasin, D., *125*
Hatsukami, D., *147*
Hays, P. A., 281, 289, 291, *300*
Healey, J. F., 282, *300*
Hechtman, L. T., 211, 213, 215, 216, 228, *232*
Hecker, J. E., 63, *94*
Heersema, P. H., *258*
Heifetz, L. J., 344, *358*
Heimberg, R. G., 89, *94*
Heine, L., 30, *61*
Heinrich, A., 305, *329*
Hemmings, K. A., 297, *301*
Henderson, J. G., 64, *95*, *123*
Herbert, M., *279*
Herrera, A. E., 281, 293, *300*
Hervis, O., 291, *303*
Himadi, W. G., 64, *92*
Himle, J., 66, *96*
Hirsch, J., 100, *124*
Hite, S., 312, 315, 317, 324, *329*
Hoffart, A., 64, 68, *94*
Hollon, S., 30, 60, 288, *301*
Hollon, S. D., 366, *383*
Holt, C., 64, *93*
Holt, P., 81, 82, *94*
Hope, D. A., 89, *94*
Hope, R. A., 128, *145*
Hopkins, J., 103, *124*
Horne, A. M., 335, *358*
Horowitz, M., 265, *277*
Hough, R. L., *300*
Howard, K. I., 289, 295, *302*
Hu, L., 283, *303*
Hughes, M., *94*, *301*

Yost, E. B., 237, *261*, 364, *384*
Young, J., 23, *25*, 55, *61*, 239, *261*, 298, *303*
Young, R. N., 256, *260*
Youngren, M. A., 30, *60*, 245, 259, 287, *301*
Yurmark, J. L., 362, *383*

Zane, N. W. S., 283, *303*
Zarate, R., 67, *97*
Zarit, S. H., 252, *261*
Zaubler, T. S., 64, *97*
Zeiss, A. M., 30, *60*, 245, 252, 253, *259*, *260*, 287, *301*
Zhao, S., 94, *301*

SUBJECT INDEX

Humor, 314, 340–341
Hyperactivity, 212, 214
Hyperventilation, 81–84
Hypothesis testing, 6, 80–81

Identification, 266, 276
Identity, fragmentation of, in dissociative
    disorders, 205–206
Imagery, 16
Immigration, as stress factor, 291
Impulsivity, 212–213, 225–226
Inattention, 212–213, 225–226
Inpatient program, and partial hospital
    program, 362–364
Integrative field, 275–276
Interactive behavior, 141
Interoceptive conditioning, 65
Interoceptive exposure, 84–86
Interpersonal connection, 190
Interpersonal strategies, 228
In vivo exposure, 12, 86–89

Journaling, 381–382
Jumping to conclusions, 249
Justifying cognitions, 336

Labeling, 249
Language, sexual, 312
Latinos, 281–283, 286, 297–298
Learning disabilities, 215
Learning organization, the, 31
Life goals, as homework assignment,
    160–162
Lifestyle, and obesity, 99–100
Logical response, encouraging, 353–354
Loss, experience of, 47–50, 237
Loss of control, and panic disorder, 75

Maintenance guides, 251
Mapping function, 274
Mastery, 12–13
    and guilt feelings, 53–55
Mastery and pleasure record, 43, 55
Masturbation, 306, 312, 319–320
Meal planning, in treatment of obesity,
    118

Medical examination requirement, 90
Medical patients, and Risk Adaptation
    Model (RAM), 263–265
Medications, 90, 382. *See also* drug treat-
    ment, for adult ADD
Mental filtering, 248
Mental health, demystifying, 276
Mental health history and impact, as
    homework for MISA clients,
    164–166
Mental health services, 285
Mental health services, use of, 283–286
Mental illness, 149–151, 153–154, 378–
    380. *See also* MISA (mentally ill
    substance abuser)
Meta-beliefs, 207–208
Mindfulness practices, 265–268, 273–274
MISA (mentally ill substance abuser),
    149–152, 154–156
Modeling, xiii, 13
Modifiability, perceptions of, 271
Mood monitoring, 10–11, 245–246
Motivation, 89, 155, 162, 273, 332–334
Movement therapy, 382
Multiple personality disorder, 180

National Comorbidity Survey (NCS),
    284

Obesity, 99–101
Occupational therapy, 382
Older Person's Pleasant Events Schedule
    (OPPES), 239–240, 246–248
Optimism, 264, 268–271, 276
Optimizing function, 274
Outcome research, on efficacy of CBT
    with ethnic minorities, 297–298
Outcomes measures, in treatment of de-
    pression, 47
Overactivity, 212–213, 225–226
Overestimation of probability, 78–79
Overgeneralization, 102, 248

Pairing, in interoceptive exposure exer-
    cises, 86
Panic, myths about, 73–76
Panic disorder, 65–69

129, 142–143. *See also* meta-
beliefs
Schizophrenia, 378–380
Security-seeking maneuvers, 336, 350
Selection of group members
for CAT parent-training group, 337–
340
for depression group, 35–37
for Latino depression group, 286
for Level 1 group for dissociative disorders, 179–181
for Level 2 group for dissociative disorders, 194–197
for medical patient group, 273
for partial hospital program, 366–367
for treatment of anxiety disorders, 89–
90
for treatment of depression, 35–37
for treatment of MISA clients, 152
for treatment of obesity, 105
for women's sexuality group, 307–309
Self-acceptance, 131, 313, 318
Self-care, emotional, 343–344, 352–356
Self-confrontation, written homework as,
159
Self-control, 177, 179–180, 187, 295
Self-diagnosis, 311
Self-disclosure, 315, 320–321, 340–341,
343
Self-efficacy, 265, 271
Self-esteem, education module for, 372–
375. *See also* Self-worth, sense of
Self-help treatment, 68
Self-image, of parents, 332–334
Self-judgments, 53
Self-management, 226–228
Self-monitoring, 76, 100
Self-pity, as personotypic affect, 336–337,
350
Self-shaming, 119–120
Self-worth, sense of, 130–131, 133, 229
Senior citizens. *See* adults, older
Sex therapy, 305–306. *See also* women's
sexuality
Sexual fantasies, 321
Sexual partners, 322–326
Sexual stereotypes, 315–317
Shame, 101–102, 119–120, 335, 340–
342, 349
as personotypic affect, 336–337

Shame-free environment, for CAT
parent-training group, 340–342
Shaping, 13
Shared empiricism, 11
Silence, pressure of, 141
Social isolation, 129, 187
Social support, 104–105, 268
Socratic questioning, 9, 22–23, 34, 52,
58
Spectatoring, 324
Staff, for partial hospital program, 365
Stages of change, 267
Stanford Eating Disorders Questionnaire,
106
State-Trait Anxiety Inventory, 18
Stimulus control, and weight loss, 102
Stress reduction, 273–274. *See also* relax-
ation techniques
Structuring, for adult ADD, 217, 221,
224–225
Substance abuse, 36, 149–151, 153–154,
257. *See also* MISA (mentally ill
substance abuser)
Substance use history, as homework for
MISA clients, 162–166
Successive approximation, 13, 244
Suicidal ideation, 51–53
Suicidal risk, 35, 47, 51–53
Suicide, group discussion of, 51–53
Survival guides, 251
Sympathy, vs. empathy, 335–336
Systematic desensitization, 12

Task focus, xiii–xv, 33, 46, 57, 59, 76,
153, 287
Teamwork, 31
Telephone screening, 35
Termination of treatment, 55–59. *See also*
follow-up; relapse prevention
Therapist, role of, 218
agenda setting, 38–39
analysis of anxiety, 70–72
building cohesiveness, 32–33
building task focus, 33
in CAT parent-training group, 340–
341, 343
dealing with loss, 49–50
as director or conductor, 34–35
discussion of guilt, 53–55

ABOUT THE EDITORS

John R. White, PhD, is an adjunct professor at the California School of Professional Psychology–Alameda, where he teaches the advanced clinical series in cognitive–behavioral therapy (CBT) and serves as consulting assistant professor at Stanford University School of Education for Counseling Psychology. After graduating from the California School of Professional Psychology and completing a National Institute of Mental Health fellowship at the University of California San Francisco Medical Center, Dr. White took two years of extramural training at the Cognitive Therapy Center of Philadelphia. He maintains a private practice in Fremont, California, and serves as director of psychological services at Fremont Hospital, where he developed its inpatient CBT program and manual. He is also the author of *Overcoming Generalized Anxiety Disorder*, an empirically based CBT treatment protocol.

Arthur S. Freeman, EdD, is professor and chair of the department of psychology and director of the doctoral program in clinical psychology at the Philadelphia College of Osteopathic Medicine. He is also professor in the core doctoral faculty and director of the cognitive therapy program of the Adler School of Professional Psychology in Chicago. Dr. Freeman completed his doctoral work at Teachers College–Columbia University and completed a postdoctoral fellowship at the Center for Cognitive Therapy at the University of Pennsylvania. He has published several books, including *Cognitive Therapy of Personality Disorders* (with Aaron T. Beck), *Clinical Applications of Cognitive Therapy*, and *The Comprehensive Casebook of Cognitive Therapy* (with Frank Dattilio). He has also published two trade books: *Woulda, Shoulda, Coulda: Overcoming Mistakes and Missed Opportunities* and *The Ten Dumbest Mistakes Smart People Make and How to Overcome Them* (both with Rose DeWolf).

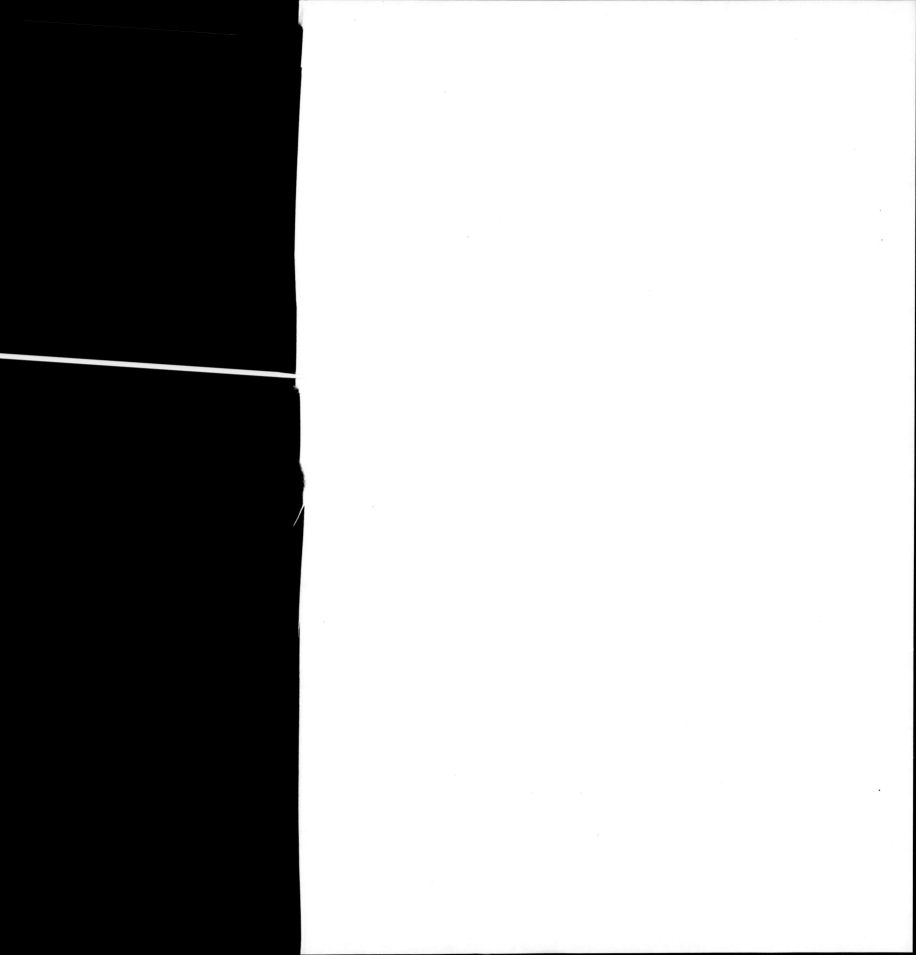